Deep Learning Pipeline

Building a Deep Learning Model with TensorFlow

Hisham El-Amir
Mahmoud Hamdy

Apress®

Deep Learning Pipeline: Building a Deep Learning Model with TensorFlow

Hisham El-Amir
Jizah, Egypt

Mahmoud Hamdy
Jizah, Egypt

ISBN-13 (pbk): 978-1-4842-5348-9
https://doi.org/10.1007/978-1-4842-5349-6

ISBN-13 (electronic): 978-1-4842-5349-6

Managing Director, Apress Media LLC: Welmoed Spahr
Acquisitions Editor: Aaron Black
Development Editor: James Markham
Coordinating Editor: Jessica Vakili

Distributed to the book trade worldwide by Springer Science+Business Media New York, 233 Spring Street, 6th Floor, New York, NY 10013. Phone 1-800-SPRINGER, fax (201) 348-4505, e-mail orders-ny@springer-sbm.com, or visit www.springeronline.com. Apress Media, LLC is a California LLC and the sole member (owner) is Springer Science + Business Media Finance Inc (SSBM Finance Inc). SSBM Finance Inc is a **Delaware** corporation.

For information on translations, please e-mail rights@apress.com, or visit www.apress.com/rights-permissions.

Apress titles may be purchased in bulk for academic, corporate, or promotional use. eBook versions and licenses are also available for most titles. For more information, reference our Print and eBook Bulk Sales web page at www.apress.com/bulk-sales.

Any source code or other supplementary material referenced by the author in this book is available to readers on GitHub via the book's product page, located at www.apress.com/978-1-4842-5348-9. For more detailed information, please visit www.apress.com/source-code.

Printed on acid-free paper

Table of Contents

About the Authors

Hisham El-Amir is a data scientist with expertise in machine learning, deep learning, and statistics. He currently lives and works in Cairo, Egypt. In his work projects, he faces challenges ranging from natural language processing (NLP), behavioral analysis, and machine learning to distributed processing. He is very passionate about his job and always tries to stay updated about the latest developments in data science technologies, attending meetups, conferences, and other events.

Mahmoud Hamdy is a machine learning engineer who works and lives in Egypt. His primary area of study is the overlap between knowledge, logic, language, and learning. He works helping to train machine learning and deep learning models to distil large amounts of unstructured, semistructured, and structured data into new knowledge about the world by using methods ranging from deep learning to statistical relational learning. He applies strong theoretical and practical skills in several areas of machine learning, to find novel and effective solutions for interesting and challenging problems in such interconnections.

About the Technical Reviewer

Vishwesh Ravi Shrimali graduated in 2018 from BITS Pilani, where he studied mechanical engineering. Since then, he has been working with BigVision LLC on deep learning and computer vision, and is also involved in creating official OpenCV courses. He has a keen interest in programming and AI, and has applied that interest in mechanical engineering projects. He has also written multiple blogs on OpenCV and deep learning on LearnOpenCV, a leading blog on computer vision. He has also co-authored *Machine Learning for OpenCV4* (2nd edition). When he is not writing blogs or working on projects, he likes to go on long walks or play his acoustic guitar.

Introduction

Artificial intelligence (AI) is the field of embeddings human thinking into computers: in other words, creating an artificial brain that mimics the functions of the biological brain. Whatever the human can do intelligently is now required to be moved into machines. First-generation AI focuses on problems that can be formally described by humans. Using AI, steps for doing something intelligent are described in a form of instructions that machines follow. Machines follow humans without changes. These features are characteristic of the first era of AI.

Humans can fully describe only simple problems such as chess, and fail to describe more complicated problems. In chess, the problem can be simply explained by representing the board as a matrix of size 8×8, describing each piece and how it moves and describing the goals. Machines will be restricted to those tasks formally described by humans. By programming such instructions, machines can play chess intelligently. Machine intelligence is now artificial. The machine itself is not intelligent, but humans have transferred their intelligence to the machine in the form of several static lines of code. "Static" means that the behavior is the same in all cases. The machine, in this case, is tied to the human and can't work on its own. This is like a master–slave relationship. The human is the master and the machines are the slaves, which just follow the human's orders and no more.

To make the machine able to recognize objects, we can give it previous knowledge from experts in a way the machine can understand. Such knowledge-based systems form the second era of AI. One of the challenges in such systems is how to handle uncertainty and unknowns. Humans can recognize objects even in different and complex environments, and are able to handle uncertainty and unknowns intelligently, but machines can't.

The Goal

Deep learning is a branch of machine learning where you model the world in terms of a hierarchy of concepts. This pattern of learning is similar to the way a human brain learns, and it allows computers to model complex concepts that often go unnoticed in other traditional methods of modeling. Hence, in the modern computing paradigm, deep learning plays a vital role in modeling complex real-world problems, especially by leveraging the massive amount of unstructured data available today.

Because of the complexities involved in a deep learning model, many times it is treated as a black box by people using it. However, to derive the maximum benefit from this branch of machine learning, one needs to uncover the hidden mystery by looking at the science and mathematics associated with it. In this book, great care has been taken to explain the concepts and techniques associated with deep learning from a mathematical as well as a scientific viewpoint. Also, the first chapter is totally dedicated to building the mathematical base required to comprehend deep learning concepts with ease. TensorFlow has been chosen as the deep learning package because of its flexibility for research purposes and its ease of use. Another reason for choosing TensorFlow is its capability to load models with ease in a live production environment using its serving capabilities.

In summary, *Deep Learning Pipeline* should provide practical expertise so you can learn deep learning pipeline from scratch in such a way that you can deploy meaningful deep learning solutions. This book will allow you to get up to speed quickly using TensorFlow and to optimize different deep learning architectures. All the practical aspects of deep learning that are relevant in any industry are emphasized in this book. You will be able to use the prototypes demonstrated to build new deep learning applications. The code presented in the book is available in the form of iPython notebooks and scripts that allow you to try out examples and extend them in interesting ways. You will be equipped with the mathematical foundation and scientific knowledge to pursue research in this field and give back to the community.

All code in the book is implemented using Python. Because native Python is complex for handling images, multiple libraries are used to help to produce an efficient implementation for applications across the chapters.

Who This Book Is For

This book is for data scientists and machine learning professionals looking at deep learning solutions to solve complex business problems, software developers working on deep learning solutions through TensorFlow, and graduate students and open source enthusiasts with a constant desire to learn.

Prerequisites

Python and all the deep learning tools mentioned in the book, from IPython to TensorFlow to model that you will use, are free of charge and can be freely downloaded from the Internet. To run the code that accompanies the book, you need a computer that uses a Windows, Linux, or Mac OS operating system. The book will introduce you step-by-step to the process of installing the Python interpreter and all the tools and data that you need to run the examples.

How this Book Is Organized

Parts

- *Part I: Introduction*—In this part, we prepare the readers by giving them all the prerequisites needed to start the journey with machine learning to deep learning.

- *Part II: Data*—As the first step of the pipeline, readers need to know everything about data, from data collection and understanding information from data to data processing and preparation.

- *Part III: TensorFlow*—In this part, we start the interesting stuff. First, we illustrate the fundamental and important concepts of deep learning; then we deep dive into the core of neural networks and the types of neural networks, describing each type; and show the important concepts of the equation of deep learning. Also, we can't forget to show a real-life example of each type.

- *Part IV: Applying What You've Learned*—This part is designed to ensure readers practice by using TensorFlow and build the pipeline.

Chapters

- *Chapter 1: A gentle introduction*—This chapter provides the big picture that shows readers what is the field that the book describes; introduction to this field; and the mathematical equations and notations that describe how machine learning works.

- *Chapter 2: Setting Up Your Environment*—This chapter introduces the programming tools and packages you need in this book and some theories to help in understanding; it also includes a bit of introduction to the Python programming language.

- *Chapter 3: A Nice Tour Through the Deep Learning Pipeline*—In chapter 3 we introduce the pipeline that the whole book is for; the deep learning approaches and subfields; the steps of the deep learning pipeline; and the extras added to TensorFlow that make it unique compared with other deep learning frameworks.

- *Chapter 4: Build Your First Toy TensorFlow App*—To make sure that we will not drop readers in the middle of the book, we show them a small example using TensorFlow that will go fast at each step of the deep learning pipeline; and make sure that the audience knows each step of the pipeline, how it is important, and how to use it.

- *Chapter 5: Defining Data*—This chapter, as its name implies, is about defining data. Readers should know what type of data they are dealing with, and that's very important so they can choose the right approach for preparing the data.

- *Chapter 6: Data Wrangling and Preprocessing*—After understanding the data, the readers now should choose the approaches and methodologies for preparing it, so this chapter helps ensure that the readers will choose the right approaches in this step.

- *Chapter 7: Data Resampling*—After cleaning and preparing the dataset, now the reader should know how to sample this dataset in the right way. Choosing the wrong samples from your data may influence the result of your models, so in this chapter we illustrate all techniques and approaches needed to sample your dataset in the right way.

- *Chapter 8: Feature Selection and Feature Engineering*—In this chapter we describe a very important topic in data step of the pipeline: feature selection and engineering. Readers should know how to select and choose the important input feature that contributes most to the output feature in which they are interested. Feature engineering is the process of using domain knowledge of the data to create features that make machine learning algorithms work. Feature selection and engineering are fundamental to the application of machine and deep learning, and readers should know when and how to use them.

- *Chapter 9: Deep Learning Fundamentals*—In this chapter we describe a very important topic in deep learning fundamentals, the basic functions that deep learning is built on. Then we try to build layers from these functions and combine these layers together to get a more complex model that will help us solve more complex problems. All that will be described by TensorFlow examples.

- *Chapter 10: Improving Deep Neural Networks*—In this chapter we describe an important topic: after building the deep learning models, the improvement starts. This chapter concerns optimization, tuning and choosing hyperparameter techniques, and weight normalization and how that will make the learning process easier and faster. After that, the reader should know how to evaluate, optimize, and tune the model parameters to reach the optimal solution and a satisfying accuracy.

- *Chapter 11: Convolutional Neural Network*—One of the important classes of deep learning is the convolutional neural network. In this chapter we illustrate everything about CNN from the one-dimensional mask to the advanced stuff like weight sharing and the difference between equivariance and invariance. We illustrate a case study using the famous dataset CIFAR-10.

- *Chapter 12: Sequential Models*—Another class of deep learning is sequential models. In this chapter we describe the problem of sequential data and the rise of recurrent neural networks, the problem and also the evolution of the GRU and LSTM, and of course we include a case study.

- *Chapter 13: Selected Topics in Computer Vision*—After finishing CNN in Part III, it's good to add some extra knowledge that makes it easier for readers when they work, like using prebuilt architectures and transfer learning.

- *Chapter 14: Selected Topics in Natural Language Processing*—This chapter fills the gaps that readers need in working with text, giving readers all the advanced approaches and techniques of natural language processing.

- *Chapter 15: Applications*—Here we show some case studies to make sure that readers get the full knowledge and understanding of how to build a pipeline, with real-life examples.

PART I

Introduction

CHAPTER 1

A Gentle Introduction

If you have ever tried to read a deep learning or even machine learning book, you will find that these books define **machine learning (ML)** as the science that teaches machines how to carry out tasks by themselves. That's a simple idea if you think of it this way, but the complexity is in the details of this mysterious science; it's within the black art of how these machines can act like humans.

Because you are reading this book now, you are probably one of the following:

1. A beginner to deep learning who wants to learn the art of deep learning in easy and straight steps

2. A developer who wants to choose a part of deep learning to work on and wants to gain the knowledge to compare between approaches to deep learning and choose the best option for him or her

3. An advanced engineer who wants to enhance their skills by learning the best practices of deep learning and how to build effective pipelines in a deep learning approach

© Hisham El-Amir and Mahmoud Hamdy 2020
H. El-Amir and M. Hamdy, *Deep Learning Pipeline*,
https://doi.org/10.1007/978-1-4842-5349-6_1

Upon starting the book, we have to make sure that you know where machine learning and deep learning come from and that's by describing the three theories: information, probability, and decision theory. After that, we will illustrate what is machine learning and what is deep learning, and also the evolution from machine learning to deep learning.

Information Theory, Probability Theory, and Decision Theory

The first question that should spark in your mind is *where does deep learning come from?*

If we wanted to write a good answer for this question, we could write another book titled *The Rise of Deep Learning*. Instead, we will show you the combination that made deep learning the state-of-art approach that many want to learn and understand how it works.

Deep learning—or we can generalize to machine learning—is built from three theories:

1. Information theory

2. Probability theory

3. Decision theory

Each of these theories contributed to the rise of the deep learning approach and made it the rich science it is today.

Information Theory

In this section, we start by answering a very good question: *what are the components of the deep learning approach?*

The first thing you do in any project is to get and prepare your dataset. And here, we start these theories by introducing some additional concepts from the field of information theory, which will also prove useful in our development of machine and deep learning approaches. We shall focus only on the key concepts, which barely scratch the surface of these theories, and we'll refer the reader elsewhere for more detailed discussions.

We begin by considering input observations and asking a question: *how much information does the model receive when it's trying to learn the pattern of the data?*

The answer depends on many things. For example you should know that information the model gains from a dataset is related to many variables, so don't be surprised if the model learned a lot more than you thought, or less. That's why this amount of information can be viewed as the "degree of surprise" on learning the value of your dataset.

Because you want to make sure that a desired model should make accurate decisions based on what it learned from a dataset, you have to ensure that the data that entered your model has the proper information that the model needs. Also, the information the model gains is a variant from another dataset, and the type of dataset may also make it hard for some models to learn the inside patterns, for example, images and text datasets. If you did not have a proper model for these data, you will never extract these information and you will never find the pattern or even learn it.

It's good to make it easier for your model to learn from any dataset by munging and cleaning the data. This will make it clear for your model to see information and also distinguish it from any noise that exists in the data; and that's what Part II of this book is about.

Part II of this book is about dealing with data, starting by defining the data and the hidden information and type of data, then how to visualize and extract the information. After seeing the truth by visualization, then you now know the road to take and you only need to make this road, and that can done by cleaning the data. At the end of this part we show you some advanced techniques to make it easier for the model to learn by extracting and engineering the features of the data to ensure that the model can see and learn the pattern.

Probability Theory

As deep learning is concerned with learning from data, it has to learn the pattern behind these data. And as you learn about this field of science, you will find yourself facing the key concept of uncertainty. While you are building a deep learning algorithm that should learn from and about a given dataset, you will find the most famous fact in the deep learning and machine learning world, which is the following:

> *There's a relationship between the certainty of any learned model on a given dataset and both noise on measurements and the finite size of the dataset.*

Let us re-illustrate it to make it clearer. Given a dataset that you are working on in some project, you tried to build a deep learning algorithm that should predict something based on the training dataset that you have. After the model had trained for a certain time, you tried to test its understanding of the dataset that it trained on, and you are surprised that it learned nothing at all.

So you asked yourself *why after all the training time did the model fail to learn?* The answer may be one of the following:

- The model is too small for the data, and that means that it cannot capture all the knowledge or the patterns from the dataset.

- The model could not capture the pattern of the dataset due to the fact that the pattern of the data is hidden through a huge variation of noise, so the model failed to understand all that.

- The model could not capture the pattern due to the small sample of your dataset, and that means the model cannot learn and generalize using a small number of observations.

So, after understanding the problems you have to face that make your model unable to perform accurately, you have another question: *how can I overcome these obstacles and make my model achieve the desired accuracy?*

The answer is behind the art of statistics, as before the invention of neural networks, statisticians used to make prediction based on a dataset.

Statisticians used what are called distributions to simulate the trend of the dataset and extract properties like the skew of the data and parameters such as the measurement of center (mean, median, and mode) and measurement of spread (variance and standard deviation). All these are on one-dimensional data, and if the data is in multidimensional space they use the covariance to see how each pair of variables goes together. They detect the correlation between each pair to detect the relationship and the association between the variable pairs. Also, they use what's called hypothesis testing to infer the result of a hypothesis performed on sample data from a dataset.

As we use deep learning to predict the future outcome based on a given observation, we use a huge combination of linear algebra and statistics as a black box to build and optimize the model.

We can't say that deep learning consists 100% of statistics. A main point to address is that deep learning is not just statistics—the same-old stuff, just with bigger computers and a fancier name. This notion comes from statistical concepts and terms that are prevalent in machine/deep learning, such as *regression, weights, biases, models*, etc. Additionally, many models approximate what can generally be considered statistical functions: the *softmax* output of a classification model consists of *logits*, making the process of training an image classifier a *logistic regression*. Also, the *least square algorithm* is a statistical approach to optimize the fitted line on linear regression.

Though the preceding paragraph is technically correct, reducing deep learning as a whole to nothing more than a subsidiary of statistics is quite wrong, and to think that deep learning just consists of statistics is a huge mistake. In fact, the comparison doesn't make much sense. Statistics is the field of mathematics that deals with the understanding and interpretation of data.

Deep learning is nothing more than a class of computational algorithms (hence its emergence from computer science). In many cases, these algorithms are completely useless in aiding with the understanding of data and assist only in certain types of uninterpretable predictive modeling. Let's take a few examples:

- In *reinforcement learning* (we will describe what it is later), the algorithm may not use a preexisting dataset at all.

- In *image processing*, referring to images as instances of a dataset with pixels as features is a bit of a clue to start with.

In Part III, we deal with everything in the model building step—how to choose, build, and train your model—providing a step-by-step guide of model choosing and creation and the best practice techniques used in the industries for building and training.

Decision Theory

We have discussed a variety of concepts from information theory and probability theory that will form the foundations for much of the subsequent discussion in this book.

In the previous section we talked about the importance of probability theory and how it is used to infer and train the model, but also we said that deep learning science does not consist only of statistics. Here we will show you another component that deep learning uses, and we will turn to a discussion about decision theory.

When we combine decision theory with probability theory, it allows us to make optimal decisions in situations involving uncertainty, such as those encountered in machine and deep learning.

Let's take an example to prove how decision theory is an important element and also describe its position in the process of building a deep learning model.

Suppose that we have a dataset that is labeled, and you want to get the function that predicts the label, given an input. This problem is called inference, and it's what probability theory is about. Let us consider that the label consists of one of two values (discrete), either true or false; the statistical term in the model you have built will infer the value of the label given its input, but you have to ensure that this choice is optimal in some appropriate sense. This is the decision step, and it is the main key concept that decision theory will tell us. It's how to make optimal decisions given the appropriate probabilities. We shall see that the decision stage is generally very simple, even trivial.

So to make sure that you have the idea, the model will use the statistics and will try to guess an output to a new given observation. The model will output a probability for each class of the label—one probability if the output is true and another if the output is false. And if we aim to minimize the chance of assigning the input observation to the wrong output label, then intuitively we would choose the class having the higher probability (confidence) value. We now show that this information is correct, and we also discuss more general criteria for making decisions.

In Part III, we also continue to talk about error measurement, how to assess the accuracy of your model, and how to evaluate your model with easy clean step. Also, as there are different types of data, we will show you a variant type of measurement for each type.

Figure 1-1 describes the difference and the correlation between the three theories. We can say that each of these theories is a necessary step for any deep learning pipeline; in other words, each theory participates in the building of any machine or deep learning model.

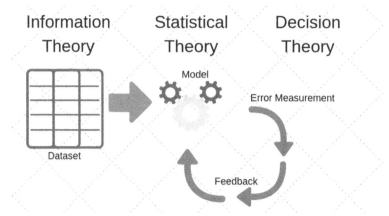

Figure 1-1. *How the three theories are correlated to each other and how they are a necessary component for deep learning pipelines. These theories describe the building process of the machine/deep learning process*

Introduction to Machine Learning

The term "machine learning" was coined by Arthur Samuel in 1959, an American pioneer in the field of computer gaming and artificial intelligence, and stated that "it gives computers the ability to learn without being explicitly programmed."

So let's start to answer a few good questions: *what is machine learning?* and *what is the difference between traditional programming and machine learning?* It's easy to get the difference between them as follows:

- *Traditional programming*: In traditional programming, we have a box that has two inputs (Input, Rule) and the traditional model generates the output based on the rule we add. Figure 1-2 shows an example diagram of traditional programming.

- *Machine learning*: In machine learning, we have a box that has two inputs (Input, Output) and the machine learning model trains to get the rule that generates the output from input. Figure 1-3 shows the machine learning programming example, and this shows how it differs from traditional programming.

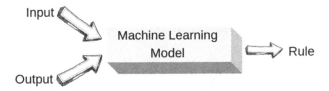

Figure 1-2. *The machine learning diagram*

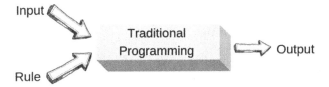

Figure 1-3. *Traditional programming diagram*

Predictive Analytics and Its Connection with Machine learning

To simplify this, we will answer the question: *what is predictive analytics?*

Predictive analytics is a commercial name for machine learning, which is used to devise complex models and algorithms that lend themselves to prediction. So machine learning is a tool for analytics! Maybe, but we can say that it's a model used by researchers, data scientists, engineers, and analysts to produce reliable decisions and results and uncover hidden insights through learning from historical relationships and trends in the dataset.

Let's consider an example. Suppose that you decide to check out that offer for a vacation; you browse through the travel agency web site and search for a hotel. When you look at a specific hotel, just below the hotel description there is a section titled "You might also like these hotels." This is a common use case of Machine Learning called a "recommendation engine." In the previous example, they think that you will like these specific hotels, based on a lot of information they already know about you (**historical dataset**). And here we will leave a question for you: *is machine learning a technique or an approach?*

Machine Learning Approaches

Machine learning has three main approaches:

1. *Supervised* learning

2. *Unsupervised* learning

3. S*emisupervised* learning

So, let us go and discuss each approach in detail.

Supervised Learning

When an algorithm learns from example data and associated target responses that can consist of numeric values or string labels, such as classes or tags, in order to later predict the correct response when posed with new examples, it comes under the category of supervised learning. This approach is indeed similar to human learning under the supervision of someone.

For example, the teacher provides good examples for the student to memorize, and the student then derives general rules from these specific examples.

Let's see it in a visualization graph (Figure 1-4) which will give you a clear illustration of supervised learning. The data is labeled (as each real-world observation/input has a certain output value), as we see in Figure 1-4. The model in supervised learning should see the data, as shown, to allow it to classify the data. The model should use the labeled data to get from Figure 1 on the left to Figure 2 on the right, or in other words, we will classify each data observation/input to a certain response/output.

In the previous example, when we explore data we see a type of supervised learning approach called Classification; there are two types actually, and they solve two problems that describe supervised learning:

- Classification

- Regression

So a good question that might come to mind is *what exactly are classification and regression?*

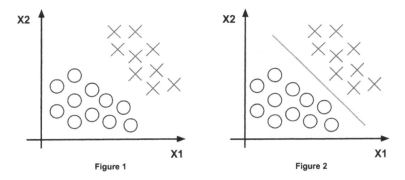

Figure 1-4. *A dataset with a model that classifies different observations (x and o) into two regions*

We define a *classification problem* as when the output variable is a category or a group, such as "black" and "white" or "spam" and "ham (no-spam)" or even X's and O's.

On the other hand, a *regression problem* is when the output variable is a real value, such as "dollars" or "height."

So if you have to choose between two or more labels, you now face a classification problem; and if you try to estimate the floating points of the output, you now face a regression problem (Figure 1-5).

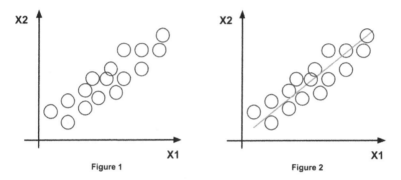

Figure 1-5. *How a regression model tries to fit the dataset*

Unsupervised Learning

Unsupervised Learning is a class of machine learning techniques to find the patterns in data. The data given to unsupervised algorithm are not labeled, which means only the input variables are given with no corresponding output variables. In unsupervised learning, the algorithms are left to themselves to discover interesting structures in the data.

In supervised learning, the system tries to learn from the previous examples that are given. On the other hand, in unsupervised learning, the system attempts to find the patterns directly from the example given. So if the dataset is labeled, it comes under a supervised problem; if the dataset is unlabeled, it is an unsupervised problem.

In unsupervised learning, the algorithms are left to themselves to discover interesting structures in the data, where you only have input data and no corresponding output variables. The easy definition for us ML engineers is that in unsupervised learning we wish to learn the inherent structure of our data without using explicitly provided labels.

But *why do we call it unsupervised learning?* We call it unsupervised learning because unlike supervised learning, there are no given correct answers and the machine itself finds the answers.

For example, suppose we have undergraduate students in a physics course and we need to predict who will pass and who will not, based on their demographic/educational factors. The model should explore the data and try to catch the patterns to get the right answer based on features it has; this is an unsupervised case.

So let's see it in Figure 1-6, which illustrates unsupervised learning. The data is labeled as we see in the graph. The model in unsupervised learning should see the data as shown in the figure, to allow it to cluster the data.

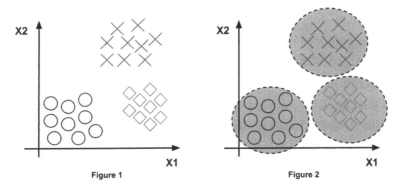

Figure 1-6. *How an unsupervised learning algorithm clusters data into groups or zones*

In Figure 1-6, we grouped data into zones. This phenomenon is called **Clustering**. Actually, we have many problems and problem-solving techniques, but the two most common problems that describe unsupervised learning are:

- Clustering

- Association

So, *what are those types?*

An **association rule learning** problem is where you want to discover rules that describe large portions of your data, such as *"people who buy X also tend to buy Y."*

A **clustering** problem is where you want to discover the inherent groupings in the data, such as grouping customers by purchasing behavior.

Semisupervised Learning

When you have a problem where you have a large amount of input data and only some of the data is labeled, this is called a *semisupervised learning* problem. These problems sit in between supervised and unsupervised learning.

Consider an example, a photo archive where only some of the images are labeled, (e.g., dog, cat, person) and the majority are unlabeled.

How does it work? You can use unsupervised learning techniques to discover and learn the structure in the input variables, then use supervised learning techniques to make best-guess predictions for the unlabeled data, feed that data back into the supervised learning algorithm as training data, and use the model to make predictions on new unseen data.

Checkpoint

To not get confused, we will make a checkpoint to summarize the difference between the machine learning approaches. Table 1-1 summarize the difference between the three approaches, supervised, unsupervised, and semisupervised learning (see also Figure 1-7).

Table 1-1. *The Three Approaches of Machine Learning—*
Summarized to Make a Checkpoint

Supervised	Unsupervised	Semisupervised
All data is labeled and the algorithms learn to predict the output from the input data.	All data is unlabeled and the algorithms learn to the inherent structure from the input data.	Some data is labeled but most of it is unlabeled, and a mixture of supervised and unsupervised techniques can be used.

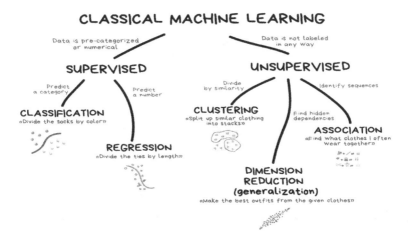

Figure 1-7. *The tree of classical machine learning*

Reinforcement Learning

Reinforcement learning is an area of machine learning. It's all about taking suitable action to maximize the reward in this situation. Reward is one of the main aspects of reinforcement learning.

For example, when you have a dog in your home and try to teach it how to sit, jump, or turn around, you start by showing the dog how to do it and then let it try itself. When you say "sit" and the dog sits, you reward it.

But if it can't understand, you don't reward it. Let's explain reinforcement. The dog is an *agent*; when you say "sit" it's an *environment* state and the agent response is called *action*. When the dog does what you say, you will give it a reward, and the dog tries to maximize this reward by understanding what you say every time. This is reinforcement learning, but the reinforcement learning is out of the scope because it requires more knowledge of mathematics.

Let's gain more understanding with Figure 1-8, which shows the environment system in reinforcement learning.

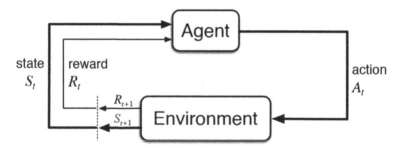

Figure 1-8. *A typical system in reinforcement learning*

As we see, the agent receives a state from the environment, and the agent performs an action. Based on this action, the environment will reward the agent or punish (not reward) it.

The agent tries to maximize these rewards as much as possible (*reinforcement learning*).

But there is some commonality between supervised and reinforcement learning, as summarized in Table 1-2.

Table 1-2. *The Commonality Between Reinforcement Learning and Supervised Learning*

Reinforcement Learning	Supervised Learning
In reinforcement learning the decision is dependent, so we give labels to sequences of dependent decisions.	In supervised learning the decisions are independent of each other, so labels are given to each decision.

From Machine Learning to Deep Learning

We now know and understand that machine learning is a subset of artificial intelligence (AI), and deep learning is a subset of machine learning. So every machine learning program is under the category of AI programs but not vice versa. The question then is *are the approaches of machine learning and AI the same?* The answer is **yes**, because every machine learning problem is an AI problem and deep learning is a subset of machine learning. Understanding this connection is fundamenatl to our book. You should keep in mind that deep learning is nothing more than methods that enhance machine learning algorithms to be more accurate and make some stages easy, like feature extractions, etc.

The easiest takeaway for understanding the difference between machine learning and deep learning is to remember that deep learning is a subset of machine learning.

Lets' See What Some Heroes of Machine Learning Say About the Field

Andrew Ng, the chief scientist of China's major search engine Baidu and one of the leaders of the Google Brain Project, shared a great analogy for deep learning with Wired Magazine: "I think AI is akin to building a rocket ship. You need a huge engine and a lot of fuel," he told Wired journalist Caleb Garling. "If you have a large engine and a tiny amount of fuel, you won't make it to orbit. If you have a tiny engine and a ton of fuel, you can't even lift off. To build a rocket you need a huge engine and a lot of fuel."

The analogy to deep learning is that the rocket engine is the deep learning models and the fuel is the huge amounts of data we can feed to these algorithms.

Nvidia: Machine learning at its most basic is the practice of using algorithms to parse data, learn from it, and then make a determination or prediction about something in the world.

Stanford: Machine learning is the science of getting computers to act without being explicitly programmed.

McKinsey & Co: Machine learning is based on algorithms that can learn from data without relying on rules-based programming.

The University of Washington: Machine learning algorithms can figure out how to perform important tasks by generalizing from examples.

Carnegie Mellon University: "The field of Machine Learning seeks to answer the question *'How can we build computer systems that automatically improve with experience, and what are the fundamental laws that govern all learning processes?'*."

Connections Between Machine Learning and Deep Learning

Machine learning and deep learning use some statistical learning methods from inside, but each method has its own approach to data extraction. Take machine learning for example: when extracting data, each instance in a dataset is described by a set of features or attributes. On the other hand, deep Learning extracts features and attributes from raw data by using a *neural network* with many hidden layers. We will see later what a neural network is and what its components are, and we'll answer these questions in detail.

Difference Between ML and DL

For the sake of simplicity and as a best practice, we are going to make the comparison between machine learning (ML) and deep learning (DL) using an example. We will start with a cats and dogs example as follows.

First, we will explain and talk about this dataset. The cat and dog dataset is set of images that in which each image (an observation) is either labeled dog if the image contains a dog, or cat if the image contains a cat.

Second, we will show the difference between the machine learning approach and the deep learning approach by applying each approach on the dataset and concluding the result of each one.

In Machine Learning

The images according to the dataset are either one of two categories: dogs or cats. The question here is *does the algorithm know which is a dog and which is a cat?*

The answer is simply that the model will try to label the pictures as one of the two categories. It will correctly classify these labels sometimes, and will incorrectly classify the other label of some images, so it will end with a disaster and very low accuracy.

This means that your model failed to learn the differences between a cat and a dog. That's because your model simply labels the pictures of dogs and cats in a way that defines specific features of *both* the animals from a general view.

Let's take an example wherin the pictures of dogs are always taken outside, so maybe if we have a picture of a cat outside, the model may recognize it as a dog because it doesn't take specific dog features into account. It sees that those pictures of dogs have a sky in them, so any picture that contains animal and sky will be considered a dog picture. This is just a simplified example.

In Deep Learning

Now, you have used the deep learning approach and you can see a huge difference in results. So, you wonder *what's the difference that made such a good effect?* Of course with some data preprocessing, you can now make the model learn the difference between the two animals by pointing the model to the animal in the image. That process is called data annotation. Thanks to that, the model can detect and correctly classify the animal in the newly entered image.

Now the model classifies the two animals, the deep learning approach uses what's called an *artificial neural network* (ANN) that sends the input (data of images) through different layers of the network, and each layer is hierarchically learning and defining specific features of each animal.

After the data is processed through layers within the neural network, the system finds the appropriate identifiers for classifying both animals from their images.

What Have We Learned Here?

One of the differences between deep learning vs. machine learning may appear in the way data is presented to the system. Machine learning algorithms almost always require structured data, whereas deep learning networks rely on layers of the ANNs.

Machine learning algorithms are built to "learn" to do things by understanding labeled data, and then use it to produce further outputs with more sets of data. However, they need to be retrained through human intervention when the actual output isn't the desired one.

Deep learning networks do not require human intervention, as the nested layers in the neural networks put data through hierarchies of different concepts, which eventually learn through their own errors. However, even these are subject to flawed outputs if the quality of data isn't good enough.

Data is the governor here. It is the quality of data that ultimately determines the quality of the result.

Why Should We Learn About Deep Learning (Advantages of Deep learning)?

Deep learning is hyped nowadays because of four main reasons:

1. *The data*: One of the things that increased the popularity of deep kearning is the massive amount of data that is available by 2018, which has been gathered over the past years and decades. This enables neural networks to really show their potential, since they get better the more data you put into them. We have questioned whether the huge amount of data is useful for machine learning too, but unfortunately not. Traditional machine learning algorithms will certainly reach a level where more data doesn't improve their performance.

2. *The power*: The computational power available nowadays enables us to process more data.

3. *The algorithms*: These recent breakthroughs in the development of algorithms are mostly due to making them run much faster than before; optimization and parallelism also made the dream come true.

4. *The marketing*: Neural networks were around for decades (proposed in 1944 for the first time) and already had some hype but also faced times where no one wanted to believe and invest in them. The phrase "deep learning" gave it a new fancy name, which made a new hype possible. This means that deep learning isn't a newly created field; you should know that it has been redeveloped again in a new decade.

Deep learning comes more popular, since machine learning algorithms require labeled data, they aren't suitable to solve complex queries which involve a huge amount of data.

Disadvantages of Deep Learning (Cost of Greatness)

1. What should be known is that deep learning requires much more data than a traditional machine learning algorithm.

2. A neural network is Black Box, meaning that you don't know how and why your neural network came up with a certain output.

3. Duration of development: it takes a lot of time to develop a neural network. Although there are libraries like Keras out there, which make the development of neural networks fairly simple, you sometimes need more control over the details of the algorithm. For example, when you try to solve a difficult problem with machine learning that no one has ever done before, you probably use TensorFlow (which we will talk about in detail in this book).

4. Neural networks are also more computationally
    expensive than traditional algorithms. State-of-
    the art deep learning algorithms, which realize
    successful training of bottomless neural networks,
    can take several weeks to train completely from
    scratch (don't worry; this is solved using transfer
    learning techniques).

Introduction to Deep Learning

So, *what is deep learning?* It's fair enough to answer that question by
saying that deep learning just means machine learning using deep neural
networks. Deep learning is a subset of machine learning but using a
human brains representation; scientists try to simulate what human brains
do by creating some algorithms. Many people say that neural networks (NNs)
and deep neural networks (DNNs) are a new approach.

Let's go back to the History of the neural network. The history of
Ddeep learning can be traced back to 1943, when Walter Pitts and Warren
McCulloch created a computer model based on the neural networks of the
human brain. They used a combination of algorithms and mathematics
they called "threshold logic" to mimic the thought process.

Then in 1965, Alexey Grigoryevich Ivakhnenko (developer of the group
method of data handling) and Valentin Grigor'evich Lapa (author of
Cybernetics and Forecasting Techniques) used models with polynomial
activation functions that were then analyzed statistically. From each layer,
the best statistically chosen features were then forwarded on to the next
layer.

1985-1990s is the second winter of AI and deep learning. Deep learning
has its own researchers; they gave more attention to deep learning.

In 1995, Dana Cortes and Vladimir Vapnik developed the support
vector machine (a system for mapping and recognizing similar data).

LSTM (long short-term memory) for recurrent neural networks (RNNs) was developed in 1997 by Sepp Hochreiter and Juergen Schmidhuber.

We don't need to spend all our time in the history of deep learning and how it is raising our world these days, but we wanted to show that deep learning wasn't invented in our days. We gave you some references to the history. Now is the time for deep learning.

Deep learning is based on the way the human brain processes information and learns. It consists of a machine learning model composed of several levels of representation, in which every level uses the information from the previous level to learn deeply. Deep learning consists of neural networks, neural networks consists of layers, and layers consist of hidden units called **perceptrons**.

Now let's see the previous structure when we put them together. First, we should see the types of neural networks, which will allow us to understand the previous structure. We have two main types of neural network (shallow and deep). Table 1-3 shows the difference between them.

Table 1-3. *Shallow vs. Deep Neural Networks*

Shallow	Deep
The word "shallow" means NOT DEEP; it has only one hidden layer.	The word "deep" means it has many hidden units.

Now we know the difference between shallow and deep. But what is a unit? What is a layer? Which is the main factor of comparison? And what are the types of layers? This is the start for deep learning; we should begin with basic function and go up to the complex module. Let's start with the unit, the simplest function of deep learning; it contains the approach of machine learning (supervised, unsupervised, semisupervised, and reinforcement). It may have an activation function (we will explore it later), like logistic regression, or regression function, or clustering function and so on. This shows that deep learning is a subset of machine learning; for now, it's a good explanation for the unit of a deep learning layer. Then, when we have more than one unit together, we create something called a layer: every unit is connected with the units in the previous layer (which is called a fully connected neural network). We have three types of layers (input, hidden (encoders), and output), so after we make units of the input layer and connect it with input data, and create new units for the next layer and connect it with the input and output layers this network is called a shallow neural network. But if we connect this hidden layer with another hidden layer, we will have a deep neural network. It seems simple enough to understand the difference between deep and shallow neural networks. But let's see an image to better understand the difference (Figure 1-9).

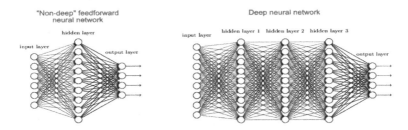

Figure 1-9. *The difference between shallow and deep neural networks*

Now let's see the types of deep neural networks:

- Feedforward neural network

- Radial basis function neural network

- Multilayer perceptron

- Convolutional neural network

- Recurrent neural network—Long short-term memory

- Modular neural network

- Sequence to sequence models

These are the most common neural networks in deep learning. We will talk about some of them in the next chapters in this book, but for now, we can learn their names and get motivated to understand them in detail.

The most common applications in deep learning:

- Computer vision and image processing research (e.g., self-driving cars).

- Natural language processing (speech recognition, machine translation, and natural language understanding)

- Recommendation engines

- Automatic colorization

- Advertising, such as social media ads and user-targeted ads

Machine Learning Mathematical Notations

After introducing the field of deep learning to you, we need to collect some math notations that will be used to prove or conclude some theories. We do not use this book for mathematical proofs or rigorous explanations, but we go more into practical aspects. We will use these math notations to write down some equations that explain why we make something in a certain way, not in another one. So let's start now; in Table 1-4 we've tried to collect all the notations that we need in this book.

$X_{i,j}$ is a notation for a constant, the smallest element in a matrix; or we can say it's the basic notation in a vector, which we use to build the vector. So what is a vector? But first, let's talk about the subscript values (i,j); they are indexing values. i^{th} is an index for rows and j^{th} is an index for columns, to allow us to get the specific value from the vector. Let's see about vectors.

While X_i is a notation for a group of constants grouped together to make a variable called a vector, in the vector we mentioned before about indexing we have i^{th} and j^{th} indexes. But X_i has only subscript i^{th}; this means that we have only one row in the vector or we have only one column. For instance, if we have one row and multiple columns, we will see it like this: $X_{1,j}$. This j means you iterate over columns. On the other hand, if we have one column and many rows, we will see it like this: $X_{i,1}$. This i means you iterate over rows. Let's make it easier: in an array you have rows and columns. If you have only one column and many rows, then $X[i][0]$; if you have one row and many columns, then $X[0][j]$.

Let's go through this a bit more. If we get some constants together we have a Vector, so if we group some vectors together, *what will we see?* It's The Matrix. X is a notation for a matrix, which is used to represent data in dimensions. When we say dimensions in matrices, we may mean columns and rows (in the case of a 2-D matrix), or maybe spaces like 2-D space. On the other hand, we can't say this matrix is 2-D when we have two columns and say 3-D when we have three columnss: it is not true at all. Next, let's see some you some special types of Matrices:

I denotes an identity matrix. An identity matrix is a matrix has its values with zeros; only the main diagonal values are ones.

X^T is a transpose matrix. A transpose matrix is a good method for matrix multiplication or inverting the matrix. We don't need to go into this complex algebra process, but you should know that it is a transpose matrix.

Table 1-4. *Summary of All Needed Notation*

Notation	Description	Usage in Machine Learning
Algebra (Numbers & Arrays)		
x	Scalar (integer or real)	$a = 3$
$\mathbf{x}$	Vector	$a = [1, 2, 3]$
$\mathbf{X}$	Matrix	$A = \begin{bmatrix} a_{ij} \end{bmatrix} = \begin{bmatrix} a_{11} & a_{12} & a_{13} & \cdots & a_{1n} \\ a_{21} & a_{22} & a_{23} & \cdots & a_{2n} \\ a_{31} & a_{32} & a_{33} & \cdots & a_{3n} \\ \cdots & \cdots & \cdots & \cdots & \cdots \\ a_{m1} & a_{m2} & a_{m3} & \cdots & a_{mn} \end{bmatrix}_{m \times n}$
I	Identity	$I_1 = [1], I_2 = \begin{bmatrix} 1 & 0 \\ 0 & 1 \end{bmatrix}, I_3 = \begin{bmatrix} 1 & 0 & 0 \\ 0 & 1 & 0 \\ 0 & 0 & 1 \end{bmatrix}, \cdots, I_n = \begin{bmatrix} 1 & 0 & 0 & 0 & \vdots & \vdots & 0 \\ 0 & 1 & 0 & 0 & \vdots & \vdots & 0 \\ 0 & 0 & 1 & 0 & \vdots & \vdots & 0 \\ 0 & 0 & 0 & 1 & \vdots & \vdots & 0 \\ 0 & 0 & 0 & 0 & \vdots & \vdots & 1 \end{bmatrix}$
X^T	Transpose matrix	

Sets & Graphs

A	A is a set	A = {1,2,3,4} this set means that it contains only 1,2,3,4 and its unique values which mean can't find repeated items in set, unlike vectors it can contain many repeated characters.
$\Re$	The set of real numbers	This means it contains all real numbers.
[a, b]	The real interval including a and b	
(a, b]	The real interval excluding a but including b	

(continued)

31

Table 1-4. (*continued*)

Notation	Description	Usage in Machine Learning
Indexing		
X_i	Element i of vector x, with indexing starting at 1	
$X_{i,j}$	Element (i, j) of matrix X	
$X_{i:}$	Row i of matrix X	
$X_{:j}$	Column i of matrix X	
$X_{i,j,k}$	Element (i, j, k) of a 3-D named *tensor* X	
$X_{:,:,i}$	2-D slice of a 3-D tensor	
x_i	Element i of the vector x	

Functions

$f : A \rightarrow B$	A function f with domain A and range B	
$f(x;\theta)$ or $f(x)$	A function of x parameterized by θ (omitted sometimes)	
$\sigma(x)$	Logistic sigmoid, i.e., $(1 + \exp(x))1$	
$g[f; x]$	A function that maps f to f(x)	
$\|X\|p$	Lpnorm of x	We will use it in the regularizations.
$\|X\|$	L2 norm of x	We will use it in the regularizations.

(continued)

Table 1-4. (*continued*)

Notation	Description	Usage in Machine Learning
Statistics		
μ	Population mean	
$\underline{x}$	Sample mean	
σ^2	Population variance	
s^2	Sample variance	
x or σ	Standard deviation	
s	Sample std dev	
$\underline{x}$	Median	

Machine Learning

X	The set of data used as training examples
Y or in some books y	The set of output examples
$\hat{y}$	Label predicted by a function f, i.e., $\hat{y} = f(x_0)$ (supervised learning)
(x^i, y^i)	The ith example pair in X (supervised learning)
$(\dot{x}, \dot{y})$	A testing pair
D	Dimension of a data point xi
K	Dimension of a label yi
J(w,b)	Cost function To calculate how your model fits data

(continued)

35

Summary

In this chapter we started with a brief introduction to machine learning, then we introduced the backbone of the field—the three theories: information, probability, and decision. After that, we illustrated the evolution from machine learning to deep learning, and we gave you an introduction to the mathematical notation used in this book.

## CHAPTER 2

Setting Up Your Environment

Now that the history and math lessons are out of the way, we must be fair and give you a dessert, so let's now prepare for the upcoming dirty work by setting our environment.

Most deep learning engineers have a development and research environment installed, ready to build and maintain deep learning models. But if you are new to this field, you may wonder about the best tool and programming language available to easily learn and effectively use to advance your career as a data scientist. We believe it's Python and TensorFlow, so in this chapter we'll be installing both.

Background

Python is an interpreted high-level programming language for general-purpose programming. Created by Guido van Rossum and first released in 1991, Python has a design philosophy that emphasizes code readability, notably using significant whitespace. It provides constructs that enable clear programming on both small and large scales. Python has conquered the scientific community and taken the lead due to the huge data processing and analysis packages in it. Also, it allows the data scientist

© Hisham El-Amir and Mahmoud Hamdy 2020
H. El-Amir and M. Hamdy, *Deep Learning Pipeline*,
https://doi.org/10.1007/978-1-4842-5349-6_2

to make fast experiments, and easy development and deployment of scientific applications. Besides all these features, Python allows us to integrate scientific experiments to desktop or web applications.

In addition to Python, there are other tools such as **R** and **MATLAB**, but what makes Python my favorite programming language is that it is open source with a huge community. Python completes your data scientist skills: it's easier for development and deployment of applications to production.

Python 2 vs. Python 3

`wiki.python.org` goes into depth on the differences between Python 2.7 and 3.3, saying that there are benefits to each. It really depends on what you are trying to achieve. But, in summation:

> *"Python 2.x is legacy, Python 3.x is the present and future of the language."*

There are subtle differences between the two. But the biggest difference is the print statement, taking the next phrase from Stack Overflow.

"The most visible (difference) is probably the way the "print" statement works. It's different enough that the same script won't be able to run on both versions at the same time, but pick one and you'll be fine."

Installing Python

Python is an open source, object-oriented and cross-platform programming language. When Python is compared with C++ or even Java as a competitor, Python wins the race due to several reasons:

- Python allows you to build a working software prototype in a very short time.

- Python is flexible, due to hundreds of packages that solve almost all of problems and fill most necessities.

For those reasons, Python became the most used language in the data scientist's toolbox (at least until we have written this book).

So let us proceed to introduce all the settings you need in order to create the data science environment to run the examples and experiments provided with this book.

Novice data scientists who have never used Python (who likely don't have the language readily installed on their machines) need to download the installer from the main website of the project first (`https://python.org/downloads/`) and then install it on their local machine.

Remember that some of the latest versions of most Linux distributions (such as *CentOS*, *Fedora*, *Red Hat Enterprise*, *Ubuntu*, and some other minor ones) have Python 2 packaged in the repository. In such a case, and in case you already have a Python version on your computer (since our examples run on Python 3), you first have to check exactly what version you are running. To do such a check, just follow these instructions:

- Open a Python shell, type python in the terminal, or click on any Python icon you find on your system.

- Then, after having Python started, test the installation by running the following code in the Python interactive shell or REPL:

```
>>> import sys
>>> print (sys.version_info)
```

- If you can read that your Python version has the major=2 attribute, it means that you are running a Python 2 instance. Otherwise, if the attribute is major=3, or if the print statement reports back to you something like v3.x.x (for instance v3.5.1), you are running the right version of Python and you are ready to move forward.

> **Note**   *REPL* stands for *read-eval-print loop*—a simple environment that takes a user's commands as an input line in a shell and outputs the result of the line by printing it.

Python Packages

Python won't come bundled with all you need, unless you take a specific premade distribution. Therefore, to install the packages you need, you can use either pip (you can install pip by following instructions here) or easy_install. Both of these tools run in the command line and make the process of installation, upgrade, and removal of Python packages a breeze. To check which tools have been installed on your local machine, run the following command:

```
$> pip
# or
$> easy_install
```

In most cases in this book, you will see packages installed using pip.

> **Note**   You might find that *pip* is in your system as pip3 and easy_install as easy_install-3, to stress the fact that both operate on packages for Python 3. For insurance, check the version $> pip --version for pip or $> easy_install --version for easy_install.

After this, you can install any Python package easily, and all its dependencies will be downloaded and installed. If you are not sure if the package is in your system or not, try to use it by importing it. If the Python interpreter raises an ImportError message, then you can be certain that the package has not been installed.

This is what happens when the NumPy library has been installed:

```
>>>import numpy
```

This happens if it's not installed:

```
>>> import numpy
Traceback (most recent call last):
File "<stdin>", line 1, in <module>
ImportError: No module named numpy
```

In this case you should install NumPy by running the following command in your terminal:

```
$> pip install
# or
$> easy_install numpy
```

IPython

IPython (Interactive Python) is a command shell—like REPL but has a nicer interface—for interactive computing in multiple programming languages. Originally developed for the Python programming language, it offers introspection, rich media, shell syntax, tab completion, and history.

IPython provides the following features:

- Interactive shells (terminal and Qt-based)

- A browser-based notebook interface with support for code, text, mathematical expressions, inline plots, and other media

- Support for interactive data visualization and use of GUI toolkits

- Flexible, embeddable interpreters to load into one's own projects

- Tools for parallel computing

Installing IPython

You can install IPython (Figure 2-1) using the following command line:

```
$> pip install ipython
```

After finishing the installation, you can run IPython using this command:

```
$> ipython
```

Note   You might find that you have to run `ipython3` instead of running just `ipython`, because *ipython3* is made for Python 3.

When you run your code lines in an IPython shell, you will find that the code is written in a line that starts with `In[1]`. This means that the shell is writing your input in line 1, and the output is written with the same syntax except it starts with `Out[1]`, for example:

```
Python 3.6.5 |Anaconda, Inc.| (default, Apr 29 2018, 16:14:56)
Type 'copyright', 'credits' or 'license' for more information
IPython 6.5.0 -- An enhanced Interactive Python. Type '?' for help.

In [ ]: ▊
```

Figure 2-1. *What IPython looks like*

Jupyter

As a data scientist or machine learning engineer, experimentation is the work approach, so fast experimentation is required. That's why **IPython** was created, but it was limited to Python programming language only until **Jupyter** was created in 2015 by Fernando Perez, in order to address the need for an interactive command shell for several languages. This new project extends the potential usability of the original IPython interface to a wide range of programming languages, such as

- Julia

- Scala

- R

For a more complete list of available kernels for Jupyter, please visit the page here `https://github.com/jupyter/jupyter/wiki/Jupyter-kernels`.

Note   You cannot mix or run the same notebook commands for different kernels; each notebook only refers to a single kernel, that is, the one it was initially created with. Consequently, on the same notebook you cannot mix languages or even versions of the same language like Python2 and Python3.

Jupyter Notebook is built off of IPython, an interactive way of running Python code in the terminal using the **REPL** model (Read-Eval-Print-Loop). The IPython kernel runs the computations and communicates with the Jupyter Notebook front-end interface.

Thanks to the great idea of kernels, which run the user's code communicated by the web-based front-end interface and provide an output of the input code to the interface itself, you can use the same interface and interactive programming style no matter what language you are using for development.

Note   Without the IPython kernel, Jupyter will not even function, even if you have installed another kernel and linked it.

Jupyter is our favored choice throughout this book, and it is used to clearly and effectively illustrate operations with scripts and data and the consequent results.

Regular IDEs are built around the cycle of

1. Writing a script

2. Running it afterward

3. Evaluating its results

Contrary to regular IDEs, Jupyter lets you write your code in chunks, named cells; run each of them sequentially; and evaluate the results of each one separately, examining both textual and graphic outputs—an advantage of this method.

- You can run a selected cell, and got an output from it.

- If a certain cell got an error or exception, other cells saves their outputs instead of running the whole script from start.

Such an approach is also particularly very good for tasks involving developing code based on data—like point 2 in the preceding list—since it automatically accomplishes the often neglected duty of documenting and illustrating how data analysis has been done, its premises and assumptions, and its intermediate and final results.

If a part of your job is to also present your work to an internal or external stakeholder in the project, Jupyter can really do the job of storytelling without any effort.

Users can easily combine code, comments, formulas, charts, interactive plots, and media such as images and videos, making each Jupyter Notebook a scientific sketchpad to find all your experimentations and their results.

Jupyter runs on all browser (such as Explorer, Firefox, or Chrome, for instance) and, when started, presents a cell waiting for code to be written in. Each block of code enclosed in a cell can be run, and its results are reported in the space just after the cell. Plots can be represented in the Notebook (inline plot) or in a separate window. In our example, we decided to plot our chart inline.

Installing Jupyter

You can find complete instructions about Jupyter installation—covering all operating systems—here (`https://jupyter.readthedocs.io/en/latest/install.html`).

If you do not have Jupyter installed on your system, you can promptly set it up using this command:

```
$> pip install jupyter
```

After installation, you can run a Jupyter kernel by calling it from the command line

```
$> jupyter notebook
```

Once the Jupyter instance has opened in the browser, you can see this page (Figure 2-2).

Figure 2-2. *The Jupyter Notebook tree file*

This is the tree page of Jupyter that you can build and control Jupyter Notebooks from. You can see the following in Figure 2-2:

- There are two notebooks in this folder.

- The notebook with the Green colored icon is running in the kernel right now.

- The notebook with the black colored icon is shut down.

- There is Upload button that lets you upload all type of files here (if you are running Jupyter on a remote server).

- With the New button you can create new notebooks or empty files or even can open a terminal.

Note   The tree page of *Jupyter* can only see the directory where the command was executed.

Now click on the New button; in the Notebooks section, choose Python 3 (other kernels may be present in the section, depending on what you installed).

You can also create a *Text File, Folder,* or open a *Terminal* (Figure 2-3).

Figure 2-3. *How to create a new file, folder, or even a terminal*

At this point your new empty notebook will look like the next screenshot (Figure 2-4), and you can start entering the commands in the cells. For instance, you may start by typing in the cell.

Figure 2-4. *The Jupyter Notebook file*

After creating a Jupyter Notebook (and that is an achievement by the way), we need to make sure that you understand some concepts about the file you have created.

What Is an ipynb File?

It will be useful to understand what this file really is.

Each *.ipynb* file is a text file that describes the contents of your Notebook in a format called JSON. Each cell and its contents, including image attachments that have been converted into strings of text, is listed therein along with some metadata. You can edit this yourself—if you know

47

what you are doing—by selecting **Edit ➤ Edit Notebook Metadata** from the menu bar in the Notebook.

There are two terms that you should notice, which may be new to you: **cells** and **kernels** are key both to understanding *Jupyter* and to what makes it more than just a word processor.

- A kernel is a "computational engine" that executes the code contained in a Notebook file.

- A cell is a container for text to be displayed in the notebook or code chunk to be executed by the Notebook's kernel.

Cells form the body of a Notebook. In the screenshot in Figure 2-5, that box with the green outline is an empty cell. There are two main cell types:

Figure 2-5. *A selected, green cell*

- A code cell contains code chunks to be executed in the kernel and displays its output below.

Note   The first cell in a new notebook by default is always a code cell.

- A **Markdown** cell contains text formatted using Markdown and displays its output in place when it is run (Figure 2-6).

Figure 2-6. *Writing a simple Python command*

So, click the Notebook *Run* button in the toolbar or press Ctrl + Enter. The result should look like Figure 2-7.

Figure 2-7. *The output of the first Python command*

Moreover, written notes can be written easily using Markdownm an effortless and fast-to-grasp markup language (`https://daringfireball. net/projects/markdown/`). Math formulas can be handled using MathJax (`www.mathjax.org/`) to render any LaTeX script inside HTML/Markdown. Its syntax has a one-to-one correspondence with HTML tags, so some prior knowledge here would be helpful but is definitely not a prerequisite.

There are many ways to write a LaTex code in a cell. The easiest way is to use the Markdown syntax simply, wrapping the equations with single $ (dollar sign) for an inline LaTeX formula, or with a double dollar sign $$ for a one-line central equation. Remember that to have a correct output, the cell should be set as Markdown. Here's an example (Figure 2-8).

This is **Markdown**

This is **Markdown**

this is : $$ f(n) = ax + b $$

this is :

$$f(n) = ax + b$$

Figure 2-8. *A simple markdown command*

Packages Used in the Book

All the packages that we are going to introduce now are strongly analytical, and used a lot in data science and machine learning projects. All these packages are made up of extensively tested and highly optimized functions for both memory usage and performance, ready to achieve any scripting operation with successful execution. A walkthrough on how to install them is provided in the following section.

NumPy

NumPy stands for (Numerical Python), which is Travis Oliphant's creation, and is the analytical backbone of the Python programming language. It provides multidimensional arrays, along with a large set of functions to operate a multiplicity of mathematical operations on these arrays. Arrays are blocks of data arranged along multiple dimensions, which implement mathematical vectors and matrices. Characterized by optimal memory allocation, arrays are useful not just for storing data, but also for fast matrix operations (vectorization).

- Website: `www.numpy.org/`

- Installation command: `pip install numpy`

- Preferred alias of importing: `import numpy as np`

SciPy

SciPy (pronounced "Sigh Pie") is open source software for mathematics, science, and engineering. The SciPy library depends on NumPy, an original project by Travis Oliphant, Pearu Peterson, and Eric Jones. SciPy completes NumPy's functionalities, offering a larger variety of scientific algorithms for linear algebra, sparse matrices, signal and image processing, optimization, Fourier transformation, and much more.

- Website: `www.scipy.org/`

- Installation command: `pip install scipy`

- Preferred alias of importing: `import scipy as sp`

Pandas

Pandas deals with everything that NumPy and SciPy cannot do. Thanks to its specific data structures, namely *DataFrames* and *Series*, pandas allows you to handle complex tables of data of different types (which is something that NumPy arrays cannot do) and time series. Thanks to Wes McKinney's creation, you will be able to easily and smoothly load data from a variety of sources. You can then slice, dice, handle missing elements, add, rename, aggregate, reshape, and finally visualize your data at will.

- Website: `https://pandas.pydata.org/`

- Installation command: `pip install pandas`

- Prefered alias of importing: `import pandas as pd`

Matplotlib

Matplotlib is a Python 2-D plotting library that produces publication quality figures in a variety of hard copy formats and interactive environments across platforms. Originally developed by John Hunter, matplotlib contains all components that are required to create quality plots from data and to visualize them interactively.

For simple plotting the *pyplot* module provides a MATLAB-like interface, particularly when combined with IPython. For the power user, you have full control of line styles, font properties, axes properties, etc, via an object-oriented interface or via a set of functions familiar to MATLAB users.

- Website: `https://matplotlib.org/`

- Installation command: `pip install matplotlib`

- Preferred alias of importing: `import matplotlib.pyplot as plt`

Note   This importing is for visualization purposes, because matplotlib contains components used for many purposes other than data visualization.

NLTK

NLTK is a leading platform for building Python programs to work with human language data. It provides easy-to-use interfaces to more than 50 corpora and lexical resources. NLTK stands for **Natural Language Toolkit**, and it provides a complete suite of functions for statistical natural language processing (NLP), starting from *tokenizers* to *part-of-speech taggers* and from *tree models* to *named-entity recognition*. Initially, Steven Bird and Edward Loper created the package as an NLP teaching infrastructure for their course at the University of Pennsylvania.

- Website: `www.nltk.org/`

- Installation command: `pip install nltk`

- Preferred alias of importing: `import nltk`

Scikit-learn

The **Scikit-learn** project started as scikits.learn, a Google Summer of Code project by David Cournapeau. Its name stems from the notion that it is a "SciKit" (SciPy Toolkit), a separately developed and distributed third-party extension to SciPy.

Scikit-learn is the core of machine learning and data science operations on Python. It offers all that you need, such as data preprocessing, supervised and unsupervised learning, model selection, validation, and error metrics.

- Website: `http://scikit-learn.org/`

- Installation command: `pip install scikit-learn`

- Preferred alias of importing: `import sklearn`

Gensim

Gensim was created by *Radim Řehůřek*, and it is a robust open source vector space modeling and topic modeling toolkit implemented in Python. It uses NumPy, SciPy, and optionally Cython for performance. Gensim is specifically designed to handle large text collections, using data streaming and efficient incremental algorithms, which differentiates it from most other scientific software packages that only target batch and in-memory processing. It implements latent semantic analysis (LSA), topic modeling by latent Dirichlet allocation (LDA), and Google's word2vec, a powerful algorithm that transforms text into vector features.

- Website: `https://radimrehurek.com/gensim/`

- Installation command: `pip install gensim`

- Preferred alias of importing: `import gensim`

TensorFlow

TensorFlow is an open source software library for dataflow programming across a range of tasks. It is a symbolic math library, and is also used for machine learning applications such as neural networks. It is used for both research and production at Google. TensorFlow was developed by the Google Brain team for internal Google use. It was released under the Apache 2.0 open source license on November 9, 2015.

- Website: `www.tensorflow.org/`

- Installation Command: `pip install tensorflow`

- Preferred alias of importing: `import tensorflow as tf`

Installing on Mac or Linux distributions

The following are the steps to install TensorFlow on Mac and Linux systems:

1. First, install pip and virtualenv (optional) if they are not already installed:

    a. For Ubuntu/Linux 64-bit:

    ```
    $ sudo apt-get install python3-pip python3-dev
    $ sudo pip3 install -U virtualenv #system-wide
    install
    ```

    b. For Mac OS X:

    ```
    $ sudo easy_install pip
    $ sudo pip install --upgrade virtualenv
    ```

2. Then you can create a virtual environment virtualenv. The following commands create a virtual environment virtualenv in the ~/tensorflow directory:

    ```
    $ virtualenv --system-site-packages ~/
    tensorflow
    ```

a. The next step is to activate virtualenv as follows:

```
$ source ~/tensorflow/bin/activate
(tensorflow)$
```

3. Henceforth, the name of the environment we're working in precedes the command line. Once activated, pip is used to install TensorFlow within it.

a. For Ubuntu/Linux 64-bit, CPU:

```
(tensorflow)$ pip install --upgrade
https://storage.googleapis.com/tensorflow/linux/
cpu/tensorflow-0.5.0-cp27-none-linux_x86_64.whl
```

b. For Mac OS X, CPU:

```
(tensorflow)$ pip install --upgrade https://storage.
googleapis.com/tensorflow/mac/tensorflow-0.5.0-py2-
none-any.whl
```

If you want to use your GPU card with TensorFlow, then install another package. I recommend you visit the official documentation to see if your GPU meets the specifications required to support TensorFlow.

---

4. Finally, when you've finished, you must disable the virtual environment:

```
(tensorflow)$ deactivate
```

Installing on Windows

If you can't get a Linux-based system, you can install Ubuntu on a virtual machine; just use a free application called VirtualBox, which lets you create a virtual PC on Windows and install Ubuntu in the latter. So, you can try the operating system without creating partitions or dealing with cumbersome procedures.

Keras

Keras is an open source neural network library written in Python. It is capable of running on top of TensorFlow, Microsoft Cognitive Toolkit, or Theano. Designed to enable fast experimentation with deep neural networks, it focuses on being user friendly, modular, and extensible.

It was developed as part of the research effort of project ONEIROS (Open-ended Neuro-Electronic Intelligent Robot Operating System), and its primary author and maintainer is François Chollet, a Google engineer.

- Website: `https://keras.io/`

- Installation command: `pip install keras`

- Preferred alias of importing: `import keras`

Summary

In this chapter we discussed the whole environment, installation, and preparation of Python; we also discussed how to install every package that will be used in the book from NumPy to TensorFlow. We illustrated the IDE you will use to develop and maintain the code for the exercises, and how to use it for both coding and documenting.

In Chapter 3 we will give a nice tour through the deep learning pipeline, introducing the pipeline step-by-step and also the deep learning approaches. We will get into some practicality with an introduction to TensorFlow.

## CHAPTER 3

A Tour Through the Deep Learning Pipeline

In Chapter 1, we saw an introduction to the deep learning field, to the theories that are the basis of the field. We also discussed the evolution of deep learning and the needed mathematical notation to succeed while reading the book, and we showed you how to install the environment needed for the projects in this book.

In this chapter, we will start with the "flavors" of deep learning, the approaches of it, and different types of neural networks. Next, we will introduce the big picture of the deep learning pipeline; we also will go through the steps of the pipeline in detail. And as always, we will break things up with some technicality, by introducing TensorFlow; we will cover basic recipes in order to understand how TensorFlow works and how to access data for this book and additional resources.

© Hisham El-Amir and Mahmoud Hamdy 2020
H. El-Amir and M. Hamdy, *Deep Learning Pipeline*,
https://doi.org/10.1007/978-1-4842-5349-6_3

Deep Learning Approaches

This deep learning introduction considers how the pioneers in this field got their intuition to make neural networks, fundamental to deep learning. When we talk about something, we want to know where it comes from or how it will work.

This will guide us to learn some biologics. From this point, we will get into neural networks and how they get the data; extract the data; and push the data to the model, which should understand the data through the three learning approaches we talked about in Chapter 1 (supervised, unsupervised, and semisupervised).

What Is Deep Learning

As we mentioned before in Chapter 1 when we discussed what deep learning is, we talked about types of deep learning, using either shallow or deep neural networks. We said that deep learning is basically neural; that we got the idea from the biological neural networks in our brain. So let us see how our brains work.

Biological Deep Learning

To understand how neural networks work and where they come from, we need to mention neurons. There are some questions you might ask yourself, such as *in human brains how does data go from our eyes and we then recognize it and then say some words that seem to make sense?* A neuron is the basic unit in our brain that has all of this information (Figure 3-1). The neuron is also the basic unit of computation in a neural network, often called a *node* or *unit*.

Mathematically speaking, a neuron receives input from some other nodes or from an external source and computes an output. Each *input* has an associated *weight* (w) and *bias* (b), which is assigned on the basis of its relative importance to other inputs. The node applies a function to the weighted sum of its inputs. The idea is that the synaptic strengths (the weights w) are learnable and control the strength of influence and its direction: excitatory (positive weight) or inhibitory (negative weight) of one neuron on another. In the basic model, the dendrites carry the signal to the cell body, where they all get summed. If the final sum is above a certain threshold, the neuron can fire, sending a spike along its axon. In the computational model, we assume that the precise timings of the spikes do not matter and that only the frequency of the firing communicates information. We model the firing rate of the neuron with an activation function (for instance, *sigmoid function*), which represents the frequency of the spikes along the axon. As we see that the representation of neutrals in our brains is most common to our neural which we will talk about it but let us see Figure 3-1.

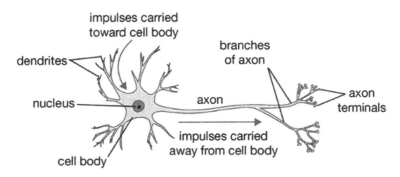

Figure 3-1. *A human neuron*

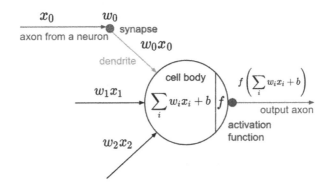

Figure 3-2. *A machine neuron*

However, the question is: *is an artificial neural network (ANN) similar to our brain's neural net?* I think the answer is "not"; ANNs don't work like our brain. An ANN is a simple crude comparison; the connections between biological networks are much more complex than those implemented by an ANN. But let us again try to define a neural network. As we define it again, we can say that:

The neural network is made of neurons (Figure 3-2). Biologically the neurons are connected through synapses and our neural network is connected together by something like synapses or the representation of them (edges), where information flows (weights for out computational model). When we train a neural network, we want the neurons to fire whenever they learn specific patterns from the data, and we model the firing rate using an activation function.

Let's get through this definition. We say that the neuron is the basic unit of computation in a neural network. A machine neuron is a representation of a human neuron; it receives input from some other nodes, or from an external source, and computes an output. Each input has an associated **weight**(w), which is assigned on the basis of its relative importance to other inputs. The node applies a function **f** (defined in the following) to the weighted sum of its inputs, as shown in Figure 3-3.

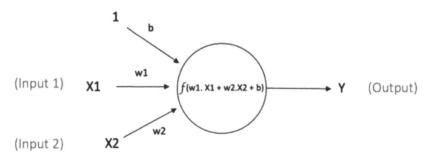

Output of neuron $= Y = f(w1. X1 + w2.X2 + b)$

Figure 3-3. *How a neuron acts*

So, we now know how a neuron in an ANN works, and its architecture. If you have any problem with math notation, you can review mathematical notation sheet in chapter one. We have a new question: *is a neuron a perceptron?* Let's see what perceptron is and get the connection between these two concepts. The perceptron is a linear classifier (binary, and by binary we mean that a single perceptron will output either a 0 or 1 label). Also, it is used in supervised learning. It helps to classify the given input data. So, let's see some characteristics of the perceptron:

- Input values or one input layer

- Weights and bias

- Net sum

- Activation function

This is actually what a neuron has: it has X as *Input* examples or observations or input layer, W as *Weights,* b as *Bias*, and sum, and a as Activation function.

So we can conclude that *perceptron* is *neuron*, so let's move forward into the neural network. The neural network isn't the only perceptron, but it contains many concepts like layers. What are layers? A layer is a group of perceptrons or neurons. But how does it work, and what are the types of layers? A layer is changed by the concept or the algorithm. This will be discussed further and you will see these concepts, but the basic definitions of layers are

- *Input nodes (input layer)*: No computation is done here within this layer; they just pass the information to the next layer (hidden layer most of the time). A block of nodes is also called a layer.

- *Hidden nodes (hidden layer)*: In hidden layers is where intermediate processing or computation is done; they perform computations and then transfer weights (signals or information) from the input layer to the following layer (another hidden layer or to the output layer). It is possible to have a neural network without a hidden layer, and we'll explain this later.

- *Output nodes (output layer)*: Here, we finally use an activation function that maps to the desired output format (e.g., Softmax for classification).

What Are Neural Networks Architectures?

We see the main three functions of layers in the neural network (input layer, hidden layer, output layer), but that can be changed through the concepts or the architectures of the neural network. It seems some layers may have only one perceptron, or many perceptrons connected together, or layers that we can't see how they work. We need to have a lot of complex mathematical equations and combinations and it's difficult to accurately get how these hidden layers work. Let's see some examples of the architectures:

Single-layer perceptron. This is the simplest feedforward neural network and does not contain any hidden layer, which means it only consists of a single layer of output nodes. This is said to be single because when we count the layers we do not include the input layer. The reason for that is because at the input layer no computations are done; the inputs are fed directly to the outputs via a series of weights. Let us discuss the multilayer perceptron first and then talk about the feedforward neural network.

Figure 3-4. *Neuron inputs, weights, and outputs*

Multilayer perceptron (MLP). This class of networks consists of multiple layers (input layer, hidden layer or layers) of computational units, usually interconnected in a feedforward way. Each neuron in one layer has direct connections to the neurons of the subsequent layer. While a single layer perceptron can only learn linear functions, a multilayer perceptron can also learn nonlinear functions.

1. *Input layer*: The input layer has three nodes. The bias node has a value of 1. The other two nodes take X_1 and X_2 as external inputs (which are numerical values depending upon the input dataset). As discussed, no computation is performed in the input layer, so the outputs from nodes in the input layer are 1, X_1, and X_2, respectively, which are fed into the hidden Layer.

2. *Hidden layer*: The hidden layer also has three nodes, with the bias node having an output value of 1. The output of the other two nodes in the hidden layer depends on the outputs from the input layer (1, X_1, and X_2) as well as the weights associated with the connections (edges). Figure 3-4 shows

the output calculation for one of the hidden nodes (highlighted). Similarly, the output from another hidden node can be calculated. Remember that f refers to the activation function. These outputs are then fed to the nodes in the output layer. So, what is a feedforward neural network?

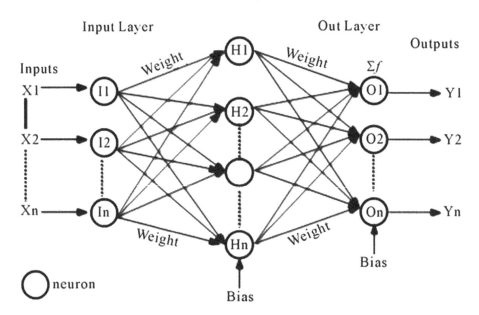

Figure 3-5. *A feedforward neural network*

Feedforward neural network (Figure 3-5). Let's start with the specific regions first, which is the basic builder of our algorithm. The feedforward neural network was the first and simplest type of ANN devised. It contains multiple neurons (nodes) arranged in layers. Nodes from adjacent layers have connections or edges between them. All these connections have weights associated with them. In a feedforward network, the information moves in only one direction—forward—from the input nodes, through the hidden nodes (if any), and to the output nodes. There are no cycles or loops in the network, and it has two types (single-layer perceptron, multilayer perceptron). Let's have a look at Figure 3-6 to see how it works and explain it in a good way.

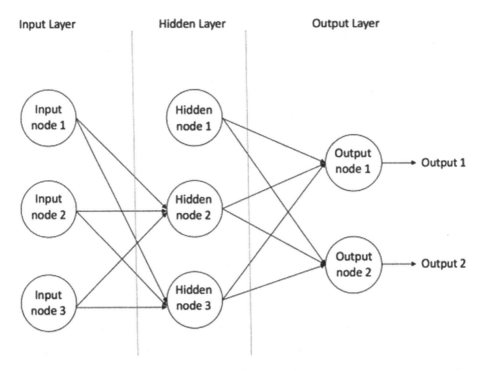

Figure 3-6. *The difference between input, hidden, and output layers*

A feedforward neural network can consist of three types of nodes:

> *Input nodes*: The input nodes provide information
> from the outside world to the network, and
> are together referred to as the "input layer." No
> computation is performed in any of the input
> nodes—they just pass on the information to the
> hidden nodes.

Hidden nodes: The hidden nodes have no direct connection with the outside world (hence the name "hidden"). They perform computations and transfer information from the input nodes to the output nodes. A collection of hidden nodes forms a "hidden layer." While a feedforward network will only have a single input layer and a single output layer, it can have zero or multiple hidden layers.

Output nodes: The output nodes are collectively referred to as the "output layer" and are responsible for computations and transferring information from the network to the outside world.

Feedforward neural networks are primarily used for supervised learning in cases where the data to be learned is neither sequential nor time dependent.

So we now know a lot about the one-direction neural network which is called a feedforward neural network, but we have many types of neural network architectures to talk about. We will discuss them in detail later in Part IV. We have **convolutional neural network**, **recurrent neural network**, and **self-organizing map (SOM)**. These are the types of neural network that can be used in any approach in deep learning—or machine learning (supervised, unsupervised, semisupervised, and reinforcement learning), as we say that deep learning is a subset of machine learning. Let's look at these layers architectures.

First, we will talk about convolutional neural networks (CNNs). CNNs (Figure 3-7) are very similar to ordinary neural networks; they are made up of neurons that have learnable weights and biases. In a convolutional neural network (CNN, or ConvNet, or shift invariant or space invariant) the unit connectivity pattern is inspired by the organization of the visual cortex. Units respond to stimuli in a restricted region of space known as the receptive field. Receptive fields partially overlap, over-covering the entire visual field. The unit response can be approximated mathematically by a convolution operation. They are variations of multilayer perceptrons that use minimal preprocessing. Their wide applications are in image and video recognition, recommender systems, and natural language processing. CNNs require large data to train on.

Second, we will talk about recurrent neural networks (RNNs). In an RNN, connections between units form a directed cycle (they propagate data forward, but also backward, from later processing stages to earlier stages). This allows it to exhibit dynamic temporal behavior. Unlike feedforward neural networks, RNNs can use their internal memory to process arbitrary sequences of inputs. This makes them applicable to tasks such as unsegmented, connected handwriting recognition, speech recognition, and other general sequence processors.

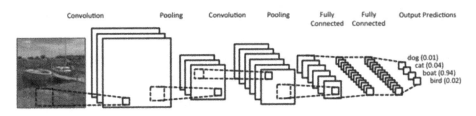

Figure 3-7. *An example of a convolution neural network*

Third is the **self-organizing map (SOM)**. It is a type of ANN that is trained using unsupervised learning to produce a low-dimensional (typically two-dimensional), discretized representation of the input space of the training samples, called a map. It is therefore a method to do dimensionality reduction. SOMs differ from other ANNs, as they apply competitive learning as opposed to error-correction learning (such as backpropagation with gradient descent), and in the sense that they use a neighborhood function to preserve the topological properties of the input space. And it is almost always used for unsupervised learning cases.

What we need you to learn in this chapter is the deep learning architectures and their forms. This is the first step of our stairs to TensorFlow and deep learning layers and how you can make these layers writeable to your project. So far we've talked about them in theoretical and academic ways. We will explore these concepts and know their purpose, and how to know of the architecture is good for your data or not. All this is discussed in our deep learning pipeline.

Deep Learning Pipeline

In the previous chapter we gave an introduction to book, to deep learning, and installed our environment. Yet we did not introduce what the book title means, so *what is the deep learning pipeline?*

Answers to this question will go along with you through the end of the book, but to be fair, you deserve an overview of the meaning of the title.

Before diving into Part II: Data, let's take a moment to look at the overall deep learning pipeline, to make sure that you understand each part correctly. Also, this will help you get situated in the larger picture of the book. To that end, we'll begin with a little musing on the basic concepts, like data and models.

Any predictive modeling, which is any deep learning project, can be broken down into five common tasks:

1. Define and prepare problem

2. Summarize and understand data

3. Process and prepare data

4. Evaluate algorithms

5. Improve results

These tasks can either be combined and used together or broken down and used apart further, but this is the general structure. To work through modeling deep learning problems in a pipeline, you need to map these tasks onto this process. Sometimes you will see these tasks renamed or presented in a different structure, but in general they have the same purpose. So, we will be stuck to this pipeline with these tasks in the exact order throughout the book.

The tasks may need to be adapted or renamed slightly to suit the Python way of doing things (e.g., Pandas for data loading, matplotlib for visualization, and TensorFlow for modeling).

In the next sections we will provide these mappings of the pipeline. We will also elaborate and illustrate each task and the types of subtasks, with examples and libraries that you can use for these types.

Define and Prepare Problem

Why do you collect data? There are questions that data you are collecting can help you answer: questions like *which stocks should I invest in?* or *how can I understand my customers?*

The answer to these questions cannot be that simple. The path from data to answers is full of false starts and dead ends, like a maze. What starts out as a promising approach may not pan out or give the wanted answer, the right answer. What was originally just a hunch may end up leading to the best solution. Deep learning pipelines are made for specific types of reasons; workflows with data are frequently multistage, iterative processes.

For instance, stock prices are observed at the exchange, aggregated by an intermediary like Thomson Reuters, stored in a database, bought by a company, converted into a data warehouse or on a Hadoop cluster, pulled out of the store by a script, subsampled, cleaned by another script, dumped to a file, and converted to a format that you can try out in your favorite modeling library in Python or any other programming language. The predictions are then dumped back out to an *EXCEL* or a *CSV* file and parsed by an evaluator or file reader engine. And the model is iterated multiple times, rewritten in C++ or Java by your production team, and run on all of the data before the final predictions are pumped out to another database.

So, we can say that this step is about understanding the problem and its domain, and to understand, collect, and load everything you need to start working on your problem. This includes

- Python modules, classes, and functions that you intend to use

- Loading your dataset from its source

This is also the home of any global configuration you might need to do. It is also the place where you might need to make a reduced sample of your dataset if it is too large to work with.

Ideally, your dataset should be small enough to build a model or create a visualization within a short period. You can always scale up well-performing models later.

Summarize and Understand Data

Data can be defined as observations of real-world phenomena, and as information that has been translated into a form that is efficient for movement or processing.

As examples, stock market data involves observations of daily stock prices, announcements of earnings by individual companies, and even opinion articles from pundits; or personal biometric data can include measurements of our minute-by-minute heart rate, blood sugar level, blood pressure, etc.

As you need to work in the domain of these observations, you have to understand this domain and these observations, which sometimes you may know as distribution. You need to summarize and visualize these observations to understand them and be able to see trends. Each piece of data provides a small window into a limited aspect of reality. The collection of all of these observations gives us a picture of the whole.

This step is about better understanding the data that you have available. This includes understanding your data through

- Descriptive statistics such as summaries

- Use of data visualizations such as plots with Matplotlib, ideally using convenience functions from Pandas

- Taking your time and using the results to prompt a lot of questions, assumptions, and hypotheses, which you can investigate later with specialized models

Process and Prepare Data

After understanding the domain and the data, you need to prepare it for the next step. So, data processing is, generally, the collection and manipulation of items of data to produce meaningful information. You can think that you have a small piece of the puzzle, and the goal is to solve it. But the picture is messy because it is composed of a thousand little pieces, and in real-life data there's always measurement noise and missing pieces. So, by processing the data, you make it easier for the model to see the clear picture and understand it very well. This is a crucial step in the pipeline, and the accuracy of the model depends on it.

This step is about preparing the data in such a way that it best exposes the structure of the problem and the relationships between your input attributes and the output variable. This includes tasks such as the following:

- Cleaning data by removing duplicates, marking missing values, and even imputing missing values

- Feature selection where redundant features may be removed and new features developed

- Data transforms where attributes are scaled or redistributed in order to best expose the structure of the problem later to learning algorithms

Start simple. Revisit this step often and cycle with the next step until you converge on a subset of algorithms and a presentation of the data that results in accurate or accurate-enough models to proceed.

Evaluate Algorithms

Trying to understand the world through data is like trying to piece together reality using a noisy, incomplete jigsaw puzzle with a bunch of extra pieces. This is where mathematical modeling—in particular statistical modeling too—comes in. The language of statistics contains concepts for many frequent characteristics of data, such as wrong, redundant, or missing. Wrong data is the result of a mistake in measurement. Redundant data contains multiple aspects that convey exactly the same information.

For instance, the day of the week may be present as a categorical variable with values of "*Saturday*," "*Sunday*," ..., "*Friday*," and again included as an integer value between 0 and 6. If this day-of-the-week information is not present for some data points, then you've got missing data on your hands.

A mathematical model of data describes the relationships between different aspects of the data. For instance, a model that predicts stock prices might be a formula that maps a company's earning history, past stock prices, and an industry to the predicted stock price. A model that recommends music might measure the similarity between users (based on their listening habits), and recommend the same artists to users who have listened to a lot of the same songs. Mathematical formulas relate numeric quantities to each other. But raw data is often not numeric. (The action "Alice bought The Lord of the Rings trilogy on Wednesday" is not numeric, and neither is the review that she subsequently writes about the book.) There must be a piece that connects the two together. This is where features come in.

This step is about finding a subset of machine learning algorithms that are good at exploiting the structure of your data (e.g., have better than average skill). This involves steps such as

- Separating out a validation dataset to use for later confirmation of the skill of your developed model. Or defining test options using scikit-learn, such as cross validation and the evaluation metric to use.

- Spot-checking a suite of linear and nonlinear machine learning algorithms

- Comparing the estimated accuracy of algorithms

On a given problem you will likely spend most of your time on this and the previous step until you converge on a set of three to five well-performing machine learning algorithms.

Improve Results

Features and models sit between raw data and the desired insights. In a machine learning workflow, we pick not only the model, but also the features. This is a double-jointed lever, and the choice of one affects the other. Good features make the subsequent modeling step easy and the resulting model more capable of completing the desired task. Bad features may require a much more complicated model to achieve the same level of performance. In the rest of this book, we will cover different kinds of features and discuss their pros and cons for different types of data and models. Without further ado, let's go.

Once you have a shortlist of machine learning algorithms, you need to get the most out of them.

There are two different ways to improve the accuracy of your models:

- Search for a combination of parameters for each algorithm using scikit-learn that yields the best results.

- Combine the prediction of multiple models into an ensemble prediction using ensemble techniques.

The line between this and the previous step can blur when a project becomes concrete. There may be a little algorithm tuning in the previous step. And in the case of ensembles, you may bring more than a shortlist of algorithms forward to combine their predictions.

Once you have found a model that you believe can make accurate predictions on unseen data, you are ready to finalize it. Finalizing a model may involve subtasks such as

- Using an optimal model tuned by scikit-learn to make predictions on unseen data

- Creating a standalone model using the parameters tuned by scikit-learn

- Saving an optimal model to file for later use

Once you make it this far, you are ready to present results to stakeholders and/or deploy your model to start making predictions on unseen data.

Fast Preview of the TensorFlow Pipeline

As we mentioned earlier, TensorFlow (TF) is an open source software library for numerical computation using data flow graphs. Nodes in the graph represent mathematical operations, while the graph edges represent the multidimensional data arrays (tensors) passed between them.

TensorFlow is available with Python and C++ support, and as we agreed in Chapter 1, we shall use Python 3 in this book for learning, as indeed Python API is better supported and much easier to learn. In the next section, we explain very briefly the main features of the TensorFlow package, with some programming examples.

TensorFlow includes various types of rich functions and features that any deep learning engineer needs in their work; the main features include the following:

- Defining, optimizing, and efficiently calculating mathematical expressions involving multidimensional arrays (tensors)

- Programming support of deep neural networks and machine learning techniques

- Transparent use of GPU computing, automating management and optimization of the same memory and the data used. You can write the same code and run it either on CPUs or GPUs. More specifically, TensorFlow will figure out which parts of the computation should be moved to the GPU.

- High scalability of computation across machines and huge data sets

Tensors—the Main Data Structure

TensorFlow bases its data management on tensors. Tensors are concepts from the field of mathematics and are developed as a generalization of the linear algebra terms of vectors and matrices.

Talking specifically about TensorFlow, a tensor is just a typed, multidimensional array, with additional operations, modeled on the tensor object.

Before going to see what the properties of tensors are, we need to teach you how to run these tensors. TensorFlow uses what's called sessions to run tensors, so let's go and see what these sessions mean.

First Session

As in Chapter 1, we installed our environment to make it easier to work on a step-by-step example throughout the book. It is time to move from theory to practice. To get an initial idea of how to use TensorFlow, open your favorite Python editor—it's recommended to use Jupyter—and write the following lines of code:

```
x = 1
y = x + 9
print(y)
import tensorflow as tf
x = tf.constant(1,name='x')
y = tf.Variable(x+9,name='y')
print(y)
```

As you can easily understand in the first three lines, the constant x, set equal to 1, is then added to 9 to set the new value of the variable y, and then the end result of the variable y is printed on the screen.

In the last four lines, we have translated according to the TensorFlow library the first three variables.

If we run the program, we have the following output:

```
10

<tensorflow.python.ops.variables.Variable object at
0x7f30ccbf9190>
```

The TensorFlow translation of the first three lines of the program example produces a different result. Let's analyze them.

First. The following statement should never be missed if you want to use the TensorFlow library. It tells us that we are importing the library and call it tf:

```
import tensorflow as tf
```

Second. We create a constant value called x, with a value equal to one:

```
x = tf.constant(1,name='x')
```

Third. Then we create a variable called y. This variable is defined with the simple equation y=x+9:

```
y = tf.Variable(x+9,name='y')
```

Fourth. Finally, print out the result:

```
print(y)
```

So *how do we explain the different result?* The difference lies in the variable definition. In fact, the variable y doesn't represent the current value of x + 9, instead, it means that when the variable y is computed, take the value of the constant x and add 9 to it. This is the reason why the value of y has never been carried out. In the next section, I'll try to fix it. So, we open the Python IDE (Figure 3-8) and enter the following lines:

```
import tensorflow as tf

x = tf.constant(1, name='x')
y = tf.Variable(x+9,name='y')

model = tf.initialize_all_variables()

with tf.Session() as session:
    session.run(model)
    print(session.run(y))
```

Figure 3-8. *TensorFlow code snippet*

Running the preceding code, the output result is finally as follows:

```
10
```

We have removed the print instruction, but we have initialized the model variables:

```
model = tf.global_variables_initializer()
```

And, mostly, we have created a session for computing values. In the next step, we run the model, created previously, and finally, run just the variable y and print out its current value.

```
with tf.Session() as session:
        session.run(model)
    print(session.run(y))
```

This is the magic trick that permits the correct result. In this fundamental step, the execution graph called the Data Flow Graph (another important feature in TensorFlow) is created in the session, with all the dependencies between the variables. The y variable depends on the variable x, and that value is transformed by adding 9 to it. The value is not computed until the session is executed.

Data Flow Graphs

If you think about it, you will find that any deep learning application is just a result of the repeated computation of complex mathematical expressions. In TensorFlow, every computation can be described using the Data Flow Graph, where each node in the graph represents the instance of a mathematical operation (multiply, divide, add, subtract, and so on), and each edge is a multidimensional data set (tensors) on which the operations are performed.

TensorFlow supports these constructs and these operators. So, let's see in detail how nodes and edges are managed by TensorFlow.

> *Node*: In TensorFlow, each node can represent an instantiation of a single operation. Each operation has at least one input and may have an output or not. For instance, the TensorFlow `tf.add()` function represents one operation, which is the addition operation: it takes two inputs and produces only one output.

> *Edges*: In TensorFlow, edges represent the data consumed or produced by a computation. There are two types of edge:

> - *Normal edges*: They are carriers of data structures (tensors), where an output of one operation (from one node) becomes the input for another operation. For example, the node `tf.matmul()` would correspond to a single node with two incoming edges (the matrices to be multiplied) and one outgoing edge (the result of the multiplication).

> - *Special edges*: These edges are not data carriers between the output of a node (operator) and the input of another node. A special edge indicates a control dependency between two nodes. Let's suppose we have two nodes A and B and special edges connecting A to B; it means that B will start its operation only when the operation in A ends. Special edges are used in Data Flow Graphs to set the happens-before relationship between operations on the tensors.

After learning the structure of the Data Flow Graph, let's now explore some features in deeper detail.

> *Operation*: This represents an abstract computation, such as adding or multiplying matrices. An operation manages tensors. It can just be polymorphic: the same operation can manipulate different tensor element types. For example, the addition of two `int32` tensors, the addition of two `float64` tensors, and so on.

> *Kernel*: This represents the concrete implementation of that operation. A kernel defines the implementation of the operation on a particular device. For example, an add matrix operation can have a CPU implementation and a GPU one. In the following section, we introduce the concept of sessions to create a model execution graph in TensorFlow. Let's explain this topic.

> *Session*: When the client program has to establish communication with the TensorFlow runtime system, a session must be created. As soon as the session is created for a client, an initial graph is created and is empty. It has two fundamental methods:

> - `session.extend`: In computation, the user can extend the execution graph, requesting to add more operations (nodes) and edges (data).

> - `session.run`: Using TensorFlow, sessions are created with some graphs, and these full graphs are executed to get some outputs, or sometimes,

subgraphs are executed thousands/millions of times in run invocations. Basically, the method runs the execution graph to provide outputs.

Dataflow has several advantages that TensorFlow leverages when executing your programs:

- *Parallelism*: By using explicit edges to represent dependencies between operations, it is easy for the system to identify operations that can execute in parallel.

- *Distributed execution*: By using explicit edges to represent the values that flow between operations, it is possible for TensorFlow to partition your program across multiple devices (CPUs, GPUs, and TPUs) attached to different machines. TensorFlow inserts the necessary communication and coordination between devices.

- *Compilation*: TensorFlow's XLA compiler can use the information in your Data Flow Graph to generate faster code, for example, by fusing together adjacent operations.

- *Portability*: The Data Flow Graph is a language-independent representation of the code in your model. You can build a Data Flow Graph in Python, store it in a SavedModel, and restore it in a C++ program for low-latency inference.

Tensor Properties

As previously discussed, TensorFlow uses a tensor data structure to represent all data. Any tensor has a static type and dynamic dimensions, so you can change a tensor's internal organization in real time.

Another property of tensors is that only objects of the tensor type can be passed between nodes in the computation graph.

Note   From now on, every time we use the word tensor, we'll be referring to TensorFlow's tensor objects.

Tensor Rank

A tensor rank represents the dimensional aspect of a tensor, but is not the same as a matrix rank. It represents the number of dimensions in which the tensor lives, and is not a precise measure of the extension of the tensor in rows/columns or spatial equivalents.

A rank one tensor is the equivalent of a vector, and a rank one tensor is a matrix. For a rank two tensor, you can access any element with the syntax t[i, j] similar to the syntax of accessing a matrix, as this rank will produce a matrix. For a rank three tensor, you would need to address an element with t[i, j, k], and so on.

In the following example, we will create a tensor, and access one of its components:

```
import tensorflow as tf
sess = tf.Session()
tens1 = tf.constant([[[1,2],[2,3]],[[3,4],[5,6]]])
print(sess.run(tens1)[1,1,0])
# 5
```

This is a tensor of rank three, because in each element of the containing matrix, there is a vector element, and that's why we need to specify three coordinates.

Table 3-1 summarizes all the variables ranks and their math entity as well as the code definition by example.

Table 3-1. *The Tensor Rank with Example*

Rank/Dimension	Math Entity	Code Definition Example
0	Scalar	scalar = 1000
1	Vector	vector = [2, 8, 3]
2	Matrix	matrix = [[4, 2, 1], [5, 3, 2], [5, 5, 6]]
3	3d-tensor	tensor = [[[4], [3], [2]], [[6], [100], [4]], [[5], [1], [4]]]

Tensor Shape

The TensorFlow documentation uses three notational conventions to describe tensor dimensionality: rank, shape, and dimension number. Table 3-2 shows how these relate to one another.

Table 3-2. *The Tensor Shape with Example*

Rank	Shape	Dimension Number	Example
0	[]	0	Scaler = 10
1	[d0]	1	Vector = [4]
2	[d0, d1]	2	Matrix = [2, 2]
3	[d0, d1, d2]	3	Tensor = [2, 2, 4]
n	[d0, ... , dn-1]	D	

Summary

Now let's do a brief recap about what we've seen and learned in this chapter. First we learned what deep learning is and about its approach, which is a subset of machine learning. We learned the basic function tools to build layers, which combine together to make a deep learning architecture. Finally, we went through the pipeline to give you a view about where the book will go, and what you will learn when you get into chapters that define it in detail. After finishing this chapter, we hope you found it valuable.

## CHAPTER 4

Build Your First Toy TensorFlow app

In the previous chapter, we answered important questions you have to know before continuing reading the book, such as: *what is TensorFlow?*, *what makes it very valuable like this?*, and *is TensorFlow easy to learn?* All these questions come to your mind and many developers too, when you see a TensorFlow word, but yes, TensorFlow is a very valuable package in deep learning. However, there are many packages like it that are compatible with deep learning.

In this chapter, we continue introducing the important concepts you need in TensorFlow. We introduce the usage of TensorFlow in the field of deep learning, and how this library helps us a lot by giving us the necessary components and functions that represent the building blocks for any deep learning model. Also, we give you two small examples of how to build a tiny neural network with TensorFlow. So, let us get started.

Basic Development of TensorFlow

Let us consider another approach, teaching you all the needed TensorFlow functionalities by walking through examples. We will start by warming up, and then we will go to the hard parts bit by bit.

Hello World with TensorFlow

To be fair enough, it's good to understand TensorFlow by seeing a working example of it, so we will go through the advanced part of TensorFlow by giving it to you in small examples.

So, the first example is to warm up the information we gave you in *Chapter* 2, we will build a small app that outputs the words "Hello, TensorFlow!"

As you see, we first import the print_function from the __future__ module to make the print of Python 2 callable as the print function in Python 3. After this, we of course have to import TensorFlow as tf, the popular alias we talked in a previous chapter. Then we initiate the hello variable that equals the tf.constant, and we set it to the word we need to print. Last, we create the session that we will use to run the whole program and we run it to print in the last line.

```python
from __future__ import print_function
import tensorflow as tf
# The value returned by the constructor represents
# the output of the Constant op.
hello = tf.constant('Hello, TensorFlow!')
# Start tf session
sess = tf.Session()
# Run the op
print(sess.run(hello))
```

So, when I first see this piece of code, I may have a question: *what is the tf.constant?* It is a good question, and tf.constant is one of many tensor type variables. But this one has an advantage, as indicated by its name: it cannot change its value through the runtime of the program. A constant has the following arguments, which can be tweaked as required to get the desired function.

- *value*: A constant value (or list) of output type *dtype*

- *dtype*: The type of the elements of the resulting tensor

- *shape*: Optional dimensions of the resulting tensor

- *name*: Optional name for the tensor

Simple Iterations

Now we have warmed up with the previous example; what we saw in this example, we discussed in Chapter 2 (constant, session).

So we need something new, and a bit harder; we need to see what more TensorFlow can do. We now have a session, constant, and variables.

In the next example, we learn to make loops in TensorFlow and make updates to certain variables. These variables simulate the model weights, and loops simulate the epochs that update the model weights.

```
# our first variable in the "global_variable" set
var = tf.Variable(0)
add_operation = tf.add(var, 1)
update_operation = tf.assign(var, add_operation)
with tf.Session() as sess:
# once define variables, you have to initialize
# them by doing this
    sess.run(tf.global_variables_initializer())
    for _ in range(3):
        sess.run(update_operation)
        print(sess.run(var))
```

Note   In this code example we did not import the TensorFlow, as we assume that you imported it in the previous example and both are in the same Python session.

First things first: we created the var variable and initiated it with tf. Variable with 0 value, then we created the add_operation variable that is a TensorFlow addition block or operation. After that we initiated the update_operation with tf.assign(var, add_operation), which simply updates the var variable by reference using the add_operation function, and all that happens when you call the update_operation variable.

Now it's time for creating the session, but if you noticed, we created the session within the with block. Why did we do that? The reason is that after initiating and running each session, we have to close it to free all the resources reserved by the program or by the TensorFlow graph. After that we ran the session sess.run(tf.global_variables_initializer()) and you can see the weird tf.global_variables_initializer() function; the main job of this function is to initialize all variables in the TensorFlow graph. So, if you run tf.Variable or tf.Placeholder—and we will see what it is later—you will see an error and that's due to the uninitiated variables. And last, we do a simple loop that iterates and updates the var variable by running update_operation.

So, how does this simulate a real-world deep learning model? When you train a model, you use variables to hold and update parameters. Variables are in-memory buffers containing tensors. We know about tensors from Chapter 2, so the question is: *is the tensor in the previous example a variable or constant?* It can't be a constant type tensor, so we have to use tf.Variable because we need a form of tensors that can be updated in the runtime of our TensorFlow graph.

Prepare the Input Data

Going a bit further, we need to simulate the input data for any model in TensorFlow. One may question how the user can enter any data to the model. We will make it harder; we will enter an image to TensorFlow. Using the imread command in **matplotlib**, we import a digital image in standard format colors (JPG, PNG, BMP, TIF):

```
import matplotlib.image as mp_image
filename = "lena.jpeg"
input_image = mp_image.imread(filename)
```

However, we can see the rank and the shape of the tensor:

```
print('input dim = {}'.format(input_image.ndim))
print('input shape = {}'.format(input_image.shape))
# input dim = 3
# input shape = (220, 220, 3)
```

You'll see the output, which is (220, 220, 3). This means the image is 220 pixels high, 220 pixels wide, and 3 colors (red, green, blue) deep. Finally, using matplotlib, it is possible to visualize the imported image (Figure 4-1):

```
import matplotlib.pyplot as plt
plt.imshow(input_image)
plt.show()
```

Figure 4-1. *The code output of the lena image*

In this example, `slice` is a bidimensional segment of the starting image, where each pixel has the RGB components, so we need a placeholder to store all the values of the slice:

```
import tensorflow as tf
my_image = tf.placeholder("uint8",[None,None,3])
```

For the last dimension, we'll need only three values. Then we use the TensorFlow operator slice to create a subimage:

```
slice = tf.slice(my_image,[10,0,0],[16,-1,-1])
```

The last step is to build a TensorFlow working session, an extra thing than the last example you saw. When we run the session, we need to feed it the placeholder we have (the data we have); we can do this by sending all the data to `feed_dict`, which will feed the input to the session (or your model perhaps):

```
with tf.Session() as session:
result = session.run(slice,feed_dict={my_image: input_image})
print(result.shape)
plt.imshow(result)
plt.show()
```

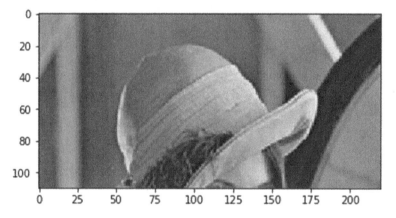

Figure 4-2. *The resulting shape is then as the image shows*

To recap, we put a summary of the tf.Placeholder and tf.Variable in Table 4-1.

Table 4-1. *A Comparison Between tf.Placeholder and tf.Variable*

Placeholder	Variable
A placeholder is a node (same as a variable) whose value can be initialized in the future. These nodes basically output the value assigned to them during runtime. A placeholder node can be assigned using the tf.placeholder() class, to which you can provide arguments such as type of the variable and/or its shape. Placeholders are extensively used for representing the training dataset in a machine learning model, as the training dataset keeps changing.	A TensorFlow variable is the best way to represent a shared, persistent state manipulated by your program. Variables are manipulated via the tf.Variable class. Internally, a tf.Variable stores a persistent tensor. Specific operations allow you to read and modify the values of this tensor. These modifications are visible across multiple tf.Sessions, so multiple workers can see the same values for a tf.Variable. Variables must be initialized before using.
Examples	
A = tf.placeholder(tf.float32, shape=(None, 3)) B = A + 5	x = tf.Variable(3, name="x") y = tf.Variable(4, name="y") f = x∗x∗y + y + 2

Doing the Gradients

TensorFlow has functions to solve other more complex tasks. For example, we will use a mathematical operator that calculates the derivative of y with respect to its expression x parameter. For this purpose, we use the `tf.gradients()` function.

Let us consider the math function $y = 2x^3$. We want to compute the gradient $\dfrac{dx}{dy}$ with respect to $x = 1$. The following is the code to compute this gradient:

```
import tensorflow as tf
x = tf.placeholder(tf.float32)
y = 2*x*x*x
grad = tf.gradients(y, x)
with tf.Session() as session:
    grad_val = session.run(grad,feed_dict={x:1})
    print(grad_val)
```

[6.0]

So, what happens in the preceding code? Let us illustrate it step by step.

1. First, import the TensorFlow library: `import TensorFlow as tf`

2. The x variable is the independent variable of the function: `x = tf.placeholder(tf.float32)`

3. Let's build the function: `y = 2*x*x`

4. Finally, we call the `tf.gradients()` function with y and x as arguments: `grad = tf.gradients(y, x)`

5. To evaluate the gradient, we must build a session: `with tf.Session() as session:`

6. The gradient will be evaluated on the variable x=1: `grad_val = session.run(var_grad,feed_dict={x:1})`

7. The grad_val value is the feed result, to be printed: `print(grad_val)`

That gives the following result: `6.0`

Linear Regression

In this section, we begin our exploration of machine learning techniques with the linear regression algorithm. Our goal is to build a model that is able to predict the values of a dependent variable from the values of one or more independent variables.

Why Linear Regression?

It's a basic machine learning algorithm. It's very justifiable to start from there. First of all, it is a very plain algorithm, so the reader can grasp an understanding of fundamental machine learning concepts such as supervised learning, cost function, and gradient descent.

Additionally, after learning linear regression, it is quite easy to understand the logistic regression algorithm, and believe it or not, it is possible to categorize that one as a small neural network. It's possible, yes; we can see it in the next chapters. In Part III we will see how neural networks work.

What Is Linear Regression?

Linear regression is a very common statistical method that allows us to learn a function or relationship from a given set of continuous data.

For example, we are given some data points of x and corresponding y, and we need to learn the relationship between them. That is called a hypothesis. The hypothesis is a statistical method that tries to predict the best model to fit the input data x. In the case of linear regression, the hypothesis is a straight line, as in the following:

$$h(x) = wx + b$$

We will now work on a project in which we will apply all the concepts we will discuss in the next chapters. In this example, we will create one approximately linear distribution; afterward, we will create a regression model that tries to fit a linear function that minimizes the error function (defined by least squares). This model will allow us to predict an outcome for an input value, given one new sample.

But before we start, let's have a hint about datasets.

Dataset Description

For this example, we will be generating a synthetic dataset consisting of a linear function with added noise.

Let's start with importing some packages:

```
import matplotlib.pyplot as plt
import numpy as np
import tensorflow as tf
```

First, we see `matplotlib.pyplot as plt`. These packages are used for visualization methods, which we will talk about later. The third, `tensorflow`, is an open source software library for dataflow programming across a range of tasks, as discussed in previous chapters.

The second, `numpy`, is a package for mathematical combinations and multiplication, but we don't need to talk about it in more detail now.

To begin, we start by generating our dataset, namely x and y. You can think of each value in x and y as points on the graph. We want NumPy to generate 101 points with a value between (-1 and 1), spread evenly. The result is a NumPy array stored in `trX`. Similarly, we also want to randomly generate y such that it has a gradient of 2 (W) and some form of randomness using `np.random.randn()`. To make things interesting, we set y-intercept b to 0.2.

```
np.random.seed(seed=47)
# Linear space of 101 and [-1,1]
trX = np.linspace(-1, 1, 101)
#Create The y function based on the x axis
trY = 2 * trX + np.random.randn(*trX.shape) * 0.4 + 0.2
```

Let's start to see how data will be plotted and how data is distributed (Figure 4-3).

```
# Create a new figure
plt.figure()
#Plot a scatter draw of the random data points
plt.scatter(trX,trY)
# Draw one line with the line function
plt.plot (trX, .2 + 2 * trX)
plt.show()
```

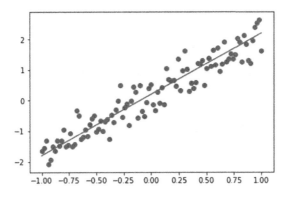

Figure 4-3. *The points of the dataset*

We construct the TensorFlow graph that helps us compute W and b. This is done in the function linear_regression(). In our formula $y = WX + b$; the x and y are nodes represented as TensorFlow placeholders.

```
# create symbolic variables
X = tf.placeholder("float", name="X")
y = tf.placeholder("float", name = "y")
```

In the first argument of **tf.placeholder**, we define the data type as float32—a common data type in the placeholder. The second argument is the **shape** of the placeholder set to **None**, as we want it to be determined during training time. The third argument lets us set the **name** for the placeholder.

We now define our model by declaring name_scope as Model. This scope groups all the variables it contains in order to form a unique entity with homogeneous entities. In this scope, we first define a function that receives the variables of the x-axis coordinates, the weight, and the bias. Then we create a new variable, objects, to hold the changing parameters and instantiate the model with the y_model variable.

```
with tf.name_scope("Model"):
  def model(X, W, b):
    # We just define the line as X*w + b0
    return tf.add(tf.multiply(X,W), b)
  # create a shared variable
  w = tf.Variable(-1.0, name="b0")
  # create a shared variable
  b = tf.Variable(-2.0, name="b1")
  y_model = model(X, W, b)
```

In the **Cost Function**, we create a new scope to include all the operations of this group and use the previously created y_model to account for the calculated y-axis values that we use to calculate the loss.

```
with tf.name_scope("CostFunction"):
  # use sqr error for cost
  cost = (tf.pow(Y-y_model, 2))
```

To define the chosen optimizer, we initialize GradientDescentOptimizer, and the step will be of 0.05, which seems like a reasonable start for convergence.

```
train_op = tf.train.GradientDescentOptimizer(0.05)
               .minimize(cost)
```

Let's create the session and initialize the variables we want to save for reviewing in TensorBoard. We will be saving one scalar variable with the error result of the last sample for each iteration. We will also save the graph structure in a file for reviewing.

```
sess = tf.Session()
init = tf.global_variables_initializer()
# you can use you own path
tf.train.write_graph(sess.graph, '/home/ubuntu/linear',
'graph.pbtxt')
cost_op = tf.summary.scalar("loss", cost)
merged = tf.summary.merge_all()
sess.run(init)
writer = tf.summary.FileWriter('/home/ubuntu/linear',
sess.graph)
```

For model training, we set an objective of 100 iterations (epochs), where we send each of the samples to the train operation of the gradient descent. After each iteration, we plot the modeling line and add the value of the last error to the summary.

```
for i in range(100):
  for (x, y) in zip(trX, trY):
    sess.run(train_op, feed_dict={X: x, Y: y})
    summary_str = sess.run(cost_op, feed_dict={X: x, Y: y})
    writer.add_summary(summary_str, i)
```

```
  b0temp=b.eval(session=sess)
  b1temp=w.eval(session=sess)
  plt.plot (trX, b0temp + b1temp * trX )
plt.show()
```

Let's see how our model is trained in a visualization chart (Figure 4-4). Note that the X data was set on the x-axis, while each line is a model trying to predict the corresponding response y for it.

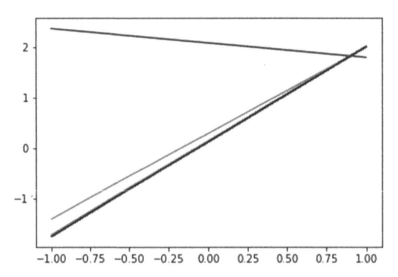

Figure 4-4. *Different lines from different models*

Now let's check the parameter results, printing the run output of the *w* and *b* variables.

```
print ("w = {}".format(sess.run(w))) # Should be around 2
print ("b = {}".format(sess.run(b))) #Should be around 0.2
```

```
Output:
w = 1.8842864
b = 0.12578306
```

It's time to graphically review the data again and the suggested final line—the final predictor line (Figure 4-5).

```
plt.scatter(trX,trY)
plt.plot (trX, sess.run(b) + trX * sess.run(w))
plt.show()
```

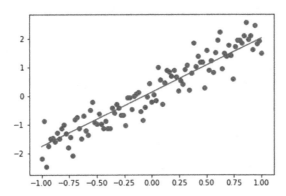

Figure 4-5. *How the model line fits the data points. Notice that the x-axis is the input data, while the y-axis is the corresponding response; also notice that the blue points are the data observations, while the line is the model trying to fit it*

Full Source Code

```
import matplotlib.pyplot as plt
import numpy as np
import tensorflow as tf

# Linear space of 101 and [-1,1]
trX = np.linspace(-1, 1, 101)
#Create The y function based on the x axis
trY = 2 * trX + np.random.randn(*trX.shape) * 0.4 + 0.2

trX = np.linspace(-1, 1, 101)
trY = 2 * trX + np.random.randn(*trX.shape) * 0.4 + 0.2
# create a y value which is approximately linear
#  but with some random noise
```

```python
plt.figure() # Create a new figure
plt.scatter(trX,trY) #Plot a scatter draw of
# the random datapoints

# Draw one line with the line function
plt.plot (trX, .2 + 2 * trX)
plt.show()

# create symbolic variables
X = tf.placeholder("float", name="X")
Y = tf.placeholder("float", name = "Y")

with tf.name_scope("Model"):
  def model(X, w, b):
    # We just define the line as X*w + b0
    return tf.add(tf.multiply(X,w), b)
  # create a shared variable
  w = tf.Variable(-1.0, name="b0")
  # create a shared variable
  b = tf.Variable(-2.0, name="b1")
  y_model = model(X, w, b)

# use sqr error for cost
with tf.name_scope("CostFunction"):
  cost = (tf.pow(Y-y_model, 2))

train_op = tf.train.GradientDescentOptimizer(0.05).
minimize(cost)


sess = tf.Session()
init = tf.global_variables_initializer()
tf.train.write_graph(sess.graph, '/home/ubuntu/linear',
'graph.pbtxt')
cost_op = tf.summary.scalar("loss", cost)
```

```
merged = tf.summary.merge_all()
sess.run(init)
writer = tf.summary.FileWriter('/home/ubuntu/linear',
sess.graph)

for i in range(100):
  for (x, y) in zip(trX, trY):
    sess.run(train_op, feed_dict={X: x, Y: y})
    summary_str = sess.run(cost_op, feed_dict={X: x, Y: y})
    writer.add_summary(summary_str, i)
  b0temp=b.eval(session=sess)
  b1temp=w.eval(session=sess)
  plt.plot (trX, b0temp + b1temp * trX )
plt.show()

print (sess.run(w)) # Should be around 2
print (sess.run(b)) #Should be around 0.2

plt.scatter(trX,trY)
plt.plot (trX, sess.run(b) + trX * sess.run(w))
```

XOR Implementation Using TensorFlow

Exclusive or exclusive disjunction is a logical operation that outputs true only when inputs differ (one is *true*, the other is *false*). We will learn something about it, but if you need to learn it in detail, you can read more about Boolean functions. In calculus, XOR is a solution for a gates problem: $A \oplus B = (A \cup B) \wedge (\sim A \cup \sim B)$. Let's see how it works (Table 4-2).

Table 4-2. *The input and output of the XOR gate*

A	B	A XOR B
0	0	0
0	1	1
1	0	1
1	1	0

This a short explanation about the XOR gate, but it's not our aim to discuss the XOR gate; our aim is to use TensorFlow to make a model XOR. Let's start some code.

We don't need to reexplain these lines of code again, as we just explained it in the linear regression example. And as always, we will start by importing the needed packages.

```
import matplotlib.pyplot as plt
import numpy as np
import tensorflow as tf
```

Let's construct the dataset as a table. We will make both A and B as columns in X_train and the result of the A XOR B function as y_train.

```
# setting required X and Y values to
# perform XOR operation
X_train = [[0,0],[0,1],[1,0],[1,1]]
y_train = [[0],[1],[1],[0]]
```

Then we will create the placeholders that we will enter the data with in the model. We will create one called X for the X_train with shape 4*2— because it has 4 rows and 2 columns, and y for y_train with shape 4*1— because it has 4 rows and it is one column. Both will have the same name of variables.

```
# create symbolic variables
X = tf.placeholder(tf.float64, shape=[4, 2],name="X")
y = tf.placeholder(tf.float64, shape=[4, 1],name="Y")
```

Let's construct some variables, like the number of training examples (number of rows) and features we have in our dataset (number of columns) and some hyperparameters, like learning rate and number of units in our model hidden layer.

```
#number of training examples (Rows)
m = np.shape(X)[0]
#number of features (Columns)
n = np.shape(X)[1]
#number of nodes in the hidden layer
hidden_s = 2
#learning rate initialization
l_r = 1
```

To build the model that should solve the XOR problem, we need to add new things like *theta* and *hidden layers*, and of course, we described the *activation functions* before. So, don't worry about this complex code; we'll explain this code in.

The neural network mainly is composed of layers, so each layer is connected by another layer. Hence, we can define every layer as the output of the earlier or previous layer multiplied by some weights, and we add some bias to it too. For instance, layer one Z_1 is equal to the output of the previous layer, which is A_0 or the input X multiplied by its weights W_1 and then bias b_1 is added. After this, the output of this layer goes through the activation function before sending it to the next layer $A_1 = Sigmoid(Z_1)$. And the process is repeated for the next layer.

So, let do one last and fast recap: in the first layer $Z_1 = W_1 * X + b_1$, and then $A_1 = Sigmoid(Z_1)$. In the next layer, or we can call it the hidden layer, $Z_2 = W_2 * A_1 + b_2$, and then $A_2 = Sigmoid(Z_2)$. So please remember this function, and we will discuss the activation function and the weights and hyperparameters in a later chapter. But for now, we want you to see an end-to-end example.

Now, let us write the model code that does the same as we described in the preceding equations. We start by building the model in a scope called *Model*; using `tf.name_scope` we can achieve this and build small scopes in our system.

```
with tf.name_scope("Model"):
def model():
      # cast tensor to new type
      # and make new variable theta1, theta2
      theta1 = tf.cast(tf.Variable(tf.random_normal([3,
      hidden_s]),name="theta1"),tf.float64)

      theta2=tf.cast(tf.Variable(tf.random_normal([hidden_
      s+1,1]),name = "theta2"),tf.float64)

      #conducting forward propagation
      a1 = tf.concat([np.c_[np.ones(m)], X], 1)
      # the weights of the first layer are multiplied
      # by the input of the first layer
      z1 = tf.matmul(a1,theta1)
      # the input of the second layer is the output of
      # the first layer passed through
      # activation function and column of biases is added
      a2 = tf.concat([np.c_[np.ones(m)],tf.sigmoid(z1)],1)
      # the input of the second layer is
      # multiplied by the weights
      z3 = tf.matmul(a2,theta2)
      # the output is passed through the activation
      # function to obtain the final probability
      h3 = tf.sigmoid(z3)
      return h3
```

Now we call the function that will build the model for us, as in the following:

```
y_model = model()
```

This cost function (Figure 4-6) is captured by the log function, such that:

$$cost = \begin{cases} -log(h(x)) & if\, y = 1 \\ -log(1 - h(x)) & if\, y = 0 \end{cases}$$

Figure 4-6. *The cost function equation*

```
with tf.name_scope("CostFunction"):
            cost=
-tf.reduce_sum(Y*tf.log(y_model)+(1-Y)*tf.log(1-y_
model),axis=1)
```

To define the chosen optimizer, we initialize `GradientDescent Optimizer`, and the step will be of 0.05, a reasonable start for convergence. But the optimizer now works with the hyperparameter learning rate.

```
train_op = tf.train.GradientDescentOptimizer(learning_rate=l_r)
            .minimize(cost)
```

Let's create the session and initialize the variables we want to save for reviewing in TensorBoard. We will be saving one scalar variable with the error result of the last sample for each iteration. We will also save the graph structure in a file for reviewing as follows:

```
sess = tf.Session()
init = tf.global_variables_initializer()
tf.train.write_graph(sess.graph, '/home/ubuntu/xor',
'graph.pbtxt')
```

```
cost_op = tf.summary.scalar("loss", cost)
merged = tf.summary.merge_all()
sess.run(init)
writer = tf.summary.FileWriter('/home/ubuntu/xor', sess.graph)
```

For model training, we set an objective of 100 iterations (epochs), where we send each of the samples to the train operation of the gradient descent. After each iteration, we plot the modeling line and add the value of the last error to the summary.

```
for i in range(100):
  sess.run(train_op, feed_dict={X: X_train, Y: Y_train})
  if i%100==0:
      print("Epoch:",i)
      print("Hyp:",sess.run(y_model,feed_dict ={X:X_train,Y:Y_
      train}))

Epoch: 0
Hyp: [[0.4708459 ]
 [0.50110425]
 [0.50382591]
 [0.51823803]]
```

Now let's check the parameter results, printing the run output of the *w* and *b* variables.

```
# Should be around 2
print ("w = {}".format(sess.run(w)))
#Should be around 0.2
print ("b = {}".format(sess.run(b)))

Output:
w = 1.7057617
b = 0.20965417
```

It's time to graphically review the data again and the suggested final line—the final predictor line.

```
plt.scatter(trX,trY)
plt.plot (trX, sess.run(b) + trX * sess.run(w))
```

Full Source Code

```
import matplotlib.pyplot as plt
import numpy as np
import tensorflow as tf

#setting required X and Y values to perform XOR operation
X_train = [[0,0],[0,1],[1,0],[1,1]]
Y_train = [[0],[1],[1],[0]]

## ADD PLOT HERE
plt.figure() # Create a new figure
plt.scatter(X_train) #Plot a scatter draw of the random
datapoints
# Draw one line with the line function
plt.show()

X = tf.placeholder(tf.float64, shape=[4, 2], name="X")
# create symbolic variables
Y = tf.placeholder(tf.float64, shape=[4, 1], name = "Y")

m = np.shape(X)[0] #number of training examples
n = np.shape(X)[1] #number of features
hidden_s = 2        #number of nodes in the hidden layer
l_r = 1             #learning rate initialization

with tf.name_scope("Model"):
  def model():
```

```
    theta1 = tf.cast(tf.Variable(tf.random_
    normal([3,hidden_s]),name = "theta1"),tf.float64)
    theta2 = tf.cast(tf.Variable(tf.random_normal([hidden_
    s+1,1]), name = "theta2"),tf.float64)
    # conducting forward propagation
    a1 = tf.concat([np.c_[np.ones(m)], X], 1)
    # the weights of the first layer are multiplied by the
    input of the first layer
    z1 = tf.matmul(a1,theta1)
    # the input of the second layer is the output of the first
    layer, passed through the activation function and column of
    biases is added
    a2 = tf.concat([np.c_[np.ones(m)],tf.sigmoid(z1)],1)
    # the input of the second layer is multiplied by the
    weights
    z3 = tf.matmul(a2,theta2)
    # the output is passed through the activation function to
    obtain the final probability
    h3 = tf.sigmoid(z3)
    return h3

  y_model = model()

with tf.name_scope("CostFunction"):
        cost = -tf.reduce_sum(Y*tf.log(y_model)+(1-Y)*tf.
        log(1-y_model),axis = 1)

train_op = tf.train.GradientDescentOptimizer(learning_rate =
l_r).minimize(cost)

sess = tf.Session()
init = tf.global_variables_initializer()
```

```
tf.train.write_graph(sess.graph, '/home/ubuntu/xor','graph.
pbtxt')
cost_op = tf.summary.scalar("loss", cost)
merged = tf.summary.merge_all()
sess.run(init)
writer = tf.summary.FileWriter('/home/ubuntu/xor', sess.graph)

for i in range(100):
  sess.run(train_op, feed_dict={X: X_train, Y: Y_train})
  if i%100==0:
      print("Epoch:",i)
      print("Hyp:",sess.run(y_model,feed_dict = {X:X_train,Y:Y_
      train}))

print (sess.run(w)) # Should be around 2
print (sess.run(b)) #Should be around 0.2

plt.scatter(trX,trY)
plt.plot (trX, sess.run(b) + trX * sess.run(w))
```

Summary

In this chapter, we broke down the theories and used illustrations with practical work and hard code with TensorFlow. We showed you the TensorFlow basics to understand its components and make it easier for you to follow this book and develop products. Then we gave you step-by-step examples, which walk you through the most needed functionalities and API of TensorFlow.

This chapter was the last one in the first part of the book. In the second part the fun begins with a data journey, taking you from data novice to data engineer with a full guide from data definition to data engineering.

PART II

Data

CHAPTER 5

Defining Data

Now that you have a basic introduction to the world of artificial intelligence, machine learning in general, and the world of deep learning in particular, you should understand how this field is very important.

After the Introduction Part, we must define some concepts that are necessary to understand to be a data scientist—or, to be specific, a deep learning engineer. In Part II we take you from data novice to a data analyst or data engineer. All the chapters in this part will be about data. For instance, this chapter defines the data and its basic concepts; it will teach you what real data looks like and the data shapes and forms it takes, with real-life examples, and so on.

In this chapter we define data, and that is equivalent to answering *what is the data?* After that, we make a small comparison among the forms of data such as *structured, semistructured*, and *unstructured*, defining them and using small examples for elaboration. After that, we talk about the ideal form of the data and why you should make your data *tidy data*.

Also, we talk about all types of data that you might face in any real-life project such as **tabular data** and its subtypes, which are *qualitative* and *quantitative*, and the *levels* of tabular data like *nominal, ordinal, interval,* and *ratio*. After that, we look at both **text** and **images** data, using examples to ensure that you understand this very well. Now, let's go to the core of the chapter.

© Hisham El-Amir and Mahmoud Hamdy 2020
H. El-Amir and M. Hamdy, *Deep Learning Pipeline*,
https://doi.org/10.1007/978-1-4842-5349-6_5

Defining Data

Data is unorganized and unprocessed facts: it might be a raw number, figures, images, words, or sounds, derived from observations or measurements. Usually, data is static in nature, a set of discrete, objective facts about events, and there is no inherent meaning in it.

In the field of data science in general, it is important to understand the different types of data for several reasons. Not only because the type of data will help to dictate the method of cleaning and processing—although choosing the best method is important—but also because knowing whether the data is unstructured or perhaps quantitative can tell you a lot about the real-world phenomenon being measured.

So, what we talk about in this chapter is called the *characteristic* of the dataset and not the *entire dataset*. And we will be very clear about which one we refer to at any given time.

Why Should You Read This Chapter?

It might seem worthless to stop and think about what type of data we have before getting into the fun stuff, like model building and maintenance in deep learning, but this is arguably one of the most important steps you need to take to perform data science.

Consider an example where we are looking at a certain dataset of people with a type of disease. In a dataset of people, if we considered the age of every patient on the dataset, we can't say that there's a patient who is zero years old; the age cannot be zero or even a negative number. Another example is a **gender** column that is denoted via an identifying number to save space. For example, perhaps *male* is denoted by 1, while *female* is 2. Without understanding that these numbers are not actually ordered numbers as we normally think about them (where 2 is greater than 1 and therefore female is greater than male), we will make terrible mistakes in our analysis.

You should apply the same principles when you use any data field pipelines. When given a dataset, it is tempting to jump right into exploring, applying statistical models, and researching the applications of deep learning in order to get results faster. However, if you don't understand the type of data that you are working with, then you might waste your time applying models that will be ineffective with that dataset.

When given a new dataset, it is always recommended to take about an hour (it might be less) to make the distinctions mentioned in the following sections.

Structured, Semistructured, and Unstructured Data

The first question you might ask about the upcoming dataset is if the data is structured or not. Let's show you the difference between structured, semistructured, and unstructured data.

- *Structured data*: is easily organized and generally stored in databases or flat files like CSV and EXCEL. Structured data generally consists of numerical information and is objective.

  Some types of structured data can be machine generated, such as data that comes from medical devices (heart rate, blood pressure), manufacturing sensors (rotation per minute, temperature), or web server logs (number of times a page is visited). Structured data can also be human-generated: data such as age, zip code, and gender.

- *Unstructured data*: continues to grow in influence in the enterprise as organizations try to leverage new and emerging data sources. These new data sources are largely made up of streaming data coming from social media platforms, mobile applications, location services, and Internet of Things technologies.

  Most data that exists in text form, including server logs and Facebook posts and its comments, is *unstructured*. Also, a genetic sequence of chemical nucleotides (for example, ACGTATTGCA) is *unstructured* even if the order of the nucleotides matters, as we cannot form descriptors of the sequence using a row/column format.

- *Semistructured data*: is a form of structured data that does not conform with the formal structure of data models associated with relational databases or other forms of data tables, but nonetheless contains tags or other markers to separate semantic elements and enforce hierarchies of records and fields within the data. Therefore, it is also known as self-describing structure.

  Semistructured data might be found in file types of JSON and XML formats.

As a data engineer or deep learning engineer, you will always prefer to work with structured data, although sometimes semistructured too. Most of us, as data scientist/machine learning engineers, build statistical and machine learning models on structured datasets that consist of columns and rows that make the model easy to follow its pattern, but they cannot work on unstructured data because unstructured data has no specific pattern or interpretation. Hence, we cannot expect our model to work with these types of data without a proper cleaning.

But what makes unstructured data so important is that it is so common on the Internet; almost 80%-90% of the world's data is unstructured data, suggesting that 80%-90% of the world's knowledge is hidden in it. This data exists in many forms like tweets, e-mails, literature, and server logs. These are generally unstructured forms of data.

We will see later how to extract knowledge from unstructured free-form datasets, and how to use preanalysis techniques, called *preprocessing,* that turn unstructured data into a clean and organized table—in other words, turn it into structured data.

Tidy Data

Tidy data is a standard way of mapping the meaning of a dataset to its structure. A dataset is messy or tidy, depending on how rows, columns, and tables are matched up with observations, variables, and types.
In **tidy data**:

1. Each variable forms a column.

2. Each observation forms a row.

3. Each type of observational unit forms a table.

This is Codd's 3rd normal form, but with the constraints framed in statistical language, and the focus put on a single dataset rather than the many connected datasets common in relational databases. **Messy data** is any other arrangement of the data.

Tidy data makes it easy for an analyst or a computer to extract needed variables, because it provides a standard way of structuring a dataset. Compare, for example, the different versions of pregnancy data: in the messy version you need to use different strategies to extract different variables. This slows analysis and invites errors. If you consider how many data analysis operations involve all of the values in a variable (every aggregation function), you can see how important it is to extract these values in a simple, standard way. Tidy data is particularly well suited for vectorized programming languages like Python, because the layout ensures that values of different variables from the same observation are always paired.

While the order of variables and observations does not affect the analysis, a good ordering makes it easier to scan the raw values. One way of organizing variables is by their role in the analysis: are values fixed by the design of the data collection, or are they measured during the course of the experiment? Fixed variables describe the experimental design and are known in advance. Computer scientists often call fixed variables *dimensions*, and statisticians usually denote them with subscripts on random variables. Measured variables are what we actually measure in a study. Fixed variables should come first, followed by measured variables, each ordered so that related variables are contiguous. Rows can then be ordered by the first variable, breaking ties with the second and subsequent (fixed) variables. This is the convention adopted by all tabular displays in this book.

Divide and Conquer

As we go further in this chapter, we can divide data into three pieces, as follows:

- Tabular data

- Text data

- Image data

You can face each type in a real-problem, so you have to be ready to understand and prepare such data types.

Tabular Data

Quantitative vs. Qualitative Data

We talked earlier about a dataset's specific characteristics and defined it, and we know that structured data comes in the form of tables or matrices, each consisting of rows and columns. Rows represent a real-world observation or case study, for example, certain patient biometrics. Columns represent data fields, for example, the patient gender field.

Each data column has its own characteristics that define the column, for example, patient gender might be either male or female if *not missing* values. So, these values of patient gender follow some representation that needs to be defined.

Note   Columns can be named *features*, *columns*, *characteristics*, or even *variables*.

All fields follow one of two data types, which are defined as follows:

- *Quantitative data*: This data can be described using numbers, and basic mathematical procedures, including addition, are possible on the set.

- *Qualitative data*: This data cannot be described using numbers and basic mathematics. This data is generally thought of as being described using "natural" categories and language.

Example—the Titanic

The sinking of the RMS Titanic is one of the most infamous shipwrecks in history. Let's say that we are processing observations of what sorts of people were likely to survive, using the following descriptors

119

(characteristics). And each of these characteristics can be classified as either quantitative or qualitative; that simple distinction can change everything. Let's take a look at each one:

- **PassengerId** - *quantitative*: Observation ID; usually takes numerical values

- **Survived** - *qualitative*: Survival (0 = No; 1 = Yes)

- **Pclass** - *qualitative*: Passenger class (1 = 1st; 2 = 2nd; 3 = 3rd)

- **Name** - *qualitative*: Passenger name

- **Sex** - *qualitative*: Passenger gender

- **Age** - *quantitative*: Passenger age

- **SibSp** - *quantitative*: Number of siblings/spouses aboard

- **Parch** - *quantitative*: Number of parents/children aboard

- **Ticket** - *qualitative*: Ticket number

- **Fare** - *quantitative*: Passenger fare

- **Cabin** - *qualitative*: Cabin ID

- **Embarked** - *qualitative*: Port of embarkation (C = Cherbourg; Q = Queenstown; S = Southampton)

So, after we categorize each column to be either q*uantitative* or *qualitative*, you might wonder why these columns are under this category. Let me give another quick example for more elaboration.

Let us consider the column Name, which represents the passenger name. This column is not expressed as a number and we cannot perform math on the name of the passenger, so it is *qualitative*. Now consider Age, which represents passenger age in numbers. We can do basic operations such as adding up the ages for all passengers and dividing it by the total number of passengers to get the passengers' **average** age, thus putting the Age column under the *Quantitative* umbrella.

Note   Even though a ticket number is being described using numbers, it is not quantitative. This is because you can't talk about the *sum* of all ticket numbers or an average ticket number. These are nonsensical descriptions.

Pretty much whenever a word is used to describe a characteristic, it is a *qualitative* factor.

Divide and Conquer

Quantitative data can be broken down one step further, into *discrete* and *continuous* quantities, that can be defined as follows:

- *Discrete variable*: is a variable whose value is obtained by counting—for example, the number of students present, because you can count the students in a certain class.

- *Continuous variable*: is a variable whose value is obtained by measuring. One example is the height of students in a class, because a student's height might be 150 cm or 150.5 cm or even 150.09 cm. The height of a person or building is a continuous number because an infinite scale of decimals is possible. Other examples of continuous data would be time and temperature.

Making a Checkpoint

So far, we have looked at the differences between structured, semistructured, and unstructured data, as well as between qualitative and quantitative characteristics.

These are simple concepts in the data science field, but these distinctions may cause a huge effect on the data scientist's analysis of a given dataset.

A small summarization   To make it simple, data as a whole can either be *structured* or *unstructured*, meaning that the data can either take on an organized row/column—*table like view*— structure with distinct features that describe each row of the dataset, or exist in a free-form state that usually must be preprocessed into a form that is easily digestible.

If data takes a *structured* format or we can say that the data is *tabled*, we can look at each column (*feature*) of the dataset as being either *quantitative* or *qualitative*. Basically, can the column be described using mathematics and numbers or not? The next part of this chapter breaks down data into four very specific and detailed levels. At each order, we will apply more complicated rules of mathematics, and in turn, we can gain a more intuitive and quantifiable understanding of the data.

The Four Levels of Data

Looking at structured data, we understand that each column (*feature*) can be one of the following four levels:

- Nominal
- Ordinal
- Interval
- Ratio

As we explain each element of this list, you will see the structure of data and the variation of columns; each element of this list comes with a practice guide of its processing and techniques used for it. But before we start explaining these techniques, we shall introduce a small statistical definition: the *measure of center*.

Measure of Center

A measure of central tendency (*measure of center*) is a value that attempts to describe a set of data by identifying the central position of the data set (as representative of a "typical" value in the set). This *one value number* describes what the data *tends to*, and for each data level the measure of center technique changes. So, let us start explaining these levels.

Note   Sometimes the *measure of center* of a feature is referred to as the *balance point* of this feature.

The Nominal Level

Let's start with the easiest one to understand, the nominal level, which consists of data that is described purely by **name** or **category**, **Nominal** scales could simply be called "*labels.*" Basic examples include *gender, nationality*, or *species*. They are not described by numbers and are therefore **qualitative**. The following are some examples:

- Your gender is at the nominal level of data. You are either a *male* or a *female.*

- The answer to "*What is your hair color?*" is also nominal, where the answer might be "*brown, black, blond, gray*, or *other.*"

Mathematical Operations Allowed for Nominal

We cannot perform mathematics at the nominal level of data except the basic *equality* and *set membership* functions, as shown in the following two examples:

- Being a *data scientist* is the same as being in the *tech industry*, but not vice versa.

- A figure described as a *square* falls under the description of being a *rectangle*, but not vice versa.

Note   A subtype of nominal scale with only two categories (e.g., male/female) is called *dichotomous.*

Measures of Center for Nominal

In order to find the *balance point* of nominal data, we generally turn to the *mode.*

The **mode** is defined as the most frequently occurring number in a data set. The mode is most useful in situations that involve categorical (qualitative) data that are measured at the nominal level.

As an example of this, consider that we collected all students in a certain school and listed their gender whether *male* or *female* as follows:

> Male, female, male, male, female, male, female, female, male, female, male

The *mode* here is male, where if you count the values you will find that there are six males and five females.

Note   Measures of center such as the *mean* and *median* do not make sense at this level, as we cannot order the observations or even add them together.

What Does It Mean to be a Nominal Level Type?

Data at the nominal level is mostly categorical in nature, like we saw in the last example male/female, because we generally can only use words to describe the data.

While data at the **nominal** level can certainly be useful, we must be careful about what insights we may draw from them. With only the **mode** as a basic *measure of center*, we are unable to draw conclusions about an average observation. This concept does not exist at this level. It is only at the next level that we may begin to perform true mathematics on our observations.

The Ordinal Level

The nominal level is not that flexible—we cannot use most mathematical operations on its observations—due to the fact that we cannot order its observations in any natural way.

So, we can say that the data that can be ordered or have a rank are in the **ordinal level** category; however, although the ordinal level provides us with a rank order, or the ability to place one observation before the other, it does not provide us with relative differences between observations. This means that while we can order the observations from first to last, we cannot execute a mathematical operation such as adding or subtracting the observations to get any real meaning.

Examples of Being Ordinal

Each scale is an incremental level of measurement, meaning each scale fulfills the function of the previous scale and all survey question scales such as **Likert, semantic differential, dichotomous**, etc.

For example, a semantic differential scale question might be "How satisfied are you with our services?" and the answer is one of the following:

- Very unsatisfied – 1

- Unsatisfied – 2

- Neutral – 3

- Satisfied – 4

- Very satisfied – 5

As you can see, the order of variables is important and so is the labeling. Very unsatisfied will always be worse than unsatisfied, and satisfied will be worse than very satisfied.

Note   At the ordinal level, the distance between variables can't be calculated. Description qualities indicate tagging properties similar to the nominal scale, in addition to which, the ordinal scale also has a relative position of variables. Origin of this scale is absent; therefore, there is no fixed start or "true zero."

What Data Is Like at the Ordinal Level

As we said about nominal level data, we can see the same here. The ordinal level is mostly categorical in nature, like we saw in the last example *satisfied/natural/unsatisfied*, because we generally can use words to describe the data order in the process.

While data at the ordinal level can certainly be useful, we must be careful about what insights we may draw from them, as you know now that the order matters. So, selecting the wrong measure of center technique may influence your results and make things go wrong. This concept does not exist at this level. It is only at the next level that we may begin to perform true mathematics on our observations.

Mathematical Operations Allowed for Ordinal

At the ordinal level, we can do more mathematical operations on data that we could not do at the nominal level data. We inherit all mathematics from the nominal level (equality and set membership) and we can also add the following to the list of operations that are allowed at the ordinal level:

- Ordering

- Comparison

Ordering refers to the natural order provided to us by the data; however, this can be tricky to figure out sometimes. For example, if you are building a recommendation engine, you can consider ordering items using each item rank to make a higher rank come first to the user, or you might think to sort these items per cost or materials and so on. This could change the order of the data, but as long as we are consistent in what defines the order, it does not matter what defines it.

Comparisons are another new operation allowed at the ordinal level. At the ordinal level, it would not make sense to say that *male* is better than *female* or vice versa. But at the ordinal level, we can make certain comparisons. For example, going back to the earlier example of a semantic differential scale, we can say that putting an "unsatisfied" on a survey is worse than putting a "neutral."

Measures of Center for Ordinal

At this level, the **median** is an appropriate way of defining the center of the data. The **mean**, however, would be impossible because division and addition are not allowed at this level. But we can use the **mode** like we did at the nominal level.

Here's a small example to elaborate the use of median. Imagine that we have conducted a survey using the satisfaction question in the earlier example; you will see results as follows:

```
5, 2, 5, 2, 4, 1, 2, 3, 1, 5, 4, 3, 4, 5,
3, 2, 5, 3, 2, 1, 4, 5, 3, 4, 4, 4, 5, 4,
3, 2, 4, 5, 4, 2, 1, 4, 5, 4, 3, 2, 1
```

Most people may argue that the mean of these scores would work just fine. But the mean would not be as mathematically viable, because if we added two scores, say a score of four plus a score of one, the sum of two does not really mean anything, and if you divided by their count, say two, the result will be out of these scale representations. If addition/subtraction among the scores doesn't make sense, the mean won't make sense either.

So, let us use *Python* to calculate both mean and median to see the effect of the observation on both of these functions (Figure 5-1). We also recommend using the **NumPy** package.

Importing numpy

```
In [1]: import numpy as np
```

np.mean()

```
In [2]: survey_results = [5, 2, 5, 2, 4, 1, 2, 3, 1, 5, 4, 3, 4, 5,
                          3, 2, 5, 3, 2, 1, 4, 5, 3, 4, 4, 4, 5, 4,
                          3, 2, 4, 5, 4, 2, 1, 4, 5, 4, 3, 2, 1, 5]
```

```
In [3]: print(np.mean(survey_results))
        3.33333333333
```

np.median()

```
In [4]: survey_results = [5, 2, 5, 2, 4, 1, 2, 3, 1, 5, 4, 3, 4, 5,
                          3, 2, 5, 3, 2, 1, 4, 5, 3, 4, 4, 4, 5, 4,
                          3, 2, 4, 5, 4, 2, 1, 4, 5, 4, 3, 2, 1, 5]
```

```
In [5]: print(np.median(survey_results))
        4.0
```

Figure 5-1. *A code example of how to calculate mean and median*

As you can see in the example in figure, using median will produces the output of 4 and this exists in the observation, so we can use it as a center of these observations. However, the mean outputs 3.33 and that's out of the data observation scale—it does not exist in the observations—and that's why we cannot use mean on ordinal level data.

Quick Recap and Check

So far, we have introduced to you two levels of data out of four:

- The nominal level

- The ordinal level

At the nominal level, we deal with data usually described using vocabulary, or you can say it's just named (although sometimes with numbers), with no order, and little use of mathematics (equality and set membership). At the ordinal level, we have data that can be described with numbers and also have a "natural" order, allowing us to put one in front of the other, and you can use comparisons and sorting on them.

The Interval Level

The **interval Level** is defined as a numerical scale where the order of the variables is known, as well as the difference between these variables. Variables that have familiar, constant, and computable differences are classified using the interval scale. It is easy to remember the primary role of this scale too. *"Interval"* indicates distance between two entities, which is what the interval scale helps in achieving.

The interval scale contains all the properties of the ordinal scale, in addition to which, it offers a calculation of the difference between variables. The main characteristic of this scale is the equidistant difference between objects.

Examples of Interval Level Data

Temperature is a great example of data at the interval level. If it is 100 degrees Fahrenheit in one country and 80 degrees Fahrenheit in another one, then the first country is 20 degrees warmer than the second. This simple example allows for so much more manipulation at this level than previous examples.

- 80 degrees is always higher than 50 degrees, and the difference between these two temperatures is the same as the difference between 70 degrees and 40 degrees.

- Also, the value of 0 is arbitrary, because negative values of temperature do exist, which makes the Celsius/Fahrenheit temperature scale a classic example of interval scale.

What Data Is Like at the Interval Level

As you can see, this data level is represented by numbers, and that seems a bit easier for the sake of analysis, but in fact you have to pay some attention to your variables. That is because in selecting the measure of center technique such as **mean,** you have a lot of outliers that may influence the conclusions you get from it.

Mathematical Operations Allowed for Interval

We can use all the operations allowed at the lower levels (equality, ordering, comparisons, and so on), along with two other notable operations:

- Addition

- Subtraction

These two new operations allow us to express the observation in a useful way.

Measures of Center for Interval

At this level, we can use the *median* and *mode* to describe this data; however, usually the most accurate description of the center of data would be the **arithmetic mean**, more commonly referred to as, simply, "the mean." Recall that the definition of the mean requires us to add together all the measurements. At the previous levels, addition was meaningless; therefore, the mean would have lost useful value. It is only at the interval level and above that the arithmetic mean makes sense.

Suppose we look at the temperature of a fridge containing a pharmaceutical company's new vaccine. We measure the temperature every hour with the following data points (in Fahrenheit; Figure 5-2).

Importing numpy

```
In [1]:  import numpy as np
```

np.mean()

```
In [8]:  fridge_temp = [31, 32, 32, 31, 28, 29, 31, 38, 32, 31, 30,
                        29, 30, 31, 28, 30, 27, 29, 32, 31, 31, 28,
                        30, 29, 33, 35, 36, 27, 33, 30, 27, 36, 31]
```

```
In [9]:  print(np.mean(fridge_temp))
```

```
         30.8484848485
```

np.median()

```
In [10]: fridge_temp = [31, 32, 32, 31, 28, 29, 31, 38, 32, 31, 30,
                        29, 30, 31, 28, 30, 27, 29, 32, 31, 31, 28,
                        30, 29, 33, 35, 36, 27, 33, 30, 27, 36, 31]
```

```
In [11]: print(np.median(fridge_temp))
```

```
         31.0
```

Figure 5-2. *A comparison of mean and median on other data*

Note how the *mean* and *median* are quite close to each other and both are around 31 degrees. The question is, *on average, how cold is the fridge?* It's about 31; however, the temperature dropped below 29 degrees but you ended up assuming that it isn't enough for it to be detrimental. This is where the measure of variation can help us understand how bad the fridge situation can be, also how it is good to choose mean or median as a representation of the center of our data.

Measures of Variation for Interval

This is a new measurement that we have not yet discussed. In data science in general, you should take into consideration not only the center of your data, but also it's variation; it is very important to mention how "spread out' the data is. The measures that describe this phenomenon are called measures of variation, or the variance.

You have likely heard of **standard deviation** before. This idea is extremely important and we should address it briefly. A measure of variation—like the standard deviation—is a number that attempts to describe how spread out the data is. Along with a measure of center, a measure of variation can almost entirely describe a dataset with only two numbers.

Standard Deviation

Standard deviation is the most common measure of variation of data at the interval level and beyond. The standard deviation can be thought of as the *average distance a data point is at from the mean*. While this description is technically and mathematically incorrect, it is a good way to think about it. The formula for standard deviation can be broken down into the following steps:

1. Find the mean of the data.

2. For each number in the dataset, subtract it from the mean and then square it.

3. Find the average of each square difference (variance).

4. Take the square root of the number obtained in step three. This is the standard deviation.

Note   The reason we want the "square difference" between each point and the mean and not the "actual difference" is because squaring the value actually puts emphasis on outliers—data points that are abnormally far away.

For example, look back at the temperature dataset. Let's find the standard deviation of the dataset (Figure 5-3).

```
np.std()
```

```
In [12]:  fridge_temp = [31, 32, 32, 31, 28, 29, 31, 38, 32, 31, 30,
                         29, 30, 31, 28, 30, 27, 29, 32, 31, 31, 28,
                         30, 29, 33, 35, 36, 27, 33, 30, 27, 36, 31]
```

```
In [13]:  print(np.std(fridge_temp))
          2.59511443224
```

Figure 5-3. *Calculating standard deviation*

All of this code led to us finding out that the standard deviation of the dataset is closer to 2.6, meaning that, on average, a data point is 2.5 degrees off from the average temperature of around 31 degrees. So, the temperature could likely dip below 29 degrees again in the near future.

Measures of variation give us a very clear picture of how spread out or dispersed our data is. This is especially important when we are concerned with ranges of data and how data can fluctuate (think of percent return on stocks). The big difference between data at this level and at the next level lies in something that is not obvious. Data at the interval level does not have a natural starting point or a natural zero. However, being at zero degrees Celsius does not mean that you have no temperature.

The Ratio Level

Finally, we will take a look at the ratio level. After moving through three different levels with differing levels of allowed mathematical operations, the ratio level proves to be the strongest of the four.

Not only can we define order and difference, the ratio level allows us to multiply and divide as well. This might not seem like much to make a fuss over but it changes almost everything about the way we view data at this level.

Examples

While Fahrenheit and Celsius are stuck in the interval level, the Kelvin scale of temperature boasts a natural zero. A measurement of zero Kelvin literally means the absence of heat. It is a nonarbitrary starting zero. We can actually scientifically say that 200 Kelvin is twice as much heat as 100 Kelvin. Money in the bank is at the ratio level. You can have "no money in the bank"; and it makes sense that $200,000 is twice as much as $100,000.

Measures of Center for Ratio

The arithmetic mean still holds meaning at this level, as does a new type of mean called the geometric mean. This measure is generally not used as much, even at the ratio level, but it's worth mentioning. It is the square root of the product of all the values.

For example, in our fridge temperature data, we can calculate the geometric mean as shown in Figure 5-4.

```
         scipy.stats.gmean
In [14]: from scipy.stats import gmean

In [15]: fridge_temp = [31, 32, 32, 31, 28, 29, 31, 38, 32, 31, 30,
                        29, 30, 31, 28, 30, 27, 29, 32, 31, 31, 28,
                        30, 29, 33, 35, 36, 27, 33, 30, 27, 36, 31]

In [16]: print(gmean(fridge_temp))
         30.7432478687
```

Figure 5-4. *The geometric mean*

Note again how it is close to the arithmetic mean and median as calculated before.

Problems with the Ratio Level

Even with all of this added functionality at this level, we must also generally make a very large assumption that actually makes the ratio level a bit restrictive. Data at the ratio level is usually nonnegative. For this reason alone, many data scientists prefer the interval level to the ratio level. The reason for this restrictive property is because if we allowed negative values, the ratio might not always make sense.

Summarizing All Levels Table 5-1

Table 5-1. *Summarizing All the Tabular Data Levels*

Support:	Nominal	Ordinal	Interval	Ratio
The sequence of variables is established	-	Yes	Yes	Yes
Mode	Yes	Yes	Yes	Yes
Median	-	Yes	Yes	Yes
Mean	-	-	Yes	Yes
Difference between variables can be evaluated	-	-	Yes	Yes
Addition and subtraction of variables	-	-	Yes	Yes
Multiplication and division of variables	-	-	-	Yes
Absolute zero	-	-	-	Yes

The diagram in Figure 5-5 may make it easy for you to understand each level's properties and how each level inherits properties from the level under it.

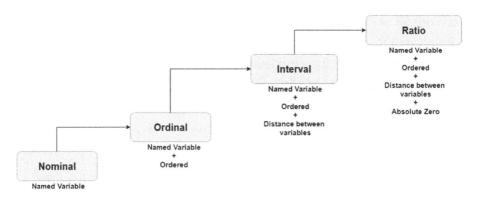

Figure 5-5. *Summary of all data levels*

Text Data

Text is a form of data that has existed for millenniums throughout human history. Including all the sacred texts influencing all the religions, all the compositions of poets and authors, all the scientific explanations by the brightest minds of their times, all the political documents that define our history and our future, and all kinds of explicit human communication, these "all" define the importance of data available in the form of what we call text.

What Is Text Processing and What Is the Level of Importance of Text Processing?

Text processing is one of the most common tasks in many ML applications. As proof, we will see some examples of text processing tasks:

- *Language translation*: Translation of a sentence from one language to another

- *Sentiment analysis*: To determine, from a text corpus, whether the sentiment toward any topic or product, etc. is positive, negative, or neutral

- *Spam filtering*: Detects unsolicited and unwanted email/messages

As we see, text has many tasks that are very important to ML applications besides speech recognition and generation. For now, we can say that we answered this question, but we should say something about text data: it has a name in machine learning, called NLP (natural language processing). But we are here to talk about text, so let's complete our scope about text types. We'll discuss structured and unstructured data, how to use this data in example by processing it and cleaning it, and see the most common techniques that used to process data. So let's continue our journey into data.

First, to simplify text data, we can modify it. Text data is basically just words. A lot of the time the first thing that you do with text is to turn it into numbers using some interesting functions like the bag-of-words formulation.

Second, *what are the tools used in text processing*? NLP is the main tool that machine learning engineers use to handle text data. So let's provide a good definition of NLP.

Natural language processing is a field in machine learning concerning the ability of a computer to understand, analyze, manipulate, and potentially generate human language.

We have many tools that are used in NLP, like NLTK (Natural Language Toolkit), which we talked about in Part I. We will get into more detail about text data in Part III when we talk about the recurrent neural network (RNN), but let's take a simple overview about text.

IMDB—Example

In this example, we work with the most common dataset in text, which is benchmarked in many kinds of research. It is The Large Movie Review Dataset (often referred to as the IMDB dataset) containing 25,000 highly polar movie reviews (good or bad), used for training and again for testing. The problem is to determine whether a given movie review has a positive or negative sentiment (Figure 5-6).

```
df.to_csv('movie_data.csv', index=False, encoding='utf-8')
```

```
df.head()
```

	review	sentiment
0	I went and saw this movie last night after bei...	1
1	Actor turned director Bill Paxton follows up h...	1
2	As a recreational golfer with some knowledge o...	1
3	I saw this film in a sneak preview, and it is ...	1
4	Bill Paxton has taken the true story of the 19...	1

Figure 5-6. *The movie data*

As we see in Figure 5-6, this data of the IMDB is just a data feature of the reviews by users about the film, with a sentiment feature or labeled feature that allow us to know if the review is a positive or negative one. That allows the model to train the combination of words that indicate a negative review or positive review.

It's an easy example that gives us a look at text data. We will talk more in the next chapters about text and how to process text data, and train it with many algorithms and use the architecture that fits the data well. For now we learned a little bit in this portion about what text data is.

Images Data

Computer vision is one of the hottest topics in artificial intelligence. It is making tremendous advances in many fields such as self-driving cars, robotics, and even various photo correction apps. Steady progress in object detection is being made every day. Vision is showing us the future of technology in general and deep learning in particular, so we can't even imagine all of its possibilities.

Computer vision basically is the science of manipulating and processing images to extract certain knowledge from it. So, this approach deals with all types of images from grayscale to multicolor scale, and from 2-dimensional to 4-dimensional scales.

Image processing performs some operations on images to get an intended manipulation. Think about what we do when we start a new data analysis. We do some data preprocessing and feature engineering. It's the same with image processing. We do image processing to manipulate the pictures for extracting some useful information from them. We can reduce noises, and control the brightness and color contrast.

Type of Images (2-D, 3-D, 4-D)

The pipeline of images may still the same for 2-D, 3-D, and 4-D data, but you have to know the different types of data you may deal with. Also you should know and understand each step you may have to deal with for any image data you might face in the future.

2-D Data

We say that images are in 2-dimensional space when each observation is composed of a 2-D matrix, and what makes the whole data is in 3-D space. Images that are 2-D most likely are gray images; that is intuitive because each pixel in 2-dimensional space is represented by only one value, and this value can be between 0 and 255. Now let us upgrade and increase the dimensional space by one, and see what happens.

3-D Data

If you increase the dimensional space by one, then the images are in 3-dimensional space, and that makes each image observation composed of a 3-D tensor, while the whole data is in 4-dimensional space and is composed of a 4-D tensor. Images that are composed of 3-D, are composed of three channels, most likely the red, green, and blue channels, making each image in this data colored. Each pixel in the image is composed of three values, one value between 0 and 225 per each channel, and we will see how to deal with this type of data in a later Chapter 11.

4-D Data

Again, if you increase the dimensional space by one, then the images are in 4-dimensional space, and that makes each image observation composed of a 4-D tensor, while the whole data is in 5-dimensional space and is composed of a 4-D tensor. Images that are composed of 4-D, are composed of three channels, most likely the red, green, and blue channels, making each image in this data colored, and taking the time variation of the image as another dimension.

For instance, biomedical images are typically volumetric images (3-D) and sometimes have an additional time dimension (4-D) and/or multiple channels (4-D–5-D) (e.g., multisequence MR images). The variation in biomedical images (Figure 5-7) is quite different from that of a natural image (e.g., a photograph), as clinical protocols aim to stratify how an image is acquired (e.g., a patient is lying on his/her back, the head is not tilted, etc.). In their analysis, we aim to detect subtle differences (i.e., some small region indicating an abnormal finding).

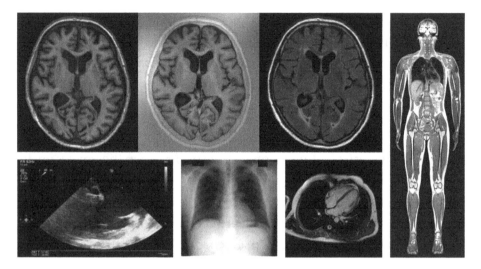

Figure 5-7. *Examples of what 4-D images look like*

Example—MNIST

The MNIST database (Modified National Institute of Standards and Technology database) is a large database of handwritten digits that is commonly used for training various image processing systems. The database is also widely used for training and testing in the field of machine and deep learning.

The MNIST database contains 60,000 training images and 10,000 testing images. Half of the training set and half of the test set were taken from NIST's training dataset, while the other half of the training set and the other half of the test set were taken from NIST's testing dataset.

The MNIST dataset (Figure 5-8) was created by "re-mixing" the samples from NIST's original datasets. The creators felt that since NIST's training dataset was taken from American Census Bureau employees, while the testing dataset was taken from American high school students, it was not well suited for statistical learning experiments.

Figure 5-8. *Sample of the MNIST dataset*

Example—CIFAR-10

In this example, we will be working on one of the most extensively used datasets in image comprehension, one that is used as a simple but general benchmark. In this example, we will build a simple CNN model to have an idea of the general structure of computations needed to tackle this type of classification problem.

This dataset consists of 40,000 images of 32×32 pixels, representing the following categories: *airplane, automobile, bird, cat, deer, dog, frog, horse, ship,* and *truck.* In this example, we will just take the first of the 10,000 image bundles to work on (Figure 5-9).

Figure 5-9. *Sample of the CIFAR-10 dataset*

Summary

The type of data that you are working with is a very large piece of data science and machine learning. It must precede most of your analysis, because the type of data you have impacts the type of analysis that is even possible! Whenever you are faced with a new dataset, the first questions you should ask about it are the following:

- Is the data organized or unorganized?

  For example, does our data exist in a nice, clean row/column structure?

- Is each column quantitative or qualitative?

  For example, are the values numbers, strings, or do they represent quantities?

- At what level of data is each column?

  For example, are the values at the nominal, ordinal, interval, or ratio level?

- If it is image data, what is the data augmentation method we need to use?

- If it is text data, what is the method we will use to transform text to numbers?

The answers to these questions will not only impact your knowledge of the data, but will also dictate the next steps of your analysis. They will dictate the types of charts you are able to use and how you interpret them in your upcoming data models. Sometimes we will have to convert from one level to another in order to gain more perspective.

In the coming chapters, we will take a much deeper look at how to deal with and explore data at different levels. By the end of this book, we will be able to not only recognize data at different levels, but we'll also know how to deal with it at these levels.

CHAPTER 6

Data Wrangling and Preprocessing

In the previous chapter, we defined what data means; we also discussed types and levels of data. So, we are now just getting into action with data! In this chapter, you'll learn how to understand and clean your dataset.

In some books or references you will find the topic of this chapter has a different name; they might call it data munging.

Munging means to manipulate or change, in a series of well-specified and reversible steps, a piece of original data to a completely different— and hopefully more useful—one. You might see some data scientist or deep learning engineers use another term to describe this process in the pipeline. These terms are almost synonymous: terms such as data wrangling or data preparation. By any name, munging is a very important part of any data engineering pipeline.

While reading this book, you will find us mentioning more jargon and technicalities taken from the fields of probability and statistics (such as probability distributions, descriptive statistics, and hypothesis testing). We will try to add a dictionary-like appendix for these terms to make sure that we are on the same page; however, our main purpose is to provide you with the essential concepts for handling deep learning projects, and it is nice if you already are familiar with some of them. But we will put an appendix in case you may need a refresh or even a straightforward

© Hisham El-Amir and Mahmoud Hamdy 2020
H. El-Amir and M. Hamdy, *Deep Learning Pipeline*,
https://doi.org/10.1007/978-1-4842-5349-6_6

introduction to any of the concepts dealt with in this or another chapter. Given such premises, in this chapter the following topics will be covered:

- The data fields pipelines (so that you'll know what is going on and what's next)

- Loading data from a file

- Selecting data you need

- Handling any missing or wrong data

- Augmenting and deleting data

- Grouping and transforming data to obtain new and meaningful information

The Data Fields Pipelines Revisited
Giving You a Reason

We recently read that The New York Times called data cleaning "janitor work" and said that 80 percent of a data scientist's time will be spent doing this kind of cleaning. As we can see in Figure 6-1, despite its importance, data cleaning has not really captured the public imagination in the same way as big data, data mining, or machine learning.

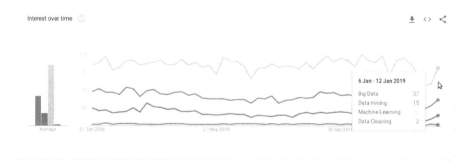

Figure 6-1. *The current trend of machine learning*

Well, unfortunately we would all be a lot better off if we just got the job done rather than ignoring it, complaining about it, and giving it various demeaning names.

Where Is Data Cleaning in the Process?

The data science process is described in six steps, as shown in the following list. Data cleaning is right in the middle, at the third step; but rather than thinking of these steps as a linear (like a waterfall), start-to-finish framework, we will revisit the steps as needed several times over in the course of a project in more of an iterative manner. It is also worth pointing out that not every project will have all the steps; for example, sometimes, we do not have a collection step or a visualization step. It really depends on the particular needs of the project.

- The first step is to come up with the problem statement. Identify the problem you are trying to solve.

- The next step is data collection and storage. Where did the data come from that is helping you answer this question? Where did you store it and in what format?

- Then comes data cleaning. Did you change the data at all? Did you delete anything? How did you prepare it for the analysis and mining step next?

- The next step is data analysis and machine learning. What kind of processing did you do to the data? What transformations? What algorithms did you use? What formulas did you apply? What deep learning algorithms did you use? In what order?

- Representation and visualization is the fifth step. How do you show the results of your work? This can be one or more tables, drawings, graphs, charts, network diagrams, word clouds, maps, and so on. Is this the best visualization to represent the data? What alternatives did you consider?

- The last step is problem resolution. What is the answer to the question or problem you posed in step 1? What limitations do you have on your results? Were there parts of the question that you could not answer with this method? What could you have done differently? What are the next steps?

Data Loading and Preprocessing

After you find the dataset you want for your project, you also know how to import the needed Python packages for the pipeline. In this section, having kept your toolbox ready, you are about to learn how to structurally load, manipulate, and process datasets using pandas and NumPy; and as you have seen in previous chapters, how to set up these packages. You are now ready to proceed to the next section.

Fast and Easy Data Loading

Let's start with pandas. The pandas library offers the most accessible and complete function to load tabular data from a file (*CSV*, comma-separated values; *TSV*, tab-separated values; *JSON*) or a *URL*.

By default, it will store data in a specialized pandas data structure, index each row, separate variables by custom delimiters, infer the right data type for each column, convert data (if necessary), as well as parse dates, missing values, and erroneous values, and do a lot of processing. The amazing part is that you can do all that with just one line of Python code; that's why it's fast and easy.

```
import pandas as pd
iris_df = pd.read_csv('Iris.csv', sep=',', decimal='.',
index_col=False)
iris_df.head()
```

	Id	SepalLengthCm	SepalWidthCm	PetalLengthCm	PetalWidthCm	Species
0	1	5.1	3.5	1.4	0.2	Iris-setosa
1	2	4.9	3.0	1.4	0.2	Iris-setosa
2	3	4.7	3.2	1.3	0.2	Iris-setosa
3	4	4.6	3.1	1.5	0.2	Iris-setosa
4	5	5.0	3.6	1.4	0.2	Iris-setosa

Figure 6-2. *The table output of the DataFrame*

```
iris_df   = pd.read_csv(iris_data, sep=',',
            decimal='.', header=None, index_col=False,
            names=['sepal_length', 'sepal_width', 'petal_length',
                'petal_width', 'target'])
```

```
import urllib
import pandas as pd
data_url  = "https://archive.ics.uci.edu/ml/machine-learning-
databases/iris/iris.data"
```

```
request   = urllib.request.Request(data_url)
iris_data = urllib.request.urlopen(request)
iris_df   = pd.read_csv(iris_data, sep=',',
                    decimal='.', header=None,
```

```
                    index_col=False,
                    names=['sepal_length', 'sepal_width',
                            'petal_length', 'petal_width',
                            'target'])
iris_df.head()
```

	sepal_length	sepal_width	petal_length	petal_width	target
0	5.1	3.5	1.4	0.2	Iris-setosa
1	4.9	3.0	1.4	0.2	Iris-setosa
2	4.7	3.2	1.3	0.2	Iris-setosa
3	4.6	3.1	1.5	0.2	Iris-setosa
4	5.0	3.6	1.4	0.2	Iris-setosa

Figure 6-3. *The table output of the online DataFrame*

As you see in the two preceding code cells (Figures 6-2 and 6-3), both of them do the same job, which is loading the data, either from a file (*CSV*, sometimes called a flat file), or from a *URL* (e.g., the cloud).

In the case of a file, you can specify: the name of the file; the character used as a separator (sep), which might be comma, tab, hash, etc...; the character used for the decimal placeholder (decimal), which might look like 10.01 in the dataset or like 10,01; whether there is a header (header) or not; and the variable names (using names and a list). pandas has some default settings of some of its parameters like the sep=',' for example, and also decimal='.'.

Note   Be careful that you do not set the sep (separator) and the decimal point for numbers with the same values, to prevent loading errors and for data-loading safety.

The resulting object, named iris, is a pandas DataFrame. It's more than a simple Python list or dictionary, and in the sections that follow, we will explore some of its features and functionalities. To get an idea of its content (to view the inner data values), you can print the first (or the last) row(s), using the following commands (Figures 6-4 and 6-5):

iris_df.head()

	sepal_length	sepal_width	petal_length	petal_width	target
0	5.1	3.5	1.4	0.2	Iris-setosa
1	4.9	3.0	1.4	0.2	Iris-setosa
2	4.7	3.2	1.3	0.2	Iris-setosa
3	4.6	3.1	1.5	0.2	Iris-setosa
4	5.0	3.6	1.4	0.2	Iris-setosa

Figure 6-4. *A table that outputs from the head() function*

Iris_df.tail(7)

	sepal_length	sepal_width	petal_length	petal_width	target
143	6.8	3.2	5.9	2.3	Iris-virginica
144	6.7	3.3	5.7	2.5	Iris-virginica
145	6.7	3.0	5.2	2.3	Iris-virginica
146	6.3	2.5	5.0	1.9	Iris-virginica
147	6.5	3.0	5.2	2.0	Iris-virginica
148	6.2	3.4	5.4	2.3	Iris-virginica
149	5.9	3.0	5.1	1.8	Iris-virginica

Figure 6-5. *The output table from the tail() function*

Note   The head/tail functions, if called without arguments, will print only five rows. If you want to get back a different number of rows, just call the function using the number of rows you want to see as an argument, as in the second of the preceding two code cells.

Next, you might want to see just the names of columns (**hint:** you can see them when you use iris.head()); to get the names of the columns, you can simply use the following method:

```
iris_df.columns
# Output:
# Index(['sepal_length', 'sepal_width', 'petal_length',
# 'petal_width', 'target'], dtype='object')

iris_df.columns = ['s_length', 's_width', 'p_length', 'p_width',
                   'target']
```

The resulting object in code cell one is a very interesting one. It looks like a *Python list*, but it actually is a *pandas index*. As suggested by the object's name, it indexes the columns' names. And in code cell two you see that you can change the column names as you want, but be careful and choose the names wisely that you are using to represent the columns.

To extract the target column (Figure 6-6), for example, you can simply do the following:

```
y = iris_df['target']
y.head()
```

```
0       Iris-setosa
1       Iris-setosa
2       Iris-setosa
3       Iris-setosa
4       Iris-setosa
Name: target, dtype: object
```

Figure 6-6. *The output series that represents the target variable*

The type of the object y is a pandas Series. Right now, think of it as a one-dimensional array or vector as mathematically represented with axis labels, as we will investigate in depth later on.

Note   For convention we use small letters for vector/array, and capital letters for matrices.

```
y = iris_df.target
```

Note   As you can see, we can get the column as a pandas DataFrame(matrix), but it is not preferred.

Now, we just understood that a pandas index class acts like a dictionary index of the table's columns.

Note that you can also get a list of columns referring to them by their indexes, as follows (Figure 6-7):

```
X = iris_df[['s_length', 's_width', 'p_length', 'p_width']]
X.head()
```

	s_length	s_width	p_length	p_width
0	5.1	3.5	1.4	0.2
1	4.9	3.0	1.4	0.2
2	4.7	3.2	1.3	0.2
3	4.6	3.1	1.5	0.2
4	5.0	3.6	1.4	0.2

Figure 6-7. *Just the selected variables output*

As you can see here the pandas DataFrame present its flexibility by letting you select the columns the way you prefer. And as you can see, the result is a pandas DataFrame.

Why such a difference in results when using the same function?

- In the first case, we asked for a column. Therefore, the output was a 1-D vector (that is, a pandas Series).

- In the second case, we asked for multiple columns and we obtained a matrix-like result (and we know that matrices are mapped as pandas DataFrames).

Note   You can simply spot the difference by looking at the heading of the output; if the columns are labeled, then you are dealing with a pandas DataFrame. On the other hand, if the result is a vector and it presents no heading, then that is a pandas Series.

So far, we have learned some common steps from the data loading process; after you load the dataset, you usually separate the *features* (predictors) and *target* (which is response) labels.

And, as you know:

- In a classification problem, target labels are the discrete/nominal numbers or textual strings that indicate the class associated with every set of features.

- In a regression problem, target labels are continuous/interval (or ratio) numbers that indicate the value associated with every set of features.

Then, the following steps require you to get an idea of how large the problem is, and therefore you need to know the size of the dataset. Typically, for each observation, we count a line, and for each feature, a column. To obtain the dimensions of the dataset, just use the attribute shape on a pandas DataFrame or Series, as shown in the following example:

```
iris_df.shape
# Outputs
# (150, 5)
```

The resulting object is a tuple that contains the size of the matrix/array in each dimension.

Note   pandas Series follow the same format (that is, a tuple with only one element)—for example, data_series.shape will output (10, 1).

However, if you want to ignore the data loading process, you can always use the preloaded datasets in the sklearn.datasets module. This module contains all types of dataset (*classification* and *regression*) you can use—for practicing and experimentation purposes only. Also, you can use some functionalities in this module to generate you own dataset too, and that will help you enhance your pipeline operation selection and experimentation process too.

```
from sklearn.datasets import load_iris

iris = load_iris()
iris_df = pd.DataFrame(iris.data, columns=iris.feature_names)
iris_df.head()
```

Missing Data

As we all know, when someone transforms a dataset from one source to another, somehow data loss happens. We cannot avoid that loss or prevent it from happening, but we can fix it or make our model learn that loss or ignore it, as we will see in the coming chapters. So now we will talk about the mysterious combination of zeros, empties, and nulls.

You probably want to know the difference between each of those. We will show you the difference using three simple scenarios to illustrate and define the meaning of zeros, empties, and nulls.

Scenario one: Imagine that you have a purse that is filled with coins, and as I ask you some questions about it, you should answer them.

If I ask you how many coins are in the purse, you observe that there are no coins in the purse. The question *how many coins are in the purse?* is unanswerable. There is no purse! The answer is not a positive value, it is not a zero value, and it is not even empty. The value is null.

Scenario two: A few hours later, you looked in the purse again and saw ten coins are in it. Wonderful; you now have an answer to the question. In this case, you can answer the question with this piece of data, and its value is 10.

After a while, you look in the purse again and discover that there are no more coins. Every single coin is gone. You look, you search, and you find the answer to *how many coins are in the purse?* is a zero value. So, you still have a piece of data and its value is now 0.

Scenario three: Just before the evening, you grab your purse from your pocket. As you walk across the street, you find your friend and he asks, "What's in the purse?" Currently, the purse is empty. There is nothing in the purse—*no coins and nothing else.* Note that the answer is not zero, because the question he asked was not a numeric one. The answer is also not **null,** because we do have a purse and we did look inside it, but there was just no answer.

Empties

Empties are a bit trickier to work with than zero, but they make a lot of sense in some cases, for instance, when working with strings. For example, suppose we have an attribute called middle name. Well, I have no middle name so I would always leave this field empty. Filling in a space or a hyphen (or making up something) for a value that is truly empty does not make a lot of sense. Space is not the same thing as empty. The correct value in the case of an empty string may, in fact, be "empty."

Is It Ever Useful to Fill Missing Data Using a Zero Instead of an Empty or Null?

Let's state the fact that it is always better to fill the missing value than to leave it empty or null. You can know the missing value in a tricky way: if this variable has a uniform distribution between 0 and 1 and it has a small peak at -1, then -1 is actually a missing value.

Depending on data sources, missing data is identified differently. pandas always identifies missing values as *NaN*. However, unless the data has been preprocessed to a degree that an analyst will encounter missing values as *NaN*, missing values can appear as a question mark (?) or a zero (0) or minus one (-1) or a blank. As a result, it is important that a data scientist always performs exploratory data analysis (EDA) first before writing any machine learning algorithm. EDA is simply a litmus test for understanding and knowing the behavior of our data.

Managing Missing Features

Sometimes a dataset can contain missing features, so there are a few options that can be taken into account:

- Removing the whole row

- Creating a submodel to predict those features

- Using an automatic strategy to input them according to the other known values

- The first option is the most drastic one and should be considered only when the dataset is quite large, the number of missing features is high, and any prediction could be risky.

- The second option is much more difficult, because it's necessary to determine a supervised strategy to train a model for each feature and, finally, to predict their value.

- Considering all the pros and cons, the third option is likely to be the best choice.

Scikit-learn offers the class Imputer, which is responsible for filling the holes using a strategy based on the mean (default choice), median, or *frequency*-mode—(the most frequent entry will be used for all the missing ones). The following snippet shows an example using the three approaches (the default value for a missing feature entry is *NaN*. However, it's possible to use a different placeholder through the parameter missing_values):

```
import pandas as pd
from sklearn.preprocessing import Imputer
titanic_df = pd.read_csv('train.csv')
titanic_df.head(2)
```

	PassengerId	Survived	Pclass	Name	Sex	Age	SibSp	Parch	Ticket	Fare	Cabin	Embarked
0	1	0	3	Braund, Mr. Owen Harris	male	22.0	1	0	A/5 21171	7.2500	NaN	S
1	2	1	1	Cumings, Mrs. John Bradley (Florence Briggs Th...	female	38.0	1	0	PC 17599	71.2833	C85	C

Figure 6-8. *The head of the Titanic dataset*

```
titanic_df.Age.isna().sum()
# Outputs
# 177
titanic_imputer = Imputer(strategy='mean')
new_age = pd.DataFrame(titanic_imputer.fit_transform([titanic_
df.Age])[0])
new_age.isna().sum()
# Outputs
# 0
```

Dealing with Big Datasets

If the dataset you want to load is too big to fit in the memory, then you have to divide it into pieces (or named chunks). This approach is sometimes called sampling, and we will see in future chapters something about that. After that, you make a batch deep learning algorithm, which works with only a part/piece of the data at once. Using a batch approach also makes sense if you just need a sample of the data. Thanks to Python, you actually can load the data in chunks. This operation is also called data streaming, since the dataset flows into a DataFrame or some other data structure as a continuous flow. As opposed to all the previous cases, the dataset has been fully loaded into the memory in a standalone step.

With pandas, there are two ways to chunk and load a file:

- The first way is by loading the dataset in chunks of the same size; each chunk is a piece of the dataset that contains all the columns and a limited number of lines, not more than as set in the function call (the chunksize parameter).

- You can also use the CSV package, which offers two functions to iterate small chunks of data from files: the reader and the DictReader functions.

Note   The output of the read_csv function in this case is not a pandas DataFrame but an iterator-like object. In fact, to get the results in memory, you need to iterate that object:

```
iris_df = pd.read_csv('Iris.csv', sep=',', decimal='.',
                      header=None, index_col=False,
                      iterator=True,
                      names=['sepal_length', 'sepal_width',
                             'petal_length', 'petal_width',
                             'target'])
iris_df.get_chunk(10).shape
# Outputs
# 10
```

There will be 14 other pieces like these, each of them of shape (10, 5). The other method to load a big dataset is by specifically asking for an iterator of it. In this case, you can dynamically decide the length (that is, how many lines to get) you want for each piece of the pandas DataFrame:

```
for chunk in iris_df:
  print('SHAPE: ', chunk.shape)
  print(chunk, '\n')
```

Accessing Other Data Formats

So far, we have worked on CSV files only. The pandas package offers similar functionality (and functions) in order to load MS Excel, HDFS, SQL, JSON, HTML, and Stata datasets. Since they're not used in all data science projects, the understanding of how one can load and handle each of them is left to you, and you can refer to the documentation available on the website. A basic example of how to load an SQL table is available in the code that accompanies the book.

Note   CSV (comma-separated) and TSV (tab-separated) are similar, as they both are considered flat files.

```
titanic_df = pd.read_excel('Titanic.xlsx')
titanic_df.head(2)
```

	PassengerId	Survived	Pclass	Name	Sex	Age	SibSp	Parch	Ticket	Fare	Cabin	Embarked
0	1	0	3	Braund, Mr. Owen Harris	male	22.0	1	0	A/5 21171	7.2500	NaN	S
1	2	1	1	Cumings, Mrs. John Bradley (Florence Briggs Th…	female	38.0	1	0	PC 17599	71.2833	C85	C

Figure 6-9. *The output of the Excel file*

Data Preprocessing

We are now able to import the dataset, even a big, problematic one. Now, we need to learn the basic preprocessing routines in order to make it feasible for the next data science step.

First, if you need to apply a function to a limited section of rows, you can create a mask (Figure 6-10). A mask is a series of Boolean values (that is, True or False) that tells whether the line is selected or not.

For example, let's say we want to select all the lines of the iris dataset that have a sepal length greater than 6. We can simply do the following:

```
threshold_mask = iris_df['sepal_length'] > 6.0
threshold_mask.head()
```

```
0     False
1     False
2     False
3     False
4     False
Name: sepal_length, dtype: bool
```

Figure 6-10. *The output of masking data*

In the preceding simple example, we can immediately see which observations are True and which are not (False), and which ones fit the selection query.

Now, let's check how you can use a selection mask on another example. We want to substitute the Iris-virginica target label with the Virginica label. We can do this by using the following two lines of code:

```
mask_target = iris_df['target'] == "Iris-virginica"
iris_df.loc[mask_target, 'target'] = "Virginica"

iris_df.target[100:105]
```

```
100       Virginica
101       Virginica
102       Virginica
103       Virginica
104       Virginica
Name: target, dtype: object
```

Figure 6-11. *The renamed data*

You'll see that all occurrences of Iris-virginica are now replaced by Virginica (Figure 6-11). The loc() method is a way to access the data of the matrix with the help of row-column indexes.

To see the new list of the labels in the target column, we can use the unique() method. This method is very handy if initially you want to evaluate the dataset:

```
iris_df.target.unique()
# Outputs
# array(['Iris-setosa', 'Iris-versicolor',
# 'Virginica'], dtype=object)
iris_df.target.nunique()
# Outputs
# 3
```

This method allows us to see the unique values inside either pandas DataFrame or Series, and the method is very helpful in the analysis process. Another way is to count the number of unique values, and that could happen by using nunique(), which will return the number of unique values in the input DataFrame/Series.

If you want to see some statistics (mean, median, and so on) about each feature (statistics about data give you some intuition about what happens in it), you can do the following steps:

- You can group each column accordingly.

- You can also apply a mask.

The pandas method groupby will produce a similar result to the GROUP BY clause in ab SQL statement. The next method to apply should be an aggregate method on one or multiple columns.

For example, the mean() pandas aggregate method is the counterpart of the AVG() SQL function to compute the mean of the values in the group. The pandas aggregate method var() calculates the variance; sum(), the summation; count(), the number of rows in the group; and so on.

Note   The result is still a pandas DataFrame; therefore, multiple operations can be chained together.

As a next step, we can try a couple of examples of groupby() in action. Grouping observations by target (that is, label), we can check the difference between the average value and the variance of the features for each group (Figures 6-12 and 6-13).

```
iris_df.groupby(['target']).mean()
```

target	sepal_length	sepal_width	petal_length	petal_width
Iris-setosa	5.006	3.418	1.464	0.244
Iris-versicolor	5.936	2.770	4.260	1.326
Virginica	6.588	2.974	5.552	2.026

Figure 6-12. *The iris groupby mean output*

```
iris_df.groupby(['target']).var()
```

target	sepal_length	sepal_width	petal_length	petal_width
Iris-setosa	0.124249	0.145180	0.030106	0.011494
Iris-versicolor	0.266433	0.098469	0.220816	0.039106
Virginica	0.404343	0.104004	0.304588	0.075433

Figure 6-13. *The iris groupby variance output*

Finally, if your dataset contains a time series (for example, in the case of a numerical target) and you need to apply a `rolling` operation to it (in the case of noisy data points), you can simply do the following:

```
pd.rolling_mean(time_series, 5)
```

This can be performed for a rolling average of the values. Alternatively, you can use the following line of code:

```
pd.rolling_median(time_series, 5)
```

Instead, this can be performed in order to obtain a rolling median of the values. In both of these cases, the window had a sample size of 5.

More generically, the `apply()` pandas method is able to perform any row-wise or column-wise operation programmatically. `apply()` should be called directly on the *DataFrame*.

- The first argument is the function to be applied row-wise or column-wise.

- The second is the axis to apply it on.

Note   The function can be a built-in, library-provided, lambda, or any other user-defined function.

As an example of this powerful method, let's now try to count how many nonzero elements there are in each line (Figure 6-14). With the apply method, this is simple:

```
import numpy as np
iris_df.apply(np.count_nonzero, axis=1).head()
```

```
0    5
1    5
2    5
3    5
4    5
dtype: int64
```

Figure 6-14. *The iris nonzero values count output*

Similarly, to compute the nonzero elements feature-wise (that is, per column; Figure 6-15), you just need to change the second argument and set it to axis=0:

```
iris_df.apply(np.count_nonzero, axis=0)
```

```
sepal_length    150
sepal_width     150
petal_length    150
petal_width     150
target          150
dtype: int64
```

Figure 6-15. *The iris nonzero values count(per column) output*

Finally, to operate element-wise, the applymap() method should be used on the *DataFrame*. In this case, just one argument should be provided: the function to apply.

For example, let's assume you're interested in the length of the string representation of each cell. To obtain that value, you should first cast each cell to a string value, and then compute the length. With applymap, this operation is very easy (Figure 6-16):

```
iris_df.applymap(lambda el: len(str(el))).head()
```

	sepal_length	sepal_width	petal_length	petal_width	target
0	3	3	3	3	11
1	3	3	3	3	11
2	3	3	3	3	11
3	3	3	3	3	11
4	3	3	3	3	11

Figure 6-16. *The iris nonzero values count output*

Data Augmentation

As we all know, the performance of any deep learning algorithm or any neural networks often improves with the amount of data available. So, the larger your dataset, the more accurate results you can find—of course with respect to other factors such as selecting the right algorithm for your problem.

Data augmentation is a technique to artificially create new training data from existing training data. This is done by applying domain-specific techniques to examples from the training data that create new and different training examples.

Image data augmentation is perhaps the most well-known type of data augmentation and involves creating transformed versions of images in the training dataset that belong to the same class as the original image.

Transforms include a range of operations from the field of image manipulation, such as shifts, flips, zooms, and much more.

The intent is to expand the training dataset with new, plausible examples. This means, variations of the training set images that are likely to be seen by the model. For example, a horizontal flip of a picture of a cat may make sense, because the photo could have been taken from the left or right. A vertical flip of the photo of a cat does not make sense and would probably not be appropriate given that the model is very unlikely to see a photo of an upside-down cat.

As such, it is clear that the choice of the specific data augmentation techniques used for a training dataset must be chosen carefully, and within the context of the training dataset and knowledge of the problem domain. In addition, it can be useful to experiment with data augmentation methods in isolation and in concert, to see if they result in a measurable improvement to model performance, perhaps with a small prototype dataset, model, and training run.

Modern deep learning algorithms, such as the convolutional neural network, or CNN, can learn features that are invariant to their location in the image. Nevertheless, augmentation can further aid in this transform invariant approach to learning and can aid the model in learning features that are also invariant to transforms, such as left-to-right to top-to-bottom ordering, light levels in photographs, and more.

Image data augmentation is typically only applied to the *training dataset*, and **not** to the *validation* or *test dataset*. This is different from data preparation such as image resizing and pixel scaling; they must be performed consistently across all datasets that interact with the model.

So, let us get started and see what we can do to get more images from the existing one. First, we need to import our packages as follows:

```
import tensorflow as tf
import matplotlib.image as mpimg
import matplotlib.pyplot as plt
```

Then, we need to load the image that we will do the experimentation on, so we can change its properties and make it seem like a new image for our model. The `tf.image` provides image augmentation functions so that all the computation is done on the GPU. In this tutorial, we use TensorFlow `eager_execution` so that we can see the augmented image directly.

```
tf.enable_eager_execution()

image_path = 'lena_forsen.png'

image_string=tf.read_file(image_path)
image=tf.image.decode_png(image_string,channels=3)
image=tf.image.convert_image_dtype(image,dtype=tf.float32)
```

Also, we need to implement the function that shows the result of all our experimentation, such that we do not have to write the same code again and again.

```
def show_image(original_image,augmented_image,title):
  fig=plt.figure()
  fig.suptitle(title)

  original_plt=fig.add_subplot(1,2,1)

  original_plt.set_title('original image')
  original_plt.imshow(original_image)

  augmented_plt=fig.add_subplot(1,2,2)
  augmented_plt.set_title('augmented image')
  augmented_plt.imshow(augmented_image)
  plt.show(block=True)
```

Now we can start our image augmentation, as our environment is ready for the process; so let us get started.

Image Crop

tf.image provides various functions for image cropping. tf.image. central_crop removes the outer parts of an image but retains the central region of the image along each dimension (Figure 6-17). If we specify central_fraction = 0.5, this function returns the central 50% of the image. Also, this function works on either a single image (image is a 3-D Tensor), or a batch of images (image is a 4-D Tensor).

central_image = tf.image.central_crop(image, central_fraction=0.7)
show_image(image, central_image, "Central Image Crop")

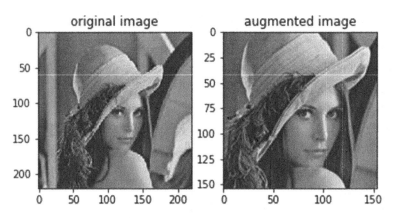

Figure 6-17. *The result of central image crop transformation*

Crop and Resize

This function extracts crops from the input image at positions defined at the bounding box locations in boxes and resizes to a common output size specified by crop_and_size.

```
im = tf.expand_dims(image, 0)
crop_and_resize = tf.image.crop_and_resize(im, boxes=[[0.0,
0.0, 0.5, 0.5]], crop_size=[256, 256], box_ind=[0])
```

```
show_image(image, tf.squeeze(crop_and_resize, 0), "Crop and
Resize")
```

The crop_and_resize operation extracts crops from the input image tensor and resizes them using either *bilinear sampling* or *nearest neighbor sampling* (possibly with aspect ratio change) to a common output size specified by crop_size. This is more general than the crop_to_bounding_box operation, which extracts a fixed size slice from the input image and does not allow resizing or aspect ratio change. Another parameter is box_ind, which is the index of each box; it is needed to specify or to be used as a pointer to each output crop image, hence the output is multiple images if there are multiple boxes.

It returns a tensor with crops from the input image at positions defined at the bounding box locations in boxes. The cropped boxes are all resized (with bilinear or nearest neighbor interpolation) to a fixed size = [crop_height, crop_width].

Finally, we need to do tf.squeeze, because the result that comes from crop_and_resize is a 4-D tensor [num_boxes, crop_height, crop_width, depth]. So, we need to transform it to a 3-D tensor.

You can find more answers about crop_and_resize (Figure 6-18) by visiting https://stackoverflow.com/questions/51843509/about-use-tf-image-crop-and-resize.

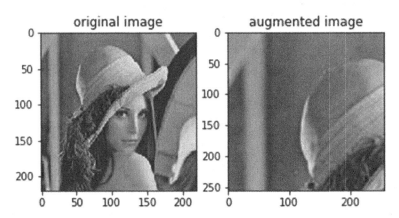

Figure 6-18. *The result of crop and resize image transformation*

Crop to Bounding Box

This is a basic edition of the crop_and_resize operation, which extracts a fixed size slice from the input image given the boundaries and does not allow resizing or aspect ratio change (Figure 6-19).

```
top_left = tf.image.crop_to_bounding_box(image, 10, 10, 90, 90)
show_image(image, top_left, "Crop to Bounding Box")
```

Crop to Bounding Box

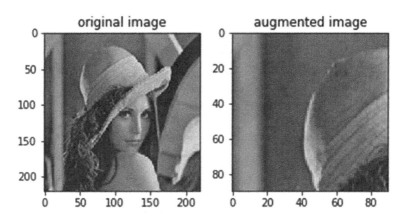

Figure 6-19. *The result of selected box crop image transformation*

Flipping

Flipping, which is important for CNN to remove certain features of the object, is available in only a particular side. For example, you don't want a CNN model to learn that an apple leaf happens only on the right side as observed in the base image. Flipping produces a different set of images from the rotation at multiples of 90 degrees (Figures 6-20 and 6-21).

```
flip_image = tf.image.flip_left_right(image)
show_image(image, flip_image, "Flip")
```

Flip

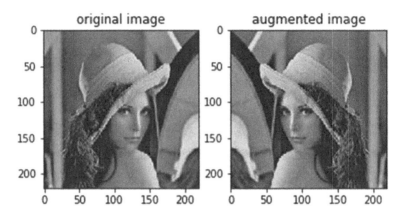

Figure 6-20. *The result of vertical flip image transformation*

```
flip_image = tf.image.flip_up_down(image)
show_image(image, flip_image, "Flip")
```

Flip

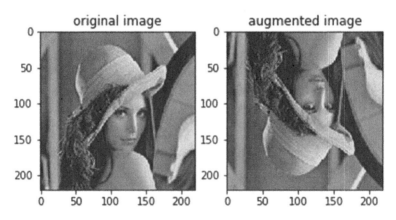

Figure 6-21. *The result of horizontal flip image transformation*

1. `random_flip_left_right()` to randomly flip an image horizontally (left to right)

2. `random_flip_up_down()` to randomly flip an image vertically (upside down)

3. `flip_up_down()` to flip an image vertically (upside down)

Rotate Image

Simply, this operation rotates an image counterclockwise by the passed angle in radians (Figure 6-22). And we can pass the radians by `math.radians`, which will calculate the radians based on the angle parameter.

```
import math

rotate_image = tf.contrib.image.rotate(image, math.
radians(270))
show_image(image, rotate_image, "Rotate Image")
```

Rotate Image

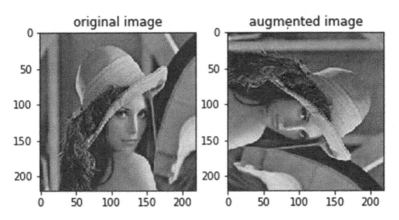

Figure 6-22. *The result of rotation image transformation*

Translation

We would like our model to recognize the object present in any part of the image. Also, the object can be present partially in the corner or edges of the image. For this reason, we shift the object to various parts of the image (Figure 6-23).

The parameter translation is a vector representing [dx, dy] or (if image has rank 4) a matrix of length num_images, with a [dx, dy] vector for each image in the batch.

```
move_image = tf.contrib.image.translate(image,
translations=[10, 10])
show_image(image, move_image, "Image Translation")
```

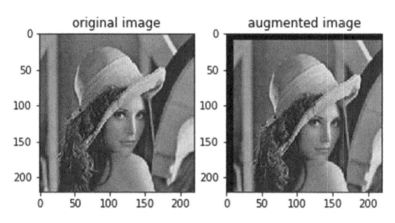

Figure 6-23. *The result of image translation*

Transform

This operation can apply the given transform matrix to the image. The transform matrix is given as a vector of length 8 that represent the wanted transformation (Figure 6-24).

```
theta = -0.2
transforms = [1, tf.sin(theta), 0, 0, tf.cos(theta), 0, 0, 0]

transform_image = tf.contrib.image.transform(image,
transforms=transforms)
show_image(image, transform_image, "Transform Image")
```

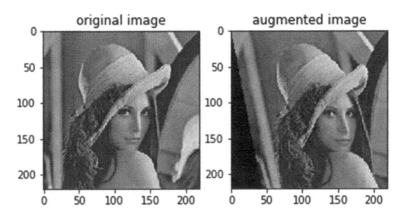

Figure 6-24. The result of image transformation

Adding Salt and Pepper Noise

Overfitting happens when your neural network tries to learn high-frequency features that may not be useful. Gaussian noise effectively distorts the high-frequency features (Figure 6-25).

```
import numpy as np
from skimage.util import random_noise

image_array = np.asarray(image)
noise_image = random_noise(image_array, mode="gaussian", var=0.01)

show_image(image, noise_image, "Noise Image")
```

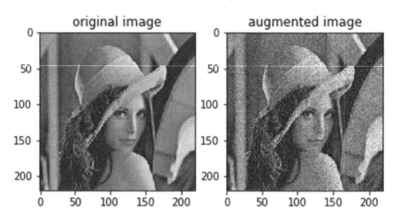

Figure 6-25. *The result of an image with salty noise*

A toned-down version of this is the salt and pepper noise, which presents itself as random black and white pixels spread through the image.

Convert RGB to Grayscale

The following function converts one or more images from RGB to grayscale (Figure 6-26).

```
gray_image = tf.image.rgb_to_grayscale(image)
show_image(image, tf.squeeze(gray_image), "Gray Image")
```

Gray Image

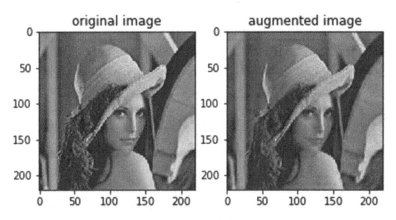

Figure 6-26. *The result of image scale conversion*

Change Brightness

The following function adjusts the brightness of RGB or grayscale images (Figure 6-27).

```
bright_image = tf.image.adjust_brightness(image, 0.2)
show_image(image, bright_image, "Bright Image")
```

181

Bright Image

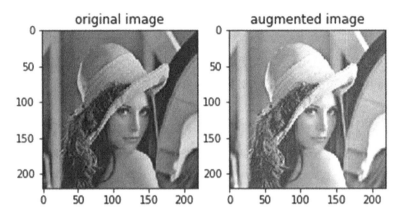

Figure 6-27. *The result of image brightness transformation*

Adjust Contrast

The following function adjusts the contrast of RGB or grayscale images (Figure 6-28).

```
contrast_image = tf.image.adjust_contrast(image, contrast_
factor=0.6)
show_image(image, contrast_image, "Contrast Image")
```

Contrast Image

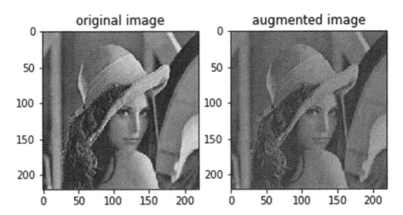

Figure 6-28. *The result of contrasting transformation*

Adjust Hue

The following function adjusts the hue of an RGB image (Figure 6-29).

```
hue_image = tf.image.adjust_hue(image, delta=0.4)
show_image(image, hue_image, "Hue Image")
```

Hue Image

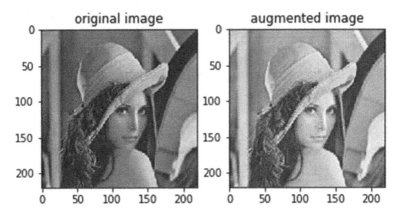

Figure 6-29. *The result of hue image transformation*

183

The image hue is adjusted by converting the image to HSV and rotating the hue channel (H) by delta. The image is then converted back to RGB. The delta must be in the interval [-1, 1].

Adjust Saturation

The image saturation is adjusted by converting the image to HSV and multiplying the saturation (S) channel by the saturation_factor and clipping. The image is then converted back to RGB (Figure 6-30).

```
saturation_image = tf.image.adjust_saturation(image, 5)
show_image(image, saturation_image, "Saturation Image")
```

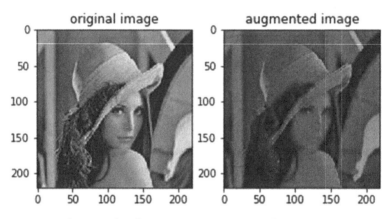

Figure 6-30. *The result of image saturation adjustment*

Categorical and Text data

As we discussed in a previous chapter; typically, you'll find yourself dealing with two main kinds of data:

- Numerical

- Categorical

Numerical data, such as temperature, amount of money, days of usage, or house number, can be composed of either floating-point numbers (such as 1.0, -2.3, 99.99, and so on) or integers (such as -3, 9, 0, 1, and so on). Each value that the data can assume has a direct relation with others, since they're comparable. In other words, you can say that a feature with a value of 2.0 is greater (actually, it is double) than a feature that assumes a value of 1.0. This type of data is very well defined and comprehensible, with binary operators such as equal to, greater than, and less than.

Categorical data is also known as nominal and ordinal data. Categorical data expresses an attribute that cannot be measured and assumes values in a finite or infinite set of values, often named levels.

For example, the weather is a categorical feature, since it takes values in a discrete set (sunny, cloudy, snowy, rainy, and foggy). Other examples are features that contain URLs, IPs, items you put in your e-commerce cart, device IDs, and so on. On this data, you cannot define the equal to, greater than, and less than binary operators and therefore, you can't rank them.

A plus point for both categorical and numerical values is Booleans. In fact, they can be seen as categorical (presence/absence of a feature) or, on the other hand, as the probability of a feature having an exhibit (has displayed, has not displayed). Since many deep learning algorithms do not allow the input to be categorical, Boolean features are often used to encode categorical features as numerical values.

Hint   You can review Chapter 5, which defines data types.

Data Encoding

Many deep learning libraries require that categorical features/columns are encoded as integer values. Although most estimators for classification/regression in Scikit-learn convert columns to integers internally, it is considered good practice to provide all data features/columns as integer arrays to avoid technical glitches.

To encode the categorical variables, we can use an approach similar to the mapping of ordinal features discussed previously. We need to remember that columns are not ordinal, and it doesn't matter which integer number we assign to a particular string-label. Thus, we can simply enumerate the class labels starting at 0:

```
class_mapping = {label:idx for idx,label in
                 enumerate(np.unique(titanic_df.Sex))}
class_mapping
# Output
# {'female': 0, 'male': 1}
```

Next, we can use the mapping dictionary to transform the categorical feature or column (Figure 6-31) into integers:

```
titanic_df['Sex'] = titanic_df['Sex'].map(class_mapping)
titanic_df['Sex'].head()
```

```
0    1
1    0
2    0
3    0
4    1
Name: Sex, dtype: int64
```

Figure 6-31. *The result of categorical transformation*

We can reverse the key-value pairs in the mapping dictionary as follows, to map the converted class labels back to the original string representation (Figure 6-32):

```
inv_class_mapping = {v: k for k, v in class_mapping.items()}
titanic_df['Sex'] = titanic_df['Sex'].map(inv_class_mapping)
titanic_df['Sex'].head()
```

```
0        male
1      female
2      female
3      female
4        male
Name: Sex, dtype: object
```

Figure 6-32. *The result of categorical inverse transformation*

Alternatively, there is a convenient LabelEncoder class directly implemented in Scikit-learn to achieve the same:

```
from sklearn.preprocessing import LabelEncoder
gender_le = LabelEncoder()
titanic_gender = gender_le.fit_transform(titanic_df.Sex)
titanic_gender[0:10]
# Outputs
# array([1, 0, 0, 0, 1, 1, 1, 1, 0, 0])
```

Note   The fit_transform method is just a shortcut for calling fit and transform separately.

And the `classes_` attribute shows you the class that the real categorical column was before encoding:

```
gender_le.classes_
# Outputs
# array(['female', 'male'], dtype=object)
```

Performing One-Hot Encoding on Nominal Features

In the previous section, we used a simple dictionary-mapping approach to convert the ordinal size feature into integers. Since Scikit-learn estimators treat class labels without any order, we used the convenient `LabelEncoder` class to encode the string labels into integers. It may appear that we could use a similar approach to transform the nominal gender column of our dataset, as follows:

```
from sklearn.preprocessing import LabelEncoder
gender_le = LabelEncoder()
titanic_gender = gender_le.fit_transform(titanic_df.Sex)
titanic_gender[0:10]
# Outputs
# array([1, 0, 0, 0, 1, 1, 1, 1, 0, 0])
```

After executing the preceding code, the first column of the NumPy array *X* now holds the new gender values, which are encoded as shown in code cell output.

If we stop at this point and feed the array to our model, we will make one of the most common mistakes in dealing with categorical data.

Can You Spot the Problem?

Although the gender values don't come in any particular order, a learning algorithm will now assume that male is larger than female. Although this assumption is incorrect, the algorithm could still produce useful results. However, those results would not be optimal.

A common workaround for this problem is to use a technique called one-hot encoding (Figure 6-33). The idea behind this approach is to create a new dummy feature for each unique value in the nominal feature column. Here, we would convert the gender feature into two new features: male and female. Binary values can then be used to indicate the particular gender of a sample; for example, a male sample can be encoded as male=1, female=0. To perform this transformation, we can use the OneHotEncoder that is implemented in the sklearn.preprocessing module:

```
from sklearn.preprocessing import OneHotEncoder
gender_ohe = OneHotEncoder()
titanic_gender_ohe = gender_ohe.fit_transform(pd.
DataFrame(titanic_gender))
titanic_gender_ohe[0:10]
# Outputs
# <10x2 sparse matrix of type '<class 'numpy.float64'>' with 10
stored elements in Compressed Sparse Row format>
```

When we initialized the OneHotEncoder, we defined the column position of the variable that we want to transform via the categorical_features parameter. By default, the OneHotEncoder returns a sparse matrix when we use the transform method, and we converted the sparse matrix representation into a regular (*dense*) NumPy array for the purposes of visualization via the toarray method.

> **Note**   Color is the first column in the feature matrix X Sparse
> matrices are simply a more efficient way of storing large datasets,
> and one that is supported by many Scikit-learn functions, which is
> especially useful if it contains a lot of zeros. To omit the `toarray`
> step, we could initialize the encoder as `OneHotEncoder(...,`
> `sparse=False)` to return a dense NumPy array.

An even more convenient way to create those **dummy** features via one-hot encoding is to use the get_dummies method implemented in pandas. Applied on a DataFrame, the get_dummies method will only convert string columns and leave all other columns unchanged:

```
pd.get_dummies(titanic_df.Sex).head()
```

	female	male
0	0	1
1	1	0
2	1	0
3	1	0
4	0	1

Figure 6-33.   *The result of one-hot encoding transformation*

A Special Type of Data: Text

Let's introduce another type of data. Text is frequently used on the Web; you can see almost every website has forms, and social media is filled with text data like *posts* and *comments*. Text is also used as input for deep learning algorithms, since it contains a natural representation of data in our language. It's so rich, that it also contains the answer to what we're looking for.

The most common algorithm used when dealing with text is to use a bag of words. According to this algorithm, every word becomes a feature and the text becomes a vector that contains nonzero elements for all the features (that is, the words) in its body. Given a text dataset, *what's the number of features?* It is simple. Just extract all the unique words in it and enumerate them. For a very rich text that uses all the English words, that number is around 600,000. If you're not going to further process it (removal of *third person, abbreviations, contractions,* and *acronyms*), you might find yourself dealing with more than that, but that's a very rare case. In a plain and simple approach, which is the target of this book, we just let Python do its best.

The dataset used in this section is textual; it's the famous 20newsgroup (for more information about this, visit 20Newsgroups (`http://qwone.com/~jason/20Newsgroups/`). It is a collection of about *20,000* documents that belong to 20 topics of newsgroups. It's one of the most frequently used (if not the top most used) datasets presented while dealing with text classification and clustering. To import it (Figure 6-34), we're going to use only its restricted subset, which contains all the science topics (medicine and space):

```
from sklearn.datasets import fetch_20newsgroups
categories = ['sci.med', 'sci.space']
twenty_sci_news = fetch_20newsgroups(categories=categories)
```

Note   The first time you run this command, it automatically downloads the dataset and places it in the $HOME/`scikit_learn_data/20news_home/` default directory.

```
print(twenty_sci_news.data[0])
```

```
From: flb@flb.optiplan.fi ("F.Baube[tm]")
Subject: Vandalizing the sky
X-Added: Forwarded by Space Digest
Organization: [via International Space University]
Original-Sender: isu@VACATION.VENARI.CS.CMU.EDU
Distribution: sci
Lines: 12


From: "Phil G. Fraering" <pgf@srl03.cacs.usl.edu>
>
> Finally: this isn't the Bronze Age, [..]
> please try to remember that there are more human activities than
> those practiced by the Warrior Caste, the Farming Caste, and the
> Priesthood.

Right, the Profiting Caste is blessed by God, and may
  freely blare its presence in the evening twilight ..


--
* Fred Baube (tm)
```

Figure 6-34. *The result of loading the 20newsgroups dataset*

The easiest way to deal with the text is by transforming the body of the dataset into a series of words. This means that for each document, the number of times a specific word appears in the body will be counted.

For example, let's make a small, easy-to-process dataset:

- doc_1: We love machine learning.

- doc_2: Machine learning is great.

In the entire dataset, which contains doc_1 and doc_2, there are only six different words: we, love, machine, learning, is, and great. Given this array, we can associate each document with a feature vector:

```
feature_doc_1 = [1 1 1 1 0 0]
feature_doc_2 = [0 0 1 1 1 1]
```

Note that we're discarding the positions of the words and retaining only the number of times the word appears in the document. That's all.

In the 20newsletter dataset, with Python, this can be done in a simple way:

```
print (twenty_sci_news.target[0])
# Outputs
# 1
print (twenty_sci_news.target_names[twenty_sci_news.target[0]])
# Outputs
# sci.space
```

First, we instantiate a CountVectorizer object. Then, we call the method to count the terms in each document and produce a feature vector for each of them, which is fit_transform. Then we can query the matrix size.

Note   The output matrix is sparse, because it's very common to have only a limited selection of words for each document (since the number of *nonzero* elements in each line is very low and it makes no sense to store all the redundant zeros).

Anyway, the output shape is (1187, 25638). The first value is the number of observations in the dataset (the number of documents), while the latter is the number of features (the number of unique words in the dataset). After the CountVectorizer transforms, each document is associated with its feature vector (Figure 6-35). Let's take a look at the first document.

```
from sklearn.feature_extraction.text import CountVectorizer
count_vect = CountVectorizer()
word_count = count_vect.fit_transform(twenty_sci_news.data)
word_count.shape
# Outputs
# (1187, 25638)
print (word_count[0])
```

```
(0, 10827)     2
(0, 10501)     2
(0, 17170)     1
(0, 10341)     1
(0, 4762)      2
(0, 23381)     2
(0, 22345)     1
(0, 24461)     1
(0, 23137)     7
(0, 21382)     1
(0, 3233)      1
(0, 10713)     1
```

Figure 6-35. *The result of count vectorizing the dataset*

You may notice that the output is a sparse vector where only nonzero elements are stored. To check the direct correspondence to words (Figure 6-36), just try the following code:

```
word_list = count_vect.get_feature_names()
for n in word_count[0].indices:
  print ('Word "%s" appears %i times' % (word_list[n],
  word_count[0, n]))
```

```
Word "from" appears 2 times
Word "flb" appears 2 times
Word "optiplan" appears 1 times
Word "fi" appears 1 times
Word "baube" appears 2 times
Word "tm" appears 2 times
Word "subject" appears 1 times
Word "vandalizing" appears 1 times
Word "the" appears 7 times
Word "sky" appears 1 times
```

Figure 6-36. *The data transformed using count vectorizer*

So Far, Everything Has Been Pretty Good, Hasn't It?

Let's move forward to another task of increasing complexity and effectiveness. Counting words is good, but we can get more info from the data with more complexity. Let's compute their frequency. It's a measure that you can compare across differently sized datasets. It gives an idea whether a word is a stop word (that is, a very common word such as a, an, the, or is) or a rare, unique one. Typically, these words are the most important because they're able to characterize an instance and the features based on these words, which are very discriminative in the learning process. To retrieve the frequency of each word in each document, we use TfidfVectorizer to compute the frequency matrix (Figure 6-37); try the following code:

```
from sklearn.feature_extraction.text import TfidfVectorizer
tf_vect = TfidfVectorizer(use_idf=False, norm='l1')
word_freq = tf_vect.fit_transform(twenty_sci_news.data)
word_list = tf_vect.get_feature_names()

for n in word_freq[0].indices:
  print ('Word "%s" has frequency %0.3f' % (word_list[n],
  word_freq[0, n]))
```

```
Word "from" has frequency 0.022
Word "flb" has frequency 0.022
Word "optiplan" has frequency 0.011
Word "fi" has frequency 0.011
Word "baube" has frequency 0.022
Word "tm" has frequency 0.022
Word "subject" has frequency 0.011
Word "vandalizing" has frequency 0.011
Word "the" has frequency 0.077
Word "sky" has frequency 0.011
Word "added" has frequency 0.011
Word "forwarded" has frequency 0.011
Word "by" has frequency 0.033
Word "space" has frequency 0.022
Word "digest" has frequency 0.011
Word "organization" has frequency 0.011
```

Figure 6-37. *The data transformed using Tfidf Vectorizer*

The sum of the frequencies is 1 (or close to 1 due to the approximation). This happens because we chose the L1 norm. In this specific case, the word frequency is a probability distribution function. Sometimes, it's nice to increase the difference between rare and common words. In such cases, you can use the L2 norm to normalize the feature vector.

An even more effective way to vectorize text data is by using Tfidf. In brief, you can multiply the term frequency of the words that compose a document by the inverse document frequency of the word itself (that is, in the number of documents it appears, or in its logarithmically scaled transformation). This is very handy to highlight words that effectively describe each document and which are a powerful discriminative element among the dataset.

Tfidf gained a lot of popularity since computers have started to process and mine text data. The majority of search engines and information retrieval software have used it mainly for its effective way to measure sentence similarity and distance, making it an optimal solution to retrieve documents from a user-inserted text search query.

```
from sklearn.feature_extraction.text import TfidfVectorizer
tfidf_vect = TfidfVectorizer()
word_tfidf = tfidf_vect.fit_transform(twenty_sci_news.data)
word_list = tfidf_vect.get_feature_names()
for n in word_tfidf[0].indices:
  print ('Word "%s" has tf-idf %0.3f' % (word_list[n],
  word_tfidf[0, n]))
```

```
Word "fred" has tf-idf 0.089
Word "twilight" has tf-idf 0.139
Word "evening" has tf-idf 0.113
Word "in" has tf-idf 0.024
Word "presence" has tf-idf 0.119
Word "its" has tf-idf 0.061
Word "blare" has tf-idf 0.150
Word "freely" has tf-idf 0.119
Word "may" has tf-idf 0.054
Word "god" has tf-idf 0.119
Word "blessed" has tf-idf 0.150
Word "is" has tf-idf 0.026
Word "profiting" has tf-idf 0.150
Word "right" has tf-idf 0.068
```

Figure 6-38. *The data after tfidf transformation*

In this example, the four most information-rich words of the first documents are caste, baube, flb, and tm (they have the highest tf-idf score). This means that their term frequency within the document is high, whereas they're pretty rare in the remaining documents. In terms of information theory, their entropy is high within the document, while it's lower considering all the documents.

So far, for each word, we have generated a feature. **What about taking a couple of words together?**

That's exactly what happens when you consider bigrams instead of unigrams. With bigrams (or generically, n-grams), the presence or absence of a word—as well as its neighbors—matters (that is, the words near it and their disposition). Of course, you can mix unigrams and n-grams and create a rich feature vector for each document. In a simple example, let's test how n-grams work:

```
text_1 = 'we love data science'
text_2 = 'data science is hard'
documents = [text_1, text_2]

count_vect_1_grams = CountVectorizer(ngram_range=(1, 1), stop_
words=[], min_df=1)
word_count = count_vect_1_grams.fit_transform(documents)
word_list = count_vect_1_grams.get_feature_names()

print ("Word list = ", word_list)
print ("text_1 is described with", [word_list[n] + "(" +
str(word_count[0, n]) + ")" for n in word_count[0].indices])

# Outputs
# Word list =   ['data', 'hard', 'is', 'love', 'science', 'we']
# text_1 is described with ['we(1)', 'love(1)',
#               'data(1)', 'science(1)']

count_vect_1_grams = CountVectorizer(ngram_range=(2, 2))
word_count = count_vect_1_grams.fit_transform(documents)
word_list = count_vect_1_grams.get_feature_names()

print ("Word list = ", word_list)
print ("text_1 is described with", [word_list[n] + "(" +
str(word_count[0, n]) + ")" for n in word_count[0].indices])
```

```
# Outputs
# Word list =  ['data science', 'is hard',
#                   'love data', 'science is', 'we love']
# text_1 is described with ['we love(1)',
#                   'love data(1)', 'data science(1)']

count_vect_1_grams = CountVectorizer(ngram_range=(1, 2))
word_count = count_vect_1_grams.fit_transform(documents)
word_list = count_vect_1_grams.get_feature_names()

print ("Word list = ", word_list)
print ("text_1 is described with", [word_list[n] + "(" +
str(word_count[0, n]) + ")" for n in word_count[0].indices])

# Outputs
# Word list =  ['data', 'data science', 'hard',
#                   'is', 'is hard', 'love', 'love data',
#                   'science', 'science is', 'we',
#                   'we love']
# text_1 is described with ['we(1)', 'love(1)',
#                   'data(1)', 'science(1)', 'we love(1)',
#                   'love data(1)', 'data science(1)']
```

The preceding example is very intuitive and combines the first and second algorithms we previously discussed. In this code cell, we used a CountVectorizer, but this algorithm is very common with a TfidfVectorizer.

Note   The number of features explodes exponentially when you use n-grams.

If you have too many features (rich text data) in your dataset (the dictionary may be too rich, there may be too many ngrams, or the computer may just be limited), you can use a trick that lowers the complexity of the problem (but you should first evaluate the trade-off performance/trade-off complexity).

It's common to use the hashing trick, where many words (or n-grams) are hashed and their hashes collide (which makes a bucket of words). Buckets are sets of semantically unrelated words but with colliding hashes. With HashingVectorizer(), as shown in the following example, you can decide the number of buckets of words you want. The resulting matrix, of course, reflects your setting:

```
from sklearn.feature_extraction.text import HashingVectorizer
hash_vect = HashingVectorizer(n_features=1000)
word_hashed = hash_vect.fit_transform(twenty_sci_news.data)
word_hashed.shape
# Outputs
# (1187, 1000)
```

> **Note** You can't invert the hashing process (since it's an irreversible summarization process).

After this transformation, you will have to work on the hashed features as they are. Hashing presents quite a few advantages:

- Allowing quick transformation of a bag of words into vectors of features

  - Hash buckets are our features in this case.

- Easily accommodating never previously seen words among the features

- Avoiding overfitting by having unrelated words collide together in the same feature

Tokenization, Stemming, and Stop Words

What Are Tokenizing and Tokenization?

Tokenizing means splitting your text into minimal meaningful units. It is a mandatory step before any kind of processing. It is the act of breaking up a sequence of strings into pieces such as words, keywords, phrases, symbols and other elements called *tokens*.

Tokens can be individual words, phrases, or even whole sentences. That's all about tokenization, actually,

We need to talk about it, but we should zoom out to see what happens from a flying camera. This camera will allow us to see what is *lexical analysis, lexing,* or *tokenization*; which is the process of converting a sequence of characters (such as in a computer program or web page) into a sequence of tokens.

A program that performs lexical analysis may be termed a lexer, tokenizer, or scanner, though the scanner is also a term for the first stage of a lexer.

We said the word *lexer* many times. So, the question is, what is a lexer? or to be rigorous, what is a *lexeme*? A lexeme is a sequence of characters in the source program that matches the pattern for a token and is identified by the lexical analyzer as an instance of that token. But we didn't really answer the question *"what is a token?"* in rigorous form. A token is a string with an assigned and thus identified meaning; it is structured as a pair consisting of a token name and an optional token value. The token name is a category of lexical unit, and common token names are:

- *identifier*: names the programmer chooses

- *keyword*: names already in the programming language

- *separator* (also known as punctuators): punctuation characters and paired-delimiters.

- *operator*: symbols that operate on arguments and produce results

201

- *literal*: numeric, logical, textual, reference literals

- *comment*: line, block

These names are not important in the scope of this book, but we tried to give you some information about the basics of tokenization. However, we do not do all of this manually; we will see some packages in Python that help us to make **tokenization** and **stemming** very easy. For now, let us see an example to get a better idea about it.

Input: Friends, Romans, Countrymen, lend me your ears.

Output: (Friends), (Romans), (Countrymen), (lend), (me), (your), (ears).

XML-Output:

```
<sentence>
  <word>Friends</word>
  <word>Romans</word>
  <word>Countrymen</word>
  <word>lend</word>
  <word>me</word>
  <word>your</word>
  <word>ears</word>
</sentence>
```

After we've seen this example, I think we have a good understanding about Tokenization. But before we get into examples, we'll see a new term called *stemming*. So, the question rings, what is stemming?

Stemming refers to reducing a word to its root form. While performing natural language processing tasks, you will encounter various scenarios where you find different words with the same root.

For example, "*compute, computer, computing, computed.*" You may want to reduce the words to their root form for the sake of uniformity. This is where stemming comes into play. Now we can see what stemming is, but what is the difference between stemming and lemmatization (Table 6-1)?

Table 6-1. *The Difference Between Stemming and Lemmatization*

Stemming	Lemmatization
Stemming is the process of reducing inflexion in words to their root forms, such as mapping a group of words to the same stem, even if the stem itself is not a valid word in the language.	Lemmatization, unlike stemming, reduces the inflected words properly, ensuring that the root word belongs to the language. In lemmatization, the root word is lemma. A lemma (plural lemmas or lemmata) is the canonical form, dictionary form, or citation form of a set of words.

Example		**Example**	
`Word`	`Porter Stemmer`	`Word`	`Lemma`
`friend`	`friend`	`He`	`He`
`friendship`	`friendship`	`was`	`wa`
`friends`	`friend`	`running`	`running`
`friendships`	`friendship`	`and`	`and`
		`eating`	`eating`
		`at`	`at`

Examples of stemmers in the NLTK are *Porter stemmer* and *Snowball stemmer*. Both of them have been implemented using different algorithms.

Let's take a quick and easy look at these two stemmers.

The Porter stemming algorithm is a process of removing the suffix form words in English; for example, we will take a word and try to get its stemmer values,

```
E.g: Connected - > connect
     Connecting - > connect
     Connector - > connect
     Connection - > connect
```

The rules for making a Porter stemmer:

(F)

Rule			Example		
SSES	→	**SS**	caresses	→	caress
IES	→	**I**	ponies	→	poni
SS	→	**SS**	caress	→	caress
S	→		cats	→	cat

This is the basis of the NLTK, which you can see more about at `www.nltk.org/`. Now we get the basic word in the phrase (token) and we get its root. Let's talk a moment about stop words. Stop Words are words that do not contain important significance to be used in search queries. Usually, these words are filtered out from search queries because they return a vast amount of unnecessary information. Each programming language will give its own list of stop words to use. Mostly they are words that are commonly used in the English language such as "as, the, be, are," etc.

We will start in the next stage on the bag-of- words algorithm and IR algorithms that help in natural language processing, like tf-idf.

The Bag-of-Words (BoW) Model

What is the BoW?

We may want to perform classification of documents, so each document is an "input" and a class label is the "output" for our predictive algorithm. Algorithms take vectors of numbers as input; therefore, we need to convert documents to fixed-length vectors of numbers. So how we can make this in machine learning algorithm isn't possible so we need a model which think about text documents in machine learning, throws away all of the order information in the words and focuses on the occurrence of words in a document. This BoW is what we need to perform this task very efficiently. We know the definition of BoW and how we can use it. Let's see how it works in a technical way.

The BoW model can be implemented by assigning each word a unique number. Then any document we see can be encoded as a fixed-length vector with the length of the vocabulary of known words. The value in each position in the vector could be filled with a count or frequency of each word in the encoded document. We are only concerned with encoding schemes that represent which words are present or the degree to which they are present in encoded documents, without any information about the order.

Let's take an example to get a better understanding about the bag of words:

1.   John likes to watch movies. Mary likes movies too.

2.   John also likes to watch football games.

Based on these two text documents, a list is constructed as follows for each document:

```
#1 "John", "likes", "to", "watch", "movies", "Mary", "likes",
"movies", "too"
```

```
#2 "John", "also", "likes", "to", "watch", "football", "games"
```

Representing each bag-of-words as a JSON object:

```
BoW1 = {"John":1,"likes":2,"to":1,"watch":1,"movies":2,
"Mary":1,"too":1};
BoW2 = {"John":1,"also":1,"likes":1,"to":1,"watch":1,
"football":1,"games":1};
```

Now see what happens when we have a new document like this:

1.   John likes to watch movies. Mary likes movies too.
        John also likes to watch football games.

So now we should take the union of BoW3=BoW1 BoW2 so we will see the output:

```
BoW3 = {"John":2,"likes":3,"to":2,"watch":2,"movies":2,"Mary":1,
    "too":1,"also":1,"football":1,"games":1}
```

After we finish this section we will try to prepare you for the next Chapter 8, which features extraction. There you will learn how to prepare your data and get information about what data you have. This will become more obvious in the next chapters.

Summary

We started this chapter by defining what is the data pipeline and elaborated where is data cleaning in the pipeline' after that we gave you a good reason why you need to clean your dataset.

After that we looked at useful techniques to make sure that we handle missing data correctly. Before we feed data to a deep learning algorithm, we also have to make sure that we encode categorical variables correctly, and we have seen how we can map ordinal and nominal features values to integer representations.

Finally, we made a case study and discussed how to use what we learned from this chapter on the Titanic dataset to prepare, clear it, and make it ready for the next step of the pipeline.

CHAPTER 7

Data Resampling

In statistics, resampling is the method that consists of drawing repeated samples from the original data. So, we can say that *resampling methods* are a tool taken from modern statistics. These methods involve repeatedly taking a sample from the training set and training the model on each sample in order to get additional information about the model.

For example, we can estimate variability of the learning of the model of interest. We can draw different samples from the training data, then each time we train the model on a given sample, we examine the difference in results. An approach like that may allow us to obtain information that would not be available to us if we trained our model only one time using all of the training dataset.

Using resampling methods might be costly and expensive by way of computational power, especially if you think about these approaches training the same model many times using a different subset of the training dataset. But nowadays computer power has grown, and the requirements of these methods are not impossible.

In this chapter we will introduce two of the most commonly used methods in data resampling: *cross-validation* and *bootstrap*. Both of these methods are very important and used a lot in many practical applications, and are an essential part of any machine learning pipeline. For example, *cross-validation* can be used to estimate the error coming from a trained model to check and evaluate its performance, or to select something called

© Hisham El-Amir and Mahmoud Hamdy 2020
H. El-Amir and M. Hamdy, *Deep Learning Pipeline*,
https://doi.org/10.1007/978-1-4842-5349-6_7

the level of flexibility. *Bootstrap* is commonly used to give us the accuracy of model parameter used in training

- **Note:** The process of evaluating the model's performance is known as *model assessment*.

- **Note:** The process of selecting the best level of flexibility is known as *model selection*.

Creating Training and Test Sets

When a dataset is large enough, it's a good practice to split it into training and test sets; the former to be used for training the model and the latter to test its performances.

You might wonder why you should do that from the beginning. Separating data into *training* and *testing* sets is an important part of evaluating data mining models. Typically, when you separate a data set into a training set and a testing set, most of the data is used for training and a smaller portion of the data is used for testing.

The methods that we will discuss in this chapter have a main responsibility, which is to randomly sample the data to help ensure that the testing and training sets are similar. By using similar data for training and testing, you can minimize the effects of data discrepancies and better understand the characteristics of the model.

After a model has been processed by using the training set, you test the model by making predictions against the test set. Because the data in the testing set already contains known values for the attribute that you want to predict, it is easy to determine whether the model's guesses are correct.

To summarize, there are two main rules in performing such an operation:

- Both datasets must reflect the original distribution.

- The original dataset must be randomly shuffled before the split phase in order to avoid a correlation between consequent elements.

Cross-Validation

In a previous chapter we illustrated the difference between the *testing error rate* and the *training error rate*. The error that comes as a result of using a certain model to predict the output of a new observation is called the *testing error rate*.

You can see that:

- The **lower** the testing error rate, the good the model is.

- The **higher** the rate is, the worse the model is.

Note   Do not forget that the testing set was **not** used to train the model.

The training error rate can be easily calculated by applying the model to the dataset used in its training. But, you will notice that this error rate is often different from the test error rate and lower too, and it's not a good measure for the model because it can underestimate the true accuracy.

As we want a good estimation of the testing error rate, we need a large testing set. But what if you cannot get a large dataset for testing? Here come some methods to estimate the testing error rate using the training dataset. In the next section we will consider a type of method that estimates the testing error rate by holding out a small subset of the training data, and not to train the model on this subset; it then uses the model to predict these subset outputs.

Validation Set Technique

The validation set technique is a very simple technique for estimating testing error rate associated with training a model on a dataset. It involves randomly dividing the available training set into two pieces: a *training set* and a *validation set* (sometimes called *hold-out set*). The model trains on a *training data piece*; after training finishes, the model is used to predict the responses/outputs for the observations in the validation set and as a result, it provides an estimate of the testing error rate (Figure 7-1).

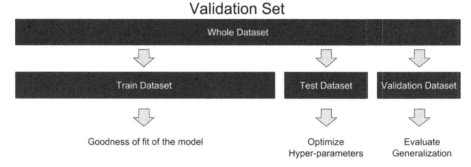

Figure 7-1. *A strategic view of how a validation set works*

The first thing we can start with is to load the dataset that we will work with in this chapter, the Iris dataset, which we introduced in a previous chapter. Then we create two variables: one for input features and another one for the target/output feature.

Note   The Iris dataset comes as preloaded dataset in a datasets module at sklearn package.

```
from sklearn import datasets
iris = datasets.load_iris()

print('X shape: {}, y shape: {}'.format(iris.data.shape, iris.
target.shape))
```

```
# Output
# X shape: (150, 4), y shape: (150, )
```

After loading the dataset into X and y variables, we also print the shape of both variables. It's now time for sampling the data to choose points that will be in the training set and ones that will be in the validation and testing sets.

So, we import from the `sklearn.model_selection` module the `train_test_split` function that will divide the data into train and test portions.

```
from sklearn.model_selection import train_test_plit
```

Then, we use it to divide both X and y into training X, y (to be called X_train, y_train) and testing X, y sets (to be called X_test, y_test).

Note   The training set will be equal to 60% of the whole dataset, and the testing set will be equal to 40% of the whole dataset.

```
X_train, X_test, y_train, y_test = train_test_split(iris.data,
iris.target, test_size=0.4, random_state=47)
```

After the divide operation is done, and all sets are created from the sampling operation, let us print the shape of all sets to see the percentage of the divide operation. As we configured it, the training data has 90 observations of 150 total observations, and this means 60% of the data; and the testing set has 60 observations, which means that it is equal to 40% of the whole dataset.

```
print('# Train => X shape: {}, y shape: {}'.format(X_train.shape,
y_train.shape))
print('# Test  => X shape: {}, y shape: {}'.format(X_test.shape,
y_test.shape))
```

```
# Output
# # Train => X shape: (90, 4), y shape: (90, )
# # Test  => X shape: (60, 4), y shape: (60, )
```

Now, we need to create the validation set, as we don't have any function that can create all of the training, validating, and testing sets in one step. We need to do the same step of dividing the data on the test set, but this time we want the divide the 40% into 20% for testing and 20% for validating, so we will divide the testing set in half. In the following code, we divided the testing set into 50% testing set and 50% validation set.

```
X_test, X_valid, y_test, y_valid = train_test_split(X_test,
y_test, test_size=0.5, random_state=47)
```

After we divide, again, we print all sets to make sure that we are in the right place. As you can see, we did not touch the training set at all, the 90 observations in the training set remain untouched, while the testing set now is 30 observations instead of 60, and there's a validation set that has 30 observations too.

```
print('# Train => X shape: {}, y shape: {}'.format(X_train.shape,
y_train.shape))
print('# Test  => X shape: {}, y shape: {}'.format(X_test.shape,
y_test.shape))
print('# Valid => X shape: {}, y shape: {}'.format(X_valid.shape,
y_ valid.shape))
```

```
# Output
# # Train => X shape: (90, 4), y shape: (90, )
# # Test  => X shape: (30, 4), y shape: (30, )
# # Valid => X shape: (30, 4), y shape: (30, )
```

The model should train on the training set, and after the learning process (training) is finished the model is used to predict the outcome (responses) for the observations (input row) in the validation set.

The resulting validation set error rate should be an estimate of the test error rate. The validation set approach is conceptually simple and easy to implement, but it has two potential drawbacks:

- The estimate of the test error rate that the validation set provides can be **highly variable**, depending on the process that selected which observation will be on the training set and which observation will be on the testing set.

- The estimate of the test error rate that the validation set provide might overestimate the test error rate. That's because we take a subset of the training and/or testing set as a validation set, and that makes the sets smaller in size, which means the model may perform worse due to fewer training observations.

So, in the next approach, we will introduce an upgrade of the validation set called *cross-validation*; this approach is especially to address the two issues just mentioned.

Leave-One-Out Cross-Validation (LOOCV)

LOOCV is very similar to a validation set and does the same job, but it was created to solve the drawbacks of a validation set.

Similar to a validation set, LOOCV splits the set of data into two parts. However, the validation set contains only a single observation (just one point of the dataset). Let us consider that this one point/observation is (x_1, y_1) and this point is used for the validation set, and all other observations $\{(x_2, y_2), ..., (x_n, y_n)\}$ are used for training the model (as training set). The model now learns from n-1 observations in the training set, and validates its learning process on only one observation. We are predicting y1 for the x1, since (x_1, y_1) is not used on the learning process (training model), and the metric used contains errors for the first point (x_1, y_1) that we describe as $E_1 = (y_1 - \hat{y}_1)^2$ for regression and $E_1 = (y_1 \neq \hat{y}_1)^2$ for classification.

Now we provide almost an unbiased estimate for the test error. But even though this error term is unbiased, it is still a poor estimate because it is highly variable; and you can sense it because we are using only one observation (x_1, y_1) for validating our model knowledge.

If we want to fix this problem, we can simply repeat the same process by selecting (x_2, y_2) as the validation set and all other observation as the training set. We train our model on $n - 1$ other observations and compute E_2 for the validation point x_2. We repeat again for (x_3, y_3), train the model, validate, and produce E_3. We do it again for (x_4, y_4) and produce E_4 and do it for all data points/observations for N times to produces N errors, $E_1, ..., E_n$. The LOOCV estimate for the test error now is the average of these N validation set error rates.

$$CV_{(N)} = \frac{1}{n} \sum_{i}^{N} E_i$$

As we can see, LOOCV has a couple of advantages that could not exist in the validation set approach:

- LOOCV has less bias than a validation set, because we repeatedly train the model on $n - 1$ data observations (and that's almost the entire dataset). That doesn't happen in the validation set approach; in the validation set approach, we take a subset of the whole dataset as the validation set and train the model on the other data subsets. So the LOOCV approach tends not to overestimate the test error rate as much as the validation set approach does.

- LOOCV produces the same results each time you run it; unlike the validation set approach, there is no randomness in the train-test splits. LOOCV repeatedly takes each data point as validation set one time and at the end calculates the mean error rate. There's no randomness generated, because you do not select the validation set observations; you simply take each observation as validation for one time and iterate.

```
from sklearn.model_selection import LeaveOneOut
```

We know that sklearn contains almost any function we need as we perform our machine learning pipeline, and it works for most of the dataset we will deal with. As a first step, we need to load the LeaveOneOut method from the model_selection module in Scikit-learn.

After loading the method, we need to load our data; for simplicity, we will use the iris preloaded dataset in the sklearn datasets module.

```
X = iris.data
y = iris.target
```

Until now, we have loaded the method and data. Now we will start the work, and we'll do that by initiating the LeaveOneOut class and getting the number of possible splits. As you see, there are 150 possible splits.

```
loo = LeaveOneOut()
loo.get_n_splits(iris.data)
```

Now we can use the loo instance for us, and we can do that by getting the starting and ending indices for both train and testing sets.

```
from train_index, test_index in loo.split(X):
    X_train, X_test = X[train_index], X[test_index]
    y_train, y_test = y[train_index], y[test_index]
```

For each iteration, the class instance will give the test one data point, and the rest will be in the training.

LOOCV may have a drawback, which concerns computational power. LOOCV can be expensive to implement, since the model has to train N times. So, if the dataset is large, this can be very time consuming, and you should consider the time the model takes to learn.

K-Fold Cross-Validation

You might think that this new approach is an upgrade to LOOCV. K-Fold CV involves randomly dividing the dataset into k equal subsets/groups and they're called *folds*. Then we take the first subset (fold) as a validation set and train the mode on the other $k - 1$ fold as a training-set. The validation error produced (let's call it E_1) is calculated from the validation set (hold-out fold). We repeat the process k times; each time, we take one different fold as the validation set and all other $k - 1$ as the training set. This process results in k estimate of the test error rate, which is $E_1, ..., E_k$, and then we take the average:

$$CV_{(N)} = \frac{1}{N} \sum_{i=1}^{N} E_i$$

You can see that LOOCV is a special case of K-Fold CV in which k is equal to N. In practice, the developer performs K-Fold CV using k=5 or k=10, but most developers do not use k=N due to computational power as we mentioned earlier.

```
from sklearn.model_selection import KFold

kf = KFold(n_split=5)
kf.get_n_split(X)
# Output
# 5
```

```
for train_index, test_index in kf.split(X):
    X_train, X_test = X[train_index], X[test_index]
    Y_train, y_test = y[train_index], y[test_index]
    Print('# Train => X shape: {} ## Test => X Shape: {}'.
    format(X_train.shape, X_test.shape))

# Output
# Train => X shape: (120, 4) ## Test => X Shape: (30, 4)
# Train => X shape: (120, 4) ## Test => X Shape: (30, 4)
# Train => X shape: (120, 4) ## Test => X Shape: (30, 4)
# Train => X shape: (120, 4) ## Test => X Shape: (30, 4)
# Train => X shape: (120, 4) ## Test => X Shape: (30, 4)
```

Bootstrap

Bootstrap is a statistical technique used for sampling data with replacement.

For now, we have a little introduction for the bootstrap technique. We will use a real example that allows you to get a better idea about data resampling with bootstrap. There are other resampling techniques like Monte Carlo, and randomization techniques, but here we will talk only about the bootstrap technique.

The bootstrap method can be used to estimate the quantity of a population. This is done by repeatedly taking small samples, calculating the statistic, and taking the average of the calculated statistics.

Bootstrap in Statistics

Bootstrap is denoted by x^*. Let's start to generate a bootstrap sample. We have N observations and need to sample them; we can get these samples from the distribution of population.

So, N observations are $x_1 = 2$, $x_2 = 1$, $x_3 = 7$, ..., $x_N = 5$ for instance.

The sample we get from N observations we can denote as vector $x(\underline{x})$ and we can make any operation in this sample, like mean $S = \theta(\underline{x})$. This action can be done without replacement, or we can do the same but with replacement. What's the difference between replacement and without replacement? With replacement means that we can repeat the same value more than one in the same observation, but without replacement we can't repeat the value in an observation more than once. Note the observation should be *IID* (independent identical distribution). Identically distributed means that there are no overall trends—the distribution doesn't fluctuate, and all items in the sample are taken from the same probability distribution. Independent means that the sample items are all independent events. So let's complete the bootstrap.

So N observations are $x_1 = 2$, $x_2 = 1$, $x_3 = 7$, ..., $x_N = 5$. The sample we get from N-observation can be denoted as Bootstrap $x(x^*)$

And we can make any operation in this sample like mean S = (x^*) but here with replacement. Let's see a figure that may make things easier.

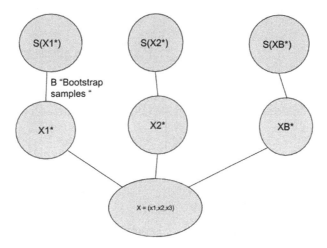

Basically, the bootstrap method is a statistical technique for estimating quantities about a population by averaging estimates from multiple small data samples.

You can see the difference between these two examples in the following image.

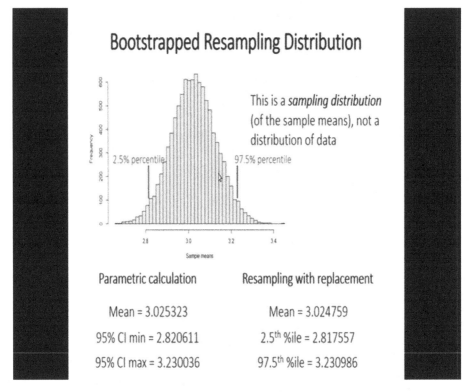

Figure 7-2. *Sample distribution*

Tips to Use Bootstrap (Resampling with Replacement)

To give you the best experience using the bootstrap technique, we summarized it into steps, and you can use these steps to create your data selection pipeline.

1. Maintains data structure but reshuffles values, extrapolating to the population

2. The procedure can sample each value multiple times, or not at all.

3. Useful for estimating statistic parameters where data are nonnormal

4. Has unknown statistical properties (e.g., PCA— we will discuss it in a later chapter).

So, let us give some thought to how this method works, get into more details about it, and see how we can make these samples. The process for building one sample can be summarized as follows:

1. Choose the size of the sample.

2. If the size of the sample is less than the chosen size:

   a. Randomly select an observation from the dataset.

   b. Add it to the sample.

The bootstrap method can calculate the quantity of population in the following steps:

1. Choose a number of bootstrap samples to perform.

2. Choose a sample size.

3. For each bootstrap sample:

   a. Draw a sample with replacement with the chosen size.

   b. Calculate the statistic on the sample.

4. Calculate the mean of the calculated sample statistics.

After setting up the theoretical toolbox, let's take an example to demonstrate how these statistical methods work.

Imagine we have a dataset with 6 observations:

```
[0.1, 0.2, 0.3, 0.4, 0.5, 0.6]
```

The first step is to choose the size of the sample. Here, we will use 4. Next, we must randomly choose the first observation from the dataset. Let's choose 0.2.

```
sample = [0.2]
```

This observation is returned to the dataset, and we repeat this step three more times.

```
sample = [0.2, 0.1, 0.2, 0.6]
```

We now have our data sample. The example purposefully demonstrates that the same value can appear zero, or one or more times in the sample. Here the observation 0.2 appears twice. An estimate can then be calculated on the drawn sample.

```
statistic = calculation([0.2, 0.1, 0.2, 0.6])
```

Those observations not chosen for the sample may be used as out-of-bag observations.

```
oob = [0.3, 0.4, 0.5]
```

In the case of evaluating a machine learning model, the model is fit on the drawn sample and evaluated on the out-of-bag sample.

```
train = [0.2, 0.1, 0.2, 0.6]
test = [0.3, 0.4, 0.5]
model = fit(train)
statistic = evaluate(model, test)
```

That concludes one repeat of the procedure. It can be repeated 30 or more times to give a sample of calculated statistics.

```
statistics = [...]
```

This sample of statistics can then be summarized by calculating a mean, standard deviation, or other summary value to give a final usable estimate of the statistic.

```
estimate = mean([...])
```

At the end of this section, we should know what sampling is, how we use it with replacement and without replacement, and the difference between them when we use it with statistical functions.

Generators

When you are working on developing a machine/deep learning model, you might experience lack of memory while feeding datasets into the model. The moment you run into memory errors when trying to take the training data into memory, you know that you have to switch your data feeding strategy.

Even state-of-the-art configurations might go out of memory sometimes to process the whole data. That is the reason why we need to find other ways to do that task efficiently. The only way to do it is by loading the data in real time; hence, we are going to show you how to generate your dataset on multiple cores in real time and feed it right away to your deep learning models.

What Are Keras Generators?

A generator is just a module in Keras, which is used to get batches of input and corresponding output on the fly during the training process.

An example is reading in a set that contains an input of 100 images, getting a corresponding 100 label vector, and then feeding this set to the GPU for the training step. We have to keep in mind that, in some cases, even the most state-of-the-art configuration won't have enough memory space to process the data the way we used to do it. That is the reason why we need to find other ways to do that task efficiently. We are going to show you how to generate your dataset on multiple cores in real time and feed it right away to your deep learning models.

Let's see an example, to get a better idea about *data_generator*, and we will talk about **train-on-the-fly** module too. Let's start with the Keras package; we need it to use generators, and now you can import it from TensorFlow too as a module.

```
// could not understood the example here
```

The example we go through is a teaching example to learn how to use this package to enhance feeding your data into your model.

Before getting started, let's go through a few organizational tips that are particularly useful when dealing with large datasets. Let **ID** be the string that identifies a given sample of the dataset. A good way to keep track of samples and their labels is to adopt the following framework:

1. Create a dictionary called `partition` where you gather

   - in `partition['train']` a list of training IDs

   - in `partition['validation']` a list of validation IDs

Create a dictionary called `labels` where for each **ID** of the dataset, the associated label is given by `labels[ID]`.

For example, let's say that our training set contains `id-1`, `id-2`, and `id-3` with respective labels 0, 1, and 2, with a validation set containing `id-4` with label 1. In that case, the Python variables partition and labels look like:

```
Partition
{'train': ['id-1', 'id-2', 'id-3'], 'validation': ['id-4']}
Labels
{'id-1': 0, 'id-2': 1, 'id-3': 2, 'id-4': 1}
```

Now we get a basic idea about how data is partitioned and labeled, and what the folder looks like to separate data, classes, and labeled data. A data/ folder is used to save your dataset in it.

```
folder/
├── my_classes.py
├── keras_script.py
└── data/
```

Data Generator

Now, let's go through the details of how to set up the Python class DataGenerator, which will be used for real-time data feeding to your Keras model.

So, let's now write the initialization function of the class as follows:

```
def __init__(self, list_IDs, labels, batch_size=32,
dim=(32,32,32),n_channels=1,n_classes=10, shuffle=True):
    #'Initialization'
    self.dim = dim
    self.batch_size = batch_size
    self.labels = labels
    self.list_IDs = list_IDs
    self.n_channels = n_channels
    self.n_classes = n_classes
    self.shuffle = shuffle
    self.on_epoch_end()
```

Now we initialize the variables we need. But let's consider every variable, dimension sizes (e.g., a volume of length 32 will have dim=(32,32,32)), number of channels, number of classes, and batch size or decide whether we want to shuffle our data at generation. And we store important information such as labels and the list of IDs that we wish to generate at each pass.

Now I need to talk about callback functions, and on_epoch_end is one of them.

But before talking about the functions we use, as we are accustomed in this book, we'll try to cover the basics about what is a callback.

A callback is a set of functions to be applied at given stages of the training procedure. You can use callbacks to get a view on internal states and statistics of the model during training. You can pass a list of callbacks (as the keyword argument callbacks) to the fit() method of the Sequential or Model classes. The relevant methods of the callbacks will then be called at each stage of the training.

Callback

One of the important modules we can use a lot is the keras.callbacks. Callback() module. This API allows you to specify which metric to monitor, such as loss or accuracy on the training or validation dataset. You can specify whether to look for an improvement in maximizing or minimizing the score. Finally, the filename that you use to store the weights can include variables like the epoch number or metric. The Keras documentation defines.

- *params*: Dictionary. Training parameters (e.g., verbosity, batch size, number of epochs...)

- *model*: an instance of keras.models.Model. Reference of the model being trained

The logs dictionary that callback methods take as an argument will contain keys for quantities relevant to the current batch or epoch.

Currently, the fit(...) method of the Sequential model class will include the following quantities in the logs that it passes to its callbacks:

- on_epoch_end: Logs include acc and loss, and optionally include val_loss (if validation is enabled in fit), and val_acc (if validation and accuracy monitoring are enabled).

- on_batch_begin: Logs include size, the number of samples in the current batch.

- on_batch_end: Logs include loss, and optionally acc (if accuracy monitoring is enabled).

For more about callbacks, you can see the documentation at http://faroit.com/keras-docs/1.1.0/callbacks/.

Now let's talk about the function on_epoch_end(); as we see, you can use it by using its parameters. Let's see an example. This function is very important in training and not just in the generator example; for example, if we train a model and this model gets an accuracy that satisfies us and it still has many epochs that will waste our time, we use on_epoch_end(). Let's get the definition of on_epoch_end().

```
class myCallback(tf.keras.callbacks.Callback):
  def on_epoch_end(self, epoch, logs={}):
    if(logs.get('acc')>0.6):
      print("\nReached 60% accuracy so cancelling training!")
      self.model.stop_training = True
```

In this example, the model will stop training after we get an accuracy of 60%, which we are satisfied with at this time so we don't need to initialize the number of epochs.

Since we are talking about generators, after we finish the initialization process it's time to continue this process into a new task. Shuffling the order in which examples are fed to the classifier is helpful, so that batches between epochs do not look alike. Doing so will eventually make our model more robust.

Another method that is core to the generation process is one that achieves the most crucial job: producing batches of data. The private method in charge of this task is called __data_generation and takes as argument the list of IDs of the target batch.

```python
def __data_generation(self, list_IDs_temp):
  'Generates data containing batch_size samples' # X :
  (n_samples, *dim, n_channels)
  # Initialization
  X = np.empty((self.batch_size, *self.dim, self.n_channels))
  y = np.empty((self.batch_size), dtype=int)

  # Generate data
  for i, ID in enumerate(list_IDs_temp):
      # Store sample
      X[i, ] = np.load('data/' + ID + '.npy')

      # Store class
      y[i] = self.labels[ID]

  return X, keras.utils.to_categorical(y, num_classes=self.n_classes)
```

During data generation, this code reads the NumPy array of each example from its corresponding file ID.npy. Since our code is multicore friendly, note that you can do more complex operations instead (e.g., computations from source files) without worrying that data generation becomes a bottleneck in the training process.

Also, please note that we used the `keras.utils.to_categorical` method to convert our numerical labels stored in y to a binary form—to be specific, one-hot vector form—(e.g., in a 6-class problem, the third label corresponds to [0 0 1 0 0 0]) suited for classification.

Now comes the part where we build up all these components together. Each call requests a batch index between 0 and the total number of batches, where the latter is specified in the __len__ method.

```
def __len__(self):
    'Denotes the number of batches per epoch'
    return int(np.floor(len(self.list_IDs) / self.batch_size))
```

A common practice is to set this value to $\dfrac{\#Samples}{Batch\ Size}$ so that the model sees the training samples at most once per epoch. Now that we have a basic understanding about data generators, we will see an example about it with a real dataset. Let's choose a simple dataset: the cats and dogs dataset, www.kaggle.com/c/dogs-vs-cats. Then the data should be in this structure:

```
data/
    training/
        class_Dog/
                class_a01.jpg
                class_a02.jpg
                ...
        class_Cat/
                class_b01.jpg
                class_b02.jpg
                ...
    validation/
        class_Dog/
```

```
                    class_a01.jpg
                    class_a02.jpg

                    ...

            class_Cat/
                    class_b01.jpg
                    class_b02.jpg

                    ...
```

Let's see a code for this data set. You don't need to understand it in detail—it will be explained in in detail Part III—but we want you to see the data generator used in a real problem.

```
from keras.preprocessing.image import ImageDataGenerator
import numpy as np

# step 1: load data

img_width = 150
img_height = 150
train_data_dir = 'data/train'
valid_data_dir = 'data/validation'

datagen = ImageDataGenerator(rescale = 1./255)

train_generator = datagen.flow_from_directory(directory=train_
data_dir,
target_size=(img_width,img_height),
classes=['dogs','cats'],
class_mode='binary',
batch_size=16)

validation_generator = datagen.flow_from_
directory(directory=valid_data_dir,
target_size=(img_width,img_height),
```

```
classes=['dogs','cats'],
class_mode='binary',
batch_size=32)

# step-2: build model
...

# Step 3: Train the Model with the Generator
training = model.fit_generator(generator=train_generator,
steps_per_epoch=2048//16, epochs=20,
validation_data=validation_generator,
validation_steps=832//16)
```

Now that we've finished this, you can have fun with generators and callbacks. Now you can either evaluate or deploy your model; it's up to you.

Summary

In this chapter we have introduced sampling techniques. Sampling is a very important step before building a model, and it ensures that the model learns the most from the selected data, not to get biased using the training data. You learned how to create a good training and testing set. We discussed several techniques, one of them being the bootstrap, which is a very strong statistical method for sampling the data. And finally, we gave a technical example of how the data generator method in Keras works on getting data and feeding it to the model.

CHAPTER 8

Feature Selection and Feature Engineering

Feature selection and engineering are important steps in a *machine learning pipeline* and involves all the techniques adopted to reduce their dimensionality. Most of the time, these steps come after cleaning the dataset.

Most algorithms have strong assumptions about the input data, and their performance can be negatively affected when raw datasets are used. Moreover, the data is seldom isotropic; there are often features that determine the general behavior of a sample, while others that are correlated don't provide any additional pieces of information. So, it's important to have a clear view of a dataset and know the most common algorithms used to reduce the number of features or select only the best ones.

In this chapter, you will learn about three fundamental techniques that will help to summarize and compress the information content of a dataset by transforming it onto a new feature subspace of lower dimensionality

© Hisham El-Amir and Mahmoud Hamdy 2020
H. El-Amir and M. Hamdy, *Deep Learning Pipeline*,
https://doi.org/10.1007/978-1-4842-5349-6_8

than the original one. Data compression is an important topic in machine learning, and it helps us to compress, store, and analyze a huge amount of data. So, we will cover the following topics:

- **Principal component analysis (PCA)** for unsupervised data compression

- **Linear discriminant analysis (LDA)** is a supervised dimensionality reduction technique for maximizing class separability

- Nonlinear dimensionality reduction via **kernel principal component analysis**

Dataset Used in This Chapter

Scikit-learn provides some built-in datasets that can be used for testing purposes. They're all available in the module `sklearn.datasets` and have a common structure:

- The `desc` instance variable contains a description about the data set you are using.

- The `data` instance variable contains the whole input set X.

- While `target` contains the labels for *classification* or response values for *regression*.

For example, considering the Boston house pricing dataset (used for regression), we have:

```
from sklearn.datasets import load_boston
boston = load_boston()
X = boston.data
y = boston.target
print('X shape: {}, and y shape: {}'.format(X.shape, y.shape))
```

```
# Output
# X shape: (506, 13), and y shape: (506,)
```

In the Boston dataset, we have

- 506 samples or observations

- 13 features or predictors

- single target or response value

In this chapter, we're going to use both the *Boston House Prices* dataset for *regression examples* and the *MNIST handwritten digit* dataset for *classification tasks.* For each concept we will describe in this chapter we will go through an example using these datasets to show you how to deal with the large number of variables and the hidden knowledge in your data.

```
from sklearn.datasets import load_digits
digits = load_digits()
X = digits.data
y = digits.target
print('X shape: {}, and y shape: {}'.format(X.shape, y.shape))
# Output
X shape: (1797, 64), and y shape: (1797,)
```

Similarly, you can import the *MNIST handwritten digit* dataset from the sklearn.datasets module; it's very simple and saves time for learning and experimentation.

The MNIST dataset provided by Scikit-learn is limited for many reasons; the first reason is to make it easier for educational purposes. If you want to experiment with the original dataset, refer to the web site http://yann.lecun.com/exdb/mnist/. Here you can download a full version that contains up to 70,000 handwritten digits already, split into training and test sets.

Scikit-learn also provides functions for creating dummy datasets from scratch:

- make_classification()

- make_regression()

- make_blobs() (*particularly useful for testing cluster algorithms*)

They're very easy to use, and in many cases it's the best choice to test a model if you do not have a dataset and without loading more complex datasets, or for educational purposes.

You can visit the sklearn datasets web site `https://scikit-learn. org/stable/da` for further information about all datasets provided by Scikit-learn.

Dimensionality Reduction—Questions to Answer

If you are working in a new project, and you have been provided with a dataset that contains dozens of variables, would you ever wonder what to do with all those variables? So, the real question is the following: *what happens when your dataset has too many variables?*

You may have faced some of these situations, or at least you might have thought of them:

- You find that most of the variables are **correlated**.

- You lose patience and decide to run a model on whole data. This returns **poor accuracy** and you feel terrible.

- You become indecisive about what to do.

- You start thinking of some strategic method to **find** a few *important variables*.

So, we need an approach that can choose important variables, or in other words, select the important variables that can affect the model and produce a good estimation for the output.

Another reason is that the feature selection and extraction topic is important to understand in the fields of statistics and data science. But when putting a lesson together for students or anyone wants to learn it, we found that the resources online were too technical, didn't fully address our needs, and/or provided conflicting information.

As a result, we wanted to put together the *"What"*, *"When,"* *"How,"* and *"Why"* of this topic and answer them in specific detail. Specifically, we wanted to present the rationale for this topic, the math under the hood, some best practices, and potential drawbacks to each method under this topic.

What Is Dimensionality Reduction?

If you've worked with a lot of variables before, you know this can cause some problems to you and the model you are building. So you may decide to select some variables that are important to help you to get the most of your dataset and will make the model reach the highest accuracy. On the other hand, you'll want to remove all the variables those will not do those things for you. To do all that—the selecting/removing process—you need to answer the following:

- Do you understand the relationships between each variable?

- Do you have so many variables that you are in danger of overfitting your model to your data, or you might be violating assumptions of whichever modeling tactics you're using?

You might ask the question *How do I take all of the variables I've collected and focus on only a few of them?* In technical terms, you want to "reduce the dimension of your feature space" by reducing the dimension of your feature space. You'll have fewer relationships between variables to consider and you are less likely to overfit your model.

Note   This doesn't immediately mean that overfitting, etc. are no longer concerns—but we're moving in the right direction!

Somewhat unsurprisingly, reducing the dimensions of the feature space is called *dimensionality reduction*. There are many ways to achieve dimensionality reduction, but most of these techniques fall into one of two classes:

- Feature elimination

- Feature extraction

Feature elimination is what it sounds like: we reduce the feature space by eliminating features. Instead of considering every single variable, we might drop all variables except the three we think will best predict what the United States' gross domestic product will look like. Advantages of feature elimination methods include simplicity and maintaining interpretability of your variables.

As a disadvantage, though, you gain no information from those variables you've dropped. If we only use last year's GDP, the proportion of the population in manufacturing jobs per the most recent American Community Survey numbers, and the unemployment rate to predict this year's GDP, we're missing out on whatever the dropped variables could contribute to our model. By eliminating features, we've also entirely eliminated any benefits those dropped variables would bring.

Feature extraction, however, doesn't run into this problem. Say we have ten independent variables. In feature extraction, we create ten "new" independent variables, where each new independent variable is a combination of each of the ten "old" independent variables. However, we create these new independent variables in a specific way and order these new variables by how well they predict our dependent variable.

You might ask *where does the dimensionality reduction come into play?* Well, we keep as many of the new independent variables as we want, but we drop the least important ones. Because we ordered the new variables by how well they predict our dependent variable, we know which variable is the most important and least important. But—and here's the kicker—because these new independent variables are combinations of our old ones, we're still keeping the most valuable parts of our old variables, even when we drop one or more of these "new" variables!

When Should I Use Dimensionality Reduction?

1. Do you want to **reduce** the number of variables, but aren't able to identify what are the important variables and what are the variables you consider to remove?

2. Do you want to ensure your variables are **independent** of one another, or there's no **correlation** between any of the *predictor/input* variables?

3. Do you care about the **interpretability** of the dataset variables?

If you answered "yes" to all three questions, then dimensionality reduction is a good approach to use. If you answered "no" to question 3, you **should not** use dimensionality reduction.

Finally, **how** and **why** are subject to the properties of each method, so they will be answered while describing and illustrating each method in the approach of dimensionality reduction.

Unsupervised Dimensionality Reduction via Principal Component Analysis (PCA)

As we explained, we can use feature extraction to reduce the number of features in a dataset. We can do that by using a feature extraction algorithm to transform or project the data onto a new feature space.

In the context of dimensionality reduction, feature extraction can be understood as an approach to data compression with the goal of maintaining most of the relevant information. Feature extraction is typically used to improve computational efficiency but can also help to reduce the curse of dimensionality.

Note   Using dimensionality reduction is very good if we are working with nonregularized models, and that's because it reduces the data complexity; hence, they are two different problems that work on similar areas.

The curse of dimensionality refers to phenomena that arise when analyzing and organizing data in high-dimensional spaces. The common theme of these problems is that when the dimensionality increases, the volume of the space increases so fast that the available data becomes sparse.

PCA is an *unsupervised linear transformation* technique that is widely used across different fields, most prominently for dimensionality reduction. Other popular applications of PCA include the following:

- Exploratory data analyses and denoising of signals in stock market trading

- The analysis of genome data and gene expression levels in the field of bioinformatics

PCA helps us to identify patterns in data based on the correlation between features. In a nutshell, PCA aims to find the direction of maximum variance in high-dimensional data and projects it onto a new subspace with equal or fewer dimensions than the original one. The orthogonal axes (principal components) of the new subspace can be interpreted as the direction of maximum variance given the constraint that the new feature axes are orthogonal to each other, as illustrated in Figure 8-1. Here, x1 and x2 are the original feature axes, and PC1 and PC2 are the principal components.

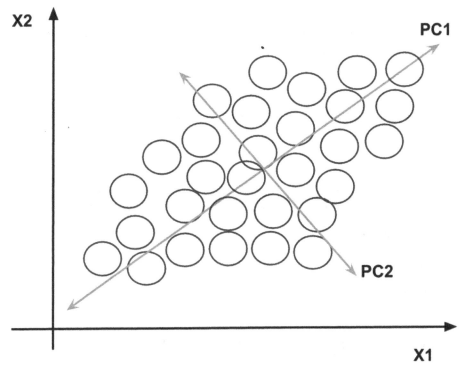

Figure 8-1. *The two-principle dimensions of the dataset*

If we use PCA for dimensionality reduction, we construct a dk-dimensional transformation matrix W. That allows us to map a sample vector x onto a new k-dimensional feature subspace that has fewer dimensions than the original d-dimensional feature space:

$$x = [x_1, x_2, \ldots, x_{d-1}, x_d], x \in R^d$$

$$\downarrow xW, W \in R^{d \times k}$$

$$z = [z_1, z_2, \ldots, z_{k-1}, z_k]$$

As a result of transforming the original d-dimensional data onto this new d-dimensional subspace (typically $k \ll d$), the first principal component has the largest possible variance, and all subsequent principal components will have the largest possible variance given that they are uncorrelated (orthogonal) to the other principal components. Note that the *PCA* directions are highly sensitive to data scaling, and we need to standardize the features *prior* to PCA if the features were measured on different scales and we want to assign equal importance to all features.

Before looking at the PCA algorithm for dimensionality reduction in more detail, let's summarize the approach in a few simple steps:

1. Standardize the d-dimensional dataset.

2. Construct the covariance matrix.

3. Decompose the covariance matrix into its eigenvectors and eigenvalues.

4. Select k eigenvectors that correspond to the k largest eigenvalues, where k is the dimensionality of the new feature subspace ($k \leq d$).

5. Construct a projection matrix W from the "top" k eigenvectors.

6. Transform the d-dimensional input dataset X using the projection matrix W to obtain the new k-dimensional feature subspace.

Total and Explained Variance

In this subsection, we will tackle the first four steps of a PCA:

- Standardizing the data

- Constructing the covariance matrix

- Obtaining the eigenvalues and eigenvectors of the covariance matrix

- Sorting the eigenvalues by decreasing order to rank the eigenvectors

Feature Selection and Filtering

As we explained earlier, the unnormalized dataset with many features contains information proportional to the independence of all features and their variance. Let's consider a small dataset with three features, generated randomly from many Gaussian distributions (Figure 8-2).

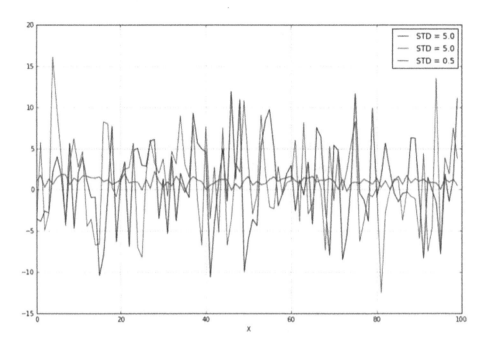

Figure 8-2. *The standard deviation of different datasets*

Even without further analysis, it's obvious that the central line (*with the lowest variance* std=0.5) is almost constant and doesn't provide any useful information. On the other hand, the other two variables carry more information, as they have a higher variance than the central line and their std=5.0.

A variance threshold is therefore a useful approach to remove all those elements whose contribution is under a predefined level. Scikit-learn provides the class VarianceThreshold that can easily solve this problem. By applying it on the previous dataset, we get the following result:

Note   The variance threshold removes the elements based on their variability and so, information.

```
X[0:3, :]
# Output:
array([[ 6.32000000e-03,    1.80000000e+01,    2.31000000e+00,
         0.00000000e+00,    5.38000000e-01,    6.57500000e+00,
         6.52000000e+01,    4.09000000e+00,    1.00000000e+00,
         2.96000000e+02,    1.53000000e+01,    3.96900000e+02,
         4.98000000e+00] ,
       [ 2.73100000e-02,    0.00000000e+00,    7.07000000e+00,
         0.00000000e+00,    4.69000000e-01,    6.42100000e+00,
         7.89000000e+01,    4.96710000e+00,    2.00000000e+00,
         2.42000000e+02,    1.78000000e+01,    3.96900000e+02,
         9.14000000e+00],
       [ 2.72900000e-02,    0.00000000e+00,    7.07000000e+00,
         0.00000000e+00,    4.69000000e-01,    7.18500000e+00,
         6.11000000e+01,    4.96710000e+00,    2.00000000e+00,
         2.42000000e+02,    1.78000000e+01,    3.92830000e+02,
         4.03000000e+00]])

from sklearn.feature_selection import VarianceThreshold
vt = VarianceThreshold(threshold=1.5)
X_t = vt.fit_transform(X)
X_t[0:3, :]

# Output
array([[ 6.32000000e-03,    1.80000000e+01,    2.31000000e+00,
         6.52000000e+01,    4.09000000e+00,    1.00000000e+00,
         2.96000000e+02,    1.53000000e+01,    3.96900000e+02,
         4.98000000e+00],
       [ 2.73100000e-02,    0.00000000e+00,    7.07000000e+00,
         7.89000000e+01,    4.96710000e+00,    2.00000000e+00,
         2.42000000e+02,    1.78000000e+01,    3.96900000e+02,
         9.14000000e+00],
```

```
[ 2.72900000e-02,    0.00000000e+00,    7.07000000e+00,
  6.11000000e+01,    4.96710000e+00,    2.00000000e+00,
  2.42000000e+02,    1.78000000e+01,    3.92830000e+02,
  4.03000000e+00]])
```

The third feature has been completely removed because its variance is under the selected threshold=1.5. There are also many univariate methods that can be used in order to select the best features according to specific criteria based on *F-tests and p-values*, such as **chi-square** or **ANOVA**. However, their discussion is beyond the scope of this book, and the reader can find further information in *Statistics* by David Freedman, Robert Pisani, and Roger Purves (Norton & Company, 2011). Two examples of feature selection that use the classes SelectKBest (which selects the *best* K-score features) and SelectPercentile (which selects only a subset of features belonging to a certain percentile) are shown next. It's possible to apply them both to regression and classification datasets, being careful to select appropriate score functions:

```
from sklearn.datasets import load_boston, load_iris
from sklearn.feature_selection import SelectKBest,
SelectPercentile, chi2, f_regression
regr_data = load_boston()
regr_data.data.shape
# Output
(506, 13)

# Init the algorithm
# This algorithm as the name,
# selects the best k features
kb_regr = SelectKBest(f_regression)
X_b = kb_regr.fit_transform(regr_data.data, regr_data.target)
X_b.shape
```

```
# Output
(506, 10)
kb_regr.scores_
# Output
array([ 88.15124178,  75.2576423, 153.95488314,   15.97151242,
112.59148028, 471.84673988, 83.47745922,   33.57957033,
85.91427767, 141.76135658, 175.10554288,   63.05422911,
601.61787111])
```

For further details about all Scikit-learn score functions and their usage, visit the Scikit-learn feature selection (`https://scikit-learn.org/stable/modules/feature_selection.html#univariate-feature-selection`).

Principal Component Analysis

In many cases, the dimensionality of the input dataset X is high and so is the complexity of every related machine learning algorithm. Moreover, the information is spread uniformly across all the features. In general, if we consider a Euclidean space, we have

$$X = \{x'_1, x'_2, \ldots, x'_{n-1}, x'_n\} \text{ where } x'_i \in R^m \wedge x'_i = x'_{i1} e_1 + \ldots + x'_{im} e_m$$

So, each point is expressed using an orthonormal basis made of m linearly independent vectors. Now, considering a dataset X, a natural question arises: *is it possible to reduce m without a drastic loss of information?* Let's consider Figure 8-3 (without any particular interpretation).

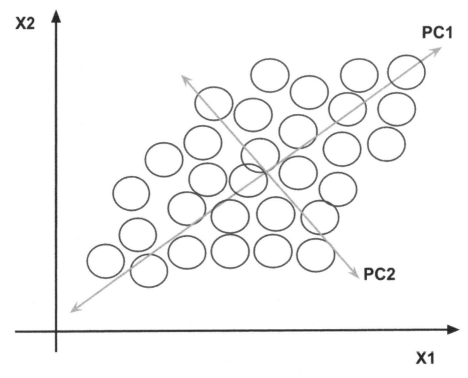

Figure 8-3. *Revisiting principle component image*

It doesn't matter which distributions generated $X = (x, y)$; however, the variance of the horizontal component is clearly higher than the vertical one. As discussed, it means that the amount of information provided by the first component is higher and, for example, if the x-axis is stretched horizontally keeping the vertical one fixed, the distribution becomes similar to a segment where the depth has lower and lower importance.

In order to assess how much information is brought by each component, and the correlation among them, a useful tool is the covariance matrix (Figure 8-4; if the dataset has zero mean, we can use the correlation matrix).

$$C = \begin{pmatrix} \sigma_1^2 & \cdots & \sigma_{1m} \\ \vdots & \ddots & \vdots \\ \sigma_{m1} & \cdots & \sigma_m^2 \end{pmatrix}$$

$$where \; \sigma_{ij} = \frac{1}{m}\sum_{k}(x_{ki} - E[X_i])(x_{kj} - E[X_j])$$

Figure 8-4. *The covariance equation*

C is symmetric and positive semidefinite, so all the eigenvalues are nonnegative, but *what's the meaning of each value?* The covariance matrix C for the previous example is symmetric; As expected, the horizontal variance is quite a bit higher than the vertical one. Moreover, the other values are close to zero. If you remember the definition and, for simplicity, remove the mean term, they represent the cross-correlation between couples of components. It's obvious that in our example, X and Y are uncorrelated (they're orthogonal), but in real-life examples, there could be features that present a residual cross-correlation. In terms of information theory, it means that knowing Y gives us some information about X (which we already know), so they share information that is indeed doubled. So, our goal is also to decorrelate X while trying to reduce its dimensionality. This can be achieved by considering the sorted eigenvalues of C and selecting the best principle component values:

So, it's possible to project the original feature vectors into this new (sub-) space, where each component carries a portion of total variance and where the new covariance matrix is decorrelated to reduce useless information sharing (in terms of correlation) among different features. In Scikit-learn, there's the PCA class, which can do all this in a very smooth way:

```
import numpy as np
import matplotlib.pyplot as plt
from sklearn.datasets import load_digits
from sklearn.decomposition import PCA
mnist = load_digits()
```

A figure with a few random MNIST handwritten digits is shown in Figure 8-5.

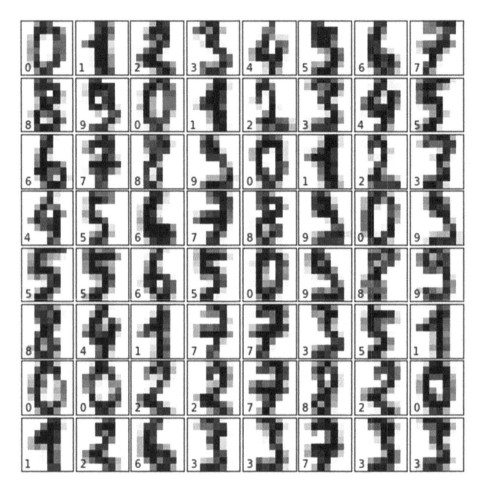

Figure 8-5. *The MNIST dataset*

Each image is a vector of 64 *unsigned int* (8 bit) numbers (0, 255), so the initial number of components is indeed 64. However, the total amount of black pixels is often predominant and the basic signs needed to write 10 digits are similar, so it's reasonable to assume both high cross-correlation and a low variance on several components. Trying with 36 principal components, we get:

```
pca = PCA(n_components=36)
proj = pca.fit_transform(digits.data)
plt.scatter(proj[:, 0], proj[:, 1], c=digits.target,
cmap="Paired")
plt.colorbar()
```

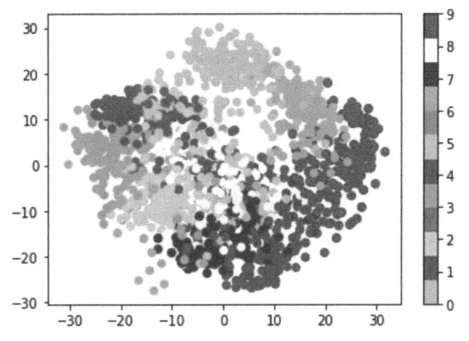

Figure 8-6. *The scatter plot of PCA output*

In order to improve performance, all integer values are normalized into the range [0, 1] and, through the parameter whiten=True, the variance of each component is scaled to one. As also the official Scikit-learn documentation says, this process is particularly useful when an isotropic distribution (any distribution has a simple shape to your eye but very complex shape to the algorithm) is needed for many algorithms to perform efficiently. It's possible to access the explained variance ratio through the instance variable explained_variance_ratio_, which shows which part of the total variance is carried by each single component:

```
pca.explained_variance_ratio_
# Output:
array([ 0.14890594, 0.13618771, 0.11794594,  0.08409979,
        0.05782415, 0.0491691,  0.04315987,  0.03661373,
        0.03353248, 0.03078806, 0.02372341,  0.02272697,
        0.01821863, 0.01773855, 0.01467101,  0.01409716,
        0.01318589, 0.01248138, 0.01017718,  0.00905617,
        0.00889538, 0.00797123, 0.00767493,  0.00722904,
        0.00695889, 0.00596081, 0.00575615,  0.00515157,
        0.00489539, 0.00428888, 0.00373606,  0.00353271,
        0.00336678, 0.0032803,  0.0030832,   0.00293777])
```

A plot for the example of MNIST digits is shown next (Figure 8-7). The bottom graph represents the variance ratio, while the top one is the cumulative variance. It can be immediately seen how the first components are normally the most important ones in terms of information, while the following ones provide details that a classifier could also discard.

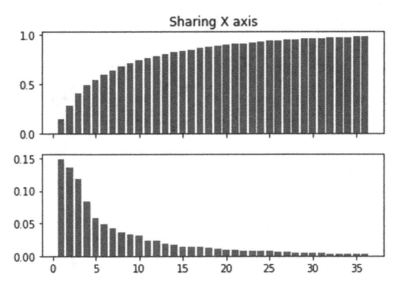

Figure 8-7. *The histogram and CDF plot of the variance per each component*

As expected, the contribution to the total variance decreases dramatically starting from the fifth component, so it's possible to reduce the original dimensionality without an unacceptable loss of information, which could drive an algorithm to learn wrong classes. In the preceding graph, there are the same handwritten digits rebuilt using the first *36 components* with whitening and normalization between *0* and *1*. To obtain the original images, we need to inverse-transform all new vectors and project them into the original space:

```
X_rebuilt = pca.inverse_transform(X_pca)
```

The result is shown in Figures 8-8 and 8-9.

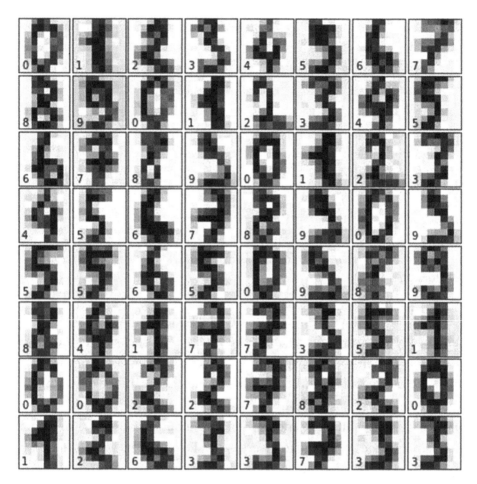

Figure 8-8. *The output of PCA inversion*

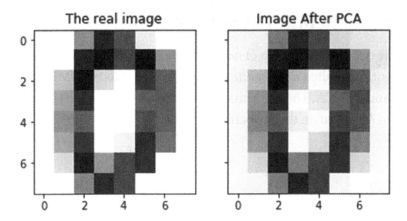

Figure 8-9. *The output of PCA inversion vs. the real image*

This process can also partially denoise the original images by removing residual variance, which is often associated with noise or unwanted contributions (almost every calligraphy distorts some of the structural elements that are used for recognition).

I suggest the reader try different numbers of components (using the explained variance data) and also n_components='mle', which implements an automatic selection of the best dimensionality ("Automatic Choice of Dimensionality for PCA" by Thomas P. Minka (NIPS, 2000: 598-604)). Scikit-learn solves the **PCA** problem with **SVD** (singular value decomposition), which can be studied in detail in *Linear Algebra* by David Poole (Brooks Cole, 2015). It's possible to control the algorithm through the parameter svd_solver, whose values are 'auto', 'full', 'arpack', and 'randomized'.

Nonnegative Matrix Factorization

When the dataset is made up of nonnegative numbers, it's possible to use a good algorithm called *nonnegative matrix factorization* (NNMF) instead of using standard PCA. The algorithm optimizes a loss function (alternatively on W and H) based on the Frobenius norm:

$$L = \frac{1}{2}\|X - WH\|^2_{Frob}, \ where \ \|A\|^2_{Frob} = \sqrt{\sum_i \sum_j |a_{ij}|^2}$$

If $dim(X) = n \times m$, then $dim(W) = n \times p$ and $dim(H) = p \times m$ with p equal to the number of requested components (the n_components parameter), which is normally *smaller than* the original dimensions n and m.

The final reconstruction is purely additive, and it has been shown that it's particularly efficient for images or text where there are normally no nonnegative elements. In the following snippet, there's an example using the Iris dataset (which is nonnegative). The init parameter can assume different values (see the documentation), which determine how the data matrix is initially processed. A random choice is for nonnegative matrices, which are only scaled (no SVD is performed):

```
from sklearn.datasets import load_iris
from sklearn.decomposition import NMF
iris = load_iris()
iris.data.shape
# Output
(150L, 4L)
```

```
nmf = NMF(n_components=3, init='random', l1_ratio=0.1)
Xt = nmf.fit_transform(iris.data)
nmf.reconstruction_err_
# Output
1.8819327624141866
```

```
iris.data[0]
# Output
array([ 5.1, 3.5, 1.4, 0.2])

Xt[0]
# Output
array([ 0.20668461, 1.09973772, 0.0098996 ])

nmf.inverse_transform(Xt[0])
# Output
array([5.10401653, 3.49666967, 1.3965409, 0.20610779])
```

NNMF, together with other factorization methods, will be very useful for more advanced techniques, such as recommendation systems and topic modeling. NNMF is very sensitive to its parameters (in particular, initialization and regularization), so I suggest reading the original documentation for further information: http://scikit-learn.org/stable/modules/generated/sklearn.decomposition.NMF.html.

Sparse PCA

Scikit-learn provides different PCA variants that can solve particular problems. I do suggest reading the original documentation. However, I'd like to mention SparsePCA, which allows exploiting the natural sparsity of data while extracting principal components. If you think about the handwritten digits or other images that must be classified, their initial dimensionality can be quite high (a 10x10 image has 100 features). However, applying a standard PCA selects only the average most important features, assuming that every sample can be rebuilt using the same components. Simplifying, this is equivalent to:

$$y_R = c_1 y_{R1} + c_2 y_{R2} + \ldots + c_{(g-1)} y_{R(g-1)} + c_g y_{Rg}$$

On the other hand, we can always use a limited number of components, but without the limitation given by a dense projection matrix. This can be achieved by using sparse matrices (or vectors), where the number of nonzero elements is quite low. In this way, each element can be rebuilt using its specific components (in most cases, they will always be the most important), which can include elements normally discarded by a dense PCA. The previous expression now becomes:

$$y_R = \left[c_1 y_{R1} + c_2 y_{R2} + \ldots + c_{(g-1)} y_{R(g-1)} + c_g y_{Rg} \right] + ZEROTERM$$

$$ZEROTERM = \left(0 \cdot y_{R(g+1)} + 0 \cdot y_{R(g+2)} + \ldots + 0 \cdot y_{R(g+n-1)} + 0 \cdot y_{R(gn)} \right)$$

Here the non-null components have been put into the first block (they don't have the same order as the previous expression), while all the other zero terms have been separated. In terms of linear algebra, the vectorial space now has the original dimensions. However, using the power of sparse matrices (provided by `scipy.sparse`), Scikit-learn can solve this problem much more efficiently than a classical PCA.

The following snippet shows a sparse PCA with 60 components. In this context, they're usually called atoms and the amount of sparsity can be controlled via *L1-norm* regularization (higher alpha parameter values lead to more sparse results). This approach is very common in classification algorithms and will be discussed in the next chapters:

```
from sklearn.decomposition import SparsePCA
spca = SparsePCA(n_components=60, alpha=0.1)
X_spca = spca.fit_transform(digits.data / 255)
spca.components_.shape
# Output
(60L, 64L)
```

For further information about SciPy sparse matrices, visit https://docs.scipy.org/doc/scipy-0.18.1/reference/sparse.html.

Kernel PCA

It's useful to mention the class KernelPCA, which performs a PCA with non-linearly separable data sets. Just to understand the logic of this approach (the mathematical formulation isn't very simple), it's useful to consider a projection of each sample into a particular space where the dataset becomes linearly separable. The components of this space correspond to the first, second, ... principal components, and a kernel PCA algorithm therefore computes the projection of our samples onto each of them. Let's consider a dataset made up of a circle with a blob inside:

```
from sklearn.datasets import make_circles
Xb, Yb = make_circles(n_samples=500, factor=0.1, noise=0.05)
```

The graphical representation is shown in Figure 8-10. In this case, a classic PCA approach isn't able to capture the nonlinear dependency of existing components (the reader can verify that the projection is equivalent to the original dataset). However, looking at the samples and using polar coordinates (therefore, a space where it's possible to project all the points), it's easy to separate the two sets, only considering the radius.

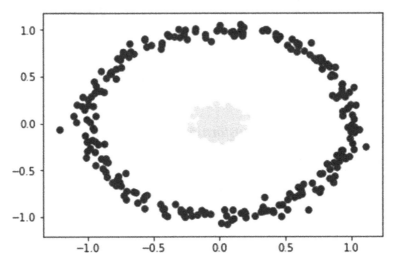

Figure 8-10. *The circular dataset we are using*

Considering the structure of the dataset, it's possible to investigate the behavior of a PCA with a radial basis function kernel. As the default value for gamma is *1.0/number of features* (for now, consider this parameter as inversely proportional to the variance of a Gaussian), we need to increase it to capture the external circle. A value of 1.0 is enough:

```
from sklearn.decomposition import KernelPCA
kpca = KernelPCA(n_components=2, kernel='rbf', fit_inverse_
transform=True, gamma=1.0)
X_kpca = kpca.fit_transform(Xb)
```

The instance variable X_transformed_fit will contain the projection of our dataset into the new space. Plotting it, we get Figure 8-11.

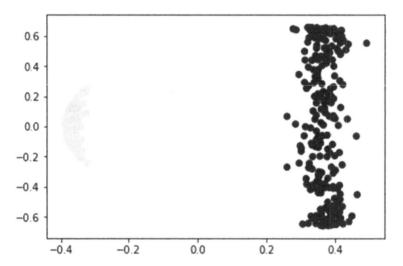

Figure 8-11. *The output transformation of the kernel PCA*

The plot shows a separation just like expected, and it's also possible to see that the points belonging to the central blob have a curve distribution because they are more sensitive to the distance from the center.

Kernel PCA is a powerful instrument when we think of our dataset as made up of elements that can be a function of components (in particular, radial-basis or polynomials) but we aren't able to determine a linear relationship among them.

For more information about the different kernels supported by Scikit-learn, visit `http://scikit-learn.org/stable/modules/metrics.html#linear-kernel`.

Atom Extraction and Dictionary Learning

Dictionary learning is a technique that allows rebuilding a sample starting from a sparse dictionary of atoms (similar to principal components). In "Online Dictionary Learning for Sparse Coding" by Julien Mairal, Francis Bach, Jean Ponce, and Guillermo Sapiro in *Proceedings of the 29th International Conference on Machine Learning (2009)* there's a description of the same online strategy adopted by Scikit-learn, which can be summarized as a double optimization problem, where:

$$X = \left\{ x'_1, x'_2, \ldots, x'_{n-1}, x'_n \right\}, \text{ where } x'_i \in R^m$$

is an input dataset and the target being to find both a dictionary D and a set of weights for each sample.

$$D \in R^{m \times k} \wedge A = \left\{ \alpha'_1, \alpha'_2, \ldots, \alpha'_{j-1}, \alpha_j \right\}, \text{ where } \alpha_j \in R^k$$

After the training process, an input vector can be computed as:

$$x'_i = D\alpha'_i$$

The optimization problem (which involves both D and alpha vectors) can be expressed as the minimization of the following loss function:

$$L(D,A) = \frac{1}{2}\sum_i \left\| x_i - D\alpha'_i \right\|_2^2 + c\left\| \alpha'_i \right\|_1$$

Here the parameter c controls the level of sparsity (which is proportional to the strength of *L1* normalization). This problem can be solved by alternating the least square variable until a stable point is reached.

In Scikit-learn, we can implement such an algorithm with the class `DictionaryLearning` (using the usual digits datasets), where `n_components`, as usual, determines the number of atoms:

```
from sklearn.decomposition import DictionaryLearning
dl = DictionaryLearning(n_components=36, fit_algorithm='lars',
transform_algorithm='lasso_lars')
X_dict = dl.fit_transform(digits.data)
```

This piece of code might take a few minutes to run, longer than any code we have written in this chapter. But don't panic; this is just one type of many other types of feature selection techniques. So if it does not work in your local machine, try Colaboratory (`https://colab.research.google.com/notebooks/welcome.ipynb#recent=true`). This will do the job for you, or you can limit the number of samples to 20 to 50; it's up to you.

Latent Dirichlet Allocation (LDA)

LDA is a shortcut of two descriptions: the first description is related to NLP, and the second one is related to data analysis. So, LDA with NLP is called **latent Dirichlet allocation**, and for data analysis it is called **linear discriminate analysis**. But this may seem a little weird. Are we talking about LDA with NLP or about LDA with data analysis? As we will see, we need to talk about LDA with NLP. But why not talk about a hot topic like linear discriminate analysis and the difference between it and PCA? PCA is a shortcut for **principle component analysis**. In this section, let's start with latent Dirichlet allocation.

Latent Dirichlet Allocation (LDA in NLP)

Before we go into the definition of LDA, we first need to know the root of this technique—topic modeling. The aim is to identify topics that best describe a set of documents. These topics will only appear during the topic modeling process, which is called a latent or unsupervised learning technique. Since LDA is the popular technique for topic modeling, let's make a definition for it. LDA imagines a fixed set of topics. Each topic represents a set of words. The goal of LDA is to map all the documents to the topics in such a way that the words in each document are mostly captured by those imaginary topics.

Let's take this definition and try to reexplain it more for simplicity. You have a set of topics; these topics have a set of words that distribute the topic; and every document has a set of topics. LDA needs to map these topics in the set X to documents in the set Y by using words. The main idea behind LDA is that each document can be described by a distribution of topics and each topic can be described by a distribution of words. So let's take an example or create an image to help with the definition of LDA.

As we said, latent Dirichlet allocation is a technique that automatically discovers topics that these documents contain. Suppose you have the following set of sentences:

- I eat fish and vegetables.

- Fish are pets.

- My kitten eats fish.

Given the preceding sentences, LDA might classify the red words under topic *F*, which we might label as "food." Similarly, blue words might be classified under a separate topic *P*, which we might label as "pets." LDA defines each topic as a bag of words, and you have to label the topics as you deem fit.

As we see, LDA has two benefits when classifying the data at the word level:

1. We can infer the content spread of each sentence by a word count, like if we see the only F in a sentence it will be 100% topic F. Let's see the statistics of our example.

    - *Sentence 1*: 100% topic F

    - *Sentence 2*: 100% topic P

    - *Sentence 3*: 33% topic P and 67% topic F

2. We can derive the proportions that each word constitutes in a given topic. For example, topic F might comprise words in the following proportions:

    - 40% eat, 40% fish, 20% vegetables, …

Now that we've gained some understanding, let's get our hands dirty with some steps about how LDA works; it works in three steps.

To illustrate these steps, imagine that you are now discovering topics in documents instead of sentences. Imagine you have two documents with the following words (Figure 8-12).

Document X	Document Y
Fish	Fish
Fish	Fish
Eat	Milk
Eat	Kitten
Vegetables	Kitten

Figure 8-12. *A table of two documents: X and Y*

3. Step 1: You tell the algorithm how many topics you think there are. You can either use an informed estimate (e.g., results from a previous analysis) or simply trial-and-error. In trying different estimates, you may pick the one that generates topics to your desired level of interpretability, or the one yielding the highest statistical certainty (i.e., log likelihood). In our previous example, the number of topics might be inferred just by eyeballing the documents.

4. Step 2: The algorithm will assign every word to a temporary topic. Topic assignments are temporary, as they will be updated in Step 3. Temporary topics are assigned to each word in a semirandom manner (according to a Dirichlet distribution, to be exact). This also means that if a word appears twice, each word may be assigned to different topics. Note that in analyzing actual documents, function words (e.g., "the," "and," "my") are removed and not assigned to any topics.

5. Step 3: The algorithm will check and update topic assignments, looping through each word in every document. For each word, its topic assignment is updated based on two criteria:

    •   How prevalent is that word across topics?

    •   How prevalent are topics in the document?

So, how do these two criteria in step three work?

First, how prevalent is that word across topics? Since the word "fish" across both documents comprises nearly half of the remaining topic F words but 0% of remaining topic P words, "fish" picked at random would more likely be about topic F (Figure 8-13).

	Document X		Document Y
F	Fish	?	Fish
F	Fish	F	Fish
F	Eat	F	Milk
F	Eat	P	Kitten
F	Vegetables	P	Kitten

Figure 8-13. *Prevalent words in both X and Y documents*

Second, how prevalent is that word across topics? Since the words in Document Y are assigned to topic F and topic P in a 50–50 ratio, the remaining "fish" word seems equally likely to be about either topic.

After this example we now know how it works. To adapt with this algorithm we will still need some mathematical information for LDA, but our aim for this book is only to gain a good understanding about an algorithm. If we need to provide some mathematics, it will be in the last part. So, we have a code example for LDA and we will continue with PCA vs. LDA.

Last, you should see that LDA is just a feature extraction technique used in NLP; it is just an automated algorithm that can read through the text documents and automatically output the topics discussed.

Code Example Using gensim

We will take a real example of the **20 Newsgroups'** dataset and use LDA to extract the naturally discussed topics.

First things first: we need to import gensim. Note that if you did not download it, please revisit Chapter 2.

```
import gensim
```

For reading the data and training the LDA model, we will use a dataset that consists of product reviews. We first create a TextCorpus, which is the component that reads documents from the file.

```
corpus = gensim.corpora.textcorpus.TextCorpus('amazon_reviews.txt')
```

Now we can train the LDA model. For details, see gensim's documentation of the class LdaModel (https://radimrehurek.com/gensim/models/ldamodel.html).

This training step will take a few minutes, depending on the efficiency of your machine and the value you set for passes.

```
model = gensim.models.LdaModel(corpus, id2word=corpus.
dictionary, alpha='auto', num_topics=10, passes=5)
```

Let's discuss the parameters of this LdaModel:

- num_topics: The number of topics we'd like to use. We set this to 10 here, but if you want, you can experiment with a larger number of topics.

- passes: The number of iterations to use in the training algorithm. Using a higher number will lead to a longer training time, but sometimes higher quality topics.

- **alpha**: A parameter that controls the behavior of the Dirichlet prior used in the model. If set to a value close to zero, the model will tend to use a fewer number of topics per document; conversely, if it's a higher value, there will be more topics per document. If set to auto, this parameter will be tuned automatically.

Inspecting topics: The function show_topic(t, n) will display the word distribution in topic *t*, sorted by the word probabilities. Then the most probable words will be shown.

```
model.show_topic(5)
# Output
[ ('film', 0.029852536),
  ('movie', 0.010055234),
  ('films', 0.004800593),
  ('horror', 0.00475024),
  ('story', 0.0038416996),
  ('scene', 0.0034877707),
  ('action', 0.0033171456),
  ('like', 0.0032384025),
  ('dvd', 0.003099864),
  ('scenes', 0.0028694542)]
```

Predicting the topics for a document: If you have a new document, you can use the trained model to estimate the topic proportions for it. This is done in two steps:

The first step is to convert the document into a matrix, and the second step is to inference.

```
doc = 'this book describes windows software'.split()
doc_vector = model.id2word.doc2bow(doc)
doc_topics = model[doc_vector]
doc_topics
```

```
# Output
[(0, 0.011552104),
 (1, 0.025947856),
 (2, 0.01148627),
 (3, 0.01466086),
 (4, 0.42382663),
 (5, 0.013418236),
 (6, 0.019740112),
 (7, 0.41398397),
 (8, 0.042892892),
 (9, 0.022491027)]
```

The result shows a predicted topic distribution. In most cases, there will be one or more dominant topics and small probabilities for the rest of the topics.

For instance, for the document this book describes, **Windows software,** we will typically get a result that this document is a mix of *book-related topics and software-related topics.* (Compare to the topic list you got above.) Again, the exact result here will vary between executions because of issues related to random number generation.

LDA vs. PCA

As we talked in the previous section about LDA (**latent Dirichlet allocation**) in NLP, now it's time to talk about LDA (**linear discriminant analysis**) but with PCA (**principal component analysis**). This comparison pf LDA vs. PCA is one of the most common ones in machine learning. We will define it as we discuss it in a simple way for anyone who doesn't have a strong mathematical background. We just need you to know the basic ideas behind this.

Again, what is principal component analysis or PCA? PCA is a dimensionality reduction method that is often used to reduce the dimensionality of large data sets, by transforming a large set of variables into a smaller one that still contains most of the information in the large set.

And what is linear discriminant analysis? LDA is a dimensionality reduction technique used as a preprocessing step in machine learning and pattern classification applications.

Now we need to know the meaning of dimensionality reduction techniques. The main goal of dimensionality reduction techniques is to reduce the dimensions by removing the redundant and dependent features by transforming the features from higher dimensional space to a space with lower dimensions.

The key to this comparison is the supervision feature: PCA uses correlation, which is aimed at unsupervised learning; LDA uses classification.

What does PCA do?

- It aims to find components that account for maximum variance in the data (including error and within-variable variance). Unlike LDA, it does not take into account class membership (i.e., unsupervised), and is used when such information is not available. Importantly, both LDA and PCA do not require any prior notion of how the variables are related among themselves, and the resulting components cannot be interpreted in terms of an underlying construct.

What does LDA do?

- This method identifies components (i.e., a linear combination of the observed variables) that maximize class separation (i.e., between-class variance) when such prior information is available (i.e., supervised). For example, you have a training set containing a variable specifying the class of each observation.

But as we compare PCA with LDA, we need to see them in figures—how they act in data. With data visualization, we can see the data, how our models react with it or our tools change in our data, and how we should tune our model parameter to get the best for our model with this data. We'll discuss data visualization in another chapter. Let's visualize the data to get more intuitions about PCA and LDA (Figures 8-14 and 8-15).

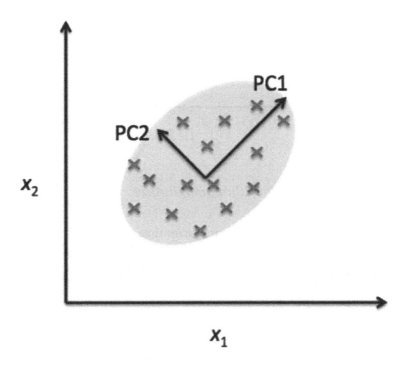

Figure 8-14. *The PCA algorithm on a dataset*

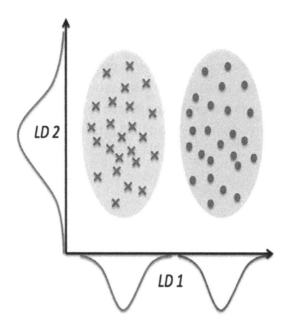

Figure 8-15. *The LDA algorithm on a dataset*

Both LDA and PCA are linear transformation techniques. As we see in the figures, LDA is just a classification, but PCA tries to get the most correlated points together. Notice that LDA is supervised, whereas PCA is unsupervised

ZCA Whitening

ZCA whitening is part of PCA. ZCA stands for **zero-phase component analysis**, which is a whitening transformation used to decorrelate (whiten) the data (image).

So, *what is whitening transformation?*

A **whitening transformation** or **sphering transformation** is a linear transformation that transforms a vector of random variables with a known covariance matrix into a set of new variables whose covariance is the identity matrix, meaning that they are uncorrelated and each have variance. The transformation is called "whitening" because it changes the input vector into a white noise vector.

It is used for data augmentation, so let's see how we can use it. As we know that ZCA is an image augmentation technique, let's talk about data augmentation first. What is data augmentation?

It is the performance of deep learning neural networks that often improves with the amount of data available.

Data augmentation is a technique to artificially create new training data from existing training data. This is done by applying domain-specific techniques to examples from the training data that create new and different training examples. Image data augmentation is perhaps the most well-known type of data augmentation and involves creating transformed versions of images in the training dataset that belong to the same class as the original image. Transforms include a range of operations from the field of image manipulation, such as shifts, flips, zooms, and much more. The intent is to expand the training dataset with new, plausible examples. This means variations of the training set images that are likely to be seen by the model.

For example, a horizontal flip of a picture of a cat may make sense, because the photo could have been taken from the left or right. A vertical flip of the photo of a cat does not make sense, and would probably not be appropriate given that the model is very unlikely to see a photo of an upside-down cat.

As such, it is clear that the choice of the specific data augmentation techniques used for a training dataset must be chosen carefully and within the context of the training dataset and knowledge of the problem domain. In addition, it can be useful to experiment with data augmentation methods in isolation and in concert to see if they result in a measurable improvement to model performance, perhaps with a small prototype dataset, model, and training run. Modern deep learning algorithms, such as the convolutional neural network, or CNN, can learn features that are invariant to their location in the image. Nevertheless, augmentation can further aid in this transform invariant approach to learning and can aid the model in learning features that are also invariant to transforms, such as left-to-right to top-to-bottom ordering, light levels in photographs, and more.

But understand that image data augmentation is typically only applied to **the training dataset**, and not to the validation or test dataset. This is different from data preparation such as image resizing and pixel scaling; they must be performed consistently across all datasets that interact with the model. Some of the data augmentation techniques are

- Horizontal and vertical shift augmentation

- Horizontal and vertical flip augmentation

- Random rotation augmentation

- Random brightness augmentation

- Random zoom augmentation

- ZCA whitening

Most of these algorithms are considered and discussed in the "Data Augmentation" section of Chapter 6.

So, we see various techniques for data augmentation but we will concentrate on ZCA whitening. A **whitening transform of** an image is a linear algebra operation that reduces the redundancy in the matrix of pixel images. Less redundancy in the image is intended to better highlight the structures and features in the image to the learning algorithm.

Typically, image whitening is performed using the PCA technique. More recently, an alternative called ZCA shows better results, leading to transformed images that keeps all of the original dimensions and, unlike PCA, result in transformed images that still look like their originals.

You can perform a ZCA whitening transform by setting the zca_ whitening argument to True.

```python
# ZCA whitening
from keras.datasets import mnist
from keras.preprocessing.image import ImageDataGenerator
from matplotlib import pyplot
from keras import backend as K
K.set_image_dim_ordering('th')
# load data
(X_train, y_train), (X_test, y_test) = mnist.load_data()
# reshape to be [samples][pixels][width][height]
X_train = X_train.reshape(X_train.shape[0], 1, 28, 28)
X_test = X_test.reshape(X_test.shape[0], 1, 28, 28)
# convert from int to float
X_train = X_train.astype('float32')
X_test = X_test.astype('float32')
# define data preparation
datagen = ImageDataGenerator(zca_whitening=True)
# fit parameters from data
datagen.fit(X_train)
# configure batch size and retrieve one batch of images
for X_batch, y_batch in datagen.flow(X_train, y_train,
batch_size=9):
        # create a grid of 3x3 images
        for i in range(0, 9):
            pyplot.subplot(330 + 1 + i)
            pyplot.imshow(X_batch[i].reshape(28, 28),
            cmap=pyplot.get_cmap('gray'))
        # show the plot
        pyplot.show()
        break
```

Summary

In this chapter, you learned about three different, fundamental dimensionality reduction techniques for feature extraction: standard PCA, LDA, and kernel PCA. Using PCA, we projected data onto a lower dimensional subspace to maximize the variance along the orthogonal feature axes while ignoring the class labels. LDA, in contrast to PCA, is a technique for supervised dimensionality reduction, which means that it considers class information in the training dataset to attempt to maximize the class separability in a linear feature space. Last, you learned about a kernelized version of PCA, which allows you to map nonlinear datasets onto a lower dimensional feature space, where the classes become linearly separable.

Equipped with these essential preprocessing techniques, you are now well prepared to learn about the best practices for building and maintaining different deep learning techniques, algorithms, and approaches each of which differs in the type of data it deals with and how it handles it. You will evaluate the performance of different models in the next chapters.

PART III

TensorFlow

CHAPTER 9

Deep Learning Fundamentals

In this chapter, we will describe a very important topic in deep learning fundamentals, the basic functions that deep learning is built on. Then we will try to build layers from these functions and combine these layers together to get a more complex model that will help us solve more complex problems, and all that will be described by TensorFlow examples.

First we will describe the smallest component of almost any deep neural network, which is the neuron and sometimes called *perceptron*. We will discuss it in some detail, and we will deep dive because there's much to cover in this chapter. Then we will illustrate the types of possible layers in a neural network, such as *input*, *hidden*, and *output* layers. As we are showing you the layers, we'll describe the difference between shallow and deep neural networks. After describing the neuron, we will show you some of the activation functions you can use to build a better neural network. Then we'll get into the learning procedure called gradient descent, an algorithm that helps learning happen. We will describe different types, such as full-batch, stochastic, and mini-batch gradient descent. And as learning happens, we need to check how good it is. We can do this with loss functions, so we will show you the different loss functions you can use to validate the learning of your model. Then we need to propagate the errors that your model makes to get better weights and good performance; and

© Hisham El-Amir and Mahmoud Hamdy 2020
H. El-Amir and M. Hamdy, *Deep Learning Pipeline*,
https://doi.org/10.1007/978-1-4842-5349-6_9

to do that, we need to show you the backpropagation algorithm and how it works. After describing this learning framework of neural networks, we think it is fair to show you some traps to avoid falling into in this area, called vanishing and exploding gradients. And last, we will go from theoretical to practical by refreshing your mind with some TensorFlow basics.

Perceptron

The most fundamental unit of a deep neural network is called *an artificial neuron*, which takes an input, processes it, passes it through an activation function like the *sigmoid*, and returns the activated output. In this section, we are only going to talk about the *perceptron* model proposed before the "*activation*" part came into the picture.

A **Perceptron** is the smallest layer in the neural network. It is a linear classifier (binary), and it is used in supervised learning. It helps to classify the given input data; the output value is f(x) calculated as $f(x) = \langle w, x \rangle + b$

where w is a vector of weights and $\langle \cdot, \cdot \rangle$ denotes the dot product. We use the dot product as we are computing a weighted sum. The sign of $f(x)$ is used to classify x as either a positive or a negative instance.

Since the inputs are fed directly to the output via the weights, the perceptron can be considered the simplest kind of feedforward network.

Before diving into the mathematics that powers this algorithm, let's see a little history on how they got the concept of the perceptron, which is neuron as we talked about in Chapter 1.

The very first step toward the perceptron we use today was taken in 1943 by Warren MuCulloch (a neuroscientist) and Walter Pitts (a logician), by mimicking the functionality of a biological neuron. Figure 9-1 describes the neuron notation.

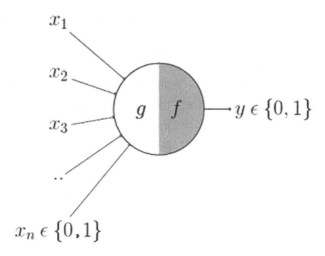

Figure 9-1. *The notation of a biological neuron*

As we see in Figure 9-1, there are two sides in this node, *g* and *f*; one of them takes the input. As we can see in the figure, *g* take a fixed size vector of data $x_1, ..., x_n$, and performs an aggregation operation. On the other hand, the *f* function makes a decision; this decision is made based on the aggregated value in *f*. Let's elaborate more on this idea.

Let's suppose that we want to predict a decision: whether to watch a random soccer game or not on TV. The inputs are all Boolean (i.e., {0, 1}) and my output variable is also Boolean {0 : *Will watch it*, 1 : *Won't watch it*}.

So, now we need to construct our data variables. Let's assume that x_1 could be *isPremierLeagueOn* (I like Premier League more), x_2 could be *isItAFriendlyGame* (I tend to care less about the friendliness), x_3 could be *isNotHome* (I can't watch it when I'm running errands, can I?), and x_4 could be *isManUnitedPlaying* (I am a big Man United fan. GGMU!)

We only have four observations about the data we have, like x_3. If x_3 is 1 (not home), then my output will always be 0 (I can't watch it when I'm running errands.), so the neuron will never fire, but we need to have a good output note at this point. As we see in the example, these inputs can either be excitatory or inhibitory. So what is the difference between them (Table 9-1)?

Table 9-1. *The Difference Between Excitatory and Inhibitory*

Excitatory	Inhibitory
Inhibitory inputs are those that have maximum effect on the decision making, irrespective of other inputs.	Inputs are NOT the ones that will make the neuron fire on its own, but they might fire it when combined together.

We need to make an equation to deduce how we can fire this perceptron and when we can't fire it. The formula is just a summation equation of all the inputs and the gave the output a domain about how we can act with the output we have (Figure 9-2).

$$g(x_1, x_2, x_3, ..., x_n) = g(\mathbf{x}) = \sum_{i=1}^{n} x_i$$

$$y = f(g(\mathbf{x})) = 1 \quad if \quad g(\mathbf{x}) \geq \theta$$
$$= 0 \quad if \quad g(\mathbf{x}) < \theta$$

Figure 9-2. *The equations that power the perceptron*

We can see that $g(x)$ is just doing a sum of the inputs—a simple aggregation—and theta here is called the thresholding parameter. For example, if I always watch the game when the sum turns out to be 2 or more, the theta is 2 here. This is called the thresholding logic.

Let's see an example of how it works with the *AND* Boolean gate (Figure 9-3).

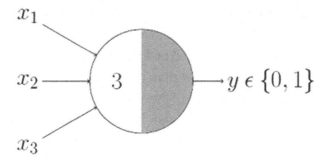

Figure 9-3. *The AND Boolean gate operation— neuron style*

An *AND* function neuron would only fire when **ALL** the inputs are ON, like when $g(x) \geq 3$. Researchers should know that the original M-P (*MuCulloch, Pitts*) neuron is not so good at everything we work with. It has some limitations, so let's see those limitations. We'll explain the M-P neuron but we may see some questions that the M-P neuron can't handle:

- What about non-Boolean (say, real) inputs? We haven't any Boolean inputs; we have ranges and variety of numbers, like $\{1, 2, 4, 5\}$.

- Do we always need to hand code the threshold? We should have some dynamic work with the threshold values.

- Are all inputs equal? What if we want to assign more importance to some inputs?

- What about functions that are not linearly separable, say, the XOR function?

We see the limitations in this model. I hope it is now clear why we are not using the M-P neuron today. Overcoming the limitations of the M-P neuron, Frank Rosenblatt, an American psychologist, proposed the classical perception model, the mighty artificial neuron, in 1958. It is a more generalized computational model than the McCulloch-Pitts neuron, where weights and thresholds can be learned over time. But what's the difference between McCulloch-Pitts and Minsky-Papert.

The perceptron model, proposed by Minsky-Papert (Figure 9-4), is a more general computational model than the McCulloch-Pitts neuron. It overcomes some of the limitations of the M-P neuron by introducing the concept of numerical weights (a measure of importance) for inputs, and a mechanism for learning those weights. Inputs are no longer limited to Boolean values, as is the case of an M-P neuron; it supports real inputs as well, which makes it more useful and generalized. This is the perceptron, the most fundamental unit of a deep neural network, called an artificial neuron.

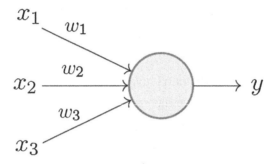

Perceptron Model (Minsky-Papert in 1969)

Figure 9-4. *The Minsky perceptron model*

Let's talk about the perceptron model and how it works in a dynamic way. As we look at the new version of the perceptron, we see one difference: we have a new variable called *weights*. We take a weighted sum of the inputs and set the output as one only when the sum is more than an arbitrary threshold (theta). However, according to the convention, instead of hand coding the thresholding parameter theta, we add it as one of the inputs, with the weight -theta as shown in the following, which makes it learnable. This is called the PLA (Perceptron Learning Algorithm); the equation will change in this way:

$$y = 1 \quad if \ \sum_{i=0}^{n} w_i x_i \geq 0$$

$$y = 0 \quad if \ \sum_{i=0}^{n} w_i x_i < 0$$

$$where, x_0 = 1 \ and \ w_0 = -\theta$$

Let's go back to our friend predicting whether I would watch a random game of soccer on TV or not using the behavioral data available. And let's assume my decision is solely dependent on three binary inputs (binary used for simplicity).

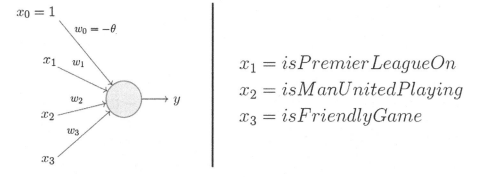

Figure 9-5. *The soccer example implementation using a perceptron*

One point about the preceding photo is that w_0 is the *bias* value. Now, let's continue the example. A soccer freak may have a very low threshold and may watch any soccer game irrespective of the league, club, or importance of the game **[theta = 0].** On the other hand, a selective viewer may only watch a soccer game that is a Premier League game, featuring a Man United game, that is not friendly **[theta = 2]**. The key points are the **weights** and the **bias**, and they will depend on the data (my viewing history, in this case).

Bias occurs when an algorithm has limited flexibility to learn the true signal from the dataset.

Let's take an example of Boolean functions using a perceptron. We will use the OR function, which is the easiest one of all Boolean functions (Figure 9-6). We will make you try to solve this equation by using the AND Boolean function, but for now, let's use OR.

x_1	x_2	OR.	
0	0	0	$w_0 + \sum_{i=1}^{2} w_i x_i < 0$
1	0	1	$w_0 + \sum_{i=1}^{2} w_i x_i \geq 0$
0	1	1	$w_0 + \sum_{i=1}^{2} w_i x_i \geq 0$
1	1	1	$w_0 + \sum_{i=1}^{2} w_i x_i \geq 0$

$$w_0 + w_1 \cdot 0 + w_2 \cdot 0 < 0 \implies w_0 < 0$$

$$w_0 + w_1 \cdot 0 + w_2 \cdot 1 \geq 0 \implies w_2 > -w_0$$

$$w_0 + w_1 \cdot 1 + w_2 \cdot 0 \geq 0 \implies w_1 > -w_0$$

$$w_0 + w_1 \cdot 1 + w_2 \cdot 1 \geq 0 \implies w_1 + w_2 > -w_0$$

Figure 9-6. *The equation of an OR Gate*

But by the way, is XOR (exclusive OR) reliable to use with the perceptron model? The answer is **no**, because we can't separate nonlinear functions to positive and negative tuples. The table of XOR is shown in Figure 9-7.

x_1	x_2	XOR	
0	0	0	$w_0 + \sum_{i=1}^{2} w_i x_i < 0$
1	0	1	$w_0 + \sum_{i=1}^{2} w_i x_i \geq 0$
0	1	1	$w_0 + \sum_{i=1}^{2} w_i x_i \geq 0$
1	1	0	$w_0 + \sum_{i=1}^{2} w_i x_i < 0$

$$w_0 + w_1 \cdot 0 + w_2 \cdot 0 < 0 \implies w_0 < 0$$

$$w_0 + w_1 \cdot 0 + w_2 \cdot 1 \geq 0 \implies w_2 > -w_0$$

$$w_0 + w_1 \cdot 1 + w_2 \cdot 0 \geq 0 \implies w_1 > -w_0$$

$$w_0 + w_1 \cdot 1 + w_2 \cdot 1 \geq 0 \implies w_1 + w_2 < -w_0$$

Figure 9-7. *The XOR Gate implementation using a perceptron*

As we see, it isn't separable output values, where in the OR function it is separable; let's see this in graphs (Figure 9-8).

$w_0 = -1, \ w_1 = 1.1, \ w_2 = 1.1$

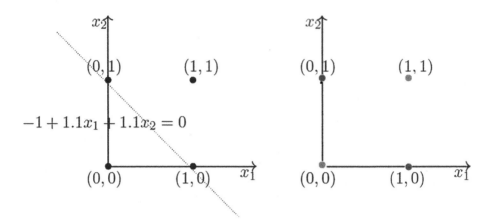

Figure 9-8. *The OR gate (left); the XOR gate (right)*

But what about a multilayer perceptron? We will talk about it later, but we should first conclude about these two approaches of perceptron (Figure 9-9)

McCulloch Pitts Neuron
(assuming no inhibitory inputs)

$$y = 1 \quad if \sum_{i=0}^{n} x_i \geq 0$$

$$= 0 \quad if \sum_{i=0}^{n} x_i < 0$$

Perceptron

$$y = 1 \quad if \sum_{i=0}^{n} w_i * x_i \geq 0$$

$$= 0 \quad if \sum_{i=0}^{n} w_i * x_i < 0$$

Figure 9-9. *The McCulloch neuron vs. perceptron*

We don't need to make a further comparison; just the preceding equations and the explanations will lead you to understand the concept. From this section, we aim to allow you get to know the perceptron learning algorithm, which is based on two types of perceptron: single perceptron and multiple perceptrons. Before we talk about the types of perceptron, we need to list the major components of a perceptron:

- *Input*: All the features become the input for a perceptron. We denote the input of a perceptron by $[x_1, ..., x_n]$, where x represents the feature value and n represents the total number of features. We also have a special kind of input called the bias. In the image (Figure 9-10), we have described the value of the bias as w_0.

- *Weights*: The values that are computed over the time of training the model. Initially, we start the value of weights with some initial value and these values get updated for each training error. We represent the weights for a perceptron by $[w_1, ..., w_n]$.

- *Bias*: A bias neuron allows a classifier to shift the decision boundary left or right. In algebraic terms, the bias neuron allows a classifier to translate its decision boundary. It aims to "*move every point a constant distance in a specified direction.*"

- *Bias helps to train the model faster and with better quality.*

- *Weighted summation*: Weighted summation is the sum of the values that we get after the multiplication of each weight w_n associated with each feature value x_n. We represent the weighted summation by $\sum_{i=0}^{n} w_i x_i$.

- *Step/activation function*: The role of activation functions is to make neural networks nonlinear. For linear classification, for example, it becomes necessary to make the perceptron as linear as possible. We will talk about this in the next sections, but it's good to know about it.

- *Output*: The weighted summation is passed to the step/ activation function, and whatever value we get after computation is our predicted output.

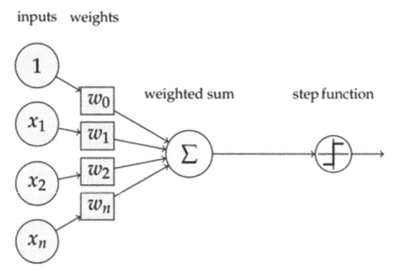

Figure 9-10. The perceptron in detail steps

Single Perceptron

A single perceptron is a basic fundamental function in the neural network, and it only works with a binary classifier. We've already talked a lot about it. But if we have more than two classes, we will want to get into the multilayer perceptron.

Multilayer Perceptron

A multilayer perceptron (MLP) contains one or more hidden layers (apart from one input and one output layer). While a single layer perceptron can only learn linear functions, a multilayer perceptron can also learn nonlinear functions (Figure 9-11).

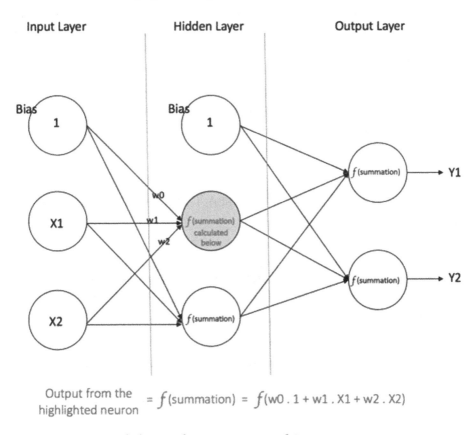

Figure 9-11. *Multilayered perceptron architecture*

- *Input layer*: The input layer has three nodes. The bias node has a value of 1. The other two nodes take X_1 and X_2 as external inputs (which are numerical values depending upon the input dataset). As discussed, no computation is performed in the input layer, so the outputs from nodes in the input layer are 1, X_1, and X_2, respectively, which are fed into the hidden layer.

- *Hidden layer*: The hidden layer also has three nodes, with the bias node having an output of 1. The output of the other two nodes in the hidden layer depends on the outputs from the input layer $(1, X_1, X_2)$ as well as the weights associated with the connections (**edges**). Then these edges are connected to the output layer.

Note   *f* refers to the activation function. These outputs are then fed to the nodes in the output layer.

- *Output layer*: The output layer has two nodes that take inputs from the hidden layer and perform similar computations as shown for the highlighted hidden node. The values calculated (Y_1 and Y_2) as a result of these computations act as outputs of the multilayer perceptron.

Recap

To recap, we learned in this section that the perceptron is the fundamental function of the neural network. When you have only one perceptron, you have a single perceptron that will solve binary classification problems; but if you have a nonlinear classification problem, you will need to use more than one perceptron to solve this problem, like OR and XOR.

Different Neural Network Layers

Before we start working with layers in the neural network, we should understand exactly what layers are. *Layer* is a general term that applies to a collection of nodes (perceptron), which contain an *activation function* (e.g., sigmoid). Patterns are presented to the network via the **input layer**, which communicates to one or more **hidden layers** where the actual processing is done via a system of weighted connections (edges). The hidden layers then link to an **output layer**.

Figure 9-12 illustrates each layer.

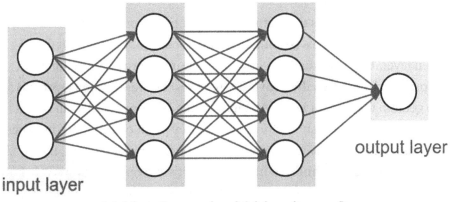

Figure 9-12. *Multilayered neural network architecture*

A neural network is made up of an input layer, one or more hidden layers, and an output layer. Every layer has one or more perceptrons, which combine together to make a layer. Every layer has a name, which describes its position.

Input Layer

The first layer in Figure 9-12 is called the *input layer*, which has nodes; the nodes of the input layer are **passive**. Passive means that they do not modify the data; they receive a single value on their input and duplicate the value to their multiple outputs. All of the input variables are represented as input nodes; each value from the input layer is duplicated and sent to all of the hidden nodes, which are contained in the **hidden layer**. This takes us to a new question: *what is the hidden layer?*

Hidden Layer(s)

All of the input variables that came from the input layer are combined across one or more nodes (summation node or activation node) in the hidden layer. This essentially creates new features, derived from the input data provided, and then through these features to a new hidden layer and so on to get into the **output layer**. All input nodes are connected to all nodes in the hidden layer. We should note that the key point of difference between shallow and deep neural networks is the number of hidden layers. If you have more than one connected hidden layer, it's a deep neural network, but if we have only one hidden layer, it's a shallow neural network. As we see, the input data is going to the hidden layer with bias and weights parameters. But is there only one way that data is weighted? The answer is **no**.

Hidden neural network layers are set up in many different ways. In some cases, weighted inputs are randomly assigned. In other cases, they are fine-tuned and calibrated through a process called backpropagation. But we have many types of neural networks (*sequence, convolution, feedforward*, etc.), so there are different ways to set up these hidden layers to generate various results. Convolutional neural networks focus on image processing; recurrent neural networks contain an element of memory; and simple feedforward neural networks work in a straightforward way on training data sets.

So, a full description of the hidden layer is: artificial neurons take in a set of weighted inputs and produce an output through an activation function. It is a typical part of nearly any neural network, in which engineers simulate the types of activities that go on in the human brain.

Output Layer

The output layer in an artificial neural network is the last layer of neurons, which produces given outputs for the program. Though they are made much like other artificial neurons in the neural network, output layer neurons may be built or observed in a different way, given that they are the last "actor" nodes on the network.

Shallow vs. Deep Neural Networks

Here we don't want to get too far into comparison. We will just consider what makes a shallow network "shallow," and the same with deep neural networks. Neural networks can be recurrent or feedforward; feedforward ones do not have any loops in their graph and can be organized in layers. If there are many layers, then we say that the network is deep.

But we have a question about what makes a neural network deep. Practically speaking, *how many layers does a network have to have in order to qualify as deep?*

Usually, if we have two or more hidden layers, we call it a *deep* neural network. In contrast, a network with only a single hidden layer is conventionally called *shallow* (Figure 9-13).

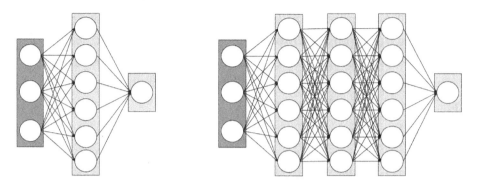

Figure 9-13. *The difference between a shallow vs. deep neural network*

We think that a shallow network *could* perform as well as the deeper ones. But there are still questions about this subject. We don't have an accurate answer, but we can produce some points for consideration about deep and shallow, and which performs the best:

1. Maybe a shallow network is more difficult to train with our current algorithms.

2. Maybe a shallow architecture does not fit the kind of problems we are usually trying to solve.

3. It can be argued that the number of units in a shallow network grows exponentially with task complexity. It may be that if you have a more complex task you want your model to fit, you need to have more neurons. So in order to be useful, a shallow network might need to have more neurons, possibly much bigger than a deep network.

These answers may be good to ponder the differences, but with a neural network you never know if using it deep or shallow may fit or not. But we will see that in a trial and error sequence. The amount of progress achieved in deep learning over the last ten years is truly amazing, but most of this progress was achieved by trial and error. We still lack very basic understanding about what exactly makes deep nets work so well. Even the list of things that people consider to be crucial for setting up an effective deep network seems to change every couple of years.

The conclusion is that we have two designs of the neural network: one if you have only one hidden layer we now talk about a shallow neural network if the hidden layers exceeded we now talk about the deep neural network, There is nothing that says you *must* use a deep neural network, but we assume it may be good for many types of complex data.

Activation Functions

Neural network activation functions are a mathematical "gate." The main concept of the activation function is the perceptron, and neural network activation functions are a crucial component of deep learning.

Activation functions determine the output of a deep learning model; its accuracy; and also the computational efficiency of training a model, which can make or break a large-scale neural network. The activation function is a very important part in neural network architecture, because activation functions have a major effect on the neural network's ability to converge and the convergence speed. In some cases, activation functions might prevent neural networks from converging in the first place. Their main purpose is to convert an input signal of a node in an ANN to an output signal.

Activation functions are mathematical equations that determine the output of a neural network. After describing the activation function, we may still want to know more about what it does. The function is attached to each neuron in the network and determines whether it should be fired or not; it does this based on whether each neuron's input is relevant for the model's prediction. Activation functions also help normalize the output of each neuron to a range between 1 and 0 or between -1 and 1.

The question is asked *what is the role of the activation function in a model?* As we saw in the previous section talking about layers, data points are transferred from the input layer to the output layer, passed by hidden layers. Each neuron has a weight, and multiplying the input number with the weight gives the output of the neuron, which is transferred to the next layer.

The activation function is located in between the input feeding the current neuron and its output going to the next layer (Figure 9-14). It can be as simple as a step function that turns the neuron output on and off, depending on a rule or threshold. Or it can be a transformation that maps the input signals into output signals that are needed for the neural network to function.

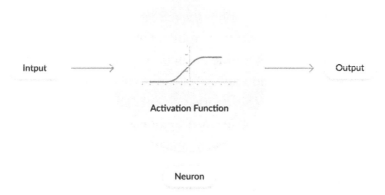

Figure 9-14. *The placement of the activation function*

Let's visualize the process, which starts from input: multiply input data with weights, add bias to them, go through the activation function, and then feed to the next layer (Figure 9-15).

Figure 9-15. *The steps of how activation works in a neuron*

So, after talking about the process, we need to know the types, how to use them, how they work, and which one is the reliable one for our neural network model.

Types of Activation Functions

There are three types of activation functions: binary step function, linear activation function, and nonlinear activation function.

First, the binary step function is a threshold-based activation function (Figure 9-16). What does this mean? It means that it depends on whether it is above or below a certain threshold value. If the neuron output is above the threshold, the activation neuron will send exactly the same signal to the next layer—and vice versa.

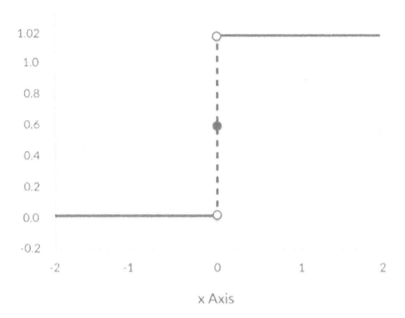

Figure 9-16. *A binary activation function*

But it is still binary, so we can't use it in multiclassification problems. It's only a trigger function and can't change any of the data that comes from the previous layer, so we need a more complex activation function. So let's talk about the next type of activation function, which is the **linear activation function** (Figure 9-17). It uses the function $A = w * x$. It takes the inputs, multiplied by the weights for each neuron, and creates an output signal proportional to the input. In one sense, a linear function is better than a step function because it allows multiple outputs, not just yes and no.

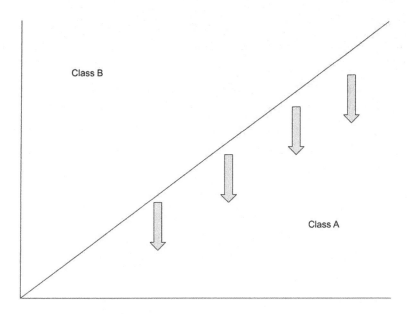

Figure 9-17. *How linear activation works*

But does the linear activation function have no problems? Of course it has. The problems lie in that it's a constant function, so we can't use the backpropagation technique (which we will talk about in the next sections) because it depends on derivatives. This is a constant function, so it has no derivative. The second thing is that it depends on its linearity. However many layers we have, it's still a linear function; we could almost say that a neural network with a linear activation function is simply a linear regression model. It has limited power and ability to handle the complexity of varying parameters of input data, which makes us need to look to a new activation function: the nonlinear activation function. Nowadays many neural network models use nonlinear activation functions. They allow the model to create complex mappings between the network's inputs and outputs, which are essential for learning and modeling complex data such as images, video, audio, and data sets that are nonlinear or have high dimensionality. They solve problems that faced the linear activation function. The types of nonlinear activation functions that are used today in neural network models are *sigmoid/logistic, tanh/hyperbolic tangent, ReLU (rectified linear unit), leaky ReLU, softmax,* and *swish.* Let's take a tour of those functions.

Sigmoid or logistic activation function: when we talk about sigmoid, we mean probability between 0 and 1 function. The main reason we use sigmoid function is that it exists between 0 and 1.

Therefore, it is especially useful for models where we have to predict the probability of an output. Since the probability of anything exists only between *the range of 0 and 1*, sigmoid is the right choice. From only 0 and 1, let's make the range wider; we can make the range from *-1 to 1*. This takes us to a new function: tanh or hyperbolic tangent activation function. This function is almost like sigmoid but the range is between -1 and 1 (Figure 9-18). The advantage is that the negative inputs will be mapped strongly negative and the zero inputs will be mapped near zero in the tanh graph. And it works very well when we work in classification between two classes. But there is a function that may be the same as sigmoid; it's called **Softmax**. This function will calculate the probabilities of each target class over all possible target classes.

Later, the calculated probabilities will be helpful for determining the target class for the given inputs. It's almost like the sigmoid function but it is divided by all the possible target classes. If the Softmax function is used for a multiclassification model, it returns the probabilities of each class and the target class will have a high probability. Its equation is:

$$Sigmoid(x) = \frac{1}{1 + exp(-x)}$$

$$softmax(x) = \frac{exp(x)}{\sum_{j=0}^{k} exp(x_j)}$$

$$tanh(x) = \frac{2}{2 + exp(-2x)} = 2 * sigmoid(2x) - 1$$

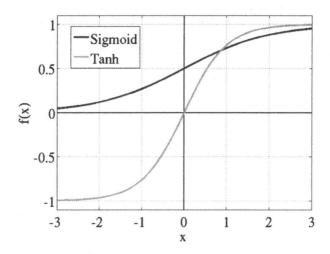

Figure 9-18. *The difference between sigmoid and tanh*

Note   Both tanh and logistic sigmoid activation functions are used in feedforward nets.

Although we have good function in the range between -1 and 1, we need to have x continuous, so now we need to work with the ReLU function. It works from zero to infinity. Let's see how it works, and why it's called *rectified*. It is called rectified because it's rectified under zero; if the value is below zero it will be zero, but if it equals 0 or above zero it will be the value itself.

The conclusion is f(z) is zero when z is less than zero and f(z) is equal to z when z is above or equal to zero.

After working with infinity, we now have to work with zero. We mainly waste all data under zero, so we create a new activation that gets some of the data under zero. It's called **leaky ReLU.**

This function works in the same direction as the ReLU function but it has some variations; it mainly tries to improve ReLU range. It works with range - infinity, infinity. That is the main variation (Figure 9-19); the equation is:

$$Relu(x) = max(0,x)$$

$$LeakyRelu(x) = max(0.01*x,x)$$

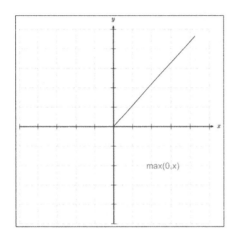 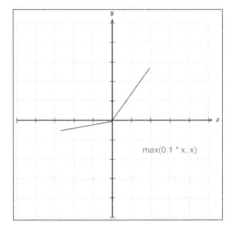

Figure 9-19. *ReLU function (left); leaky ReLU function (right)*

As we see in the preceding equations, the variation in function is that the first parameter in ReLU is equal to x multiplied by 0, as every parameter below 0 will equal zero. In leaky ReLU, x is multiplied by 0.01, so for every parameter below zero you will have a negative target for this input. Google created a new activation function called **swish**; it performs better than *ReLU* with a similar level of computational efficiency (Figure 9-20). Its equation is:

$$Swish(x) = \frac{x}{1 - exp(-x)}$$

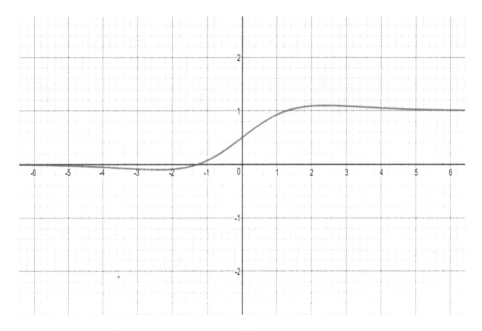

Figure 9-20. *The swish activation function*

Recap

After all, an activation function is just a perceptron. It works to allow neural networks to learn: it should be in the output layer, it may be in hidden layers, but it has never been in the input layer.

Gradient Descent

This is the main core of machine learning—the way we work to decrease the loss function. Let's get an in-depth description of gradient descent; you can have more than one description with different meanings, but let's see the abstract definition of gradient descent. Gradient descent is an optimization algorithm used to minimize some function by iteratively moving in the direction of steepest descent, as defined by the negative of the gradient. In machine learning, gradient descent is an optimization algorithm used to find the values of parameters (coefficients) of a function (f) that minimizes a cost function (loss). We talk about the cost function in the next sections. Gradient descent is best to use when the parameters cannot be calculated analytically (e.g., using linear algebra) and must be searched for by an optimization algorithm.

We will not write the gradient descent algorithm manually, as it is already implemented in packages like Keras. But we need to understand the concept of how we optimize the cost function. Cost function is simply equal to *Loss* = (*actual output − predicted output*). Let's see how gradient descent minimizes the cost function. Gradient descent is an efficient optimization algorithm that attempts to find a local or global minimum of a function. Gradient descent enables a model to learn the gradient or direction that the model should take in order to reduce errors (differences between actual y and predicted y). The direction in the simple linear regression example refers to how the model parameters **B** *(bias or intercept)* and **W** *(slope or coefficient)* should be tweaked or corrected to further reduce the cost function. As the model iterates, it gradually converges toward a minimum where further tweaks to the parameters produce little or zero changes in the loss, also referred to as convergence, where $y = WX + B$. Let's see Figure 9-20 to illustrate this linear function.

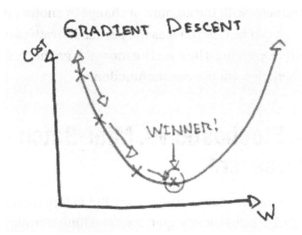

Figure 9-21. *A gradient descent step to the minimum point*

Let's explain what happened in this graph. A random position on the surface of the graph is the cost of the current values of the coefficients (cost). The bottom of the graph is the cost of the best set of coefficients, the minimum of the function. Now you will iterate in the cost to get to the goal, which is to continue to try different values for the coefficients, evaluate their cost, and select new coefficients that have a slightly better (lower) cost. Repeating this process enough times will lead to the bottom of the graph, and you will know the values of the coefficients that result in the minimum cost.

Recap

Gradient descent is a way to optimize the cost by trying to get the minimum optimal values in the cost function. This concept has many applications like mini-batch, full batch, and stochastic gradient descent, and we will see them in the next sections. Gradient descent is a very popular optimization technique in machine learning and deep learning and it can be used with most, if not all, of the learning algorithms. A gradient is basically the slope of a function: the degree of change of a parameter with the amount of change in another parameter. Mathematically, it can be described as the partial derivatives of a set of parameters with respect to its inputs. The more the gradient, the steeper the slope. Gradient descent is a convex function.

Batch vs. Stochastic vs. Mini-Batch Gradient Descent

Now, let's look further into those three types. But before we start, we have to remind you that the goal of all supervised machine learning algorithms is to best estimate a *target function (f)* that maps *input data (X)* onto *output variables (Y)*. This describes all classification and regression problems.

Batch Gradient Descent

The concept behind batch gradient descent is to update the parameters of neural networks once. This process happens after the training example is finished, that is, after all the training examples have been passed through the **network**.

For instance, if the training dataset contains 100 training examples, then the parameters of the neural network are updated once the training of all 100 examples is finished. Table 9-2 lists advantages and disadvantages of batch gradient descent.

Table 9-2. *Pros/Cons of Batch Gradient Descent*

Advantages	Disadvantages
It produces a more stable gradient descent convergence and stable error gradient than stochastic gradient descent.	The entire training set can be too large to process in the memory, therefore, additional memory might be needed.
It is computationally efficient, as all computer resources are not being used to process a single sample but rather are being used for all training samples.	Depending on computer resources, it can take too long for processing all the training samples as a batch.
It enhances the steps toward the minimum of loss function, due to updating the parameters by computing the average of all the training samples rather than the value of a single sample.	

We can see that with batch gradient, it is all about the resources you have.

Stochastic Gradient Descent

In this method, one training sample (example) is passed through the neural network at a time and the parameters (weights) of each layer are updated with the computed gradient. The parameters of all the layers of the network are updated after every training sample. Let's take an example: you have 1,000 training samples, so you now have 1,000 updated parameters and every parameter is updated after every individual sample. Table 9-3 lists advantages and disadvantages of stochastic gradient descent. Following is the equation for stochastic gradient descent; it is iterated over "n" times for "n" training samples in the training set.

$$\theta_j := \theta_j - \alpha \frac{\partial}{\partial \theta_j} J(\theta).$$

Table 9-3. *Pros/cons of Stochastic Gradient Descent*

Advantages	Disadvantages
It is computationally fast, as only one sample is processed at a time.	It can take the gradient descent into other directions, because its frequent updating to local minimum is very noisy.
In this type, we have many updates. That means the frequent updates of the steps taken toward the minima of the loss function have oscillations, which can help to get out of local minimums of the loss function.	It loses the advantage of vectorized operations, as it deals with only a single example at a time.
It is easier to fit into memory, due to a single training sample being processed by the network.	Frequent updates are computationally expensive, due to using all resources for processing one training sample at a time.

As we see, every optimization has its advantages and disadvantages, which must be considered when choosing which type of gradient descent to use. Now let's talk about the final type we've mentioned in this section, the mini-batch gradient descent.

Mini-batch Gradient Descent

Mini-batch gradient is a hybrid system between stochastic and batch gradient descent. It is a variation of the gradient descent algorithm that splits the training dataset into small batches that are used to calculate model error and update model coefficients. What mini-batch seeks to do is to find the balance between what stochastic does and the efficiency of batch gradient. Table 9-4 lists advantages and disadvantages of this type.

Ultimately, we only need to know that all this will work to optimize model learning and change the equation of cost function to allow the model to get the best accuracy while reducing the error rate.

Table 9-4. *The Pros/Cons of Mini-batch Gradient Descent*

Advantages	Disadvantages
The model update frequency is higher than batch gradient descent, which allows for a more robust convergence, avoiding local minima.	You need to configure the "mini-batch size" hyperparameter for the learning algorithm.
The batched updates provide a computationally more efficient process than stochastic gradient descent.	Error information must be accumulated across mini-batches of training examples, as with batch gradient descent.

Note   The most used gradient is the mini-batch gradient descent, especially in deep learning.

Recap

In this section, we learned the types of gradient descent. As we see, every type has its advantages and disadvantages, so we need to choose between them and see what will enhance our model more. We said before that mini-batch is the state of the art in deep learning nowadays; that may change in the future, but for now we will use it in deep learning. We hope you had fun with this section on gradient optimizers.

Loss function and Backpropagation

To simplify the neural network algorithm, we can say that any neural network can be presented as a black box with two methods, learning and predicting, as described in Figure 9-22.

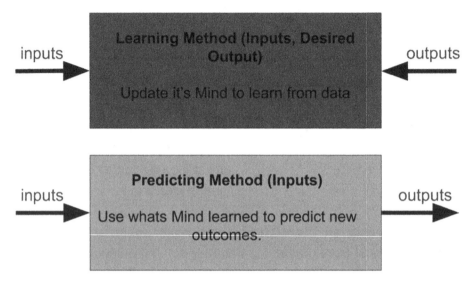

Figure 9-22. *The difference between training and predicting methods*

Our main concern in this part of the book is the learning process, which takes the inputs and the desired outputs and updates its internal state accordingly, so the calculated output gets as close as possible to the desired output.

In order to achieve this, we will decompose the learning process into its several building blocks or steps, which can be stated in the following order:

1. Model initialization

2. Forward propagation

3. Compute loss

4. Compute differentiation

5. Back propagation

6. Update the weights.

7. Iterate from step 2 to 6 until convergence.

The first step is **model initialization** before any learning procedure happens. This step is the initial hypothesis, or we can say the random guess. In this step, the model you will build will guess a random output for a given input. Thus, a *random initialization* of the model is a common practice. In order to understand this analogy, take for instance a person who has never played soccer in his life. The very first time he tries to shoot the ball, he just shoots it randomly.

The natural step to do after *initializing* the model with random weights is to check its performance. And to check the model performance we need first to make it work on the inputs we pass them through the network layer and we compare the model output with the actual output straightforwardly. This step is called **forward-propagation**, because the calculation flow is going in the natural forward direction from the input through the neural network to the output.

At this stage, on the one hand we have the model output of the randomly initialized neural network. On the other hand, we have the actual output we would like the network to learn, the real output of input data we feed to the neural network. Returning to the example of our soccer player shooting for the first time, the model output will be the final position of the ball (most of the time it will be out/missed), and the actual output would be that the ball goes inside the goal. In the beginning, our player is just shooting randomly. Let's say the ball went out—or to the right side of the goal—most of the time. What he can learn from this is that he needs to shoot a bit more to the left and focus his aim to the goal area next time he trains. In order to be able to generalize to any problem, we define what we call **loss function**.

Basically, it is a performance metric on how well the neural network manages to reach its goal of generating outputs as close as possible to the desired values. The most intuitive loss function is simply *loss* = (*actual output − model output*).

Obviously, we can use any optimization technique that modifies the internal weights of neural networks in order to minimize the total loss function that we previously defined. These techniques can include greedy search or even a simple brute-force search, but the most used technique is to go to the optimal weights that minimize the loss to its minimum value step by step using **differentiation**.

Using searching techniques or even brute-force might work if the model has only very few parameters and we don't care much about precision. However, if we are training a neural network over an array of 600x600 inputs (like in image processing), we can very easily reach models with millions of weights to optimize and brute-force can't even be imaginable, since it's a pure waste of computational resources!

Basically, differentiation deals with the derivative of the loss function. In mathematics, the derivative of a function at a certain point gives the rate or the speed at which this function is changing its values at this point. In order to see the effect of the derivative, we can ask ourselves how much the total error will change if we change the internal weight of the neural network with a certain small value δW.

You model might be composed of only one layer inside the neural network between the inputs and the outputs. But in many cases, more layers are needed, in order to reach more variations in the functionality of the neural network. For sure, we can always create one complicated function that represents the composition of all the layers of the network. Although in most cases composing the functions is very hard; plus, for every composition one has to calculate the dedicated derivative of the composition (which is not at all scalable and very error prone). In order to solve the problem, luckily for us, the derivative is decomposable, thus it can be **backpropagated**. We have the starting point of errors, which is the loss function, and we know how to derive it. So if we know how to derive each function from the composition, we can propagate back the error from the end to the start.

As we presented earlier, the derivative is just the rate at which the error changes, relative to the weight changes.

Note   In real-life problems we shouldn't **update the weights** with such big steps. Since there are a lot of nonlinearities, any big change in weights will lead to chaotic behavior. We should not forget that the derivative is only local at the point where we are calculating the derivative.

Thus, a general rule of weight updates is the delta rule:
NewWeight = OldWeight − CalculatedDerivative ∗ LearningRate The learning rate is introduced as a constant (usually very small), in order to force the weight to get updated very smoothly and slowly (to avoid big steps and chaotic behavior).

Since we update the weights with a small delta step at a time, it will take several iterations in order to learn. This is very similar to genetic algorithms, where after each generation we apply a small mutation rate and the fittest survives. In a neural network, after each iteration the gradient descent force updates the weights toward less and less global loss function. The similarity is that the delta rule acts as a mutation operator, and the loss function acts as a fitness function to minimize. The difference is that in genetic algorithms, the mutation is blind. Some mutations are bad, some are good, but the good ones have a higher chance to survive. However, the weight updates in neural networks are smarter, since they are guided by the decreasing gradient force over the error.

Loss Function

The loss function is the metric that helps a network understand whether it is learning in the right direction. To frame the loss function in simple words, consider it as the test score you achieve in an examination. Say you appeared for tests with several questions on a certain subject: what metrics would you use to understand your performance on this test? Obviously, the test score. Assume you answered all the questions, comparing your answers for each question with the right answer will give you a score metric that assesses your performance on the subject itself. Assuming you scored 56, 60, 78, 90, and 96 out of 100 in five consecutive language tests, you would clearly see that improving test scores are an indication of how well you are performing. Had the test scores been decreasing, then the verdict would be that your performance is decreasing and you would need to change your studying methods or materials to improve.

Similarly, *how does a network understand whether it is improving its learning process in each iteration?* It uses the loss function, which is analogous to the test score. The loss function essentially measures the loss from the target. Say you are developing a model to predict whether a student will pass or fail, and the chance of passing or failing is defined by the probability. So, 1 would indicate that he will pass with 100% certainty and 0 would indicate that he will definitely fail.

The model learns from the data and predicts a score of 0.87 for the student to pass. So, the actual loss here would be 1.00 – 0.87 = 0.13. If it repeats the exercise with some parameter updates in order to improve and now achieves a loss of 0.40, it would understand that the changes it has made are not helping the network to appropriately learn. Alternatively, a new loss of 0.05 would indicate that the updates or changes from the learning are in the right direction.

Based on the type of data outcome, we have several standard loss functions defined in both machine and deep learning. For regression use cases (e.g., where the end prediction would be a continuous number like the marks scored by a student, the number of product units sold by a shop, the number of calls received from customers in a contact center), here are some popular loss functions available:

Mean Squared Error - Average squared difference between the actual and predicted value.

The squared difference makes it easy to penalize the model more for a higher difference. So, a difference of 3 would result in a loss of 9, but difference of 9 would return a loss of 81.

The mathematical equivalent would be

$$\sum_{i=0}^{n} \frac{(Actual - Predicted)^2}{k}$$

TensorFlow equivalent

```
tf.losses.mean_squared_error(labels, predictions)
```

Mean Absolute Error is the average absolute error between actual and predicted.

The mathematical equivalent would be

$$\sum_{i=0}^{n} |Actual - Predicted|$$

TensorFlow equivalent is

```
tf.metrics.mean_absolute_error(labels, predictions)
# OR
tf.losses.absolute_difference(labels, predictions)
```

Similarly, a few other variants are

- MAPE – Mean absolute percentage error

```
tf.keras.losses.mean_absolute_percentage_error(labels, predictions)
```

- MSLE – Mean square logarithmic error

```
tf.keras.losses.mean_squared_logarithmic_error(labels,
predictions)
```

For categorical outcomes, your prediction would be for a class, like whether a student will pass (1) or fail (0), whether the customer will make a purchase or not, whether the customer will default on payment or not, and so on. Some use cases may have multiple classes as an outcome, like classifying types of disease (Type A, B, or C); classifying images as cats, dogs, cars, horses, landscapes; and so on.

In such cases, the losses defined in the preceding cannot be used due to obvious reasons. We would need to quantify the outcome of the class as probability and define losses based on the probability estimates as predictions.

A few popular choices for losses for categorical outcomes in Keras are as follows:

Binary cross-entropy defines the loss when the categorical outcome is a binary variable, that is, with two possible outcomes: (Pass/Fail) or (Yes/No).

The mathematical form would be

$$Loss = -\left[y * log(\hat{y}) + (1 - y) * log(1 - \hat{y})\right]$$

TensorFlow equivalent is

```
tf.backend. binary_crossentropy(y_actual, y_predicted)
```

Categorical cross-entropy defines the loss when the categorical outcomes is nonbinary, that is, more than two possible outcomes: (Yes/No/Maybe) or (Type 1/ Type 2/... Type n).

The mathematical form would be $Loss = \sum_{j=0}^{m}\sum_{i=0}^{n} y_{ij} * log(\hat{y}_{ji})$

TensorFlow equivalent is

```
tf.keras.losses.categorical_crossentropy(y_actual, y_predicted)
# OR
tf.losses.softmax_cross_entropy(y_actual, y_predicted)
```

Backpropagation

Understanding the backpropagation algorithm can take some time. If you are looking for a fast implementation of a neural network, you can skip this section, as modern libraries have the capability to autodifferentiate and perform the entire training procedure. However, understanding this algorithm would definitely give you insights into problems related to deep learning (learning problems, slow learning, exploding gradients, and diminishing gradients).

Gradient descent is a powerful algorithm, yet it is a slow method when the number of weights increases. In the case of neural networks having parameters in the range of thousands, training each weight with respect to the loss function—or, rather, formulating the loss as a function of all the weights—becomes painstakingly slow and extremely complex to use for practical purposes.

Thanks to the path-breaking paper by Geoffrey Hinton and his colleagues in 1986, we have an extremely fast and beautiful algorithm that helps us to find the partial derivative of the loss with respect to each weight. This algorithm is the workhorse of the training procedure for every deep learning algorithm. More detailed information can be found here: www.cs.toronto.edu/~hinton/backprop.html.

It is the most efficient possible procedure to compute the exact gradient, and its computational cost is always of the same $O()$ complexity as computing the loss itself. The proof of backpropagation is beyond the scope of this book; however, the intuitive explanation of the algorithm can give you an excellent insight into its complex working.

For backpropagation to work, two basic assumptions are made regarding the error function:

1. Total error can be written as a summation of individual errors of training samples/minibatch, $E = \sum_k E_k$.

2. Error can be written as a function of outputs of the network.

Backpropagation consists of two parts:

3. Forward pass, wherein we initialize the weights and make a feedforward network to store all the values

4. Backward pass, which is performed to have the stored values update the weights.

Partial derivatives, chain rules, and linear algebra are the main tools required to deal with backpropagation (Figure 9-23).

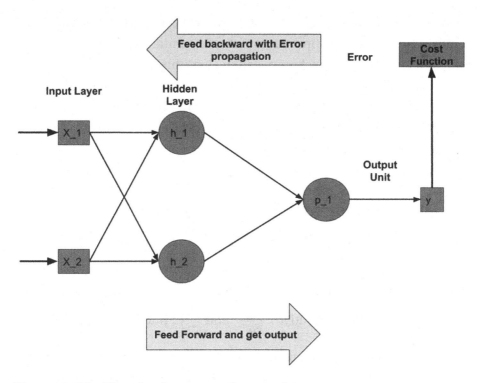

Figure 9-23. *How backpropagation works*

Initially, all the edge weights are randomly assigned. For every input in the training dataset, the ANN is activated and its output is observed. This output is compared with the desired output that we already know, and the error is "propagated" back to the previous layer. This error is noted, and the weights are "adjusted" accordingly. This process is repeated until the output error is below a predetermined threshold.

Once the preceding algorithm terminates, we have a "learned" ANN, which we consider to be ready to work with "new" inputs. This neural network is said to have learned from several examples (labeled data) and from its mistakes (error propagation).

Curious readers should investigate the original paper on backpropagation. We have provided a list of resources and blogs to understand the algorithm in greater depth. However, when it comes to implementation, you will hardly write your own code on backpropagation, as most of the libraries support automatic differentiation, and you won't really want to tweak the backpropagation algorithm.

In layman's language, in backpropagation, we try to sequentially update the weights, first by making a forward pass on the network, after which we first update the weights of the last layer, using the label and last layer outputs, then subsequently use this information recursively on the layer just before and proceed.

The Four Fundamental Equations Behind Backpropagation

Backpropagation is about understanding how changing the weights and biases in a network changes the cost function. Ultimately, this means computing the partial derivatives $\frac{\partial C}{\partial w_{jk}^l}$ and $\frac{\partial C}{\partial b_j^l}$. But to compute those, we first introduce an intermediate quantity, δ_j^l, which we call the *error* in the jth neuron in the lth layer. Backpropagation will give us a procedure to compute the error δ_j^l, and then will relate δ_j^l to $\frac{\partial C}{\partial w_{jk}^l}$ and $\frac{\partial C}{\partial b_j^l}$.

To understand how the error is defined, imagine there is a red square in our neural network (red square in Figure 9-24).

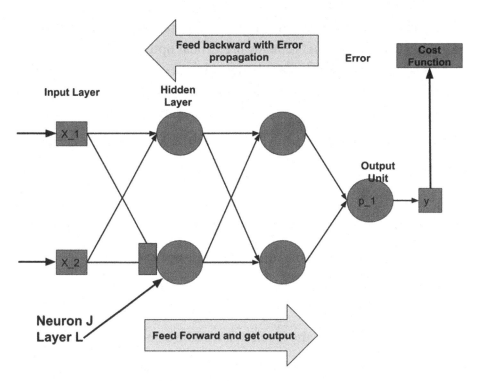

Figure 9-24. *The neuron J in Layer L through the backpropagation process*

The red square sits at the jth neuron in layer l. As the input to the neuron comes in, the red square messes with the neuron's operation. It adds a little change Δz_j^l to the neuron's weighted input, so that instead of outputting $\sigma\left(z_j^l\right)$, the neuron outputs $\sigma\left(z_j^l + \Delta z_j^l\right)$. This change propagates through later layers in the network, finally causing the overall cost to change by an amount $\frac{\partial C}{\partial z_j^l}\Delta z_j^l$.

Now, this square is a good red square, and is trying to help you improve the cost, that is, trying to find a Δz_j^l that makes the cost smaller. Suppose $\frac{\partial C}{\partial z_j^l}$ has a large value (either positive or negative). Then the red square can lower the cost quite a bit by choosing Δz_j^l to have the opposite sign to $\frac{\partial C}{\partial z_j^l}$. By contrast, if $\frac{\partial C}{\partial z_j^l}$ is close to zero, then the red square can't improve the cost much at all by perturbing the weighted input z_j^l. So, as far as the red square can tell, the neuron is already pretty near optimal.

This is only the case for small changes Δz_j^l, of course. We'll assume that the red square is constrained to make such small changes. And so, there's a heuristic sense in which $\dfrac{\partial C}{\partial z_j^l}$ is a measure of the error in the neuron.

Motivated by this story, we define the error δ_j^l of neuron j in layer l by $\delta_j^l = \dfrac{\partial C}{\partial z_j^l}$.

To continue, we use δ^l to denote the vector of errors associated with layer l. Backpropagation will give us a way of computing δ^l for every layer, and then relating those errors to the quantities of real interest, $\dfrac{\partial C}{\partial w_{jk}^l}$ and $\dfrac{\partial C}{\partial b_j^l}$. You might wonder why the red square is changing the weighted input z_j^l. Surely, it'd be more natural to imagine the red square changing the output activation a_j^l, with the result that we'd be using $\dfrac{\partial C}{\partial a_j^l}$ as our measure of error. In fact, if you do, these things work out quite similarly to the discussion following. But it turns out to make the presentation of backpropagation a little more algebraically complicated. So, we'll stick with $\delta_j^l = \dfrac{\partial C}{\partial z_j^l}$ as our measure of error.

In classification problems like *MNIST,* the term "**error**" is sometimes used to mean the classification failure rate. For example, if the neural net correctly classifies 96.0 percent of the digits, then the error is 4.0 percent. Obviously, this has quite a different meaning from our δ vectors. In practice, you shouldn't have trouble telling which meaning is intended in any given usage.

Our target: Backpropagation is based around four fundamental equations. Together, those equations give us a way of computing both the error δ^l and the gradient of the cost function. I state the four equations later. Be warned, though: you shouldn't expect to instantaneously assimilate the equations. Such an expectation will lead to disappointment. In fact, the backpropagation equations are so rich, that understanding them well requires considerable time and patience as you gradually delve deeper into the equations. The good news is that such patience is repaid many times over. And so, the discussion in this section is merely a beginning, helping you on the way to a thorough understanding of the equations.

Here's a preview of the ways we'll delve more deeply into the equations later in the chapter: I'll give a short proof of the equations, which helps explain why they are true; we'll restate the equations in algorithm-like form as pseudocode, and see how the pseudocode can be implemented as real, running Python code; and, in the final section of the chapter, we'll develop an intuitive picture of what the backpropagation equations mean, and how someone might discover them from scratch. Along the way we'll return repeatedly to the four fundamental equations, and as you deepen your understanding, those equations will come to seem comfortable and, perhaps, even beautiful and natural.

Here's an equation for the error in the output layer, δ^L. The components of δ^L are given by

$$\delta_j^L = \frac{\partial C}{\partial a_j^L} \sigma'\left(z_j^L\right) \qquad \text{(Equation 1)}$$

This is a very natural expression. The first term on the right, $\dfrac{\partial C}{\partial a_j^L}$, just measures how fast the cost is changing as a function of the jth output activation. If, for example, C doesn't depend much on a particular output neuron, j, then δ_j^L will be small, which is what we'd expect. The second term on the right, $\sigma'\left(z_j^L\right)$, measures how fast the activation function σ is changing at z_j^L.

Notice that everything in Equation 1 is easily computed. In particular, we compute z_j^L while computing the behavior of the network, and it's only a small additional overhead to compute $\sigma'(z_j^L)$. The exact form of $\dfrac{\partial C}{\partial a_j^L}$ will, of course, depend on the form of the cost function. However, provided the cost function is known, there should be little trouble computing $\dfrac{\partial C}{\partial a_j^L}$. For example, if we're using the quadratic cost function, then $C = \dfrac{1}{2}\sum_j \left(a_j^L - y_j\right)^2$, and so $\dfrac{\partial C}{\partial a_j^L} = \left(a_j^L - y_j\right)$, which obviously is easily computable.

Equation 1 is a component-wise expression for δ^L. It's a perfectly good expression, but not the matrix-based form we want for backpropagation. However, it's easy to rewrite the equation in a matrix-based form, as $\delta^L = \nabla_a C \odot \sigma'(z^L)$ (Equation 1 a).

Here, $\nabla_a C$ is defined to be a vector whose components are the partial derivatives $\dfrac{\partial C}{\partial a_j^L}$. You can think of $\nabla_a C$ as expressing the rate of change of C with respect to the output activations. It's easy to see that Equation 1 a and Equation 1 are equivalent, and for that reason from now on we'll use Equation 1 interchangeably to refer to both equations. As an example, in the case of the quadratic cost we have $\nabla_a C = a^L - y$, and so the fully matrix-based form of Equation 1 becomes $\delta^L = (a^L - y) \odot \sigma'(z^L)$. As you can see, everything in this expression has a nice vector form, and is easily computed using a library such as *NumPy*.

Here is an equation for the error δ^l in terms of the error in the next layer, δ^{l+1}. In particular,

$$\delta^l = \left(\left(w^{l+1}\right)^T \delta^{l+1}\right) \odot \sigma'\left(z^l\right) \qquad \text{(Equation 2)}$$

where $(w^{l+1})^T$ is the transpose of the weight matrix w^{l+1} for the $(l+1)^{th}$ layer. This equation appears complicated, but each element has a nice interpretation. Suppose we know the error δ^{l+1} at the $(l+1)^{th}$ layer. When we apply the transpose weight matrix, $(w^{l+1})^T$, we can think intuitively of this as moving the error backward through the network, giving us some sort of measure of the error at the output of the lth layer. We then take the Hadamard product $\odot\sigma'(z')$. This moves the error backward through the activation function in layer l, giving us the error δ^l in the weighted input to layer l.

By combining Equation 2 with Equation 1, we can compute the error δ^l for any layer in the network. We start by using Equation 1 to compute δ^L, then apply Equation 2 to compute δ^{L-1}, then Equation 2 again to compute δ^{L-2}, and so on, all the way back through the network.

Here's an equation for the rate of change of the cost with respect to any bias in the network. In particular,

$$\frac{\partial C}{\partial b_j^l} = \delta_j^l \qquad \text{(Equation 3)}$$

That is, the error δ_j^l is exactly equal to the rate of change $\dfrac{\partial C}{\partial b_j^l}$. This is great news, since Equation 1 and Equation 2 have already told us how to compute δ_j^l. We can rewrite Equation 3 in shorthand as $\dfrac{\partial C}{\partial b} = \delta$, where it is understood that δ is being evaluated at the same neuron as the bias b.

Here is an equation for the rate of change of the cost with respect to any weight in the network: In in particular,

$$\frac{\partial C}{\partial w_{jk}^l} = a_k^{l-1}\delta_j^l \qquad \text{(Equation 4)}$$

This tells us how to compute the partial derivatives $\dfrac{\partial C}{\partial w_{jk}^l}$ in terms of the quantities δ^l and a^{l-1}, which we already know how to compute. The equation can be rewritten in a less index-heavy notation as $\dfrac{\partial C}{\partial w} = a_{in}\delta_{out}$, where it's understood that a_{in} is the activation of the neuron input to the weight w, and δ_{out} is the error of the neuron output from the weight w. Zooming in to look at just the weight, w, and the two neurons connected by that weight, we can depict this as shown in Figure 9-25.

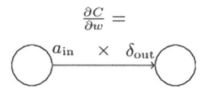

Figure 9-25. *The backpropagation connection between two neurons*

A nice consequence of the equation $\frac{\partial C}{\partial w} = a_{in}\delta_{out}$ is that when the activation a_{in} is small, $a_{in} \approx 0$, the gradient term $\frac{\partial C}{\partial w}$ will also tend to be small. In this case, we'll say the weight learns slowly, meaning that it's not changing much during gradient descent. In other words, one consequence of Equation 4 is that weights output from low-activation neurons learn slowly.

There are other insights along these lines, which can be obtained from Equation 1 to Equation 4. Let's start by looking at the output layer. Consider the term $\sigma'\left(z_j^L\right)$ in Equation 1. Recall from the graph of the sigmoid function in the last chapter that the σ function becomes very flat when $\sigma\left(z_j^L\right)$ is approximately 0 or 1. When this occurs, we will have $\sigma'\left(z_j^L\right) \approx 0$. And so, the lesson is that a weight in the final layer will learn slowly if the output neuron is either low activation (≈ 0) or high activation (≈ 1). In this case, it's common to say the output neuron has saturated and, as a result, the weight has stopped learning (or is learning slowly). Similar remarks also hold for the biases of output neuron.

We can obtain similar insights for earlier layers. In particular, note the $\sigma'(z^l)$ term in Equation 2. This means that δ_j^l is likely to get small if the neuron is near saturation. And this, in turn, means that any weights input to a saturated neuron will learn slowly.

This reasoning won't hold if $(w^{l+1})^T \delta^{l+1})$ has large enough entries to compensate for the smallness of $\sigma'(z_j^l)$. But I'm speaking of the general tendency.

Summing up, we've learned that a weight will learn slowly if either the input neuron is low-activation or if the output neuron has saturated (i.e., is either high- or low-activation).

None of these observations is too greatly surprising. Still, they help improve our mental model of what's going on as a neural network learns. Furthermore, we can turn this type of reasoning around. The four fundamental equations turn out to hold for any activation function, not just the standard sigmoid function (that's because, as we'll see in a moment, the proofs don't use any special properties of σ). So, we can use these equations to design activation functions that have particular desired learning properties. As an example, suppose we were to choose a (nonsigmoid) activation function σ so that σ' is always positive and never gets close to zero. That would prevent the slowdown of learning that occurs when ordinary sigmoid neurons saturate. Later in the book we'll see examples where this kind of modification is made to the activation function. Keeping the four equations (Equations 1 to 4) in mind can help explain why such modifications are tried, and what impact they can have (Figure 9-26).

$$\delta^L = \nabla_a C \odot \sigma'(z^L)$$

$$\delta^l = ((w^{l+1})^T \delta^{l+1}) \odot \sigma'(z^l)$$

$$\frac{\partial C}{\partial b_j^l} = \delta_j^l$$

$$\frac{\partial C}{\partial w_{jk}^l} = a_k^{l-1} \delta_j^l$$

Figure 9-26. *Summing up all of the four equations*

Exploding Gradients

What are exploding gradients?

An error gradient is the direction and magnitude calculated during the training of a neural network that is used to update the network weights in the right direction and by the right amount.

In deep networks or recurrent neural networks, error gradients can accumulate during an update and result in very large gradients. These in turn result in large updates to the network weights, and in turn, an unstable network. At an extreme, the values of weights can become so large as to overflow and result in NaN values.

The explosion occurs through exponential growth by repeatedly multiplying gradients through the network layers that have values larger than 1.0.

What is the problem with exploding gradients?

In deep multilayer perceptron networks, exploding gradients can result in an unstable network that at best cannot learn from the training data and at worst results in NaN weight values that can no longer be updated.

Exploding gradients can make learning unstable. In recurrent neural networks, exploding gradients can result in an unstable network that is unable to learn from training data and at best a network that cannot learn over long input sequences of data.

The exploding gradients problem refers to the large increase in the norm of the gradient during training. Such events are due to the explosion of the long-term components

How do you know if you have exploding gradients? There are some subtle signs that you may be suffering from exploding gradients during the training of your network, such as:

- The model is unable to get traction on your training data (e.g., poor loss).

- The model is unstable, resulting in large changes in loss from update to update.

- The model loss goes to NaN during training.

If you have these types of problems, you can dig deeper to see if you have a problem with exploding gradients. There are some less subtle signs that you can use to confirm that you have exploding gradients.

- The model weights quickly become very large during training.

- The model weights go to NaN values during training.

- The error gradient values are consistently above 1.0 for each node and layer during training.

How can we fix exploding gradients? There are many approaches to addressing exploding gradients; this section lists some best practice approaches that you can use.

Re-Design the Network Model

In deep neural networks, exploding gradients may be addressed by redesigning the network to have fewer layers.

There may also be some benefit in using a smaller batch size while training the network.

In recurrent neural networks, updating across fewer prior time steps during training, called truncated backpropagation through time, may reduce the exploding gradient problem.

Use Long Short-Term Memory Networks

In recurrent neural networks, gradient exploding can occur given the inherent instability in the training of this type of network, for example, via backpropagation through time that essentially transforms the recurrent network into a deep multilayer perceptron neural network.

Exploding gradients can be reduced by using the LSTM memory units and, perhaps, related gated-type neuron structures.

Adopting LSTM memory units is a new best practice for recurrent neural networks for sequence prediction.

Use Gradient Clipping

Exploding gradients can still occur in very deep multilayer perceptron networks with a large batch size and LSTMs with very long input sequence lengths.

If exploding gradients are still occurring, you can check for and limit the size of gradients during the training of your network.

This is called gradient clipping. Dealing with the exploding gradients has a simple but very effective solution: clipping gradients if their norm exceeds a given threshold.

Specifically, the values of the error gradient are checked against a threshold value and clipped or set to that threshold value if the error gradient exceeds the threshold.

To some extent, the exploding gradient problem can be mitigated by gradient clipping (thresholding the values of the gradients before performing a gradient descent step).

Use Weight Regularization

Another approach, if exploding gradients are still occurring, is to check the size of network weights and apply a penalty to the network's loss function for large weight values.

This is called weight regularization and often an L1 (absolute weights) or an L2 (squared weights) penalty can be used.

Using an L1 or L2 penalty on the recurrent weights can help with exploding gradients.

Vanishing Gradients

The vanishing gradients problem is one example of unstable behavior that you may encounter when training a deep neural network.

It describes the situation where a deep multilayer feedforward network or a recurrent neural network is unable to propagate useful gradient information from the output end of the model back to the layers near the input end of the model.

The result is the general inability of models with many layers to learn on a given dataset, or they might prematurely converge to a poor solution.

Many fixes and workarounds have been proposed and investigated, such as alternate weight initialization schemes, unsupervised pretraining, layer-wise training, and variations on gradient descent. Perhaps the most common change is the use of the rectified linear activation function that has become the new default, instead of the hyperbolic tangent activation function that was the default through the late 1990s and 2000s.

In this section, you will discover how to diagnose a vanishing gradient problem when training a neural network model, and how to fix it using an alternate activation function and weight initialization scheme.

Vanishing Gradients Problem

For instance, a neural network is trained using stochastic gradient descent. This involves first calculating the prediction error made by the model and using the error to estimate a gradient used to update each weight in the network so that less error is made next time. This error gradient is propagated backward through the network from the output layer to the input layer.

It is desirable to train neural networks with many layers, as the addition of more layers increases the capacity of the network, making it capable of learning a large training dataset and efficiently representing more complex mapping functions from inputs to outputs.

A problem with training networks with many layers (e.g., deep neural networks) is that the gradient diminishes dramatically as it is propagated backward through the network. The error may be so small by the time it reaches layers close to the input of the model, that it may have very little effect. As such, this problem is referred to as the "vanishing gradients" problem.

Vanishing gradients make it difficult to know in which direction the parameters should move to improve the cost function.

In fact, the error gradient can be unstable in deep neural networks and not only vanish, but also explode, where the gradient exponentially increases as it is propagated backward through the network. This is referred to as the "exploding gradient" problem.

The term vanishing gradient refers to the fact that in a feedforward network (FFN) the backpropagated error signal typically decreases (or increases) exponentially as a function of the distance from the final layer.

Vanishing gradients is a particular problem with recurrent neural networks because the update of the network involves unrolling the network for each input time step, in effect creating a very deep network that requires weight updates. A modest recurrent neural network may have 200-to-400 input time steps, resulting conceptually in a very deep network.

The vanishing gradients problem may be manifest in a multilayer perceptron by a slow rate of improvement of a model during training and perhaps premature convergence (e.g., continued training does not result in any further improvement). Inspecting the changes to the weights during training, we would see more change (i.e., more learning) occurring in the layers closer to the output layer and less change occurring in the layers close to the input layer.

There are many techniques that can be used to reduce the impact of the vanishing gradients problem for feedforward neural networks, most notably alternate weight initialization schemes and use of alternate activation functions.

Different approaches to training deep networks (both feedforward and recurrent) have been studied and applied (in an effort to address vanishing gradients), such as pretraining, better random initial scaling, better optimization methods, specific architectures, orthogonal initialization, etc.

In this section, we will take a closer look at the use of an alternate weight initialization scheme and activation function to permit the training of deeper neural network models.

Weight initialization: Update the deep MLP with tanh activation to use Xavier uniform weight initialization and report the results.

Learning algorithm: Update the deep MLP with tanh activation to use an adaptive learning algorithm such as Adam and report the results.

Weight changes: Update the tanh and ReLU examples to record and plot the L1 vector norm of model weights each epoch as a proxy for how much each layer is changed during training and compare results.

Study model depth: Create an experiment using the MLP with tanh activation and report the performance of models as the number of hidden layers is increased from 1 to 10.

Increase breadth: Increase the number of nodes in the hidden layers of the MLP with tanh activation from 5 to 25, and report performance as the number of layers are increased from 1 to 10.

TensorFlow Basics

In Part I, we discussed TensorFlow from installation to its basics; we also showed how to build a fully functional model using a toy dataset. We did all this in the introduction part to make you feel that it's easier than you think to learn deep learning and start using TensorFlow. But now we need to show you the needed fundamentals of TensorFlow, going through the same headers but with some depth; for instance, we will reillustrate the use of different types of tensor (i.e., placeholder, variable, and constant, giving you the concrete tools that you will use to build any TensorFlow deep learning models.

So, in this section, we are going to discuss the difference between placeholder, variable, and constant tensor types, and also show you the properties of tensors. After that we are going to show you the optimization framework and approaches that TensorFlow uses in almost any deep learning models, going throw the learning rate and understanding the mini-batch approach. Last, we will show you the most important optimizers in TensorFlow.

Placeholder vs. Variable vs. Constant

As we described in Part I, placeholders, variables, and constants are key tools for using computational graphs in TensorFlow. So, we have to understand the differences and when to best use them to our advantage.

One of the most important distinctions to make with the data is whether it is a placeholder or a variable. Variables are the parameters of the algorithm and TensorFlow keeps track of how to change these to optimize the algorithm. Placeholders are objects that allow you to feed in data of a specific type and shape and depend on the results of the computational graph, such as the expected outcome of a computation. On the other hand, constants have a simple use: while you build a huge model, you are going to use some functions that do something for you: matrices multiplication or any computational operation. Here you can use the constant for these operations to help you do it inside the computational graph.

Another important distinction is that in TensorFlow the differences between constants and variables are that when you declare some constant, its value can't be changed in the future (also the initialization should be with a value, not with an operation). Nevertheless, when you declare a variable, you can change its value in the future with tf.assign() method (and the initialization can be achieved with a value or operation).

The main way to create a variable is by using the Variable() function, which takes a tensor as an input and outputs a variable. This is the declaration, and we still need to initialize the variable. Initializing is what puts the variable with the corresponding methods on the computational graph. Here is an example of creating and initializing a variable:

```
my_var = tf.Variable(tf.zeros([2,3]))
sess = tf.Session()
initialize_op = tf.global_variables_initializer ()
sess.run(initialize_op)
```

Placeholders are just holding the position for data to be fed into the graph. Placeholders get data from a `feed_dict` argument in the session. To put a placeholder in the graph, we must perform at least one operation on the placeholder. We initialize the graph, declare x to be a placeholder, and define y as the identity operation on x, which just returns x. We then create data to feed into the x placeholder and run the identity operation. It is worth noting that TensorFlow will not return a self-referenced placeholder in the feed dictionary. The code is shown here and the resulting graph is shown in the next section:

```
sess = tf.Session()
x = tf.placeholder(tf.float32, shape=[2,2])
y = tf.identity(x)
x_vals = np.random.rand(2,2)
sess.run(y, feed_dict={x: x_vals})
# Note that sess.run(x, feed_dict={x: x_vals})
# will result in a self referencing error.
```

We can see what the code looks like in detail with just one variable, initialized to all zeros. The gray shaded region is a very detailed view of the operations and constants involved. The main computational graph with less detail is the smaller graph outside of the gray region in the upper right corner. For more details on creating and visualizing graphs. Note that TensorFlow will not return a self-refernced placeholder in the feed dictionary. In technical speech, running `sess.run(x, feed_dict={x: x_vals})` in the following graph will return an error .

Gradient-Descent Optimization Methods from a Deep-Learning Perspective

We think that before diving into the TensorFlow optimizers, which is a very important topic, it's also important to understand a few key points regarding full-batch gradient descent and stochastic gradient descent, including their drawbacks. That is so that one can know and understand the need to compare and choose from variants of these optimizers.

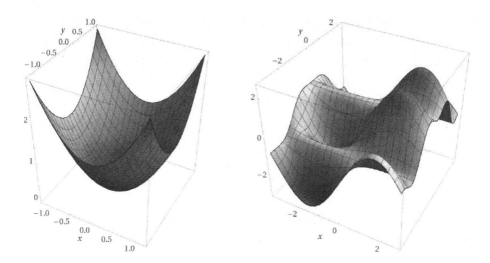

Figure 9-27. *The difference between many cost functions*

The cost function for a linear neuron with a least square error is quadratic (Figure 9-27). When the cost function is quadratic, the direction of the gradient resulting from the full-batch gradient-descent method gives the best direction for cost reduction in a linear sense, but it doesn't point to the minimum unless the different elliptical contours of the cost function are circles. In cases of long elliptical contours, the gradient components might be large in directions where less change is required and small in directions where more change is required to move to the minimum point.

The problem with this condition is that if we take small steps by making the learning rate small, the gradient descent would take a while to converge, whereas if we were to use a big learning rate, the gradients would change direction rapidly in directions where the cost function had curvature, leading to oscillations. The cost function for a multilayer neural network is not quadratic but rather is mostly a smooth function. Locally, such nonquadratic cost functions can be approximated by quadratic functions, and so the problems of gradient descent inherent to elliptical contours still prevail for nonquadratic cost functions.

339

The best way to get around this problem is to take larger steps in those directions in which the gradients are small but consistent, and take smaller steps in those directions that have big but inconsistent gradients. This can be achieved if, instead of having a fixed learning rate for all dimensions, we have a separate learning rate for each dimension.

Another big problem with neural networks is that the cost functions are mostly nonconvex, so the gradient-descent method might get stuck at local minimum points, leading to a suboptimal solution.

Note   The nonconvex nature of the neural network is the result of the hidden layer units that have nonlinear activation functions, such as sigmoid.

Full-batch gradient descent uses the full dataset for the gradient computation. While this is good for convex cost surfaces, it has its own problems in cases of nonconvex cost functions. For nonconvex cost surfaces with full-batch gradients, the model is going to end up with the minima in its basin of attraction. If the initialized parameters are in the basin of attraction of a local minimum that doesn't provide good generalization, a full-batch gradient would give a suboptimal solution.

With stochastic gradient descent, the noisy gradients computed may force the model out of the basin of attraction of the bad local minima—one that doesn't provide good generalization—and place it in a more optimal region. Stochastic gradient descent with single data points produces very random and noisy gradients. Gradients with mini-batches tend to produce much more stable estimates of gradients when compared with gradients of single data points, but they are still noisier than those produced by the full batches.

Ideally, the mini-batch size should be carefully chosen such that the gradients are noisy enough to avoid or escape bad local minima points but stable enough to converge at global minima or a local minimum that provides good generalization.

In Figure 9-28, the dotted arrows correspond to the path taken by stochastic gradient descent (SGD), while the continuous arrows correspond to the path taken by full-batch gradient descent. Full-batch gradient descent computes the actual gradient at a point, and if it is in the basin of attraction of a poor local minimum, gradient descent almost certainly ensures that the local minima L is reached. However, in the case of stochastic gradient descent, because the gradient is based on only a portion of the data and not on the full batch, the gradient direction is only a rough estimate. Since the noisy rough estimate doesn't always point to the actual gradient at point C, stochastic gradient descent may escape the basin of attraction of the local minima and fortunately land in the basin of a global minima. Stochastic gradient descent may escape the global minima basin of attraction too, but generally if the basin of attraction is large and the mini-batch size is carefully chosen so that the gradients it produces are moderately noisy, stochastic gradient descent is most likely to reach the global minima G (as in this case) or some other optimal minima that has a large basin of attraction. For nonconvex optimization, there are other heuristics as well, such as momentum, which when adopted along with stochastic gradient descent increases the chances of the SGD's avoiding shallow local minima. Momentum generally keeps track of the previous gradients through the velocity component. So, if the gradients are steadily pointing toward a good local minimum that has a large basin of attraction, the velocity component would be high in the direction of the good local minimum. If the new gradient is noisy and points toward a bad local minimum, the velocity component would provide momentum to continue in the same direction and not get influenced by the new gradient too much.

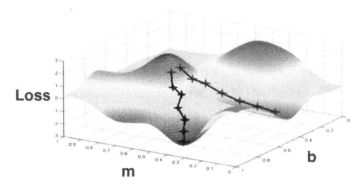

f (x) = nonlinear function of x

Figure 9-28. *The steps of SGD algorithms*

Another impediment to optimizing nonconvex cost functions is
the presence of saddle points. The number of saddle points increases
exponentially with the dimensionality increase of the parameter space of
a cost function. Saddle points are stationary points (i.e., points where the
gradient is zero) but are neither a local minimum nor a local maximum
point. Since the saddle points are associated with a long plateau of points
with the same cost as that of the saddle point, the gradient in the plateau
region is either zero or very close to zero. Because of this near-zero
gradient in all directions, gradient-based optimizers have a hard time
coming out of these saddle points. Mathematically, to determine whether
a point is a saddle point, the Eigenvalues of the Hessian matrix of the cost
function must be computed at the given point. If there are both positive
and negative Eigenvalues, then it is a saddle point.

Learning Rate in the Mini-batch Approach to Stochastic Gradient Descent

When there is high redundancy in the dataset, the gradient computed on a mini-batch of data points is almost the same as the gradient computed on the whole dataset, provided the mini-batch is a good representation of the entire dataset. In such cases, computing the gradient on the whole dataset can be avoided, and instead the gradient on the mini-batch of data points can be used as the approximate gradient for the whole dataset. This is the mini-batch approach to gradient descent, which is also called mini-batch stochastic gradient descent. When, instead of using a mini-batch, the gradients are approximated by one data point, it is called online learning or stochastic gradient descent. However, it is always better to use the mini-batch version of stochastic gradient descent over online learning, since the gradients for the mini-batch method are less noisy compared with the online mode of learning. Learning rate plays a vital role in the convergence of mini-batch stochastic gradient descent. The following approach tends to provide good convergence:

- Start with an initial learning rate.

- Increase the learning rate if the error reduces.

- Decrease the learning rate if the error increases.

- Stop the learning process if the error ceases to reduce.

Summary

As we will see in the next section, the different optimizers adopt an adaptive learning-rate approach in their implementations.

## CHAPTER 10

Improving Deep Neural Networks

Optimizers in TensorFlow

We're still on the subject of gradient descent. But let's now talk about gradient optimization, because of its importance to gradient descent. It is an optimization method for finding the minimum of a function, and it's important in deep learning. It works to update the weights of the neural network through backpropagation.

So what are the optimizations of the types of gradient descent we talked about previously (batch, mini-batch, and stochastic)? Let's start by talking about the benefits of these optimization methods:

1. Modifying the learning rate component, α

2. Modifying the gradient component, $\partial L/\partial w$

3. Modifying both (α, and $\partial L/\partial w$)

We mention $\partial L/\partial w$ as a function of the gradient (wnew=w- α $\partial L/\partial w$). This is the equation that optimizers try to optimize. To start, I think every optimizer is an optimizer of the optimizer. That's a very weird phrase but it's true, for example, Adadelta and RMSprop are optimizers of Adagrad. Let's see an image that may help show the connections between all optimizers (Figure 10-1).

© Hisham El-Amir and Mahmoud Hamdy 2020
H. El-Amir and M. Hamdy, *Deep Learning Pipeline*,
https://doi.org/10.1007/978-1-4842-5349-6_10

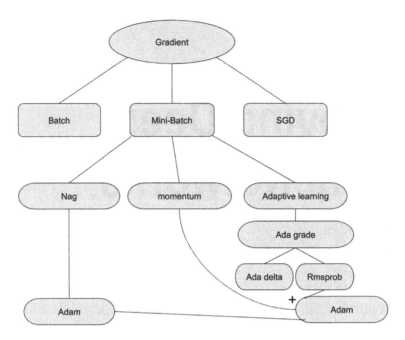

Figure 10-1. *The optimizers tree*

The most used type of optimizer in deep learning is mini-batch. We talked before about why it's the most used, so let's now get into the adaptive learning rate algorithms, Nesterov accelerated gradient (NAG) and momentum, and adaptive learning methods.

Usage:

```
train_op = tf.train.GradientDescentOptimizer (learning_rate).
minimize(cost)
```

The Notation to Use

t -> is for time step
w -> weight/parameter which we want to update
α -> learning rate
∂L/∂w -> gradient of L, the loss function to minimize

Momentum

This gradient optimizer has a variable that makes the gradient converge very fast, as it does not depend only on the current gradient to update the weight. Gradient descent with momentum replaces the current gradient with V (which stands for velocity), the exponential moving average of current and past gradients. Momentum-based methods introduce a component called velocity V that dampens the parameter update when the gradient computed changes sign, whereas it accelerates the parameter update when the gradient is in the same direction of velocity. This introduces faster convergence as well as fewer oscillations around the global minima, or around a local minimum that provides good generalization. The update rule for momentum-based optimizers is as follows:

$$w_{t+1} = w_t - \alpha V_t$$
$$V_t = \beta V_{t-1} + (1 - \beta)\frac{\partial L}{\partial w_t}$$

Default value $\beta = 0.9$, where α is the momentum parameter and η is the learning rate. The terms v_i^t and v_i^{t+1} represent the velocity at iterations t and $(t + 1)$, respectively, for the ith parameter. Similarly, v_i^t and v_i^{t+1} represent the weight of the ith parameter at iterations t and $(t + 1)$, respectively, when the cost function reaches the local minimum. When we use gradient descent, the parameters are stopped updating and in this local minimum, but when we use the momentum we will see that the parameters don't stop updating. For example, the velocity is still updating because it can't be a zero value. The prior velocity would drive the algorithm out of the local minima, considering the local minima has a small basin of attraction. The velocity or the momentum of gradient descent would be in that direction, as v_i^{t+1} would be nonzero because of the nonzero velocity from prior gradients. Also, if the prior gradients consistently pointed toward a global minimum or a local minimum with good generalization and a reasonably large basin of attraction, the velocity or the momentum of gradient descent would be in that direction. So, even if there were a bad local minimum with a small basin of attraction, the momentum component would not only drive the algorithm out of the bad local minima but also would continue the gradient descent toward the global minima or the good local minima.

Usage:

```
train_op = tf.train.MomentumOptimizer.(learning_
rate=0.001,momentum=0.9,use_nesterov=False)
```

Nesterov Accelerated Gradient

After momentum had gained in popularity, a similar update was implemented using Nesterov accelerated gradient (NAG; Sutskever et al., 2013). This update utilizes V, the exponential moving average of what I would call projected gradients.

$$w_{t+1} = w_t - \alpha V_t$$
$$V_t = \beta V_{t-1} + (1-\beta)\frac{\partial L}{\partial w^*}$$

The last term in the second equation is a projected gradient. This value can be obtained by going **one step ahead** using the previous velocity. This means that for this time step t, we have to carry out another forward propagation before we can finally execute the backpropagation. Here's how it goes:

1. Update the current weight w to a projected weight
   w* using the previous velocity.

$$w^* = w_t - \alpha V_{t-1}$$

2.   Carry out forward propagation, but using this projected weight.

3.   Obtain the projected gradient $\partial L/\partial w^*$.

4.   Compute V and w accordingly.

Note   The original Nesterov accelerated gradient paper (Nesterov, 1983) was not about stochastic gradient descent and did not explicitly use the gradient descent equation. Hence, a more appropriate reference is the aforementioned publication by Sutskever et al. in 2013, which described NAG's application in stochastic gradient descent.

Adagrad

Adaptive gradient (Adagrad) is mostly like gradient descent but with some modifications. Instead of having a global learning rate, the learning rate is normalized for each dimension on which the cost function is dependent. The learning rate in each iteration is the global learning rate divided by the l2 norm of the prior gradients up to the current iteration for each dimension. It works on the learning rate component by dividing the learning rate by the square root of S, which is the cumulative sum of current and past squared gradients.

Sometimes sparse features that don't show up much in the data can be very useful to an optimization problem. However, with basic gradient descent or stochastic gradient descent, the learning rate gives equal importance to all the features in each iteration. Since the learning rate is the same, the overall contribution of nonsparse features would be much more than that of sparse features. Hence, we end up losing critical information from the sparse features. With Adagrad, each parameter is updated with a different learning rate.

349

The sparser the feature is, the higher its parameter update would be in an iteration. This is because for sparse features the quantity would be less and the overall learning rate would be high. It may be a very good use in NLP or image processing because of data sparsity. Let's see the equation that makes what we're saying sensible: S is initialized by 0.

$$S_t = S_{t-1} + \left[\frac{\partial L}{\partial wt} \right]^2$$

$$w_{t+1} = w_t - \frac{\alpha}{\sqrt{S_t + \epsilon}} \cdot \frac{\partial L}{\partial w_t}$$

So, we note in this section that we try to adapt the learning rate to get the minima of cost function, one of the main reasons for creating these optimizations. Instead of a common learning rate for all parameters, we want to have separate learning rate for each. So Adagrad keeps the sum of squares of parameter-wise gradients and modifies individual learning rates using this. As a result, parameters occurring more often have smaller gradients.

Adadelta

Adadelta is an extension of Adagrad and it also tries to lessen Adagrad's aggressive, monotonically reducing of the learning rate, it also focuses on the learning rate component. Adadelta is probably short for **"adaptive delta,"** where delta here refers to the difference between the current weight and the newly updated weight. In Adadelta we do not need to set the default learning rate, as we take the ratio of the running average of the previous time steps to the current gradient.

$$D_t = \beta D_{t-1} + (1-\beta)[\Delta w_t]^2$$

$$S_t = \beta S_{t-1} + (1-\beta)\left[\frac{\partial L}{\partial wt}\right]^2$$

$$w_{t+1} = w_t - \frac{\sqrt{D_{t-1} + \epsilon}}{\sqrt{S_t + \epsilon}} \cdot \frac{\partial L}{\partial w_t}$$

Usage:

```
train_op = tf.train.AdadeltaOptimizer(learning_rate=0.001,
rho=0.95, epsilon=1e-08)
```

where decay represents α, epsilon represents ε, and η represents the learning rate.

RMSprop

Root mean square prop or RMSprop (Hinton et al., 2012) is another adaptive learning rate that is an improvement of Adagrad. Instead of taking the cumulative sum of squared gradients like in Adagrad, we take the exponential moving average of these gradients.

$$S_t = \beta S_{t-1} + (1-\beta)\left[\frac{\partial L}{\partial wt}\right]^2$$

$$w_{t+1} = w_t - \frac{\alpha}{\sqrt{S_t + \epsilon}} \cdot \frac{\partial L}{\partial w_t}$$

Taking an overall view, we will see that RMSprop is mostly like Adadelta but it has one difference. The difference between Adadelta and RMSprop is that Adadelta removes the use of the learning rate parameter completely by replacing it with D, the exponential moving average of squared deltas.

Usage:

```
train_op = tf.train.RMSPropOptimizer(learning_rate=0.001,
decay =0.9, momentum=0.0, epsilon=1e-10)
```

Adam

Adaptive moment estimation, or Adam (Kingma & Ba, 2014), is a combination of momentum and RMSprop. It acts upon the gradient component by using V, the exponential moving average of gradients (like in momentum) and the learning rate component by dividing the learning rate α by the square root of S, the exponential moving average of squared gradients (like in RMSprop).

$$\hat{V}_t = \frac{V_t}{1-\beta_1^t}$$

$$\hat{S}_t = \frac{S_t}{1-\beta_2^t}$$

$$w_{t+1} = w_t - \frac{\alpha}{\sqrt{\hat{S}_t} + \in} \cdot \hat{V}_t$$

Note The ^ terms are actually bias-corrected averages to ensure that the values are not biased toward 0.

Proposed default values by the authors:

$\alpha = 0.001$

$\beta_1 = 0.9$

$\beta_2 = 0.999$

$\varepsilon = 10^{-8}$

Adam is computationally efficient and has very little memory requirements. The Adam optimizer is one of the most popular gradient descent optimization algorithms.

Usage:

```
train_op=tf.train.AdamOptimizer(learning_rate=0.001,beta1=0.9,
beta2=0.999,epsilon=1e-08)
```

Nadam (Adam + NAG)

Nadam is employed for noisy gradients or gradients with high curvatures. The learning process is accelerated by summing up the exponential decay of the moving averages for the previous and current gradient, Nadam makes use of Nesterov to update the gradient one step ahead by replacing the previous $\hat{V}$ in the earlier equation with the current $\hat{V}$:

$$w_{t+1} = w_t - \frac{\alpha}{\sqrt{\hat{S}_t + \epsilon}} \left(\beta_1 \hat{V}_t + \frac{1-\beta_1}{1-\beta_1^t} \cdot \frac{\partial L}{\partial w_t} \right)$$

Where

$$\hat{V}_t = \frac{V_t}{1-\beta_1^t}$$

$$\hat{S}_t = \frac{S_t}{1-\beta_2^t}$$

Where

$$V_t = \beta_1 V_{t-1} + (1-\beta_1)\frac{\partial L}{\partial w_t}$$

$$S_t = \beta_2 V_{t-1} + (1-\beta_2)\left[\frac{\partial L}{\partial w_t}\right]^2$$

353

Default values (taken from Keras):

$\alpha = 0.002$

$\beta_1 = 0.9$

$\beta_2 = 0.999$

$\varepsilon = 10^{-7}$

Usage:

```
train_op = tf.train.MomentumOptimizer (learning_
rate=0.001,momentum=0.9,use_nesterov=False)
```

Choosing the Learning Rate

Choosing the hyperparameters learning rate is one of the hyperparameters. Deep learning neural networks are trained using the stochastic gradient descent and mini-batch algorithms. So, stochastic gradient descent is an optimization algorithm that estimates the error gradient for the current state of the model, using examples from the training dataset. It then updates the weights of the model using the backpropagation of errors algorithm, referred to simply as backpropagation. The amount that the weights are updated during training is referred to as the step size or the "learning rate." Specifically, the learning rate is a configurable hyperparameter used in the training of neural networks that has a small positive value, often in the range *between 0.0 and 1.0.*

Now that we know what the learning rate is, we need to see how we can change it during the training phase. In this phase, the backpropagation of error estimates the amount of error for which the weights of a node in the network are responsible. Instead of *updating the weight with the full amount, it is scaled by the learning rate.* This means that a learning rate of 0.1, a traditionally common default value, would mean that weights in the network are updated 0.1 * (estimated weight error). So the question is *can we configure the learning rate to get the best possible learning rate for our model?* Unfortunately, no. But the learning rate is the best hyperparameter you should tune in your model if you have time. In my opinion it the best hyperparameter and deserves attention. Unfortunately, we cannot analytically calculate the optimal learning rate for a given model on a given dataset. Instead, a good (or good enough) learning rate must be discovered via trial and error. You may think you can configure the best learning rate, but I say you should listen to more people and books:

- The initial learning rate. This is often the single most important hyperparameter, and one should always make sure that it has been tuned. If there is only time to optimize one hyperparameter and one uses stochastic gradient descent, then this is the hyperparameter that is worth tuning. See "Practical Recommendations for Gradient-Based Training of Deep Architectures" in *Neural Networks: Tricks of the Trade. Lecture Notes in Computer Science*, vol 7700 (Springer, 2012).

- In general, it is not possible to calculate the best learning rate a priori. See page 72 of *Neural Smithing: Supervised Learning in Feedforward Artificial Neural Networks* by Russell D. Reed and Robert J. Marks II (MIT Press, 1998).

You can see more books, but there are some things we can use that allow us to tune the learning rate parameter. Diagnostic plots can be used to investigate how the learning rate impacts the rate of learning and learning dynamics of the model. One example is to create a line plot of loss over training epochs during training. The line plot can show many properties, such as the rate of learning over training epochs (e.g., fast or slow). Has the model learned too quickly (sharp rise and plateau) or is it learning too slowly (little or no change)? Is the learning rate too large via oscillations in the loss?

Configuring the learning rate is challenging and time-consuming. Or you can try **grid search**. This can help to both highlight an order of magnitude where good learning rates may reside, as well as describe the relationship between learning rate and performance. It is common to grid search learning rates on a log scale from 0.1 to 10-5 or 10-6. When plotted, the results of such a sensitivity analysis often show a "U" shape, where loss decreases (performance improves) as the learning rate is decreased with a fixed number of training epochs to a point where loss sharply increases again because the model fails to converge. Or you can use the learning rate schedule: the way in which the learning rate changes over time (training epochs) is referred to as the learning rate schedule or learning rate decay. Perhaps the simplest learning rate schedule is to decrease the learning rate linearly from a large initial value to a small value. This allows large weight changes at the beginning of the learning process and small changes or fine-tuning toward the end of the learning process. Another option is to use the adaptive learning rate, in which the performance of the model on the training dataset can be monitored by the learning algorithm and the learning rate can be adjusted in response. The simplest implementation may be to make the learning rate smaller once the performance of the model plateaus, such as by decreasing the learning rate by a factor of two or an order of magnitude. Although no single method works best on all problems, there are three adaptive learning rate methods that have proved to be robust over many types of neural network architectures and problem types. They are Adagrad, RMSprop, and Adam, and all maintain and adapt learning rates for each of the weights in the model. At last, we should know that we can't choose the best learning rate but we can try to scale it to get the best result. In my opinion, the deep learning community may invite an analytical tool that makes us choose the best learning rate, but it's a very complicated choice to make.

Dropout Layers and Regularization

We want to regularize the overfitting of a neural network. When we talk about regularization, we refer to the model as having a large variance and a small bias. That is, the model is sensitive to the specific examples, the statistical noise, in the training dataset. A model with large weights is more complex than a model with smaller weights. It is a sign of a network that may be overly specialized in training data. In practice, we prefer to choose simpler models to solve the problem. We prefer models with smaller weights. But we need to remember that, in deep learning, when fitting a neural network model we must learn the weights of the network (i.e., the model parameters) using stochastic gradient descent and the training dataset. The longer we train the network, the more specialized the weights will become, overfitting the training data. The weights will grow in size in order to handle the specifics of the examples seen in the training data. Large weights make the network unstable. Although the weight will be specialized to the training dataset, minor variation or statistical noise on the expected inputs will result in large differences in the output.

We will now talk about the neural network dropout layer. This layer can be used with most types of layers, such as dense fully connected layers, convolutional layers, and recurrent layers such as the long short-term memory network layer. It works with all of the hidden layers and with the input layer, but not with the output layer. The term "dropout" refers to dropping out units (hidden and visible) in a neural network (Figure 10-2). It drops some nodes or neurons to dump the variance in weights of a cost function that we're trying to regularize. A new hyperparameter is introduced that specifies the probability at which outputs of the layer are dropped out, or inversely, the probability at which outputs of the layer are retained. The interpretation is an implementation detail that can differ from paper to code library. A common value is a probability of 0.5 for retaining the output of each node in a hidden layer and a value close to 1.0, such as 0.8 (this is called rate or make_prop), for retaining inputs from the visible layer. Some notes to help work with this layer: the dropout rate lets us know how many nodes we will drop in this layer, so the default interpretation of the dropout hyperparameter is the probability of training a given node in a layer, where 1.0 means no dropout and 0.0 means no outputs from the layer.

A good value for dropout in a hidden layer is between 0.5 and 0.8. Input layers use a larger dropout rate, such as of 0.8.

Like other regularization methods, dropout is more effective on those problems where there is a limited amount of training data and the model is likely to overfit the training data. Problems where there is a large amount of training data may see less benefit from using dropout.

When using dropout regularization, it is possible to use larger networks with less risk of overfitting. In fact, a large network (more nodes per layer) may be required, as dropout will probabilistically reduce the capacity of the network. We can see that the dropout makes something happen in our neural network, as it divides the number of nodes by the probability of dropout we initialized, so the number of nodes is equal (#nodes in neural network/probability). A good rule of thumb is to divide the number of nodes in the layer before dropout by the proposed dropout rate and use that as the number of nodes in the new network that uses dropout. For example, a network with 100 nodes and a proposed dropout rate of 0.5 will require 200 nodes (100 / 0.5) when using dropout.

Usage:

```
tf.layers.dropout(inputs, rate=0.5, noise_shape=None,
seed=None, training=False, name=None)
```

Dropout consists of randomly setting a fraction rate of input units to 0 at each update during training time, which helps prevent overfitting. The units that are kept are scaled by 1 / (1 - rate), so that their sum is unchanged at training time and inference time.

— TensorFlow official docs

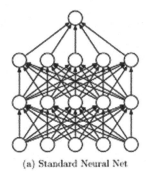
(a) Standard Neural Net

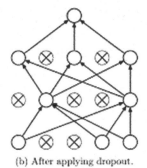
(b) After applying dropout.

Figure 10-2. *How dropout works*

Normalization Techniques

Normalization has always been an active area of research in deep learning. Normalization techniques can decrease your model's training time by a huge factor. Let's state some of the benefits of using normalization. It is called "normalization" because it tries to dump all the data into the same scale: it normalizes each feature so that they maintain the same contribution as every feature, because some features have a higher numerical value than others. This way, our network can be unbiased (to higher value features). By scaling the data in the same scale, it makes the optimization faster, because normalization doesn't allow weights to explode all over the place and restricts them to a certain range.

Normalization helps networks with regularization (only slightly, not significantly). This is in getting our model to train effectively, but this isn't as easy as it sounds. So we will ask ourselves some questions about what makes normalization not so easy; what normalization technique we should use; and, most common, which norm technique would be the best trade-off for computation and accuracy for our network. The answers may be found within a host of normalization techniques. So let's look at them.

Batch Normalization

Let's explore what we mean by "batch" and why we should use it. For a start, we should know that we normalize the input layer by adjusting and scaling the activations. For example, when we have features from 0 to 1, and some from 1 to 1000, we should normalize them to speed up learning. If the input layer is benefiting from it, why not do the same thing for the values in the hidden layers, which are changing all the time, and get ten times or more improvement in the training speed. Batch normalization allows each layer of a network to learn by itself a little bit more independently of other layers. Batch has many good benefits. One is that we can use higher learning rates, because batch normalization makes sure that there's no activation that's gone really high or really low. And that means things that previously couldn't get to train will start to train. It reduces overfitting because it has a slight regularization effect. Similar to **dropout**, it adds some noise to each hidden layer's activations. Batch normalization is a method that normalizes activations in a network across the mini-batch of a definite size. For each feature, batch normalization computes the mean and variance of that feature in the mini-batch. It then subtracts the mean and divides the feature by its mini-batch standard deviation (Figure 10-3).

$$E_x = \frac{1}{m} \sum_{i=1}^{j} \mu_B^{(i)} \qquad \text{Inference mean}$$

$$Var_x = \left(\frac{m}{m-1} \right) \frac{1}{m} \sum_{i=1}^{j} \sigma_B^{2(i)} \qquad \text{Inference variance}$$

$$y = \frac{\gamma}{\sqrt{Var_x + \epsilon}} x + \left(\beta + \frac{\gamma E_x}{\sqrt{Var_x + \epsilon}} \right) \qquad \text{Inference scaling/shifting}$$

Figure 10-3. *The difference between inferences*

Notice that γ and β are learned during training along with the original parameters of the network.

But is there a problem with this technique? Yes, there are many problems—not in general, but with some specific things. The first is with RNN, which we will talk about in Chapter 12. In an RNN, the recurrent activations of each time-step will have a different story to tell (i.e., statistics). This means that we have to fit a separate batch norm layer for each time-step. This makes the model more complicated and space-consuming, because it forces us to store the statistics for each time-step during training. So now, how can we use it with TensorFlow?

```
import tensorflow as tf

is_train = tf.placeholder(tf.bool, name="is_train");

x_norm = tf.layers.batch_normalization(x, training=is_train)

update_ops = tf.get_collection(tf.GraphKeys.UPDATE_OPS)
with tf.control_dependencies(update_ops):
    train_op = optimizer.minimize(loss)
```

So, that is the batch normalization technique we can use in our deep neural network. There are many more normalization techniques in deep learning. Let's talk about weight normalization.

Weight Normalization

In batch normalization we normalize the activation function, but now we will normalize the weight. Weight normalization is a method developed by OpenAI, in which weight normalization reparametrizes the weights of any layer in the neural network in the following way:

$$w = \frac{g}{\|v\|} v$$

It separates the weight vector from its direction. This has a similar effect as in batch normalization with variance. As for the mean, the developers of this weight normalization combine mean-only batch normalization and weight normalization to get the desired output even in small mini-batches. It means that they subtract out the mean of the minibatch, but do not divide by the variance.

Finally, what we need to know is that they use weight normalization instead of dividing by variance.

Layer Normalization

Layer normalization is a method developed by Geoffrey Hinton. Compared with weight normalization, layer normalization is slightly harder to grasp intuitively. It normalizes input across the features instead of normalizing input features across the batch dimension in batch normalization. So, when we talk about batch normalization, Batch normalization normalizes the input features across the batch dimension. So, we might say at this point that batch and layer normalization may be similar in some way. Let's see the following equations to explore that (Figure 10-4):

$$\text{Batch normalization}$$

$$\mu_j = \frac{1}{m} \sum_{i=1}^{m} x_{ij}$$
$$\sigma_j^2 = \frac{1}{m} \sum_{i=1}^{m} (x_{ij} - \mu_j)^2$$
$$\hat{x_{ij}} = \frac{x_{ij} - \mu_j}{\sqrt{\sigma_j^2 + \epsilon}}$$

$$\text{Layer Normalization}$$

$$\mu_i = \frac{1}{m} \sum_{j=1}^{m} x_{ij}$$
$$\sigma_i^2 = \frac{1}{m} \sum_{j=1}^{m} (x_{ij} - \mu_i)^2$$
$$\hat{x_{ij}} = \frac{x_{ij} - \mu_i}{\sqrt{\sigma_i^2 + \epsilon}}$$

Figure 10-4. *The layer and batch normalization*

The equations seem almost identical, so what is the difference? The difference is that in batch normalization, the statistics are computed across the batch and are the same for each example in the batch. In contrast, in layer normalization, the statistics are computed across each feature and are independent of other examples.

Let's see an image (Figure 10-5).

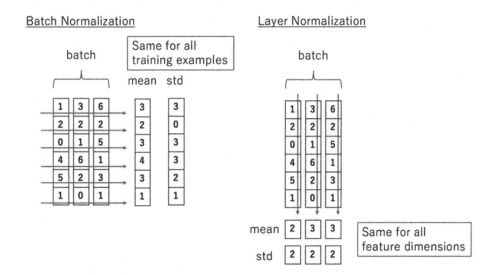

Figure 10-5. *An example of batch and layer normalization*

It solves the problem in batch normalization, as layer normalization performs better than the batch norm in the case of RNNs. But the similarity doesn't end at this point; there is one more similarity to layer normalization called *instance normalization*.

Instance Normalization

Layer normalization and instance normalization are very similar to each other. However, the difference between them is that instance normalization normalizes across each channel in each training example instead of normalizing across input features in a training example. Unlike batch normalization, the instance normalization layer is applied at test time as well (due to the nondependency of mini-batch). This technique was originally devised for style transfer. The problem that instance normalization tries to address is that the network should be agnostic to the contrast of the original image. Experimental results show that instance normalization performs well on style transfer when replacing batch normalization. Recently, instance normalization has also been used as a replacement for batch normalization in GANs (generative adversarial networks).

Group Normalization

Group normalization, as its name suggests, normalizes over a group of channels for each training example. We can say that group norm is in between instance and layer normalization. How does this hypertechnique work? When we put all the channels into a single group, group normalization becomes layer normalization and when we put each channel into a different group, it becomes instance normalization. Though layer normalization and instance normalization were both effective on RNNs and style transfer, respectively, they were still inferior to batch normalization for image recognition tasks. Group normalization was able to achieve much closer performance to batch normalization with a batch size of 32 on ImageNet, and outperformed it on smaller batch sizes. For tasks like object detection and segmentation that use much higher resolution images (and therefore cannot increase their batch size due to memory constraints), group normalization was shown to be a very effective normalization method. So the question is, if we can only use layer normalization or instance normalization, what makes us use the hypertechnique between them? The answer is very easy: we need what layer normalization adds. One of the implicit assumptions that layer normalization makes is that *all channels are* **equally important** when computing the mean. This assumption is not always true in convolutional layers. So, we need to use an instance that make neurons near the edge of an image and neurons near the center of an image have very different activation statistics. This means that computing different statistics for different channels can give models much needed flexibility. Channels in an image are not completely independent though, so being able to leverage the statistics of nearby channels is an advantage that group normalization has over instance normalization (Figure 10-6).

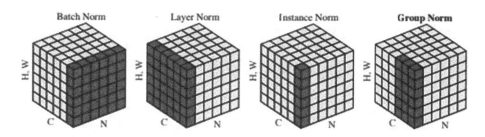

Figure 10-6. *Different normalization techniques*

Now that we've finish talking about some of the normalization techniques in deep learning, we need to say that there are more techniques to normalize the deep learning layers, and the deep learning community is still working on methods that enhances performance and prevent overfitting. In the next chapters we will discuss the applications of deep learning convolution and sequence models, with case studies about them. We are getting to the end of the pipeline, which you can make yourself.

Summary

In this chapter, we worked with optimization techniques that optimize the learning rate and make gradients reach the optimum local minimum. We talked about dropout—the regularization technique in a neural network—and how it is very useful, and the connection between it and normalization. We learned that normalization is a very good tool in deep learning, that it comes from statistics and makes the neural network more adaptable to data by scaling it. We saw how we can choose the most important hyperparameter learning rate and its connection with adaptive learning. In the next few chapters we will talk about models, the last stage in the deep learning pipeline; we will have some applications about deep learning, and we will talk about some case studies. So we hope you had a good workout with this chapter.

## CHAPTER 11

Convolutional Neural Network

In the previous chapters, we studied fully connected multilayer neural networks and their training, using backpropagation. In a typical multilayer neural network layer, with n input nodes and m neurons, we need to learn $n \times m$ parameters or weights. While a multilayer neural network may perform well in some cases—in particular, for those where the features of different dimensions are independent—there are some additional properties in the connection architecture that we might desire. For example, if it is known that the dimensions of the input data are strongly correlated or that the size of multilayer neural networks (both the number of layers and the number of neurons in each layer) must be limited for computational considerations, should there be any architectural changes introduced to a standard multilayer neural network to accommodate this additional constraint about the data or the network complexity?

Deep learning has flourished in recent years in the processing of unstructured data, especially images, text, audio, and speech. Taking convolutional neural networks (CNNs) into consideration, it works like magic when the data is images. Whenever there is a topology associated with the data, convolutional neural networks do a good job of extracting the important features out of the images.

© Hisham El-Amir and Mahmoud Hamdy 2020
H. El-Amir and M. Hamdy, *Deep Learning Pipeline*,
https://doi.org/10.1007/978-1-4842-5349-6_11

From an architectural perspective, CNNs are inspired by multilayer perceptrons; by imposing local connectivity constraints between neurons of adjacent layers, CNNs exploit local spatial correlation. The core element of convolutional neural networks is the processing of data through the convolution operation. Convolution of any signal with another signal produces a third signal that may reveal more information about the signal than the original signal itself.

What is a Convolutional Neural Network

A convolutional neural network (CNN) is a deep learning algorithm that can take in an input image, assign importance (learnable weights and biases) to various aspects/objects in the image, and be able to differentiate one from the other. The preprocessing required in a CNN is much lower as compared with other classification algorithms. Although in primitive methods filters are hand engineered, with enough training, CNNs have the ability to learn these filters/characteristics.

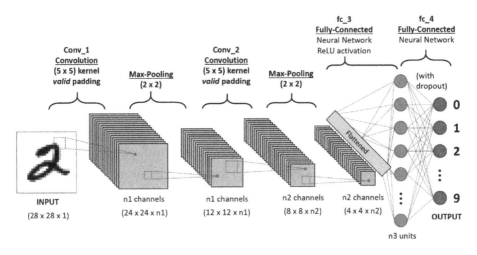

Figure 11-1. *An example of a CNN*

The architecture of a convolutional neural network (Figure 11-1) is analogous to that of the connectivity pattern of neurons in the human brain and was inspired by the organization of the visual cortex. Individual neurons respond to stimuli only in a restricted region of the visual field known as the *receptive field*. A collection of such fields overlaps to cover the entire visual area.

Convolution Operation

The convolution of a temporal or spatial signal with another signal produces a modified version of the initial signal. The modified signal may have better feature representation than the original signal, suitable for a specific task. For example, by convolving a grayscale image as a 2-D signal with another signal, generally called a filter or kernel, an output signal can be obtained that contains the edges of the original image. Edges in an image can correspond to object boundaries, changes in illumination, changes in material property, discontinuities in depth, and so on, which may be useful for several applications. Knowledge about the linear time-invariant or shift-invariant properties of systems helps one appreciate the convolution of signals better. We will discuss this first before moving on to convolution itself.

One-Dimensional Convolution

Intuitively, convolution measures the degree of overlap between one function and the reversed and translated version of another function. In the discrete case, $y(t) = x(t) * h(t) = \sum_{i=-\infty}^{+\infty} x(i)h(t-i)$

Similarly, in the continuous domain the convolution of two functions can be expressed as $y(t) = x(t) * h(t) = \int_{i=-\infty}^{+\infty} x(i)h(t-i)di$

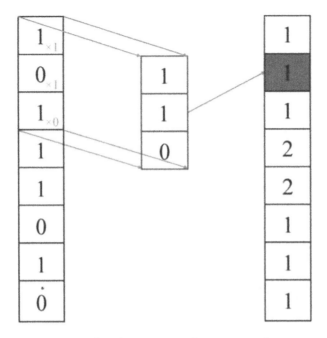

Figure 11-2. *An example of 1-D convolution masking*

Figure 11-2 shows how the equation of 1-dimensional convolution works in simple terms. Intuitively, it works like a mask that moves over the data input, which is the left vector. In each moving step it takes three neighbors, applies the masking values over the three, and assigns the output of the whole equation to a single scaler in the output vector.

You can see that in its first steps the mask takes the first three neighbors/pair in the input vector, which are $[1, 0, 1]$, then multiplies them by the mask values $[1, 1, 0][1, 1, 0]$. The multiplication is a vector-wise operation that multiplies the first input with its equivalent, the mask, and then multiplies the second input with the second one on the mask, and so on. After three multiplications happen, we add all three outputs of these operations, and the final result will be a single scalar that is assigned to the second element of the output vector. Wait a second: you wonder now why we assign the output to the second element in the right output vector, because it is not the first step. The first step was taking the input pair and adding to them a zero padding, generating the input pair [0, 1, 0].

Seeing the convolution in such way makes it easier to understand than the preceding equations. Also, you now may understand why the convolution is important, as you change the mask values to extract certain knowledge from data input. But if you do not understand or see how convolution may extract knowledge/features until now, you will see how in a few minutes.

Two-Dimensional Convolution

As we described, convolution involves both one-dimensional and two-dimensional operations; one-dimensional is referred to as 1-D convolution or just convolution. Otherwise, if the convolution is performed between two-dimensions spanning along two mutually perpendicular dimensions (i.e., if the single observation is two-dimensional in nature or, practically speaking, it is an image or matrix), then it will be referred to as 2-D convolution. This concept can be extended to involve multidimensional matrices, due to which we can have multidimensional convolution.

In the image/computer vision domain, convolution is performed by multiplying and accumulating the instantaneous values of the overlapping samples corresponding to two input images, one of which is flipped. This definition of 1-D convolution is applicable even for 2-D convolution except that, in the latter case, one of the inputs is flipped twice.

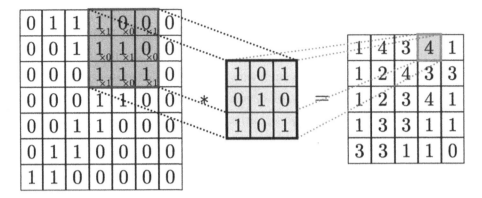

Figure 11-3. *2-D convolution masking*

Figure 11-3 shows the kind of operation that is extensively used in the field of digital image processing, wherein the 2-D matrix representing the image will be convolved with a comparatively smaller matrix called 2-D kernel.

Padding and Stride

Before going deeper into convolution, you need to know one extra thing; actually there are two important concepts you need to know and fully grasp. Both padding and stride can change the way your model sees the input observation; also, changing their parameters impacts the shape of the output feature map.

Although the convolutional layer is very simple, it is capable of achieving sophisticated and impressive results. Nevertheless, it can be challenging to develop an understanding for how the shape of the filters impacts the shape of the output feature map and how related configuration hyperparameters such as padding and stride should be configured.

In a convolution operation we have a kernel, and to make the final output of the operation more informative we use padding in an image matrix or any kind of input array. Adding padding to the input makes the kernel start giving more information to the edges of the input observation, thus making all the information and features hidden in edges of the input appear in our output.

There are three types of padding, stated as follows:

- *Padding full*: This type shows the importance of extracting the information from the edges of the input. When you use full padding on the input, it makes the kernel in the convolution operation treat each pixel with the same priority, which means the kernel steps over the edges with the same amount as the center pixels.

- *Padding same*: In this type of padding, we need to make the output observation shape from convolution operation get the same shape as the input observation. For instance, if we have a 32×32 image as input, the output will have the same shape, 32×32.

- *Padding valid*: Simply, valid convolution means no padding at all, and this may work for you as a dimensionality reduction for an input observation (image). For instance, an image with 32×32 input with kernel filter of 3×3 will generate a 30×30 output image.

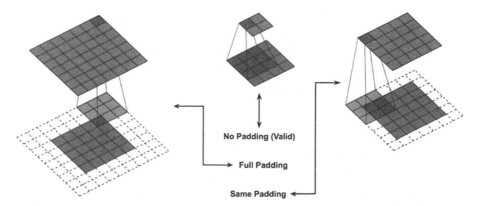

Figure 11-4. *The difference between valid, full, and same padding*

In Figure 11-4 you can see that on the left the full-padding to the input matrix makes the filter walk on each real-value (blue) of the matrix equally. So, in the figure the filter will walk/moves/slides on each blue pixel nine times wherever the pixel position is, and that creates a bigger output matrix size that will have all the representation and more features extracted. On the other hand, using no padding or valid padding will create the smallest output, as the filter only walks on the input matrix as it is; that means that there are pixels the filter will visit only one time and ones that the filter will visit many times. However, if you want the output to be equal to your input matrix, you can consider using same padding, and that will create an output matrix that is similar in shape to the input matrix.

On the other side, stride controls how the filter convolves around the input volume. In the examples we had earlier, the filter convolves around the input volume by shifting one unit at a time. The amount by which the filter shifts is the stride. In that case, the stride was implicitly set at 1. Stride is normally set in a way so that the output volume is an integer and not a fraction. Let's look at an example. Let's imagine a 7×7 input volume, a 3×3 filter (disregard the 3rd dimension for simplicity), and a stride of 1. This is the case that we're accustomed to. As you can see in Figure 11-5, the filter walks through the input with two pixels stepping to the right, and to the bottom too, and this will make the output matrix much smaller, as the overlaps between steps are reduced.

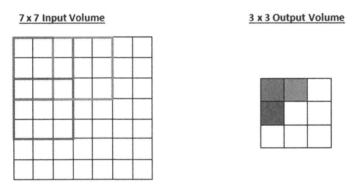

7 x 7 Input Volume   **3 x 3 Output Volume**

Figure 11-5. *The difference between the Valid, Full, Same Padding*

Common Image-Processing Filters

Let's discuss image-processing filters commonly used on 2-D images. Make sure to be clear with notations, since the natural way of indexing an image doesn't align well with how one would prefer to define the x and y axes. Whenever we represent an image-processing filter or an image in the coordinate space, n_1 and n_2 are the discrete coordinates for the x and y directions. The column index of the image in NumPy matrix form coincides nicely with the x axis, whereas the row index moves in the opposite direction of the y axis. Also, it doesn't matter which pixel location one chooses as the origin for the image signal while doing convolution. Based on whether zero padding is used or not, one can handle the edges accordingly. Since the filter kernel is of a smaller size, we generally flip the filter kernel and then slide it over the image, not the other way around.

Mean and Median Filters

The mean filter or average filter is a low-pass filter that computes the local average of the pixel intensity at any specific point. Figure 11-6 shows you how the mean filter is calculated in different types, based on what the application is going to use.

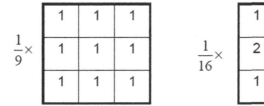

Figure 11-6. *How the mean filter is calculated*

Here, the matrix entry h22 corresponds to the entry at the origin. So, at any given point, the convolution will represent the average of the pixel intensities at that point. The following code illustrates how one can convolve an image with an image-processing filter such as the mean filter.

Please note that in many Python implementations, we would be using OpenCV to perform basic operations on the image, such as reading the image, converting the image from RGB format to grayscale format, and so on. OpenCV is an open source image-processing package that has a rich set of methodologies for image processing. Readers are advised to explore OpenCV or any other image-processing toolbox in order to get accustomed to the basic image-processing functions.

First things first: we need to import all the needed packages and functions to make sure that there's no import error on the way. We will import cv2 for OpenCV operations, matplotlib for viewing the image, NumPy for creating the filter and any matrix operation, and finally convolve2d from scipy.signal for convolution operation.

```
# IMPORTING PACKAGES
import cv2
import matplotlib.pyplot as plt
import numpy as np
from scipy.signal import convolve2d
```

After loading the packages, we now need to load the image that we want to make the operations on. The Lena Forsen image is one of the most famous images in the image processing field. In the following code we will load it, and then transform it into a gray image for the sack of simplicity.

```
# LOADING AND TRANSFORMING IMAGE
img = cv2.imread('/content/lena_forsen.png')
gray = cv2.cvtColor(img, cv2.COLOR_BGR2GRAY)
plt.imshow(gray,cmap='gray')
```

Figure 11-7 shows the loaded image in grayscale.

Figure 11-7. *The gray loaded image*

After loading the image, we need to add some noise to it, to see how the filter will somehow fix the noise. In the following code we will add a type of noise called Gaussian noise. Then we will try to fix it.

```
# PROCESSING IMAGE
mean = 0
var = 100
sigma = var**0.5
row,col = 220, 220
gauss = np.random.normal(mean,sigma,(row,col))
gauss = gauss.reshape(row,col)
gray_noisy = gray + gauss
plt.imshow(gray_noisy,cmap='gray')
```

Now, after we add the noise, we need to know how the noise will affect the image quality. In Figure 11-8, you will see the image with the noise all over it.

Figure 11-8.   *The Guassian noise on the image*

```
# CREATE AND APPLY MEAN FILTER
Hm = np.array([[1,1,1],[1,1,1],[1,1,1]])/float(9)
Gm = convolve2d(gray_noisy,Hm,mode='same')
plt.imshow(Gm,cmap='gray')
```

At the end, we will create and apply the mean filter to the image; we will use convolve2d for that purpose, to apply the filter to the image. In Figure 11-9 you can see the resulting image of the operation from the preceding code.

Figure 11-9. *The image after the mean filter*

The mean filter is mostly used to reduce the noise in an image. If there is some white Gaussian noise present in the image, the mean filter will reduce the noise, since it averages over its neighborhood, hence the white noise of the zero mean will be suppressed. As we can see from Figure 11-9, the Gaussian white noise is reduced once the image has been convolved with the mean filter. The new image has fewer high-frequency components and thus is relatively less sharp than the image before convolution, but the filter has done a good job of reducing the white noise.

One the other hand, a 2-D median filter replaces each pixel in a neighborhood with the median pixel intensity in that neighborhood, based on the filter size. The median filter is good for removing salt and pepper noise. This type of noise presents itself in images in the form of black and white pixels, and is generally caused by sudden disturbances while capturing the images. The following code illustrates how salt and pepper noise can be added to an image, and then how the noise can be suppressed using a median filter.

First, we select some random indices to do the operations (adding the noise) on it.

```
np.random.seed(0)
gray_sp = gray*1
sp_indices = np.random.randint(0,21,[row,col])
```

Then we will iterate over the indicis and set the values on the image to either 0 or 255, creating a salt-like noise. The following code describes the iteration, and Figure 11-10 shows the result of the noise on the image.

```
for i in range(row):
  for j in range(col):
    if sp_indices[i,j] == 0:
      gray_sp[i,j] = 0
    if sp_indices[i,j] == 20:
      gray_sp[i,j] = 255
plt.imshow(gray_sp,cmap='gray')
```

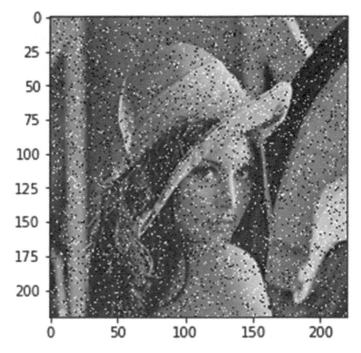

Figure 11-10. *The salt and pepper noise on the image*

Now we need to remove the salty noise from the image. Lucky for us, cv2 has an implementation of the image. The following code describes how to use it.

```
gray_sp_removed = cv2.medianBlur(gray_sp,3)
plt.imshow(gray_sp_removed,cmap='gray')
```

Figure 11-11. *The median filter effect on the noise in the image*

As we can see, the salt and pepper noise has been removed by the median filter (Figure 11-11).

Gaussian Filter

The Gaussian filter is a modified version of the mean filter, where the weights of the impulse function are distributed normally around the origin. Weight is highest at the center of the filter and falls normally away from the center. A Gaussian filter can be created with the following code. As we can see, the intensity falls in a Gaussian fashion away from the origin. The Gaussian filter, when displayed as an image, has the highest intensity at the origin and then diminishes for pixels away from the center. Gaussian filters are used to reduce noise by suppressing the high-frequency components. However, in its pursuit of suppressing the high-frequency components, it ends up producing a blurred image, called Gaussian blur.

In Figure 11-12, the original image is convolved with the Gaussian filter to produce an image that has Gaussian blur. We then subtract the blurred image from the original image to get the high-frequency component of the image. A small portion of the high-frequency image is added to the original image to improve the sharpness of the image.

```
f = np.zeros((20,20))
for i in range(20):
  for j in range(20):
    f[i,j] = np.exp(-((i-10)**2 + (j-10)**2)/10)
plt.imshow(f,cmap='gray')
```

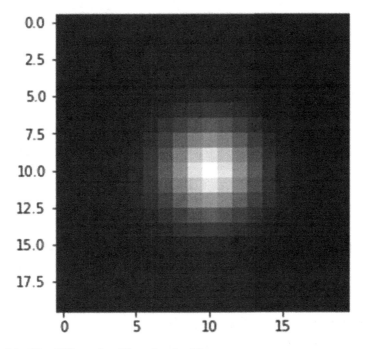

Figure 11-12. *What the filter looks like*

As you can see in Figure 11-12, it seems that the filter focuses on the middle pixel. After applying this filter on the image, you can see in Figure 11-13 that the image blurred. The following code describes how to apply the filter on the image.

```
gray_blur = convolve2d(gray,f,mode='same')
plt.imshow(gray_blur,cmap='gray')
```

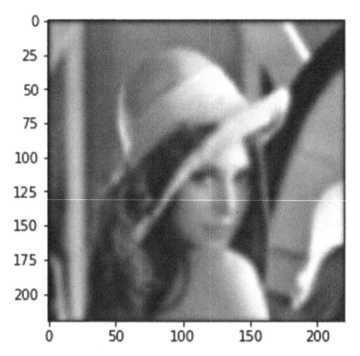

Figure 11-13. *The image after applying the filter*

The following code describes how to get back one step, enhancing the image to its real state. And Figure 11-14 shows the image returned to its real state without the blurring.

```
gray_enhanced = gray + 0.025*gray_blur
plt.imshow(gray_enhanced,cmap='gray')
```

Figure 11-14. *The image after enhancement*

Sobel Edge-Detection Filter

The Sobel operator, sometimes called the Sobel–Feldman operator or
Sobel filter, is used in image processing and computer vision, particularly
within edge detection algorithms where it creates an image emphasizing
edges.

The output response of a Sobel edge convolution detector along
both the horizontal and vertical axes can be expressed by the following
Gx and *Gy* matrices, respectively. The Sobel detectors are extensions of
the horizontal and vertical gradient filters just illustrated. Instead of only
taking the gradient at the point, it also takes the sum of the gradients at
the points on either side of it. Also, it gives double weight to the point of
interest. See Figure 11-15.

-1	0	+1
-2	0	+2
-1	0	+1

Gx

+1	+2	+1
0	0	0
-1	-2	-1

Gy

Figure 11-15. *The Sobel filter along with the two axes*

The convolution of the image with the Sobel filters is illustrated in the following code:

```
Hx = np.array([[ 1,0, -1],[2,0,-2],[1,0,-1]],dtype=np.float32)
Gx = convolve2d(gray,Hx,mode='same')
plt.imshow(Gx,cmap='gray')
```

Figure 11-16 shows the result of the preceding code. In the figure you can see that some of the edges appear strongly, and that's because the filter used can be considered a half filter. If you continue, you can see that the final result contains all the edges in the image.

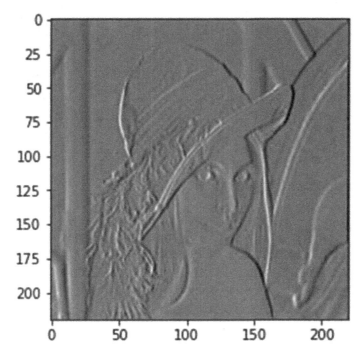

Figure 11-16. *The image after applying the X-axis filter*

And here is the other half filter, the Y-axis filter. Here you will find that the result may be similar to the result of the preceding code, but with some focus you can see some differences between the results (Figure 11-17).

```
Hy = np.array([[ -1,-2, -1],[0,0,0],[1,2,1]],dtype=np.float32)
Gy = convolve2d(gray,Hy,mode='same')
plt.imshow(Gy,cmap='gray')
```

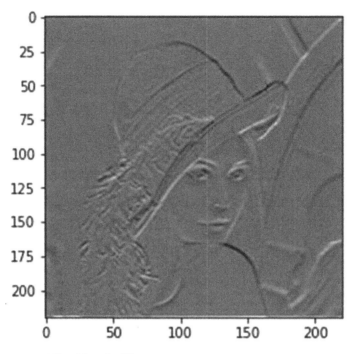

Figure 11-17. *The Y-axis filter*

Now, by combining the both filters (but squared), you will see the wanted result. In Figure 11-18 you can see the output of the following code; the result shows how the edges of the images look.

```
G = (Gx*Gx + Gy*Gy)**0.5
plt.imshow(G,cmap='gray')
```

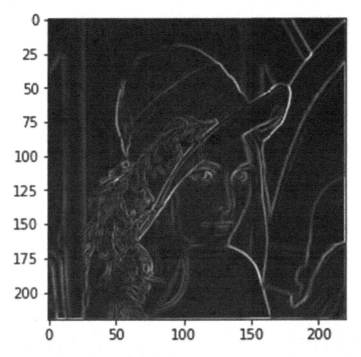

Figure 11-18. *The edges of the image*

The preceding code has the logic required to convolve the image with the Sobel filters. The *horizontal Sobel* filter detects edges in the horizontal direction, whereas the *vertical Sobel* filter detects edges in the vertical direction. Both are high-pass filters, since they attenuate the low frequencies from the signals and capture only the high-frequency components within the image. Edges are important features for an image, and help one detect local changes within an image. Edges are generally present on the boundary between the two regions in an image, and are often the first step in retrieving information from images. We saw this in the outputs of the preceding codes.

The equation that runs the combination between both halves of the filter is:

$$C(x,y) = \sqrt{\left(I_x(x,y)\right)^2 + \left(I_y(x,y)\right)^2}$$

where $C(x, y)$ denotes the pixel intensity function for the combined Sobel filter, and $I_y(x, y)$ denotes the pixel intensity of the image obtained through the vertical Sobel filter.

Identity Transform

The filter for identity transform through convolution is as follows.

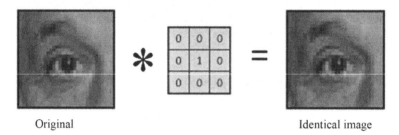

Original   Identical image

Figure 11-19. *The identity filter*

Figure 11-19 illustrates a unity transform through convolution. The implementation is like the mean filter, but with a simple modification: instead of a mean filter with 1/9 at each value of the filter pixel, we put just 1 in the middle pixel, and all others are 0s.

Convolutional Neural Networks

Convolutional neural networks (CNNs) are based on the convolution of images, and detect features based on filters that are learned by the CNN through training. For example, we don't apply any known filter, such as the ones for the detection of edges or for removing Gaussian noise, but through the training of the convolutional neural network the algorithm learns image-processing filters on its own that might be very different from normal image-processing filters. For supervised training, the filters are learned in such a way that the overall cost function is reduced as much as possible. Generally, the first convolutional layer learns to detect edges, while the second may learn to detect more complex shapes that can be formed by combining different edges, such as circles and rectangles, and so on. The third layer and beyond learn much more complicated features based on the features generated in the previous layer.

The good thing about convolutional neural networks is the sparse connectivity that results from weight sharing, which greatly reduces the number of parameters to learn. The same filter can learn to detect the same edge in any given portion of the image through its equivariance property, which is a great property of convolution useful for feature detection.

Layers of Convolutional Neural Networks

The following are the typical layers of a convolutional neural network:

- *Input layer*: will hold the pixel intensity of the image. For example, an input image with width 64, height 64, and depth 3 for the red, green, and blue color channels (RGB) would have input dimensions of 64x64x3.

- *Convolutional layer*: will take images from the preceding layers and convolve with them the specified number of filters to create images called output feature maps. The number of output feature maps is equal to the specified number of filters. Until now, CNNs in TensorFlow have used mostly 2-D filters; however, 3-D convolution filters have been introduced recently.

391

- *Activation functions*: For CNNs they are generally ReLUs, which we discussed in a previous chapter. The output dimension is the same as the input after passing through the ReLU activation layers. The ReLU layer adds nonlinearity in the network and at the same time provides nonsaturating gradients for positive net inputs.

- *Pooling layer*: will downsample the 2-D activation maps along the height and width dimensions. The depth or the number of activation maps is not compromised and remains the same.

- *Fully connected layers*: contain traditional neurons that receive different sets of weights from the preceding layers; there is no weight sharing between them as is typical for convolution operations. Each neuron in this layer will be connected either to all the neurons in the previous layer or to all the coordinate-wise outputs in the output maps through separate weights. For classification, the class output neurons receive inputs from the final fully connected layers.

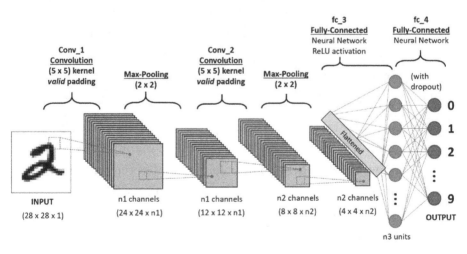

Figure 11-20. *A simple CNN*

Figure 11-20 illustrates a basic CNN that uses one convolutional layer, and one pooling layer followed by a fully connected layer and, finally, the output classification layer. The network tries to detect the number inside the image, which is 2. The output unit can be taken to have a sigmoid activation function, since it's a binary classification problem for images. Generally, for most of the CNN architectures, a few to several convolutional layer-ReLU layer-pooling layer combinations are stacked one after another before the fully connected layers. We will discuss the different architectures at a later point in time. For now, let's look at the different layers in much more detail.

Input Layer

The input to this layer is images. Generally, the images are fed in batches as four-dimensional tensors, where the first dimension is specific to the image index, second and third dimensions are specific to the height and width of the image, and the fourth dimension corresponds to the different channels. For a colored image, generally we have the *red* (R), *green* (G), and *blue* (B) channels, while for grayscale images we have only one channel. The number of images in a batch would be determined by the mini-batch size chosen for the mini-batch stochastic gradient descent. The batch size is one for stochastic gradient descent. The inputs can be fed to the input layer in mini-batches through TensorFlow placeholder `tf. placeholder` at runtime

Convolutional Layer

Convolution is the heart of any CNN network. TensorFlow supports both 2-D and 3-D convolutions. However, 2-D convolutions are more common, since 3-D convolutions are computationally memory intensive. The input images or intermediate images in the form of output feature maps are 2-D convolved with 2-D filters of the size specified. 2-D convolution happens along the spatial dimensions, whereas there is no convolution along the depth channel of the image volume. For each depth channel, the same number of feature maps is generated, and then they are summed together along the depth dimension before they pass through the *ReLU* activations. These filters help to detect features in the images. The deeper the convolutional layer is in the network, the more complicated features it learns. For instance, the initial convolutional layer might learn to detect edges in an image, while the second convolutional layer might learn to connect the edges to form geometric shapes such as circles and rectangles. The even deeper convolutional layers might learn to detect more complicated features; for example, in cat vs. dog classification it might learn to detect eyes, nose, or other body parts of the animals.

In a CNN, only the size of the filters is specified; the weights are initialized to arbitrary values before the start of training. The weights of the filters are learned through the CNN training process, hence they might not represent the traditional image-processing filters such as *mean, median, Gaussian, Sobel* or other kinds of filters. Instead the learned filters would be such that the overall loss function defined is minimized or a good generalization is achieved based on the validation. Although it might not learn the traditional edge detection filter, it would learn several filters that detect edges in some form, since edges are good feature detectors for images.

Some of the terms with which one should be familiar while defining the convolutional layer are as follows:

> *Filter size*: Filter size defines the height and width of the filter kernel. A filter kernel of size 3 × 3 would have nine weights. Generally, these filters are initialized and slid over the input image for convolution without flipping these filters. Technically, when convolution is performed without flipping the filter kernel, it's called cross-correlation

and not convolution. However, it doesn't matter, as we can consider the filters learned as a flipped version of image processing filters.

Stride: The stride determines the number of pixels to move in each spatial direction while performing convolution. In normal convolution of signals, we generally don't skip any pixels and instead compute the convolution sum at each pixel location, hence we have a stride of 1 along both spatial directions for 2-D signals. However, one may choose to skip every alternate pixel location while convolving, and thus choose a stride of 2. If a stride of 2 is chosen along both the height and the width of the image, then after convolving the output image would be approximately 1/4 of the input image sizes. Why it is *approximately* 1/4 and not exactly 1/4 of the original image or feature-map sizes will be covered in our next topic of discussion.

Padding: When we convolve an image of a specific size by a filter, the resulting image is generally smaller than the original image. For example, if we convolve a 5×5 2-D image by a filter of size 3 × 3, the resulting image is 3 × 3.

Padding is an approach that appends zeros to the boundary of an image to control the size of the output of convolution. The convolved output image length L' along a specific spatial dimension is given by

$$L' = \frac{L - K + 2P}{S} + 1$$

where L denotes the Length of the input image in a specific dimension and K is length of the kernel/filter in a specific dimension, while P denotes zeros padded along a dimension in either end and S stands for stride of the convolution.

In general, for a stride of 1 the image size along each dimension is reduced by $(K-1)/2$ on either end, where K is the length of the filter kernel along that dimension. So, to keep the output image the same as that of the input image, a pad length of $(K-1)/2$ would be required.

In TensorFlow, padding can be chosen as either "**VALID**" or "**SAME**." **SAME** ensures that the output spatial dimensions of the image are the same as those of the input spatial dimensions in cases where a stride of 1 is chosen. It uses zero padding to achieve this. It tries to keep the zero pad length even on both sides of a dimension, but if the total pad length for that dimension is odd, the extra length is added to the right for the horizontal dimension and to the bottom for the vertical dimension.

For recap, **VALID** doesn't use zero padding; hence, the output image dimension would be smaller than the input image dimensions, even for a stride of 1.

```
def conv2d(x,W,b,strides=1):
  x = tf.nn.conv2d(x,W,strides=[1,strides,strides,1],padding=
  'SAME')
  x = tf.nn.bias_add(x,b)
  return tf.nn.relu(x)
```

Pooling Layer

A pooling operation on an image generally summarizes a locality of an image, the locality being given by the size of the filter kernel—also called the receptive field. The summarization generally happens in the form of max pooling or average pooling. In max pooling, the maximum pixel intensity of a locality is taken as the representative of that locality. In average pooling, the average of the pixel intensities around a locality is taken as the representative of that locality. Pooling reduces the spatial dimensions of an image. The kernel size that determines the locality is generally chosen as 2 × 2, whereas the stride is chosen as 2. This reduces the image size to about 1/4 the size of the original image.

```
def maxpool2d(x,stride=2):
  return tf.nn.max_pool(x, ksize=[1,stride,stride,1],
strides=[1,stride,stride,1], padding='SAME')
```

Backpropagation Through the Convolutional and Pooling Layers

In an earlier chapter we introduced the backpropagation algorithm and we described the backward path for perceptrons. Now we will try to understand how the backward pass for a single convolutional layer works, by taking a simple case wherein the number of channels is one across all computations.

Backpropagation through a convolutional layer is much like backpropagation for a multilayer perceptron network. The only difference is that the weight connections are sparse, since the same weights are shared by different input neighborhoods to create an output feature map. Each output feature map is the result of the convolution of an image or a feature map from the previous layer, with a filter kernel whose values are the weights that we need to learn through backpropagation. The weights in the filter kernel are shared for a specific input–output feature-map combination.

The following convolution operation takes an input X of size $3x3$ using a single filter W of size 2 × 2 without any padding, and stride = 1, generating an output H of size 2 × 2. Also note that, while performing the forward pass, we will cache the variables X and filter W. This will help us while performing the backward pass (Figure 11-21).

X_11	X_12	X_13
X_21	X_22	X_22
X_31	X_32	X_33

W_11	W_12
W_21	W_22

h_11	h_12
h_21	h_22

Figure 11-21. *The input, weights, and output of the convolutional layer*

$$h_{11} = W_{11}X_{11} + W_{12}X_{12} + W_{21}X_{21} + W_{22}X_{22}$$

$$h_{12} = W_{11}X_{12} + W_{12}X_{13} + W_{21}X_{22} + W_{22}X_{23}$$

$$h_{21} = W_{11}X_{21} + W_{12}X_{22} + W_{21}X_{31} + W_{22}X_{32}$$

$$h_{22} = W_{11}X_{22} + W_{12}X_{23} + W_{21}X_{32} + W_{22}X_{33}$$

Note   Here, we are performing the convolution operation without flipping the filter. This is also referred to as the cross-correlation operation in literature. The preceding figure is provided just for the sake of clarity.

Before moving further, make note of the following notations.

$$\partial h_{ij} \text{represents } \frac{\partial L}{\partial h_{ij}}$$

$$\partial w_{ij} \text{represents } \frac{\partial L}{\partial w_{ij}}$$

Now, for implementing the backpropagation step for the current layer, we can assume that we get ∂h as input (from the backward pass of the next layer), and our aim is to calculate ∂w and ∂x. It is important to understand that ∂x (or ∂h for the previous layer) would be the input for the backward pass of the previous layer. This is the core principle behind the success of backpropagation.

398

$$\partial W_{11} = X_{11}\partial h_{11} + X_{12}\partial h_{12} + X_{21}\partial h_{21} + X_{22}\partial h_{22}$$

$$\partial W_{12} = X_{12}\partial h_{11} + X_{13}\partial h_{12} + X_{22}\partial h_{21} + X_{23}\partial h_{22}$$

$$\partial W_{21} = X_{21}X_{11} + X_{22}\partial h_{12} + X_{31}\partial h_{21} + X_{32}\partial h_{22}$$

$$\partial W_{22} = X_{22}X_{11} + X_{23}\partial h_{12} + X_{32}\partial h_{21} + X_{33}\partial h_{22}$$

Each weight in the filter contributes to each pixel in the output map. Thus, any change in weight in the filter will affect all the output pixels. Thus, all these changes add up to contribute to the final loss. Therefore, we can easily calculate the derivatives as follows.

Weight Sharing Through Convolution and Its Advantages

Weight sharing through convolution greatly reduces the number of parameters in the convolutional neural network. Imagine we created a feature map of size $k \times k$ from an image of $n \times n$ size with full connections instead of convolutions. There would be k^2n^2 weights for that one feature map alone, which are a lot of weights to learn. Instead, since in convolution the same weights are shared across locations defined by the filter kernel size, the number of parameters to learn is reduced by a huge factor. In cases of convolution, as in this scenario, we just need to learn the weights for the specific filter kernel. Since the filter size is relatively small with respect to the image, the number of weights is reduced significantly. For any image, we generate several feature maps corresponding to different filter kernels. Each filter kernel learns to detect a different kind of feature. The feature maps created are again convolved with other filter kernels to learn even more complex features in subsequent layers.

Translation Equivariance and Invariance

The convolution operation provides translational equivariance. That is, if a feature Z_1 in an input produces a specific feature Z_2 in the output, then even if feature Z_1 is translated around in the image, feature Z_2 would continue to be generated at different locations of the output (Figure 11-22).

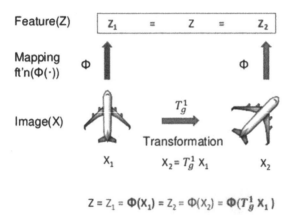

Figure 11-22. *Invariance*

Equivariance

: Mapping preserves algebraic structure of transformation

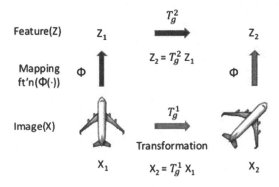

$Z_1 \neq Z_2$ but keeps the relationship $Z_2 = T_g^2 Z_1 = T_g^2 \Phi(X_1) = \Phi(T_g^1 X_1)$

: Invariance is special case of equivariance where T_g^2 is the identity.

Figure 11-23. *Equivariance*

Convolution still produces the same feature for the digit, irrespective of the translation. This property of convolution is called translational equivariance. In fact, if the digit is represented by a set of pixel intensities, x, and f is the translation operation on x, while g is the convolution operation with a filter kernel, then the following holds true for convolution: $g(f(x)) = f(g(x))$.

In our case, $f(x)$ produces the translated plan in the Figure 11-23 and the translated plan is convolved through g to produce the activated feature for the same plan, as seen in the other figure. This activated feature for the plan (i.e., $(f(x))$) could also have been achieved by translating the activated figure (i.e., $g(x)$) through the same translation f.

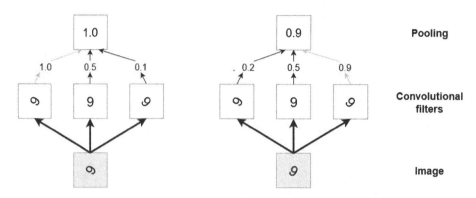

Figure 11-24. *The advantage of the pooling layer that solves the invariance*

Pooling provides some form of translational invariance based on the receptor field kernel size of the pooling. Let's take the case of max pooling. The digits in Figure 11-24 at a specific position are detected through convolution filters in both sides but are not equal, and that's the problem of the convolutional layers; but if you took a closer look you can see that the pooling layers extract a similar value to each other. In this way, max pooling provides some translational invariance to feature detection if the translation distance is not very high with respect to the size of the receptor field or kernel for max pooling.

Similarly, average pooling takes the average of the values in a locality of a feature map based on the size of the receptor field kernel. So, if a specific feature is detected by high values in its feature map in a locality—let's say at regions of edges—then the averages would continue to be high even if the image were a little translated.

Case Study—Digit Recognition on the CIFAR-10 Dataset

The first thing to do in any project or experiment is import all the needed packages. We will import TensorFlow and NumPy for all the deep learning model building and matrix operations; also, we need matplotlib for plotting the analysis and results. And we will load the rebuilt CIFAR-10 dataset in the keras.dataset module in TensorFlow for the sake of ease and simplicity.

```
import tensorflow as tf
import numpy as np
import matplotlib.pyplot as plt
from tensorflow.keras.datasets import cifar10
import time
import math

%matplotlib inline
```

After importing all the packages, we now need to load the dataset, and if you are using this for the first time, it is probably going to download the dataset in your machine.

```
(x_train, y_train), (x_test, y_test) = cifar10.load_data()

x_train.shape
```

After doing all this, you are ready to build the model. We are going to build a class that should define the model and run it too, as well as extracting the analysis and reporting the progress. The class CifarNet contains three functions as follows:

- *Init*: Function that is responsible for getting and setting conv variables (weights)

- *Forward*: Function that is responsible for creating the model architecture

403

- *Run*: Function that runs the model and returns the report of running

```
# define net
class CifarNet():
    def __init__(self):
        # conv layer
        # H2 = (H1 - F + 2P)/S +1
        # (32-5)/1 + 1 = 28
        # 28x28x32 = 25088
        # To ReLu (?x16x16x32) -> MaxPool (?x16x16x32) ->
        affine (8192)
        self.Wconv1 = tf.get_variable("Wconv1", shape=[5, 5,
        3, 32])
        self.bconv1 = tf.get_variable("bconv1", shape=[32])
        # (32-5)/1 + 1 = 28
        # 28x28x64 = 50176
        self.Wconv2 = tf.get_variable("Wconv2", shape=[5, 5,
        32, 64])
        self.bconv2 = tf.get_variable("bconv2", shape=[64])
        # affine layer with 1024
        self.W1 = tf.get_variable("W1", shape=[3136, 1024])
        self.b1 = tf.get_variable("b1", shape=[1024])
        # affine layer with 10
        self.W2 = tf.get_variable("W2", shape=[1024, 10])
        self.b2 = tf.get_variable("b2", shape=[10])

    def forward(self, X, y, is_training):
        # conv2d
        # ReLu
        # conv2d
        # ReLu
```

```
# maxpool
# Batch Norm
# Affine
# Batch Norm
# ReLu
# Affine
# dropout
# Batch Norm

# conv layer
# H2 = (H1 - F + 2P)/S +1
# (32-5)/1 + 1 = 28
# 28x28x32 = 25088
# To ReLu (?x16x16x32) -> MaxPool (?x16x16x32) ->
affine (8192)

# define our graph (e.g. two_layer_convnet) with stride 1
conv1 = tf.nn.conv2d(X, self.Wconv1, strides=[1, 1, 1,
1], padding='SAME') + self.bconv1
print(conv1.shape)
# ReLU Activation Layer
relu1 = tf.nn.relu(conv1)
print(relu1)
# Conv
conv2 = tf.nn.conv2d(relu1, self.Wconv2, strides=[1, 2,
2, 1], padding='VALID') + self.bconv2
print(conv2.shape)
# ReLU Activation Layer
relu2 = tf.nn.relu(conv2)
print(relu2)
# 2x2 Max Pooling layer with a stride of 2
```

```
maxpool = tf.layers.max_pooling2d(relu2, pool_
size=(2,2), strides=2)
print(maxpool.shape)
maxpool_flat = tf.reshape(maxpool,[-1,3136])
# Spatial Batch Normalization Layer (trainable
parameters, with scale and centering)
bn1 = tf.layers.batch_normalization(inputs=maxpool_
flat, center=True, scale=True, training=is_training)
# Affine layer with 1024 output units
affine1 = tf.matmul(bn1, self.W1) + self.b1
print(affine1.shape)
# vanilla batch normalization
affine1_flat = tf.reshape(affine1,[-1,1024])
bn2 = tf.layers.batch_normalization(inputs=affine1,
center=True, scale=True, training=is_training)
print(bn2.shape)
# ReLU Activation Layer
relu2 = tf.nn.relu(bn2)
print(relu2.shape)
# dropout
drop1 = tf.layers.dropout(inputs=relu2, training=is_
training)
# Affine layer from 1024 input units to 10 outputs
affine2 = tf.matmul(drop1, self.W2) + self.b2
# vanilla batch normalization
affine2_flat = tf.reshape(affine2,[-1,3136])
self.predict = tf.layers.batch_normalization
(inputs=affine2, center=True, scale=True, training=is_
training)
print(self.predict.shape)
return self.predict
```

```python
def run(self, session, loss_val, Xd, yd,
              epochs=1, batch_size=64, print_every=100,
              training=None, plot_losses=False,
              isSoftMax=False):
    # have tensorflow compute accuracy
    if isSoftMax:
        correct_prediction = tf.nn.softmax(self.predict)
    else:
        correct_prediction = tf.equal(tf.argmax(self.
        predict,1), y)
    accuracy = tf.reduce_mean(tf.cast(correct_prediction,
    tf.float32))

    # shuffle indicies
    train_indicies = np.arange(Xd.shape[0])
    np.random.shuffle(train_indicies)

    training_now = training is not None

    # setting up variables we want to compute (and
    optimizing)
    # if we have a training function, add that to things we
    compute
    variables = [mean_loss, correct_prediction, accuracy]
    if training_now:
        variables[-1] = training

    # counter
    iter_cnt = 0
    for e in range(epochs):
        # keep track of losses and accuracy
        correct = 0
        losses = []
```

```python
# make sure we iterate over the dataset once
for i in range(int(math.ceil(Xd.shape[0]/batch_
size))):
    # generate indicies for the batch
    start_idx = (i*batch_size)%Xd.shape[0]
    idx = train_indicies[start_idx:start_idx+batch_
    size]

    # create a feed dictionary for this batch
    feed_dict = {X: Xd[idx,:],
                 y: yd[idx],
                 is_training: training_now }
    # get batch size
    actual_batch_size = yd[idx].shape[0]

    # have tensorflow compute loss and correct
    predictions
    # and (if given) perform a training step
    loss, corr, _ = session.run(variables,feed_
    dict=feed_dict)

    # aggregate performance stats
    losses.append(loss*actual_batch_size)
    correct += np.sum(corr)

    # print every now and then
    if training_now and (iter_cnt % print_every)
    == 0:
        print("Iteration {0}: with minibatch
        training loss = {1:.3g} and accuracy of
        {2:.2g}"\
              .format(iter_cnt,loss,np.sum(corr)
              /actual_batch_size))
    iter_cnt += 1
```

```
        total_correct = correct/Xd.shape[0]
        total_loss = np.sum(losses)/Xd.shape[0]
        print("Epoch {2}, Overall loss = {0:.3g} and
        accuracy of {1:.3g}"\
                .format(total_loss,total_correct,e+1))
        if plot_losses:
            plt.ylabel('minibatch loss')
            plt.show()
    return total_loss, total_correct
```

Now we need to run the class. First we will initialize the class and create X and y variables for the dataset.

```
tf.reset_default_graph()
X = tf.placeholder(tf.float32, [None, 32, 32, 3])
y = tf.placeholder(tf.int64, [None, 1])
is_training = tf.placeholder(tf.bool)

net = CifarNet()
```

Then we will call the forward function to create the model architecture as follows.

```
net.forward(X,y,is_training)
```

After that, we will create all the needed hyperparameters the model uses, such as learning rate, optimizer type, etc.

```
# Annealing the learning rate
global_step = tf.Variable(0, trainable=False)
starter_learning_rate = 1e-3
end_learning_rate = 5e-3
decay_steps = 10000
```

```
learning_rate = tf.train.polynomial_decay(starter_learning_
              rate, global_step, decay_steps, end_learning_
              rate, power=0.5)

exp_learning_rate = tf.train.exponential_decay(starter_
learning_rate, global_step, 100000, 0.96, staircase=True)

# Feel free to play with this cell
mean_loss = None
optimizer = None

# define our loss
cross_entr_loss = tf.nn.softmax_cross_entropy_with_
logits(labels=tf.one_hot(y,10), logits=net.predict)
mean_loss = tf.reduce_mean(cross_entr_loss)

# define our optimizer
optimizer = tf.train.AdamOptimizer(exp_learning_rate)

# batch normalization in tensorflow requires this extra dependency
extra_update_ops = tf.get_collection(tf.GraphKeys.UPDATE_OPS)
with tf.control_dependencies(extra_update_ops):
    train_step = optimizer.minimize(mean_loss, global_
step=global_step)
```

Now we will train the model with 10 epochs as a start, to check if the model is running correctly. If you have low computational power, we recommend you run the model with just 1 or 2 epochs to test if it's functionally running correct.

```
# train with 10 epochs
sess = tf.Session()
try:
```

```
    with tf.device("/gpu:0") as dev:
        sess.run(tf.global_variables_initializer())
        print('Training')
        net.run(sess, mean_loss, x_train, y_train, 10, 64, 200,
        train_step, True)
        print('Validation')
        net.run(sess, mean_loss, x_test, y_test, 1, 64)
except tf.errors.InvalidArgumentError:
    print("no gpu found, please use Google Cloud if you want
    GPU acceleration")
```

If the model is running correctly, you will see the following output per each epoch the model passes (Figure 11-25).

```
Iteration 0: with minibatch training loss = 2.79 and accuracy
of 6.4
Iteration 200: with minibatch training loss = 1.46 and accuracy
of 6.1
Iteration 400: with minibatch training loss = 1.47 and accuracy
of 6.3
Iteration 600: with minibatch training loss = 1.49 and accuracy
of 6.3
Epoch 1, Overall loss = 1.4 and accuracy of 6.55
```

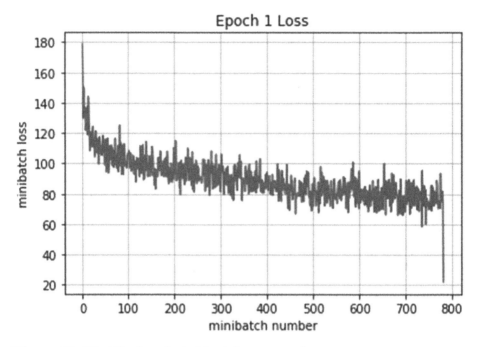

Figure 11-25. *The loss/mini-batch per epoch*

With the preceding basic convolutional neural network, which comprises two convolutional–max pooling–ReLU pairs along with a fully connected layer before the final output softmax unit, we can achieve a test-set high accuracy in just 20 to 30 epochs. And if you have low computational power, you can always use the cloud to train a larger bunch of epochs.

One more thing to emphasize is the importance of tuning the model with the correct set of hyperparameters and prior information. Parameters such as learning rate selection can be very tricky, since the cost function for neural networks is generally nonconvex. A large learning rate can lead to faster convergence to a local minimum but might introduce oscillations, whereas a low learning rate will lead to very slow convergence. Ideally, the learning rate should be low enough that network parameters can converge to a meaningful local minimum, and at the same time it should be high

412

enough that the models can reach the minima faster. Generally, for the preceding neural network a learning rate of 0.01 is a little on the higher side, but since we are only training the data on 20 epochs, it works well. A lower learning rate wouldn't have achieved such a high accuracy with just 10 epochs. Similarly, the batch size chosen for the mini-batch version of stochastic gradient descent influences the convergence of the training process. A larger batch size might be good, since the gradient estimates are less noisy; however, it may come at the cost of increased computation. One also needs to try out different filter sizes as well as experiment with different numbers of feature maps in each convolutional layer. The kind of model architecture we choose works as prior knowledge to the network.

Summary

In this chapter, we introduced the fundamental of how neural networks deal with images—data-matrices in general—and we introduced the modification needed for it. We showed you the transformation from regular image processing techniques and filters to convolutional neural networks and discussed it in detail.

In the next chapter, we will go through how neural networks deal with sequences and text data.

CHAPTER 12

Sequential Models

Recurrent Neural Networks

So why do we need a recurrent neural network (RNN)? Let's try to answer that with an example, or analogy. When reading a new article, people have two options. First, if they can't understand it, they can read articles that the new article is based on, for background information. Otherwise, they *do* understand the new article, based on some prior knowledge of the subject, without an immediate need to read similar articles. In both cases, their ability to understand the new article is enabled by some preexisting or preaquired knowledge. But they don't need to go back to the phase of learning alphabets or numbers; they only need to know what this article is about. This is the way recurrent neural networks work.

RNNs add an interesting twist to basic neural networks. The neural network takes in a fixed size vector as input, which limits its usage in situations that involve a "series" type input with no predetermined size. RNNs are designed to take a series of inputs with no predetermined limit on size. But one may wonder if you can just repeat the traditional neural network. Yes you can, but you will miss the concept of series. Series means every input is a neighbor to another input. So, if you repeat this neural network more than once, you will miss the series. Inputs mean many inputs to the neural network, not series input, so the RNN is a sequential model network. An RNN remembers the past, and its decisions are influenced by what it has learned from the past. Let's say that basic

© Hisham El-Amir and Mahmoud Hamdy 2020
H. El-Amir and M. Hamdy, *Deep Learning Pipeline*,
https://doi.org/10.1007/978-1-4842-5349-6_12

feedforward networks "remember" things too; they remember things they learned during training. For example, an image classifier learns what a "1" looks like during training and then uses that knowledge to classify things in production. Now let's see about the RNN and its types.

RNNs can take one or more input vectors and produce one or more output vectors, and the output(s) are influenced by **weights applied on inputs and "hidden" state vectors** representing the context based on prior input(s) and output(s). So, the same input could produce a different output, depending on **previous inputs in the series.** This is the "series" aspect of an RNN. Now, *how can we create the layers of an RNN?* First of all, the RNN looks quite similar to a traditional neural network except that a memory state is added to the neurons. Imagine a simple model with only one neuron, fed by a batch of data. In a traditional neural network, the model produces the output by multiplying the input with the weight and the activation function. With an **RNN**, this output is sent back to itself a number of times. **Time step** is the amount of time the output becomes the input of the next matrices multiplication. Let's visualize what happens. Say the network is composed of one neuron. The network computes the matrices multiplication between the input and the weight and adds nonlinearity with the activation function. It becomes the output at $t - 1$. This output is the input of the second matrices multiplication.

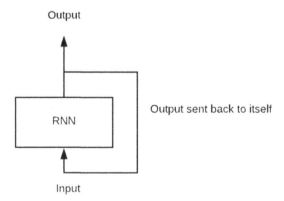

***Figure 12-1.** The abstraction of an RNN*

Figure 12-1 shows an abstract explanation of when you have an input and an output; input means batch, but batch per time. Figure 12-2 shows the RNN cell in more detail.

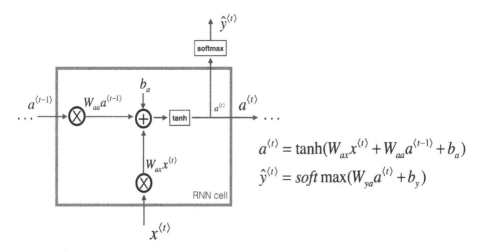

$$a^{\langle t \rangle} = \tanh(W_{ax}x^{\langle t \rangle} + W_{aa}a^{\langle t-1 \rangle} + b_a)$$
$$\hat{y}^{\langle t \rangle} = soft\max(W_{ya}a^{\langle t \rangle} + b_y)$$

Figure 12-2. *The details inside an RNN*

Now let's explain it in detail, but we will look at it from end to start. We cache the output from *softmax* and the output from *tanh*. You can say we save $\hat{y}^t$ and a^t to the cache to use it in the next state. The next state will take those two parameters as input and multiply the (a) parameter, which will be the a^{t-1} with the weight of this state. At the same time, we multiply the input vector with the weight of this state, combine those two parameters with the bias, and apply the tanh activation function on them. This will generate the next activation (a) and apply *softmax* on it to generate the predicted (y), and cache them to the next state of RNN and back again with this cycle from end to start.

So, now that we've seen only one cell and had a brief look at its functions, let's connect this cell with other cells and get a big recurrent neural network. You will see that in real life the sequence of data goes from the input and generates new output every time step. This is an RNN, which depends on time and a series of data. Figure 12-3 will make the idea more visible.

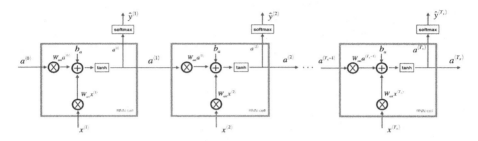

Figure 12-3. *A sequence of RNN cells*

This figure explains how the connection between the activation is generated from a state, goes through the next state, and generates a new predicted output (y). This makes a series, as we talked about previously. Now that you know the structure of the RNN, you should know that there is more than one type of RNN. You need to know the size of the input the RNN needs and the size of the output that you predicted from the RNN.

We have three types of RNN. The first type is fully recurrent networks. In this type the layered topology of a multilayer perceptron is preserved, but every element has a weighted connection to every other element in the architecture and has a single feedback connection to itself. Not all connections are trained, and the extreme nonlinearity of the error derivatives means conventional backpropagation will not work, so the backpropagation through time approach or stochastic gradient descent is employed.

The next type is recursive neural networks. First, you should know that recurrent neural networks are linear architecturally; the recursion promotes branching in hierarchical feature spaces and the resulting network architecture mimics this as training proceeds. Training is achieved with gradient descent by subgradient methods.

The last type is the neural history compressor. Jüergen *Schmidhuber* reported a very deep learner, first in 1991, that was able to perform credit assignment over hundreds of neural layers by unsupervised pretraining for a hierarchy of RNNs. Each RNN is trained unsupervised to predict the next input. Then, only inputs generating an error are feedforward, conveying new information to the next RNN in the hierarchy, which then processes at a slower, self-organizing time scale.

It was shown that no information is lost, just compressed. The RNN stack is a "deep generative model" of the data. The data can be reconstructed from the compressed form.

Before we finish this section, we need to talk about the five types of RNN architecture (Figure 12-4). Each type is best for certain uses, like many to many as an encoder or decoder and many to one for LSTM. So let's talk about each type and what it consists of. One to one is recursive, but it takes only one input and produces only one output. The next type is one to many: it takes one input and produces many outputs. Many to one has many inputs and generates only one output. Many to many actually has two types, or two architectures: one is called many to many. One of them is fully connected, which is used in video recognition; the second type is partially connected, which is used in machine translation.

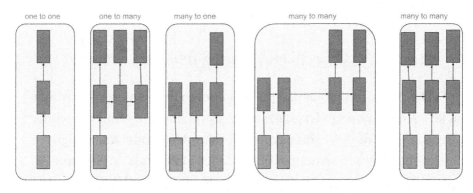

Figure 12-4. *The different types of sequences architectures*

Unfortunately, we know that RNN is supposed to carry the information up to time. However, it is quite challenging to propagate all this information when the time step is too long. When a network has too many deep layers, it becomes untrainable. This problem is called the vanishing gradient problem. If you remember, the neural network updates the weight using the gradient descent algorithm. The gradients grow smaller when the network progresses down to lower layers. This all is useful information to know about RNNs and their architectures. But simply put, an RNN is just a sequential model that we use in language models because we need sequential, or series, in a language model. So let's talk about language modeling and how RNNs are important in it.

Language Modeling

For simplification, language modeling is the task of predicting the next word or character in a document. A language model is a conditional distribution on the identifier of the ith word in a sequence, given the identities of all previous words. In language modeling, the probability of a sequence of words is computed through the product rule of the intersection of events. The probability of a sequence of words $\{w_1, w_2, w_3, ..., w_n\}$ of length n is given as follows:

$$P\left(w_1,\ w_2,\ w_3, ..., w_n\right) = P\left(w_1\right)P\left(w_2|w_1\right)P\left(w_3|w_1^2\right)...P\left(w_n|w_1^{n-1}\right)$$

So, language models assign probabilities to the sequences of words. But let's see the types of language models and how the sequence works with each type. We have three types. The simplest model that assigns these probabilities to sentences or sequence of words is an **N-Gram**. An N-gram is a sequence of N words; a *bi-gram* (or **bigram**) is a two-word sequence of words like "please turn," "turn your," or "your homework"; and a tri-gram (or trigram) is a three-word sequence of words like "please turn your," or "turn your homework." But what's the key connection between them and the RNN, or sequence model? Let's start with the easiest one: an N-gram's task is to compute $P(w|h)$, the probability of a word $w*$ given some history $h*$. Suppose the history $h*$ is "*its water is so transperant that*" and we want to know the probability that the next word is the, it can be represented as:

$$P(the|its\ water\ is\ so\ transperant\ that)$$

One way to estimate the preceding function is through the relative frequency counts, where we would take a substantial corpus, count the number of times we see "its water is so transperant that," and then count the number of times it is followed by "the":

$$P(its\ water\ is\ so\ transperant\ that) = \frac{C(its\ water\ is\ so\ transperant\ that\ the)}{C(its\ water\ is\ so\ transperant\ that)}$$

But it isn't feasible to do this task; we have many groups and we need to perform this task every single group! So, you do it by using the chain rule of probability:

$$P(w_1, \ldots, w_n) = P(w_1)P(w_2|w_1)P(w_3|w_1^2)P(w_n|w_1^{n-1})$$

This serves as the base procedure of the N-Gram model, where instead of computing the probability of a word given its entire history, we will approximate the history by just the last few words. The bigram model approximates the probability of a word given all the previous words, by using only the conditional probability of the preceding word. We approximate it with the probability $P(w_1 | w_{n-1})$; like the example of "the" and "that," you can do in a bi-gram $P(the | that)$. You can do it by using the conditional probability:

$$P(w_n|w_1^{n-1}) \approx P(w_n|w_{n-1})$$

A *trigram model* models language as a second-order Markov process, making the computationally convenient approximation that a word depends only on the previous two words. And you can use it with this equation:

$$P\left(w_1^{n-1}\right) = P\left(w_n \mid w_{n-1}, w_n\right)$$

So these are the language models in natural language processing (NLP). But we didn't talk about *uni-gram*, as we don't need it for the sequence models, so at the end, we will see how RNN works with the language model and the importance of RNN in the language model, the aim of the language model is to predict the next word, so in N-gram we condition the word we need to predict based on the previous words. Therefore, the main reason for using an RNN is it's sequential. This is analogous to the fact that the human brain does not start thinking from scratch for every word we say. Our thoughts have persistence. We'll give this property of persistence to the neural network with the use of an RNN.

A good example is "I had a good time in France. I also learned to speak some _____". If we want to predict what word will go in the blank, we have to go all the way to the word France and then conclude that the most likely word will be French. In other words, we have to have some memory of our previous outputs and calculate new outputs based on our past outputs. Another advantage of using RNNs for language modeling is that, due to memory constraints, they are limited to remembering only a few steps back. This is ideal because the context of the word can be captured in the 8–10 words before it. We don't have to remember 50 words of context, although RNNs can be used for arbitrarily long sequences if you have enough memory at your disposal. And don't forget the design of the RNN (Figure 12-5).

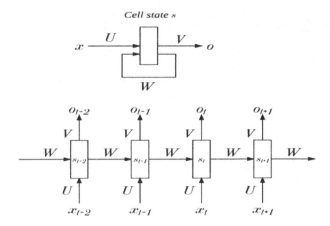

Figure 12-5. *The unroll of the RNN sequence*

In RNNs, the output at each step is conditioned on all previous words; hence, RNNs do a better job than the n-gram models at language model tasks. To understand this, let's look at the working principals of a generative recurrent neural network while considering a sequence $(X = \{x_1, x_2, ..., x_n\})$ of length n. The RNN updates its hidden state ht recursively as ht=f(ht−1,xt). The hidden state h_{t-1} has information accumulated for the sequence of words $\{x_1, x_2, ..., x_{t-1}\}$, and when the new word in the sequence x_t arrives the updated sequence information $\{x_1, x_2, ..., x_t\}$ is encoded in h_t through the recursive update.

Now we must predict the next word based on the word sequence seen so far.

So now that we know the RNN is important for the language model task and have a good explanation for this type of RNN, we will talk about LSTM, GRU this the updates of the RNN in this chapter But for now let's see how a new task works with an RNN—backpropagation through time (BPTT).

Backpropagation Through Time

Backpropagation through time, or BPTT, is the application of the backpropagation training algorithm to a recurrent neural network applied to sequence data like a time series. A recurrent neural network is shown one input each time step and predicts one output. Backpropagation for recurrent neural networks is the same as that for feedforward neural networks; the only difference is that the gradient is the sum of the gradient with respect to the log loss at each step. So, after having input and output every time step, errors are then calculated and accumulated for each time step. The network is rolled back up and the weights are updated.

Each time step of the unrolled recurrent neural network may be seen as an additional layer given the order dependence of the problem, and the internal state from the previous time step is taken as an input on the subsequent time step. Based on the predicted output and the actual output labels, the loss and the corresponding error at each time step is computed. The error at each time step is backpropagated to update the weights. So, any weight update is proportional to the sum of the gradients' contribution from errors at all the T time steps. So, let's go through some calculations about the loss function of RNNs. We mentioned before the tanh function and *softmax* function, so now let's go through the loss function. We also defined our loss, or error, to be the cross-entropy loss, given by:

$$E_t\left(y_t, \hat{y}_t\right) = -y_t \log \hat{y}_t$$
$$E\left(y, \hat{y}\right) = \sum_t E_t\left(y_t, \hat{y}_t\right)$$
$$= -\sum_t y_t \log \hat{y}_t$$

Here, y_t is the correct word at time step t, and y_t is our prediction. We typically treat the full sequence (sentence) as one training example, so the total error is just the sum of the errors at each time step (word). Let's see an illustration of an RNN (Figure 12-6) to learn how to calculate the BPTT—the backpropagation.

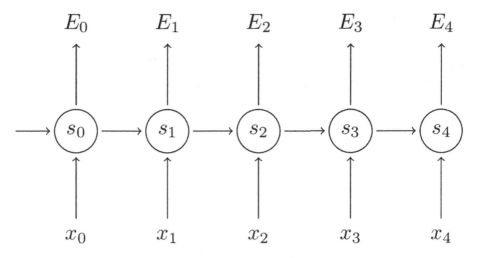

Figure 12-6. *Simple architecture of a model to describe back-propagation in it*

This is not a new idea, since we actually learned about it in the previous chapters. But let's remember that we need to calculate the gradients of the error with respect to our parameters U, V, and W and then learn good parameters using stochastic gradient descent. Just as we sum up the errors, we also sum up the gradients at each time step for one training example:

$$\frac{\partial E}{\partial W} = \sum_t \frac{\partial E_t}{\partial W}$$

To calculate these gradients, we use the chain rule of differentiation. That's the backpropagation algorithm when applied backward, starting from the error. We'll use E_3 as a figure, just to have concrete numbers to work with.

$$\frac{\partial E_3}{\partial V} = \frac{\partial E_3}{\partial \hat{y}_3}\frac{\partial \hat{y}_3}{\partial V}$$
$$= \frac{\partial E_3}{\partial \hat{y}_3}\frac{\partial \hat{y}_3}{\partial z_3}\frac{\partial z_3}{\partial V}$$
$$= (\hat{y}_3 - y_3) \otimes s_3$$

425

In the preceding, $z_3 = Vs_3$, and *circled multiplication* is the outer product of two vectors. That's intuitive, but the point is that E_3V only depends on the values at the current time step: $\hat{y}_3$, y_3, s_3. If you have these, calculating the gradient for V is a simple matrix multiplication. But the key point is to have this at first, as in the above calculation where $\dfrac{\partial z_3}{\partial V}$ really depends on those three variables, so now let's get more in-depth with calculations. $s_3 = tanh\,(Ux_t + Ws_2)$ depends on s_2, which depends on W and s_1, and so on. So, if we take the derivative with respect to W, we can't simply treat s_3 as a constant! We need to apply the chain rule again and what we really have is this:

$$\frac{\partial E_3}{\partial W} = \sum_{k=0}^{3} \frac{\partial E_3}{\partial \hat{y}_3} \frac{\partial \hat{y}_3}{\partial s_3} \frac{\partial s_3}{\partial s_k} \frac{\partial s_k}{\partial W}$$

We sum up the contributions of each time step to the gradient. In other words, because W is used in every step up to the output we care about, we need to backpropagate gradients from $t = 3$ through the network all the way to $t = 0$. Let's see a visualization (Figure 12-7) to get a better understanding about it. You already know about backpropagation; the only key difference is the time between backpropagation and BPTT.

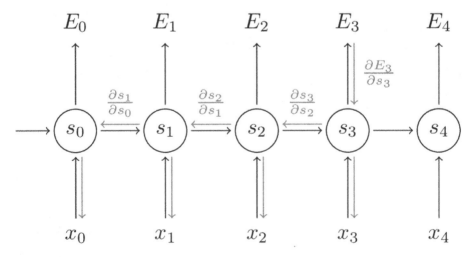

***Figure 12-7.** Feed backward backpropagation*

Note   This is exactly the same as the standard backpropagation algorithm that we use in deep feedforward neural networks. The key difference is that we sum up the gradients for W at each time step.

In a traditional neural network, we don't share parameters across layers, so we don't need to sum anything. But in my opinion, BPTT is just a fancy name for standard backpropagation on an unrolled RNN. But we have a problem with this: BPTT can be computationally expensive as the number of time steps increases. If input sequences are comprised of thousands of time steps, then this will be the number of derivatives required for a single update weight update. This can cause weights to vanish or explode (go to zero or overflow) and make slow learning and model skill noisy. This gets us to a new version of BPTT that tries to eliminate or minimize the challenges that BPPT has. So, TBPTT (truncated backpropagation through time) is developed. TBPTT is a modified version of the BPTT training algorithm for recurrent neural networks, wherein the sequence is processed one time step at a time, and periodically (k1 time steps) the BPTT update is performed back for a fixed number of time steps (k2 time steps). So, we see it depends on the two variables: k1 and k2.

- **k1:** The number of forward-pass time steps between updates. Generally, this influences how slow or fast training will be, given how often weight updates are performed.

- **k2:** The number of time steps to which to apply BPTT. Generally, it should be large enough to capture the temporal structure in the problem for the network to learn. Too large a value results in vanishing gradients.

Let's go through how TBPTT works, with parameters k1 and k2. We have four standard approaches; the last approach is divided into two approaches, as we see in the following:

- **TBPTT(n,n):** Updates are performed at the end of the sequence across all time steps in the sequence (e.g., classical BPTT).

- **TBPTT(1,n):** Time steps are processed one at a time, followed by an update that covers all time steps seen so far (e.g., classical TBPTT by Williams and Peng).

- **TBPTT(k1,1):** The network likely does not have enough temporal context to learn, relying heavily on internal state and inputs.

- **TBPTT(k1,k2),** where k1<k2<n: Multiple updates are performed per sequence, which can accelerate training.

- **TBPTT(k1,k2),** where k1=k2: A common configuration where a fixed number of time steps are used for both forward and backward-pass time steps (e.g., 10s to 100s).

In libraries like TensorFlow and Keras, things look similar and h defines the vectorized fixed length of the time steps of the prepared data. In real life, with coding, you will not do this calculation yourself, but we need you to understand what happens in the background of this equation. Now we will have a case study that makes the sequence model more obvious. Try it yourself.

Vanishing and Exploding Gradient Problems in RNN

We saw in the previous section that BPTT has many problems with time. If you have a large time series, you can have many problems that fall under the term vanishing and exploding. The key difference between RNNs and neural networks is time. The error propagates backward from output to input layer, propagating the input error gradient. With deeper neural networks, issues can arise from backpropagation, such as vanishing and exploding gradients. So, let's review with a quick definition of **vanishing gradients**. As we go back to the lower layers, the gradient often gets smaller, eventually causing weights to never change at lower layers. **Exploding gradients** are the opposite of vanishing gradients; gradient explode on the way back.

Let's see if the RNN gradient will suffer more from vanishing or exploding. In my opinion it will be vanishing, because of RNNs' large and complex structures. So, let's lay out the problem and get a solution for it. The aim of RNNs is to learn long dependencies so that the interrelations between words that are far apart are captured. For example, the actual meaning that a sentence is trying to convey may be captured well by words that are not in close proximity to each other. Let's assume the input sequence to the network is a nine-word sentence: "I grew up in France; I speak French fluently." We can see from the example that for the RNN to predict the word "French," which comes at the end of the sequence, it would need information from the word "France," which occurs further back near the beginning of the sentence. This kind of dependence between sequence data is called long-term dependencies, because the distance between the relevant information "France" and the point where it is needed to make a prediction "French" is very wide. Unfortunately, in practice, as this distance becomes wider, RNNs have a hard time learning these dependencies because they encounter either a vanishing or exploding gradient problem.

So, RNNs should be able to learn those dependencies, but they suffer from this inherent problem: failing to capture long-distance dependencies between words. This is because the gradients in instances of long sequences have a high chance of either going to zero or going to infinity very quickly. When the gradients drop to zero very quickly, the model is unable to learn the associations or correlations between events that are temporally far apart. The equations derived for the gradient of the cost function with respect to the weights of the hidden memory layers will help us understand why this vanishing gradient problem might take place. These problems arise during the training of a deep network when the gradients are being propagated back in time all the way to the initial layer. The gradients coming from the deeper layers have to go through continuous matrix multiplications because of the chain rule. As they approach the earlier layers, if they have small values (<1), they shrink exponentially until they vanish and make it impossible for the model to learn; this is the vanishing gradient problem. On the other hand, if they have large values (>1), they get larger and eventually blow up and crash the model; this is the exploding gradient problem. So, the definitions of vanishing and exploding gradient are as follows:

- **Exploding gradients:** When gradients explode, the gradients could become NaN because of the numerical overflow, or we might see irregular oscillations in training cost when we plot the learning curve.

- **Vanishing gradients:** The basic RNN model has many local influences because of recurrent neural networks as the earlier information. As the RNN weights vanishes thought time and information is lost.

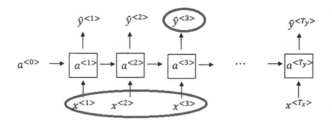

Figure 12-8. *All previous inputs participate to generate the current output*

In Figure 12-8, the output $\hat{y}^{<3>}$ is mainly influenced by a value close to $\hat{y}^{<3>}$. This local influence makes an output which is later in the sequence to be affected by earlier input in the sequence.

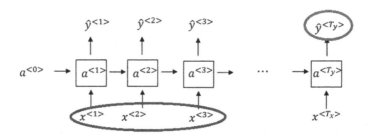

Figure 12-9. *All previous inputs participate to generate the current output*

In Figure 12-9, the output y<Ty> cannot be influenced by the early inputs in the sequences ($x^{<1>}$, $x^{<2>}$, $x^{<3>}$). It was hard for the error to backpropagate to the beginning of the sequence. This is the weakness of the basic RNN. So, now that we know about the problems of vanishing and exploding gradients, we need to solve them.

The Solution to Vanishing and Exploding Gradients Problems in RNNs

Let's start with exploding gradients. A solution to fix this is to apply gradient clipping, which places a predefined threshold on the gradients to prevent them from getting too large. By doing this, it doesn't change the direction of the gradients; it only changes its length. We can see this in Figure 12-10.

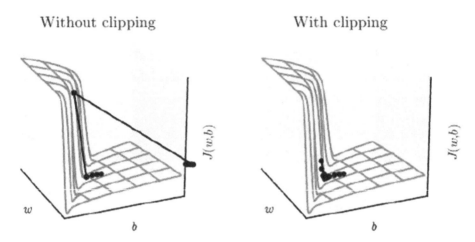

Figure 12-10. *Gradient steps with and without clipping*

So, we should get to the point that we try to enhance the gradient to reach the local minima as fast as it can without getting any errors, meaning overfitting, underfitting, vanishing, or exploding. So the solution looks easy for exploding, but not so easy for vanishing. We have two solutions for vanishing. First, we will talk about identity RNN architecture, where the network weights are initialized to the identity matrix and the activation functions are all set to ReLU. This ends up encouraging the network computations to stay close to the identity function. This works well because, when the error derivatives are being propagated backward through time, they remain constants of either 0 or 1; hence, they aren't likely to suffer from vanishing gradients. The second, widely used, solution is LSTM. Long short-term memory architecture is a variant of the regular recurrent network, which was designed to make it easy to capture long-term dependencies in sequence data. The standard RNN operates in such a way that the hidden state activation is influenced by the other local activations closest to them, which corresponds to "short-term memory." But the network weights are influenced by the computations that take place over entire long sequences, which corresponds to "long-term memory." Hence, the RNN was redesigned so that it has an activation state that can also act as weights and preserve information over long distances, hence the name "long short-term memory."

We may need to learn more about LSTM, so in the next section we will talk about it. But before we end this section, let's recap. Vanishing means that your model tries to learn, but it can't because it goes so slowly; but if you let it complete training, it may get to optimal minima, or may not. Exploding is the way that the model goes away from the optimal minima: it will go away more and more and it won't get to its optimal minima, and we can't reduce the cost function—the core of what we're trying to do. So, let's go to the next section and talk about LSTM.

Long Short-Term Memory

LSTM networks are just an advanced version of plain RNNs. These networks are capable of remembering long-term dependencies. They are designed to remember information for long periods of time without having to deal with the vanishing gradient problem. They were invented by Sepp Hochreiter and Jürgen Schmidhuber in 1997 and were refined and popularized by many people in their following work. They work tremendously well on a large variety of problems and are now widely used. We know that an RNN is very simple compared with LSTM, and LSTM is used to solve vanishing problems, so let's talk about the architecture (Figure 12-11). All RNNs have the form of a chain of repeating modules of the neural network. In standard RNNs, this repeating module will have a very simple structure, such as a single tanh layer.

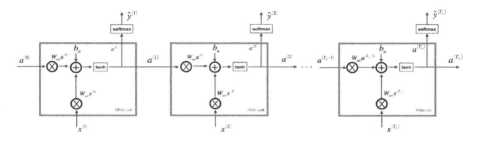

Figure 12-11. *The architecture of LSTM*

LSTMs also have this chain-like structure, but the repeating module has a different structure. Instead of having a single neural network layer, there are four, interacting in a very special way.

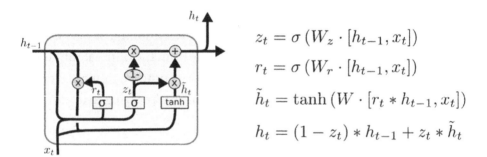

$$z_t = \sigma\left(W_z \cdot [h_{t-1}, x_t]\right)$$

$$r_t = \sigma\left(W_r \cdot [h_{t-1}, x_t]\right)$$

$$\tilde{h}_t = \tanh\left(W \cdot [r_t * h_{t-1}, x_t]\right)$$

$$h_t = (1 - z_t) * h_{t-1} + z_t * \tilde{h}_t$$

Figure 12-12. *How an LSTM cell works*

Let's talk about the core behind LSTM and what happens to input from the first state to the last one. We won't go to the equations at first; we'll just talk about the diagram (Figure 12-13). Let's start with the line above. It runs straight down the entire chain, with only some minor linear interactions. It's very easy for information to just flow along it, unchanged from the previous state, to generate new C_t to the next state, as in Figure 12-13.

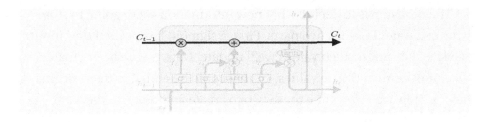

Figure 12-13. *How memory step works in LSTM*

LSTM can add or forget or update by using gates. These gates can change in this straight line. Let's build the LSTM architecture together step-by-step with data going through the input.

The first step in our LSTM is to decide what information we're going to throw away from the cell state. This decision is made by a sigmoid layer called the "forget gate layer." It looks at h_{t-1} and x_t, and outputs a number between 0 and 1 for each number in the cell state C_{t-1}.

A_1 when it is 1 represents "completely keep this" while a 0 represents "completely get rid of this." We know that the sigmoid function, which is 0 or 1, is an activation function, so the input is multiplied by it. If it is zero, this means that this input is neglected; but if it's one, this means we should care about this input. You can see an example in Figure 12-14.

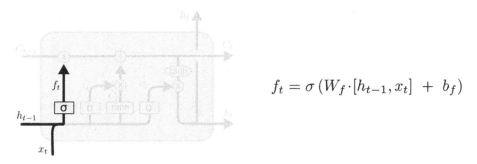

$$f_t = \sigma \left(W_f \cdot [h_{t-1}, x_t] \; + \; b_f \right)$$

Figure 12-14. *The forget cell and how it works*

435

The next step is to decide what new information we're going to store in the cell state. This has two parts. First, a sigmoid layer called the "input gate layer" decides which values we'll update. Next, a *tanh* layer creates a vector of new candidate values, C_t, that could be added to the state. In the next step, we'll combine these two to create an update to the state (Figure 12-15).

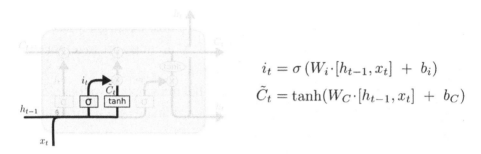

$$i_t = \sigma\left(W_i \cdot [h_{t-1}, x_t] + b_i\right)$$
$$\tilde{C}_t = \tanh(W_C \cdot [h_{t-1}, x_t] + b_C)$$

Figure 12-15. *How LSTM updates its memory*

It's now time to update the old cell state, C_{t-1}, into the new cell state, C_t. We multiply the old state by f_t, forgetting the things we decided to forget earlier. Then we add $i_t * C_t$. This represents the new candidate values, scaled by how much we decided to update each state value (Figure 12-16).

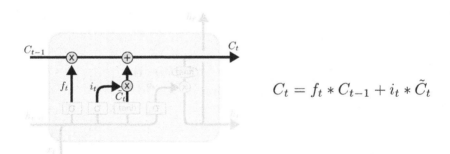

$$C_t = f_t * C_{t-1} + i_t * \tilde{C}_t$$

Figure 12-16. *The combination of forget and updating LSTM memory*

Finally, we need to decide what we're going to output. This output will be based on our cell state, but will be a filtered version. First, we run a sigmoid layer, which decides what parts of the cell state we're going to output. Then, we put the cell state through tanh (to push the values to between −1 and 1) and multiply it by the output of the sigmoid gate, so that we only output the parts we decided to (Figure 12-17).

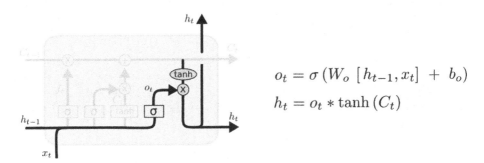

$$o_t = \sigma \left(W_o \left[h_{t-1}, x_t \right] + b_o \right)$$
$$h_t = o_t * \tanh \left(C_t \right)$$

Figure 12-17. *How LSTM calculates the output*

Besides this general use LSTM layer, many papers have been written updating this version:

1. One popular LSTM variant, introduced by F. A. Gers and Jürgen Schmidhuber (2000), is adding "peephole connections." This means that we let the gate layers look at the cell state (Figure 12-18).

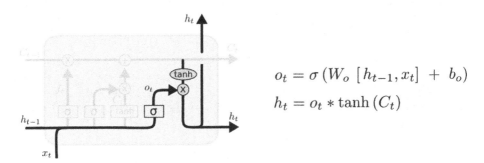

$$f_t = \sigma \left(W_f \cdot \left[C_{t-1}, h_{t-1}, x_t \right] + b_f \right)$$
$$i_t = \sigma \left(W_i \cdot \left[C_{t-1}, h_{t-1}, x_t \right] + b_i \right)$$
$$o_t = \sigma \left(W_o \cdot \left[C_t, h_{t-1}, x_t \right] + b_o \right)$$

Figure 12-18. *How LSTM tooks at memory and how it uses it*

2. Use coupled forget and input gates. Instead of separately deciding what to forget and what we should add new information to, we make those decisions together. We only forget when we're going to input something in its place. We only input new values to the state when we forget something older (Figure 12-19).

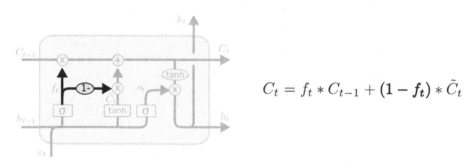

$$C_t = f_t * C_{t-1} + (1 - f_t) * \tilde{C}_t$$

Figure 12-19. *The output of forget/update memory activation function*

So, you can see that anyone can update this and adapt LSTM to handle their cases. We've learned about LSTM and its four functions; the main point is that LSTM can solve exploding and vanishing gradient problems.

Case Study—Digit Identification on the MNIST Dataset

Gated Recurrent Unit

In the section on LSTM, we said that it solves vanishing gradient problems. We now have a great new architecture called Gated Recurrent Unit (GRU), introduced by Cho, et al. in 2014. GRU aims to solve the vanishing gradient problem that comes with a standard RNN. GRU can also be considered as a variation on LSTM because both are designed similarly and, in some cases, produce equally excellent results. GRU uses so-called update gate and reset gate. Basically, these are two vectors that decide what information should be passed to the output. The special thing about them is that they can be trained to keep information from long ago, without washing it through time or removing information that is irrelevant to the prediction. So, let's see the unit of GRU in a visualization model (Figure 12-20)

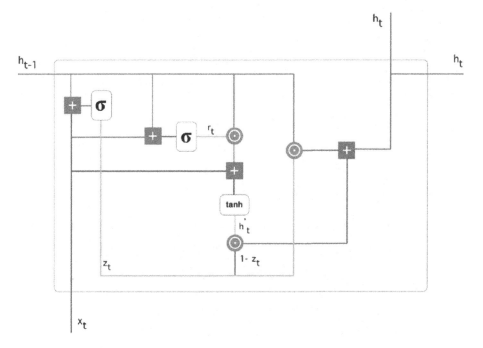

Figure 12-20. *The GRU unit architect*

Let's look at each gate individually,

1. **Update gate:** We start with calculating the update gate z_t for time step t (Figure 12-21).

$$z_t = \sigma(W^{(z)}x_t + U^{(z)}h_{t-1})$$

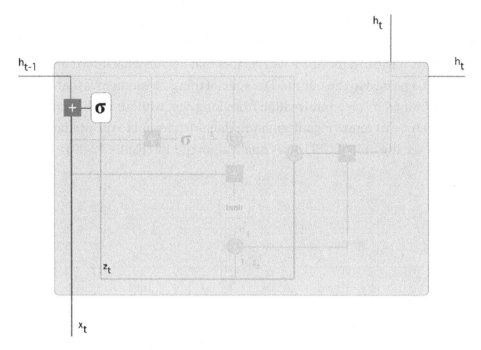

Figure 12-21. *The first step of the GRU unit, the update gate*

When x_t is plugged into the network unit, it is multiplied by its own weight, $W(z)$. The same goes for ht-1, which holds the information for the previous $t - 1$ units and is multiplied by its own weight, $U(z)$. Both results are added together and a sigmoid activation function is applied to squash the result between 0 and 1. The update gate helps the model to determine how much of the past information (from previous time steps) needs to be passed along to the future. That is really powerful, because the model can decide to copy all the information from the past and eliminate the risk of vanishing gradient problem. We will see the usage of the update gate later on. For now, remember the formula for z_t.

2. **Reset gate:** Essentially, this gate is used by the model to decide how much of the past information to forget.

$$r_t = \sigma(W^{(r)}x_t + U^{(r)}h_{t-1})$$

You see that this formula is almost like the update gate, but there is a difference in the values of variables and the gate position in the architecture. Let's see the gate in Figure 12-22.

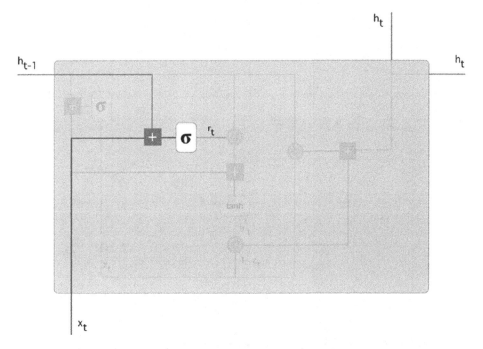

Figure 12-22. *The reset gate in GRU unit*

As before, we plug in h_{t-1} and x_t, multiply them with their corresponding weights, sum the results, and apply the sigmoid function.

441

3. **Current memory content:** This is a new memory; we introduce a new memory content that will use the reset gate to store the relevant information from the past.

$$h_t' = \tanh\left(Wx_t + r_t \odot Uh_{t-1}\right)$$

This works in four steps (Figure 12-23).

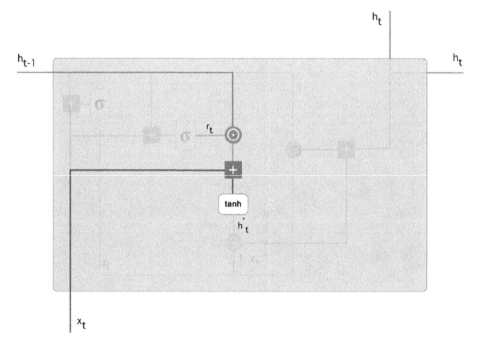

Figure 12-23. *How LSTM uses the memeory*

We do an element-wise multiplication of h_{t-1} and r_t and then sum the result with the input, x_t. Finally, *tanh* is used to produce h_t. So, after describing what happens in in the image, we need to go in details. The first step is to multiply the input x_t with a weight W and h_{t-1}

442

with a weight U. Then the second step calculates the Hadamard (element-wise) product between the reset gate r_t and Uh_{t-1}. That will determine what to remove from the previous time steps. Then we sum them up in the third step and apply the tanh activation function in the last step.

4. **Final memory at current time step:** This is the last step in the GRU; the network needs to calculate the h_t vector, which holds information for the current unit and passes it down to the network. In order to do that, the update gate is needed. It determines what to collect from the current memory content, h_t, and what from the previous steps, h_{t-1}.

$$h_t = z_t \odot h_{t-1} + (1 - z_t) \odot h_t'$$

Now let's see how this memory works. Apply element-wise multiplication to the update gate z_t and h_{t-1}, then apply element-wise multiplication to $(1 - z_t)$ and h_t (Figure 12-24). So far, we can sum the results from the previous two steps.

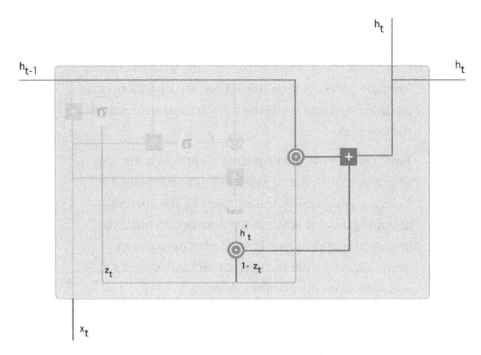

Figure 12-24. What happens to memory state at the final step

You can see how z_t is used to calculate $(1 - z_t)$, which, combined with h_t produces a result in the dark red line. z_t is also used with h_{t-1} in an element-wise multiplication. Finally, h is a result of the summation of the outputs corresponding to the bright and dark red lines. So after we've seen how the procedure works in GRU and that it's almost like LSTM, we now need to get some comparison between them—not an actual comparison, but we'll try to get some key points that allow us to choose. It is very hard to choose between them, but let's note some points to consider.

5. GRU and LSTM have comparable performance, and there is no simple way to recommend one or the other for a specific task.

444

6. GRUs are faster to train and need fewer data to generalize.

7. When there is enough data, LSTM's greater expressive power may lead to better results.

8. Like LSTMs, GRUs are drop-in replacements for the simple RNN cell.

Those were just some key points; you can research more about them. So we now know the upgrades of the basic RNN neural network: LSTM and GRU. They are widely used those days, so make sure you use them. In the next section we will see a new application of RNN, Bidirectional RNN (Bi-RNN).

Bidirectional RNN (Bi-RNN)

Bidirectional RNNs are a special type of RNN that makes use of both the past and future states to predict the output label at the current state. A bidirectional RNN combines two RNNs, one of which runs forward from left to right and the other of which runs backward from right to left. A high-level architecture diagram of a bidirectional RNN is depicted in Figure 12-25.

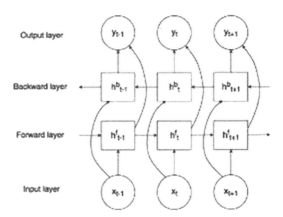

Figure 12-25. Bi-directional RNN architecture

Bidirectional RNNs are really just two independent RNNs put together. The input sequence is fed in normal time order for one network, and in reverse time order for another. The outputs of the two networks are usually concatenated at each time step, though there are other options (e.g., summation).

This structure allows the networks to have both backward and forward information about the sequence at every time step. The concept seems easy enough. But when it comes to actually implementing a neural network that utilizes a bidirectional structure, confusion arises.

It has some issues: not actually issues, but some confusion. The first confusion is about the way to forward the outputs of a bidirectional RNN to a dense neural network. For normal RNNs we could just forward the outputs at the last time step. The second confusion is about the returned hidden states. In seq2seq models, we'll want hidden states from the encoder to initialize the hidden states of the decoder.

Summary

In this chapter, we talked about sequence models, and how they became so good with language models. We also talked about the problems that face the RNN, like vanishing and exploding. Then we looked into LSTM and GRU, which solve vanishing and exploding gradient problems with sequence models because they can handle the long dependences in language models. We then talked about the common application in a sequence model called bidirectional RNN, and saw its advantages.

PART IV

Applying What You've Learned

## CHAPTER 13

Selected Topics in Computer Vision

After finishing Part III of *Deep Learning Pipeline*, you are ready now to build your pipeline. You now see the whole picture, but it's fair to tell you that you are missing some parts in each approach, and we will fill the gaps by giving you some advanced concepts in both natural language processing and computer vision. Then we will give you some examples, using different types of datasets to ensure that you can apply a deep learning pipeline correctly and easily.

Now, after finishing Chapter 11 in Part III, it's good to add some extra knowledge that makes it easier for the reader when they work. We'll be discussing and using prebuilt model architectures that made a state-of-the-art accurate prediction and produced a very high accuracy in competitions. We'll also discuss a new concept—transfer learning. This concept will help you to save both time and computational power, and we will show you the guidelines for using transfer learning with different models.

© Hisham El-Amir and Mahmoud Hamdy 2020
H. El-Amir and M. Hamdy, *Deep Learning Pipeline*,
https://doi.org/10.1007/978-1-4842-5349-6_13

Different Architectures in Convolutional Neural Networks

The challenging part of using convolutional neural networks (CNNs) in practice is how to design model architectures that best use these simple elements: the layer types, the loss function, the optimizer, and all the hyperparameters. All these are the issues you may find challenging when you are attempting to build a good model.

A useful approach to learning how to design effective CNN architectures is to study successful applications. This is particularly straightforward to do because of the intense study and application of CNNs through the past 10 to 20 years for the ImageNet Large Scale Visual Recognition Competition, or ILSVRC. This challenge resulted in both rapid advancement in the state of the art for very difficult computer vision tasks, and the development of general innovations in the architecture of CNN models.

In this section, we will go through a few widely used CNN architectures used today. These network architectures can be used in many tasks such as classification, but also, with minor modifications, segmentation, localization, and detection. Also, there are pretrained versions of each of these networks that enable the community to do transfer learning or fine-tune the models. Except LeNet, almost all the CNN models have won the ImageNet competition for classification of a thousand classes.

We will begin with the LeNet-5, which is often described as the first successful and important application of CNNs prior to the ILSVRC. Then we'll look at three other winning architectural innovations for CNNs developed for the ILSVRC, namely: AlexNet, VGG, and ResNet.

By understanding these milestone models and their architecture or architectural innovations from a high-level, you will develop both an appreciation for the use of these architectural elements in modern applications of CNN in computer vision, and be able to identify and choose architecture elements that may be useful in the design of your own models.

LeNet

The first successful CNN was developed by Yann LeCunn in 1990 for classifying handwritten digits successfully for OCR-based activities such as reading ZIP codes, checks, and so on. LeNet5 is the latest offering from Yann LeCunn and his colleagues. It takes in 32×32 size images as input and passes them through a convolutional layer to produce six feature maps of size 28×28. The six feature maps are then subsampled to produce six output images of size 14×14. Subsampling can be thought of as a pooling operation. The second convolutional layer has 16 feature maps of size 10×10, while the second subsampling layer reduces the feature map sizes to 5×5. This is followed by two fully connected layers of 120 and 84 units, respectively, followed by the output layer of ten classes corresponding to ten digits.

This model was developed for use in a handwritten character recognition problem and demonstrated on the MNIST standard dataset, achieving approximately 99.2% classification accuracy (or 0.8% error rate). The network was then described as the central technique in a broader system referred to as Graph Transformer Networks.

Compared with modern applications, the number of filters is also small, but the trend of increasing the number of filters with the depth of the network also remains a common pattern in modern usage of the technique.

The flattening of the feature maps and interpretation and classification of the extracted features by fully connected layers also remains a common pattern today. In modern terminology, the final section of the architecture is often referred to as the classifier, whereas the convolutional and pooling layers earlier in the model are referred to as the feature extractor.

Figure 13-1 represents the LeNet5 architecture diagram.

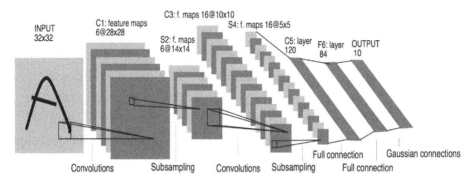

Figure 13-1. *The architecture of LeNet*

One of the key features that make this architecture different from the previous work is that the pooling though subsampling takes 2×2 neighborhood patches and sums up the four-pixel intensity values. The sum is scaled by a trainable weight and a bias, and then fed through a sigmoid activation function. This is a little different from what is done for max pooling and average pooling.

Another key feature is that the filter kernel used for convolution is of size 5×5, and the output units are radial basis function (RBF) units instead of the softmax function. The 84 units of the fully connected layers had 84 connections to each of the classes and hence, 84 corresponding weights. The 84 weights/class represent each class's characteristics. If the inputs to those 84 units are very close to the weights corresponding to a class, then the inputs are more likely to belong to that class.

In a softmax we look at the dot product of the inputs to each of the class's weight vectors, while in RBF units we look at the Euclidean distance between the input and the output class representative's weight vectors. The greater the Euclidean distance, the smaller the chance of the input belonging to that class. The same can be converted to probability by exponentiating the negative of the distance and then normalizing over the different classes.

The Euclidean distances over all the classes for an input record would act as the loss function for that input (Figure 13-2). Let $x = [x_1, x_2, ..., x_{83}, x_{84}]^T \in R^{84 \times 1}$ be the output vector of the fully connected layer. For each class, there would be 84 weight connections. If the representative class's weight vector for the ith class is $w_i \in R^{84 \times 1}$, then the output of the ith class unit can be given by the following:

$$d(x, w_i) = \sum_{j=1}^{84} (x_j - w_{ij})^2$$

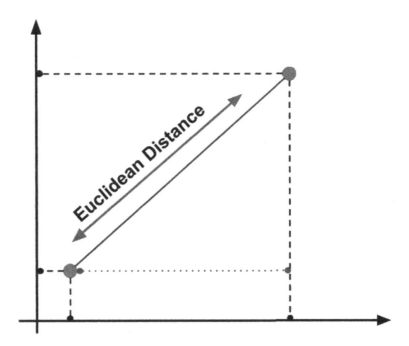

Figure 13-2. *How Euclidean distance works*

AlexNet

The work that perhaps could be credited with sparking renewed interest in neural networks, and the beginning of the dominance of deep learning in many computer vision applications, was the 2012 paper by Alex Krizhevsky, et al. titled "ImageNet Classification with Deep Convolutional Neural Networks." It won the 2012 ImageNet ILSVRC. It was the first time that a CNN architecture beat other methods by a huge margin. Their network achieved an error rate of 15.4% on its top five predictions as compared with a 26.2% error rate for the second-best entry.

Important in the design of AlexNet was a suite of methods that were new or successful, but not widely adopted at the time. Now they have become standards when using CNNs for image classification.

AlexNet made use of the rectified linear activation function, or ReLU, as the non-linearity after each convolutional layer, instead of S-shaped functions such as the logistic or tanh that were common up until that point. Also, a softmax activation function was used in the output layer, now a staple for multiclass classification with neural networks.

The architectural diagram of AlexNet is represented in Figure 13-3. AlexNet consists of five convolutional layers, max pooling layers, and dropout layers, and three fully connected layers in addition to the input and output layer of a thousand class units.

The average pooling used in LeNet-5 was replaced with a max pooling method, although in this case, overlapping pooling was found to outperform the nonoverlapping pooling that is commonly used today (e.g., stride of pooling operation is the same size as the pooling operation, e.g., 2×2 pixels). To address overfitting, the newly proposed dropout method was used between the fully connected layers of the classifier part of the model to improve generalization error.

The inputs to the network are images of size $224 \times 224 \times 3$. The first convolutional layer produces 96 feature maps corresponding to 96 filter kernels of size $11 \times 11 \times 3$, with strides of four-pixel units. The second convolutional layer produces 256 feature maps corresponding to filter kernels of size $5 \times 5 \times 48$. The first two convolutional layers are followed by max pooling layers, whereas the next three convolutional layers are placed one after another without any intermediate max pooling layers.

The fifth convolutional layer is followed by a max pooling layer, two fully connected layers of 4096 units, and finally, a softmax output layer of one thousand classes. The third convolutional layer has 384 filter kernels of size 3 × 3 × 256, whereas the fourth and fifth convolutional layers have 384 and 256 filter kernels each of size 3 × 3 × 192.

A dropout of 0.5 was used in the last two fully connected layers. You will notice that the depth of the filter kernels for convolutions is half the number of feature maps in the preceding layer for all but the third convolutional layer. And this is because the model was split into two pipelines to train on the GPU hardware of the time.

However, if you observe carefully, for the third convolutional activity there is cross-connectivity for convolution, so the filter kernel is of dimension 3 × 3 × 256 and not 3 × 3 × 128. The same kind of cross-connectivity applies to the fully connected layers, and hence, they behave as ordinary fully connected layers with 4096 units.

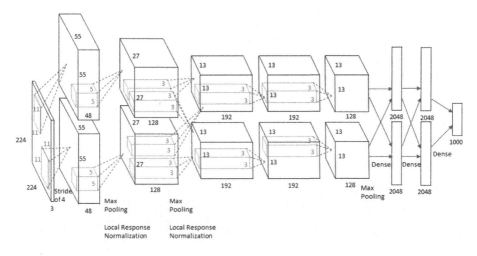

Figure 13-3. *The architecture of AlexNet*

We can summarize the key aspects of the architecture relevant in modern models as follows:

- Use of the ReLU activation function after convolutional layers and softmax for the output layer

- Use of max pooling instead of average pooling

- Use of dropout regularization between the fully connected layers

- Pattern of convolutional layer fed directly to another convolutional layer

- Use of data augmentation

VGG

An important work that sought to standardize architecture design for deep convolutional networks and developed much deeper and better performing models in the process was the 2014 paper titled "Very Deep Convolutional Networks for Large-Scale Image Recognition" by Karen Simonyan and Andrew Zisserman.

Their architecture is generally referred to as VGG after the name of their lab, the Visual Geometry Group at Oxford. Their model was developed and demonstrated in the same ILSVRC competition—in this case, the ILSVRC-2014 version of the challenge.

The first important difference that has become a de facto standard is the use of a large number of small filters. Specifically, filters with the size 3×3 and 1×1 with the stride of one, different from the large sized filters in LeNet-5 and the smaller but still relatively large filters and large stride of four in AlexNet.

Max pooling layers are used after most, but not all, convolutional layers, learning from the example in AlexNet. Yet all pooling is performed with the size 2×2 and the same stride; that too has become a de facto standard. Specifically, the VGG networks use examples of two, three, and even four convolutional layers stacked together before a max pooling layer is used. The rationale was that stacked convolutional layers with smaller filters approximate the effect of one convolutional layer with a larger sized filter, (e.g., three stacked convolutional layers with 3 × 3 filters approximates one convolutional layer with a 7 × 7 filter).

Another important difference is the very large number of filters used. The number of filters increases with the depth of the model, although it starts at a relatively large number of 64 and increases through 128, 256, and 512 filters at the end of the feature extraction part of the model.

A number of variants of the architecture were developed and evaluated, although two are referred to most commonly, given their performance and depth. They are named for the number of layers: they are the VGG-16 and the VGG-19 for 16 and 19 learned layers, respectively.

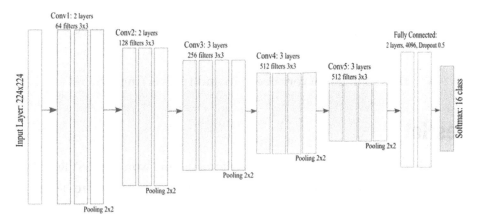

Figure 13-4. *The architecture of VGG*

Figure 13-4 represents the architecture of VGG16. The input to the network is images of size 224 × 224 × 3. The first two convolutional layers produce 64 feature maps, each followed by max pooling. The filters for convolution are of spatial size 3 × 3, with a stride of 1 and pad of 1. Max pooling is of size 2 × 2, with a stride of 2 for the whole network. The third and fourth convolutional layers produce 128 feature maps, each followed by a max pooling layer. The rest of the network follows in a similar fashion, as shown in Figure 13-4. At the end of the network there are three fully connected layers of 4096 units, each followed by the output softmax layer of a thousand classes. Dropout is set at 0.5 for the fully connected layers. All the units in the network have ReLU activations.

We can summarize the key aspects of the architecture that are relevant in modern models as follows:

- Use of very small convolutional filters (e.g., 3 × 3 and 1 × 1 with a stride of one)

- Use of max pooling with a size of 2 × 2 and a stride of the same dimensions

- The importance of stacking convolutional layers together before using a pooling layer to define a block

- Dramatic repetition of the convolutional-pooling block pattern

- Development of very deep (16 and 19 layer) models

ResNet

ResNet is a 152-layer-deep CNN from Microsoft that won the ILSVRC 2015 competition with an error rate of only 3.6%, which is perceived to be better than the human error rate of 5–10%.

A final important innovation in CNNs that we will review was proposed by Kaiming He, et al. in their 2016 paper titled "Deep Residual Learning for Image Recognition."

Their model had an impressive 152 layers. Key to the model design is the idea of residual blocks that make use of shortcut connections. These are simply connections in the network architecture where the input is kept as-is (not weighted) and passed on to a deeper layer (e.g., skipping the next layer).

ResNet implements residual blocks as follows: after each series of convolution–ReLUs–convolution operations, the input to the operation is fed back to the output of the operation. In traditional methods, while doing Convolution and other transformations, we try to fit an underlying mapping to the original data to solve the classification task.

Again, a residual block is a pattern of two convolutional layers with ReLU activation, where the output of the block is combined with the input to the block (e.g., the shortcut connection). A projected version of the input is used via 1 × 1 if the shape of the input to the block is different from the output of the block, the so-called 1 × 1 convolution. These are referred to as projected shortcut connections, compared with the unweighted or identity shortcut connections.

However, with ResNet's residual block concept, we try to learn a residual mapping and not a direct mapping from the input to output. Formally, in each small block of activities we add the input to the block to the output. This is illustrated in Figure 13-5. This concept is based on the hypothesis that it is easier to fit a residual mapping than to fit the original mapping from input to output.

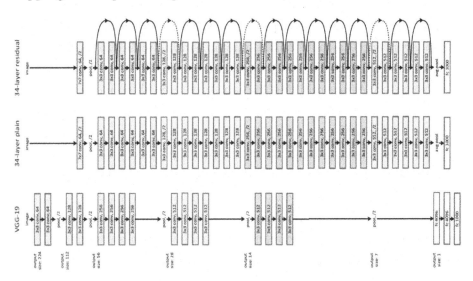

Figure 13-5. *How ResNet works*

We can summarize the key aspects of the architecture relevant to modern models as follows:

- Use of shortcut connections

- Development and repetition of the residual blocks

- Development of very deep (152-layer) models

Transfer Learning

A neural network is trained on data. This network gains knowledge from this data, which is compiled as "*weights*" of the network. These weights can be extracted and then transferred to any other neural network. Instead of training the other neural network from scratch, we **"transfer"** the learned features.

Transfer learning in a broad sense refers to storing knowledge gained while solving a problem, and using that knowledge for a different problem in a similar domain. Transfer learning has been hugely successful in the field of deep learning for a variety of reasons. Deep learning models in general have a huge number of parameters because of the nature of the hidden layers and the connectivity scheme within the different units.

To train such a huge model, lots of data is required or the model will suffer from overfitting problems. In many problems, the huge amount of data required to train the model is not available, but the nature of the problem requires a deep learning solution in order to have a reasonable impact. For instance, in image processing for object recognition, deep learning models are known to provide state-of-the-art solutions. In such cases, transfer learning can be used to generate generic features from a pretrained deep learning model, and then use those features to build a simple model to solve the problem. So, the only parameters for this problem are the ones used to build the simple model.

What Is a Pretrained Model, and Why Use It?

Simply put, a pretrained model is a model created by someone else to solve a similar problem. Instead of building a model from scratch to solve a similar problem, you use the model trained on other problem as a starting point.

So, pretrained models are generally trained on a huge corpus of data and thus have reliable parameters. When we process images through several layers of convolutions, the initial layers learn to detect very generic features such as curls and edges. As the network grows deeper, the convolutional layers in the deeper layers learn to detect more complex features relevant to the specific kind of dataset.

For example, say you want to build a self-learning car. You can spend years to build a decent image recognition algorithm from scratch or you can take an inception model (a pretrained model) from Google that was built on ImageNet data to identify images in those pictures. A pretrained model may not be 100% accurate in your application, but it saves the huge efforts required to reinvent the wheel.

As another example, in a classification, the deeper layers would learn to detect features such as eyes, nose, face, and so forth. Let's assume we have a VGG19 architecture model trained on one thousand categories of the ImageNet dataset. Now, if we get a smaller dataset that has fewer categories of images similar to those of the VGG19 pretrained model dataset, we can use the same VGG19 model up to the fully connected layer and then replace the output layer with the new classes. Also, we keep the weights of the network fixed until the fully connected layer, and only train the model to learn the weights from the fully connected layer to the output layer.

This is because the dataset's nature is the same as the smaller dataset. Thus, the features learned in the pretrained model through the different parameters are good enough for the new classification problem, and we only need to learn the weights from the fully connected layer to the output

461

layer. This is a huge reduction in the number of parameters to learn, and it will reduce the overfitting. Had we trained the small dataset using VGG19 architecture, it might have suffered from severe overfitting because of the large number of parameters to learn on a small dataset. What do you do when the dataset's nature is very different from that of the dataset used for the pretrained model?

Well, in that case, we can use the same pretrained model but fix only the parameters for the first couple of sets of convolutions–ReLUs–max pooling layers and then add a couple of convolutions–ReLU–max pooling layers that would learn to detect features intrinsic to the new dataset. Finally, we would have to have a fully connected layer followed by the output layer. Since we are using the weights of the initial sets of convolutions–ReLUs–max pooling layers from the pretrained VGG19 network, the parameters with respect to those layers need not be learned. As mentioned earlier, the early layers of convolution learn very generic features, such as edges and curves, which are applicable to all kinds of images. The rest of the network would need to be trained to learn specific features inherent to the specific problem dataset.

How to Use a Pretrained Model?

What is our objective when we train a neural network? We wish to identify the correct weights for the network by multiple forward and backward iterations. By using pretrained models that have been previously trained on large datasets, we can directly use the weights and architecture obtained and apply the learning on our problem statement. This is how *transfer learning* works. We "*transfer the learning*" of the pretrained model to our specific problem statement.

We should be very careful while choosing what pretrained model to use in an individual case. If the problem statement we have at hand is very different from the one on which the pretrained model was trained, the prediction we would get would be very inaccurate. For example, a model previously trained for speech recognition would work horribly if we tried to use it to identify objects.

We are lucky that many pretrained architectures are directly available for us as preloaded weights or in the Keras library. The **Imagenet** dataset, for example, has been widely used to build various architectures, since it is large enough (1.2M images) to create a generalized model.

These pretrained networks demonstrate a strong ability to generalize to images outside the given dataset via transfer learning. We make modifications in the preexisting model by fine-tuning the model. Since we assume that the pretrained network has been trained quite well, we would not want to modify the weights too soon and too much. While modifying, we generally use a learning rate smaller than the one used for initially training the model.

Ways to Fine-Tune the Model

1. **Feature extraction:** We can use a pretrained model as a feature extraction mechanism. We can remove the output layer (the one that gives the probabilities for being in each of the 1,000 classes) and then use the entire network as a fixed feature extractor for the new data set.

2. **Use the Architecture of the pretrained model:** We can use the architecture of the model while we initialize all the weights randomly, and train the model according to our dataset again.

3. **Train some layers while freezing others:** Another way to use a pretrained model is to train it partially. We can keep the weights of initial layers of the model frozen while we retrain only the higher layers. We can try to test how many layers are to be frozen and how many to be trained.

Pretrained VGG19

In this section, we are going to demonstrate how to use the pretrained VGG19 model. Using such a great model with this less amount of training will help you to solve complex problems with less effort. So, let's import the packages that we will use in this example.

```
from urllib.request import urlretrieve
from os.path import isfile, isdir
from tqdm import tqdm
import tarfile
import pickle
import numpy as np
import matplotlib.pyplot as plt

import skimage
import skimage.io
import skimage.transform

import tensorflow as tf
import tensornets as nets
```

After importing all the packages, we need to download the CIFAR-10 dataset. This is the dataset we used before in Chapter 11. You can check how we built the model, and how much time and computational power we payed to train the model.

Now, after you import the packages we are going to use and loaded the CIFAR-10 dataset, it's now time to build the model.

We first have to create the input/output variables, and also the hyperparameters we will use in the model building.

```
x = tf.placeholder(tf.float32, shape=(None, 224, 224, 3),
name='input_x')
y = tf.placeholder(tf.float32, shape=(None, 10), name='output_y')
```

```
learning_rate = 0.00001
epochs = 7
batch_size = 32
```

We will use VGG19 with softmax_cross_entropoy loss, of course, and the AdamOptimizer for optimizing the model.

```
logits = nets.VGG19(x, is_training=True, classes=10)
model = tf.identity(logits, name='logits')

loss = tf.losses.softmax_cross_entropy(y, logits)
train = tf.train.AdamOptimizer(learning_rate=learning_rate).
minimize(loss)

correct_pred = tf.equal(tf.argmax(model, 1), tf.argmax(y, 1))
accuracy = tf.reduce_mean(tf.cast(correct_pred, tf.float32),
name='accuracy')
```

If you called print_outputs of the logits, you will see the model architecture summary. It's similar to the Keras model.summary function that shows each layer name, type, its input and output, and the number of parameters per each layer.

```
logits.print_outputs()
```

```
# Output
Scope: vgg19
conv1/1/conv/BiasAdd:0 (?, 224, 224, 64)
conv1/1/Relu:0 (?, 224, 224, 64)
conv1/2/conv/BiasAdd:0 (?, 224, 224, 64)
conv1/2/Relu:0 (?, 224, 224, 64)
conv1/pool/MaxPool:0 (?, 112, 112, 64)
conv2/1/conv/BiasAdd:0 (?, 112, 112, 128)
conv2/1/Relu:0 (?, 112, 112, 128)
```

```
conv2/2/conv/BiasAdd:0 (?, 112, 112, 128)
conv2/2/Relu:0 (?, 112, 112, 128)
conv2/pool/MaxPool:0 (?, 56, 56, 128)
conv3/1/conv/BiasAdd:0 (?, 56, 56, 256)
conv3/1/Relu:0 (?, 56, 56, 256)
conv3/2/conv/BiasAdd:0 (?, 56, 56, 256)
conv3/2/Relu:0 (?, 56, 56, 256)
conv3/3/conv/BiasAdd:0 (?, 56, 56, 256)
conv3/3/Relu:0 (?, 56, 56, 256)
conv3/4/conv/BiasAdd:0 (?, 56, 56, 256)
conv3/4/Relu:0 (?, 56, 56, 256)
conv3/pool/MaxPool:0 (?, 28, 28, 256)
conv4/1/conv/BiasAdd:0 (?, 28, 28, 512)
conv4/1/Relu:0 (?, 28, 28, 512)
conv4/2/conv/BiasAdd:0 (?, 28, 28, 512)
conv4/2/Relu:0 (?, 28, 28, 512)
conv4/3/conv/BiasAdd:0 (?, 28, 28, 512)
conv4/3/Relu:0 (?, 28, 28, 512)
conv4/4/conv/BiasAdd:0 (?, 28, 28, 512)
conv4/4/Relu:0 (?, 28, 28, 512)
```

Now let us print the model summary using print_summary; we will see the total layers in the model, the total weights, and the number of parameters.

```
logits.print_summary()
Scope: vgg19
Total layers: 19
Total weights: 114
Total parameters: 418,833,630
```

Now, after we've built the model architecture, and checked the total parameters and total layers in the model, we are ready to train it and see what will happen.

```
save_model_path = './image_classification'

print('Training...')
with tf.Session() as sess:
    # Initializing the variables
    sess.run(tf.global_variables_initializer())
    print('global_variables_initializer ... done ...')
    sess.run(logits.pretrained())
    print('model.pretrained ... done ... ')

    # Training cycle
    print('starting training ... ')
    for epoch in range(epochs):
        # Loop over all batches
        n_batches = 5
        for batch_i in range(1, n_batches + 1):
            for batch_features, batch_labels in load_
            preprocess_training_batch(batch_i, batch_size):
                sess.run(train, {x: batch_features, y: batch_
                labels})

            print('Epoch {:>2}, CIFAR-10 Batch {}:  '.
            format(epoch + 1, batch_i), end='')

            # calculate the mean accuracy over all validation
            dataset
            valid_acc = 0
            for batch_valid_features, batch_valid_labels in
            batch_features_labels(tmpValidFeatures, valid_
            labels, batch_size):
```

```
            valid_acc += sess.run(accuracy, {x:batch_valid_
            features, y:batch_valid_labels})

        tmp_num = tmpValidFeatures.shape[0]/batch_size
        print('Validation Accuracy: {:.6f}'.format(valid_
        acc/tmp_num))

    # Save Model
    saver = tf.train.Saver()
    save_path = saver.save(sess, save_model_path)
```

If this code step is running correctly for you, then we can say "well done to you." Now the model is training as in the output below, and after it finishes, you will see the result in Figure 13-6.

```
Training...
global_variables_initializer ... done ...
model.pretrained ... done ...
starting training ...
Epoch  1, CIFAR-10 Batch 1:  Validation Accuracy: 0.510000
Epoch  1, CIFAR-10 Batch 2:  Validation Accuracy: 0.719000
Epoch  1, CIFAR-10 Batch 3:  Validation Accuracy: 0.770200
Epoch  1, CIFAR-10 Batch 4:  Validation Accuracy: 0.814000
Epoch  1, CIFAR-10 Batch 5:  Validation Accuracy: 0.832000
Epoch  2, CIFAR-10 Batch 1:  Validation Accuracy: 0.841600
Epoch  2, CIFAR-10 Batch 2:  Validation Accuracy: 0.850000
Epoch  2, CIFAR-10 Batch 3:  Validation Accuracy: 0.868000
Epoch  2, CIFAR-10 Batch 4:  Validation Accuracy: 0.856600
Epoch  2, CIFAR-10 Batch 5:  Validation Accuracy: 0.857400
```

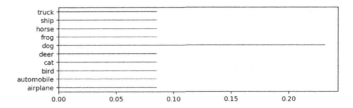

Figure 13-6. *The prediction of the left image*

Summary

In this chapter, we learned about advanced operations in CNNs, and how state-of-art architecture models such as LeNet, AlexNet, VGG, and ResNet work.

Further, we discussed what transfer learning is, and how to perform transfer learning using the pretrained versions of these CNNs. In the next chapter, we will discuss some selected topics in natural language processing and how they are useful for you to know and understand.

CHAPTER 14

Selected Topics in Natural Language Processing

In the previous chapter, we showed you some advanced concepts in computer vision such as state-of-art architectures and the transfer learning approach. It is important for you to understand these concepts when you are about to build a model to do a certain task for you.

In this chapter, we will discuss some concepts in natural language processing (NLP) that are necessary to fully understand the sequential methods, which are considered to be the traditional methods of NLP. They are relied on by the bag-of-words model and the vector space of words model.

One of the key areas for NLP is the syntactic and semantic analysis of language. Syntactic analysis refers to how words are grouped and connected in a sentence. The main tasks in syntactic analysis are tagging parts of speech, detecting syntactic classes (such as verbs, nouns, and noun phrases), and assembling sentences by constructing syntax trees. Semantic analysis refers to complex tasks such as finding synonyms, or performing word-verb disambiguation.

© Hisham El-Amir and Mahmoud Hamdy 2020
H. El-Amir and M. Hamdy, *Deep Learning Pipeline*,
https://doi.org/10.1007/978-1-4842-5349-6_14

Vector Space Model

In NLP information-retrieval systems, a document is generally represented as simply a vector of the count of the words it contains. For retrieving documents similar to a specific document, either the cosine of the angle or the dot product between the document and other documents is computed. The cosine of the angle between two vectors gives a similarity measure based on the similarity between their vector compositions. To illustrate this fact, let us look at two vectors, $x, y = R^{2 \times 1}$, shown as $x = [2\ 3]^T$ and $y = [4\ 5]^T$.

Although vectors x and y are different, their cosine similarity is the maximum possible value of 1. This is because the two vectors are identical in their component compositions. The ratio of the first component to the second component for both vectors is 2/32/3; hence, content composition-wise they are treated as being similar. Therefore, documents with high cosine similarity are generally considered similar in nature.

Let's say we have two sentences: *Doc*1 = [*The dog chased the cat*] and *Doc*2 = [*The cat was chased down by the dog*]. The number of distinct words in the two sentences would be the vector space dimension for this problem. The distinct words are *The, dog, chased, the, cat, down, by,* and *was*. So, we can represent each document as an eight-dimensional vector of word counts (Table 14-1).

Table 14-1. *Words per Document Example*

Word/Doc	The	Dog	Chased	Cat	Down	By	Was
Doc 1	1	1	1	1	0	0	0
Doc 2	1	1	1	1	1	1	1

If we represent *Doc*1 by v_1 and *Doc*2 by v_2, then the cosine similarity can be expressed as $\cos(v_1, v_2) = \dfrac{v_1^T v_2}{\|v_1\|\|v_2\|}$ (Figure 14-1) and the Euclidean distance is expressed as $d(v_1, v_2) = \sqrt{\sum(v_1 - v_2)^2}$ (Figure 14-2), where $\|v_1\|$ is the magnitude or the l_2 norm of the vector v_1. As stated earlier, cosine similarity gives a measure of the similarity based on the component composition of each vector. If the components of the document vectors are in somewhat similar proportion, the cosine distance would be high. It doesn't take the magnitude of the vector into consideration.

In certain cases, when the documents are of highly varying lengths, the dot product between the document vectors is taken instead of the cosine similarity. This is done when, along with the content of the document, the size of the document is also compared. For instance, we can have a tweet in which the words *global* and *economics* might have word counts of 1 and 2, respectively, while a newspaper article might have word counts of 50 and 100, respectively, for the same words. Assuming the other words in both documents have insignificant counts, the cosine similarity between the tweet and the newspaper article would be close to 1. Since the tweet sizes are significantly smaller, the word counts proportion of 1 : 2 for global and economics doesn't really compare to the proportion of 1 : 2 for these words in the newspaper article.

Hence, it doesn't really make sense to assign such a high similarity measure to these documents for several applications. In that case, taking the dot product as a similarity measure rather than the cosine similarity helps, since it scales up the cosine similarity by the magnitude of the word vectors for the two documents.

For comparable cosine similarities, documents with higher magnitudes would have higher dot product similarity, since they have enough text to justify their word composition. The word composition for small texts might just be by chance and not be a true representation of its intended representation. For most applications where the documents are of comparable lengths, cosine similarity is a fair enough measure.

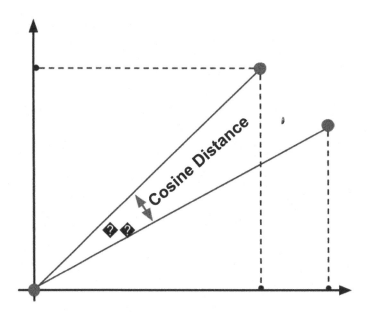

Figure 14-1. *How cosine distance works*

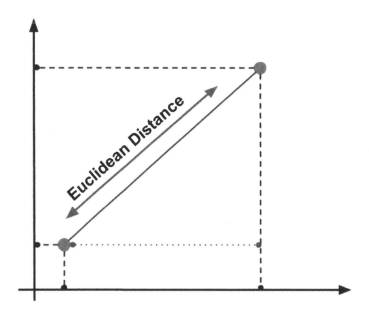

Figure 14-2. *How Euclidean distance works*

Vector Representation of Words

Just as the documents are expressed as vectors of different word counts, a word in a corpus can also be expressed as a vector, with the components being counts the word has in each document.

Other ways of expressing words as vectors would be to have the component specific to a document set to 1 if the word is present in the document or 0 if the word doesn't exist in the document.

Reusing the same example, a word can be expressed as a two-dimensional vector $[1\ 1]^T$ in the corpus of two documents. In a huge corpus of documents, the dimensionality of the word vector would be large as well. Like document similarity, word similarity can be computed through either cosine similarity or dot product.

Another way to represent words in a corpus is to one-hot encode them. In that case, the dimensionality of each word would be the number of unique words in the corpus. Each word would correspond to an index that would be set to 1 for the word, and all other remaining entries would be set to 0. So, each would be extremely sparse. Even similar words would have entries set to 1 for different indexes, so any kind of similarity measure would not work.

To represent word vectors better so that the similarity of the words can be captured more meaningfully, and also to render less dimensionality to word vectors, Word2Vec was introduced.

Word2Vec

Word2Vec is an intelligent way of expressing a word as a vector by training the word against words in its neighborhood. Words that are contextually like the given word would produce high cosine similarity or dot product when their Word2Vec representations are considered.

Generally, the words in the corpus are trained with respect to the words in their neighborhood to derive the set of the Word2Vec representations. The two most popular methods of extracting Word2Vec representations are the CBOW (continuous bag of words) method and the Skip-Gram method. The core idea behind CBOW is expressed in Figure 14-3.

Continuous Bag of Words

The Word2Vec family of models is unsupervised. This means that you can just give it a corpus without additional labels or information and it can construct dense word embeddings from the corpus. But you will still need to leverage a supervised, classification methodology once you have this corpus to get to these embeddings. But we will do that from within the corpus itself, without any auxiliary information. We can model this CBOW architecture now as a deep learning classification model such that we take in the ***context words as our input, X*** and try to predict the ***target word, Y***. In fact, building this architecture is simpler than the Skip-gram model where we try to predict a whole bunch of context words from a source target word.

The CBOW method tries to predict the center word from the context of the neighboring words in a specific window length. Let's look at the following sentence and consider a window of five as a neighborhood.

"The cat jumped over the fence and crossed the road."

In the first instance, we will try to predict the word *jumped* from its neighborhood *the cat over the*. In the second instance, as we slide the window by one position, we will try to predict the word *over* from the neighboring words *cat jumped the fence*. This process would be repeated for the entire corpus.

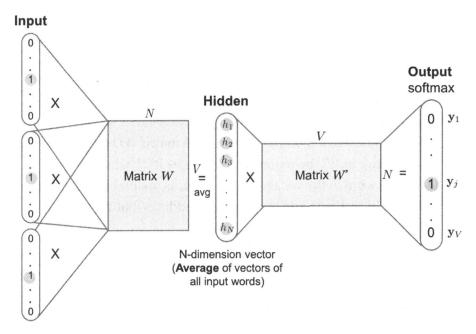

Figure 14-3. *The CBOW model*

As shown in Figure 14-3, the CBOW model is trained on the context words as input and the center word as the output. The words in the input layer are expressed as one-hot encoded vectors, where the component for the specific word is set to 1 and all other components are set to 0. The number of unique words V in the corpus determines the dimensionality of these one-hot encoded vectors, hence $x(t) \in R^{V \times 1}$. Each one-hot encoded vector $x(t)$ is multiplied by the input embeddings matrix $WI \in R^{N \times V}$ to extract the word embeddings vector $u(k) \in R^{N \times 1}$ specific to that word. The index k in $u(k)$ signifies that $u(k)$ is the word embedded for the kth word in the vocabulary. The hidden-layer vector h is the average of the input embeddings vectors for all the context words in the window, therefore $h \in R^{N \times 1}$ has the same dimension as that of the word embeddings vectors.

$$h = \frac{1}{l-1} \sum_{j=(i-2)\,j\neq i}^{(i+1)} (WI)x^j$$

where l is the length of the window size.

Similarly, all the word embeddings vectors for the input words are extracted, and their average is the output of the hidden layer. The output of the hidden layer h is supposed to represent the embeddings of the target word. All the words in the vocabulary have another set of word embeddings housed in the output embeddings matrix $WO \in R^{V \times N}$. Let the word embeddings in WO be represented by $v(i) \in R^{N \times 1}$, where the index i denotes the jth word in the vocabulary in order, as maintained in both the one-hot encoding scheme and the input embeddings matrix.

$$[WO][h] = \left[v_1^T h, v_2^T h, \ldots, v_i^T h, \ldots, v_v^T h \right]$$

The dot product of the hidden-layer embeddings h is computed with each of the v^j or v_i for simplicity by multiplying the matrix WO by h. The dot product, as we know, would give a similarity measure for each of the output words embeddings v^j *where* $j \in R^N$ and the hidden-layer computed embeddings h. The dot products are normalized to probability through a softmax and, based on the target word w^t, the categorical cross-entropy loss is computed and backpropagated through gradient descent to update the matrices' weights for both the input and output embeddings matrices.

The softmax output probability for the jth word of the vocabulary, $w_{(j)}$, given the context words, is given by the following:

$$p\left(w = w^i \mid h\right) = p^i = \frac{e^{v_i^T h}}{\sum_k^V e^{v_k^T h}}$$

If the actual output is represented by a one-hot encoded vector y, then the loss function for the particular combination of target word and its context words can be given by the following:

$$C = \sum_{i}^{v} y_i \log\left(p^i\right)$$

The different p^i are dependent on the input and output embeddings matrices' components, which are parameters to the cost function C. The cost function can be minimized with respect to these embeddings parameters through backpropagation gradient-descent techniques. To make this more intuitive, let's say our target variable is *cat*. If the hidden-layer vector h gives the maximum dot product with the outer matrix word embeddings vector for *cat* while the dot product with the other outer word embeddings is low, then the embeddings vectors are more or less correct. So, very little error or *log* loss will be backpropagated to correct the embeddings matrices. However, let's say the dot product of h with *cat* is less, and that of the other outer embeddings vectors is more; the loss of the softmax is going to be significantly higher, and thus more errors/log loss are going to be backpropagated to reduce the error.

Implementing Continuous Bag of Words

The CBOW TensorFlow implementation has been illustrated in this section. The neighboring words within a distance of two from either side are used to predict the middle word. The output layer is a big softmax over the entire vocabulary. The word embeddings vectors are chosen to be of size 128. The detailed implementation is outlined in the following code. See also Figure 14-4.

The first thing in the code is that we need to import the needed packages, and as always, these packages include TensorFlow.

```python
import numpy as np
import tensorflow as tf
from sklearn.manifold import TSNE
import matplotlib.pyplot as plt
%matplotlib inline
```

Then we need to put in the utility functions; these functions will help us a lot in processing text data such as text to vector transformations and more.

```python
def one_hot(ind,vocab_size):
    rec = np.zeros(vocab_size)
    rec[ind] = 1
    return rec

def create_training_data(corpus_raw,WINDOW_SIZE = 2):
    words_list = []
    for sent in corpus_raw.split('.'):
        for w in sent.split():
            if w != '.':
                words_list.append(w.split('.')[0])
    words_list = set(words_list)
    word2ind = {}
    ind2word = {}
    vocab_size = len(words_list)
    for i,w in enumerate(words_list): # Build the dictionaries
        word2ind[w] = i
        ind2word[i] = w

    print(word2ind)
    sentences_list = corpus_raw.split('.')
    sentences = []
    for sent in sentences_list:
```

```
    sent_array = sent.split()
    sent_array = [s.split('.')[0] for s in sent_array]
    sentences.append(sent_array)

  data_recs = []

  for sent in sentences:
    for ind,w in enumerate(sent):
      rec = []
      for nb_w in sent[max(ind - WINDOW_SIZE, 0) : min(ind +
      WINDOW_SIZE, len(sent)) + 1] :
        if nb_w != w:
          rec.append(nb_w)
        data_recs.append([rec,w])

  x_train,y_train = [],[]

  for rec in data_recs:
    input_ = np.zeros(vocab_size)
    for i in range(WINDOW_SIZE-1):
      input_ += one_hot(word2ind[ rec[0][i] ], vocab_size)
    input_ = input_/len(rec[0])
    x_train.append(input_)
    y_train.append(one_hot(word2ind[ rec[1] ], vocab_size))
  return x_train,y_train,word2ind,ind2word,vocab_size
```

Then we load the data. To simplify this process, we put in a dummy paragraph for the sack of ease. You can put a real data if you want to.

```
corpus_raw = "Deep Learning has evolved from Artificial
Neural Networks, which has been there since the 1940s. Neural
Networks are interconnected networks of processing units called
artificial neurons that loosely mimic axons in a biological
brain. In a biological neuron, the dendrites receive input
```

signals from various neighboring neurons, typically greater than 1000. These modified signals are then passed on to the cell body or soma of the neuron, where these signals are summed together and then passed on to the axon of the neuron. If the received input signal is more than a specified threshold, the axon will release a signal which again will pass on to neighboring dendrites of other neurons. Figure 3-1 depicts the structure of a biological neuron for reference. The artificial neuron units are inspired by the biological neurons with some modifications as per convenience. Much like the dendrites, the input connections to the neuron carry the attenuated or amplified input signals from other neighboring neurons. The signals are passed on to the neuron, where the input signals are summed up and then a decision is taken what to output based on the total input received. For instance, for a binary threshold neuron an output value of 1 is provided when the total input exceeds a pre-defined threshold; otherwise, the output stays at 0. Several other types of neurons are used in artificial neural networks, and their implementation only differs with respect to the activation function on the total input to produce the neuron output. In the different biological equivalents are tagged in the artificial neuron for easy analogy and interpretation."

Then we will use our functions to process the data, transforming it to x_train and y_train, and also extract some info like vocab_size.

```
corpus_raw = (corpus_raw).lower()
x_train,y_train,word2ind,ind2word,vocab_size= create_training_
data(corpus_raw,2)
```

Now, after loading and processing the data, we need to implement the CBOW. But first we need to set the parameters and create variables.

```
emb_dims = 128
learning_rate = 0.001

x = tf.placeholder(tf.float32,[None,vocab_size])
y = tf.placeholder(tf.float32,[None,vocab_size])

W = tf.Variable(tf.random_normal([vocab_size,emb_dims],mean=0.0,
stddev=0.02,dtype=tf.float32))
b = tf.Variable(tf.random_normal([emb_dims],mean=0.0,stddev=0.02,
dtype=tf.float32))
W_outer = tf.Variable(tf.random_normal([emb_dims,vocab_size],
mean=0.0,stddev=0.02,dtype=tf.float32))
b_outer = tf.Variable(tf.random_normal([vocab_size],mean=0.0,
stddev=0.02,dtype=tf.float32))
```

Now, let's create the model.

```
hidden = tf.add(tf.matmul(x,W),b)
logits = tf.add(tf.matmul(hidden,W_outer),b_outer)
cost = tf.reduce_mean(tf.nn.softmax_cross_entropy_with_
logits(logits=logits, labels=y))
optimizer = tf.train.AdamOptimizer(learning_rate=learning_
rate).minimize(cost)
```

And, after creating the architecture, let's create the graph and run the model.

```
epochs,batch_size = 100,10
batch = len(x_train)//batch_size
# train for n_iter iterations
with tf.Session() as sess:
  sess.run(tf.global_variables_initializer())
```

```
for epoch in range(epochs):
  batch_index = 0
  for batch_num in range(batch):
    x_batch = x_train[batch_index: batch_index +batch_size]
    y_batch = y_train[batch_index: batch_index +batch_size]
    sess.run(optimizer,feed_dict={x: x_batch,y: y_batch})
    print('epoch:',epoch,'loss :', sess.run(cost,feed_
    dict={x: x_batch,y: y_batch}))
W_embed_trained = sess.run(W)
```

If the model is working, we will see this output.

```
epoch: 0 loss : 4.867816
epoch: 1 loss : 1.1019261
epoch: 2 loss : 0.7556237
epoch: 3 loss : 0.5196438
epoch: 4 loss : 0.47611102
```

After running the model and finishing the epochs, we can use the
following code to plot the model.

```
W_embedded = TSNE(n_components=2).fit_transform(W_embed_
trained)
plt.figure(figsize=(10,10))
for i in range(len(W_embedded)):
  plt.text(W_embedded[i,0],W_embedded[i,1],ind2word[i])
plt.xlim(-150,150)
plt.ylim(-150,150)
```

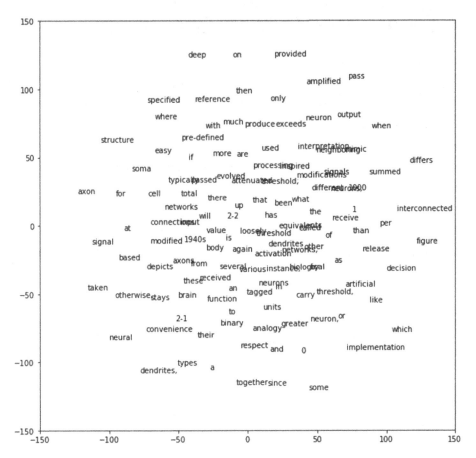

Figure 14-4. *The TSNE of the CBOW*

The word embeddings learned have been projected to a 2-D
plane through the TSNE plot. The TSNE plot gives a rough idea of the
neighborhood of a given word. We can see that the word embeddings
vectors learned are reasonable. For instance, the words *deep* and *learning*
are very close to each other. Similarly, the words *biological* and *references*
are also very close to each other.

Skip-Gram Model for Word Embeddings

Skip-gram models work the other way around. Instead of trying to predict the current word from the context words, as in CBOW, in Skip-gram models the context words are predicted based on the current word. Generally, given a current word, context words are taken in its neighborhood in each window. For a given window of five words, there would be four context words that one needs to predict based on the current word. Figure 14-5 shows the high-level design of a Skip-gram model. Much like CBOW, in the Skip-gram model one needs to learn two sets of word embeddings: one for the input words and one for the output context words. A Skip-gram model can be seen as a reversed CBOW model.

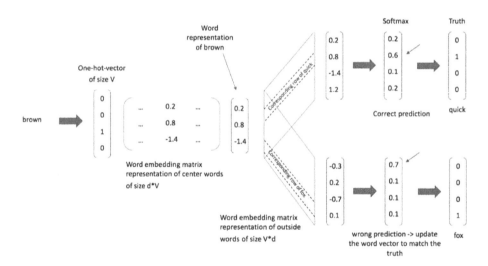

Figure 14-5. *How Skip-gram works*

In the CBOW model, the input to the model is a one-hot encoded vector $x^i \in R^{V \times 1}$ for the current word, where V is the size of the vocabulary of the corpus. However, unlike CBOW, here the input is the current word and not the context words. The input x^i, when multiplied by the input word embeddings matrix WI, produces the word embeddings vector $u^k \in R^{N \times 1}$, given that x^t represents the kth word in the vocabulary list. N, as before, represents the word embeddings dimensionality. The hidden-layer output h is nothing but u^k.

The dot product of the hidden-layer output h is computed with every word vector $v(j)$ of the outer embeddings' matrix $WO \in R^{V \times N}$ by computing $[WO][h]$ just as in CBOW. However, instead of one softmax output layer, there are multiple softmax layers based on the number of context words that we are going to predict. For example, in Figure 14-5 there are four softmax output layers corresponding to the four context words. The input to each of these softmax layers is the same set of dot products in $[WO][h]$, representing how similar the input word is to each word in the vocabulary.

$$[WO][h] = \left[v_1^T h, v_2^T h, \ldots, v_i^T h, \ldots, v_v^T h \right]$$

Similarly, all the softmax layers would receive the same set of probabilities corresponding to all the vocabulary words, with the probability of the jth word w^j given the current or the center word w^k being given by the following:

$$p\left(w^j \mid w^k\right) = p^i = \frac{e^{v_j^T w^k}}{\sum_k^V e^{v_k^T w^k}}$$

If there are four target words, and their one-hot encoded vectors are represented by $y^{j-2}, y^{j-1}, y^{j+1}, y^{j+2} \in R^{v \times 1}$, then the total loss function C for the word combination would be the summation of all four softmax losses as represented here:

$$C = - \sum_{m=t-2\, m \neq t}^{t+2} \sum_j^V y_j^m \log\left(p^j\right)$$

Gradient descent using backpropagation can be used to minimize the cost function and derive the input and output embeddings matrices' components.

Here are a few salient features about the Skip-gram and CBOW models:

- For Skip-gram models, the window size is not generally fixed. Given a maximum window size, the window size at each current word is randomly chosen so that smaller windows are chosen more frequently than larger ones. With Skip-gram, one can generate a lot of training samples from a limited amount of text, and infrequent words and phrases are also very well represented.

- CBOW is much faster to train than Skip-gram and has slightly better accuracy for frequent words.

- Both Skip-gram and CBOW look at local windows for word co-occurrences and then try to predict either the context words from the center word (as with Skip-gram) or the center word from the context words (as with CBOW). So, basically, we observe in Skip-gram that locally within each window the probability of the co-occurrence of the context word w_C and the current word w_t, given by $P(w_c|w_t)$, is assumed to be proportional to the exponential of the dot product of their word embeddings vectors.

- where u and v are the input and output word embeddings vectors for the current and context words, respectively. Since the co-occurrence is measured locally, these models miss utilizing the global co-occurrence statistics for word pairs within certain window lengths. Next, we are going to explore a basic method to look at the global co-occurrence statistics over a corpus, and then use SVD (singular value decomposition) to generate word vectors.

Implementing Skip-Gram

In this section, we will illustrate the Skip-gram model for learning word vector embeddings with a TensorFlow implementation. The model is trained on a small dataset for easy representation. However, the model can be used to train large corpuses as desired. As illustrated in the Skip-gram section, the model is trained as a classification network. However, we are more interested in the word embeddings matrix than in the actual classification of words. The size of the word embeddings has been chosen to be 128. The detailed code is represented as follows. Once the word embeddings vectors are learned, they are projected via TSNE on a two-dimensional surface for visual interpretation.

As always, we have to import the needed packages, including TensorFlow.

```
import numpy as np
import tensorflow as tf
from sklearn.manifold import TSNE
import matplotlib.pyplot as plt
%matplotlib inline
```

And we import the utility functions—all of them.

```
def one_hot(ind,vocab_size):
  rec = np.zeros(vocab_size)
  rec[ind] = 1
  return rec

def create_training_data(corpus_raw,WINDOW_SIZE = 2):
  words_list = []
  for sent in corpus_raw.split('.'):
    for w in sent.split():
      if w != '.':
        words_list.append(w.split('.')[0])
```

```python
words_list = set(words_list)
word2ind = {}
ind2word = {}
vocab_size = len(words_list)
for i,w in enumerate(words_list): # Build the dictionaries
  word2ind[w] = i
  ind2word[i] = w

print(word2ind)
sentences_list = corpus_raw.split('.')
sentences = []
for sent in sentences_list:
  sent_array = sent.split()
  sent_array = [s.split('.')[0] for s in sent_array]
  sentences.append(sent_array)

data_recs = []

for sent in sentences:
  for ind,w in enumerate(sent):
    rec = []
    for nb_w in sent[max(ind - WINDOW_SIZE, 0) : min(ind +
    WINDOW_SIZE, len(sent)) + 1] :
      if nb_w != w:
        rec.append(nb_w)
      data_recs.append([rec,w])

x_train,y_train = [],[]

for rec in data_recs:
  input_ = np.zeros(vocab_size)
  for i in range(WINDOW_SIZE-1):
    input_ += one_hot(word2ind[ rec[0][i] ], vocab_size)
  input_ = input_/len(rec[0])
```

```
    x_train.append(input_)
    y_train.append(one_hot(word2ind[ rec[1] ], vocab_size))
  return x_train,y_train,word2ind,ind2word,vocab_size
```

After this, we need to load the data. For simplicity, we will use the same paragraph used in the previous example, so you have to load it or load your own data. And do not forget to process it.

Then, we need to set the parameters and create the needed variables such as training input and output, weights, and biases for the model.

```
emb_dims = 128
learning_rate = 0.0001
epochs,batch_size = 100,10
batch = len(x_train)//batch_size

x = tf.placeholder(tf.float32,[None,vocab_size])
y = tf.placeholder(tf.float32,[None,vocab_size])

W = tf.Variable(tf.random_normal([vocab_size,emb_dims],
mean=0.0,stddev=0.02,dtype=tf.float32))
b = tf.Variable(tf.random_normal([emb_dims],mean=0.0,
stddev=0.02,dtype=tf.float32))
W_outer = tf.Variable(tf.random_normal([emb_dims,vocab_size],
mean=0.0,stddev=0.02,dtype=tf.float32))
b_outer = tf.Variable(tf.random_normal([vocab_size],mean=0.0,
stddev=0.02,dtype=tf.float32))
```

Now we are ready to create the Skip-gram model. Let's build it.

```
hidden = tf.add(tf.matmul(x,W),b)
logits = tf.add(tf.matmul(hidden,W_outer),b_outer)
cost = tf.reduce_mean(tf.nn.softmax_cross_entropy_with_
logits(logits=logits, labels=y))
optimizer = tf.train.AdamOptimizer(learning_rate=learning_
rate).minimize(cost)
```

Now you can run the model, the same as the previous model in the CBOW example, and see the result using the TSNE plot. We will leave this job for you as an exercise.

GloVe

Now we'll discuss one of the newer methods of creating vector space models of word semantics, more commonly known as word embeddings. GloVe, coined from Global Vectors, is a model for distributed word representation. The model is an unsupervised learning algorithm for obtaining vector representations for words. This is achieved by mapping words into a meaningful space where the distance between words is related to semantic similarity. Training is performed on aggregated global word–word co-occurrence statistics from a corpus, and the resulting representations showcase interesting linear substructures of the word vector space. It was developed as an open source project at Stanford. As a log-bilinear regression model for unsupervised learning of word representations, it combines the features of two model families, namely the global matrix factorization and local context window methods.

GloVe is a pretrained, readily available, word embeddings vectors library from Stanford University. The training method for GloVe is significantly different from those for CBOW and Skip-gram. Instead of basing predictions on local-running windows for words, GloVe uses global word-to-word co-occurrence statistics from a corpus to train the model and derive the GloVe vectors. Pretrained GloVe word embeddings are available at `https://nlp.stanford.edu/projects/glove/`.

In NLP, global matrix factorization is the process of using matrix factorization methods from linear algebra to perform rank reduction on a large term-frequency matrix. These matrices usually represent either term–document frequencies, in which the rows are words and the columns are documents (or sometimes paragraphs), or term–term frequencies, which have words on both axes and measure co-occurrence. Global matrix factorization applied to term-document frequency matrices is more commonly known as latent semantic analysis (LSA). In latent semantic analysis, the high-dimensional matrix is reduced via singular value decomposition (SVD).

Like SVD methods, GloVe looks at the global co-occurrence statistics, but the relation of the word and context vectors with respect to the co-occurrences count is a little different. If there are two words wi and wj and a context word w_k, then the ratio of the probabilities $P(w_k|w_i)$ and $P(w_k|w_j)$ provide more information than the probabilities themselves.

1. Collect word co-occurrence statistics in the form of word co-occurrence matrix X. Each element Xij of such a matrix represents how often word i appears in the context of word j. Usually we scan our corpus in the following manner: for each term we look for context terms within some area defined by a *window_size* before the term and a *window_size* after the term. Also, we give less weight for more distant words, usually using this formula:

$$decay = \frac{1}{offset}$$

2. Define soft constraints for each word pair:

$$w_i^T w_j + b_i + b_j = log\left(X_{ij}\right)$$

3. Here, w_i = vector for the main word, w_j = vector for the context word, and b_i, b_j are scalar biases for the main and context words.

4. Define a cost function.

$$J = \sum_i^V \sum_j^V f\left(X_{ij}\right)\left(w_i^T w_j + b_i + b_j - log\left(X_{ij}\right)\right)^2$$

Here, f is a weighting function, which helps us to prevent learning only from extremely common word pairs. The GloVe authors chose the following function:

$$f\left(X_{ij}\right)=\{\left(\frac{X_{ij}}{x_{max}}\right)^{\propto} \ \ if \ X_{ij} < XMAX \ 1 \ \ otherwise$$

Summary

In this chapter we discussed the traditional methods of natural language processing.

In the next and final chapter, we will show you some examples of how to build a deep learning pipeline on three different datasets: one on a tabular dataset; another on images; and the final one on text data, showing you a TensorFlow model from the ground up with progressive documentation.

CHAPTER 15

Applications

Case Study—Tabular Dataset
Understanding the Dataset

In this section, we are going to understand the dataset. By understanding, we mean that we are going to extract any information we can get from this data and we are going to exercise on "Titanic: Machine Learning from Disaster" from Kaggle (www.kaggle.com/c/titanic). I was also inspired to do some visual analysis of the dataset from some other resources I came across. So, let us start coding.

If you browse the dataset page on Kaggle, you will notice that the page gives information about the details of the passengers aboard the Titanic, and a column on survival of the passengers. Those who survived are represented as "1" and those who did not survive are represented as "0". The goal of this exercise is to determine if, with the other features/information about the passengers, it is possible to determine those who are likely to survive.

To check any hypothesis you have in mind, you need a good visualization, to see the information inside the data. Data visualization allows decision makers to see relationships among multidimensional datasets, and provides new ways to understand data through the use of heat maps, fever charts, and other rich graphical representations.

H. El-Amir and M. Hamdy, *Deep Learning Pipeline,*
https://doi.org/10.1007/978-1-4842-5349-6_15

Let us first import all the needed packages. You are free to use another package, but these are the ones recommended to get the job done.

```
import pandas as pd
import numpy as np
import matplotlib.pyplot as plt
import seaborn as sns
import tensorflow as tf
```

If you do not remember the preceding packages, here is a small summary about three of them, but do not hesitate to return to the introduction part and read about all the packages this book contains.

- **pandas** is a great library that deals with everything that NumPy and SciPy cannot do. Thanks to its specific data structures, namely DataFrames and Series, pandas allows you to handle complex tables of data of different types and time series. Also, you can then slice, dice, handle missing elements, add, rename, aggregate, reshape, and finally visualize your data as well.

- **matplotlib** is a Python 2-D plotting library that produces publication quality figures in a variety of hard copy formats and interactive environments across platforms. Also, it contains all components that are required to create quality plots from data and visualize them interactively. For simple plotting, the pyplot module provides a MATLAB-like interface.

- **Seaborn** is a Python data visualization library based on matplotlib. It provides a high-level interface for drawing attractive and informative statistical graphics.

Scratching the Surface

After loading all needed packages, we need to load the dataset; of course we will use pandas to load it as follows:

```
titanic_df = pd.read_csv('./input/titanic/train.csv')
titanic_df.head()
```

The head() function will print the first five rows of the DataFrame that contain the dataset (Figure 15-1).

	PassengerId	Survived	Pclass	Name	Sex	Age	SibSp	Parch	Ticket	Fare	Cabin	Embarked
0	1	0	3	Braund, Mr. Owen Harris	male	22.0	1	0	A/5 21171	7.2500	NaN	S
1	2	1	1	Cumings, Mrs. John Bradley (Florence Briggs Th...	female	38.0	1	0	PC 17599	71.2833	C85	C
2	3	1	3	Heikkinen, Miss. Laina	female	26.0	0	0	STON/O2. 3101282	7.9250	NaN	S
3	4	1	1	Futrelle, Mrs. Jacques Heath (Lily May Peel)	female	35.0	1	0	113803	53.1000	C123	S
4	5	0	3	Allen, Mr. William Henry	male	35.0	0	0	373450	8.0500	NaN	S

Figure 15-1. *The pandas DataFrame that contains the Titanic dataset*

Note   If you wonder why you don't see a similar table, that's because we have **Jupyter** as the IDE. So, try to download it and install it.

Now, before we start visualizing the dataset, we need a bit of information about each column of this dataset, and we can achieve this by calling the info() function from the DataFrame.

```
titanic_df.info()
```

This function outputs the summary of the dataset. The summary contains column names, types and number of non-null entries, and it outputs the size of the DataFrame in memory as follows (Figure 15-2).

```
<class 'pandas.core.frame.DataFrame'>
RangeIndex: 891 entries, 0 to 890
Data columns (total 12 columns):
PassengerId    891 non-null int64
Survived       891 non-null int64
Pclass         891 non-null int64
Name           891 non-null object
Sex            891 non-null object
Age            714 non-null float64
SibSp          891 non-null int64
Parch          891 non-null int64
Ticket         891 non-null object
Fare           891 non-null float64
Cabin          204 non-null object
Embarked       889 non-null object
dtypes: float64(2), int64(5), object(5)
memory usage: 83.6+ KB
```

Figure 15-2. *Titanic DataFrame column information*

Now we can start visualizing each column and see if we can extract any knowledge from it or not.

Let us warm up with the Sex column, which seems simple because it consists of only male/female entries. So let us count them up by using the factorplot(). This function takes the case sensitive column name, the DataFrame, and kind count, because we just need to count them up (Figure 15-3).

```
sns.factorplot('Sex',data=titanic_df,kind='count')
```

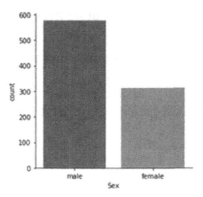

Figure 15-3. *A sex count visualization*

We can see that the count of males is almost double the count of females, but we know that the number of females who survived is greater than the number of males who survived. We can prove it by visualizing the count of survivors and see the number of survived/not survived males and females (Figure 15-4).

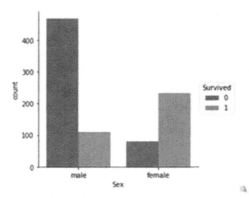

Figure 15-4. *The sex/survived count*

We can do that by using the same factorplot(), adding to it one more parameter which is hue, as follows:

```
sns.factorplot('Sex',kind='count',data=titanic_df,hue='Survived')
```

We can now prove the percentage of survived/not survived of both males and females, just by looking at two visualization charts.

The next step is to make things more complex, by adding the Pclass column to the equation (Figure 15-5).

```
sns.factorplot('Pclass',data=titanic_df,kind='count')
```

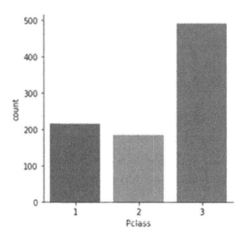

Figure 15-5. *The Pclass count*

This column represents the class reserved for each passenger, either *1 = first, 2 = second, or 3 = third class*. If you look at the chart, you can see that almost half of the passengers are in third class. I think it make sense that most passengers are in third class, in an expensive type of transportation.

Now, let's see the count of each Sex through each Pclass, and we will do the same as we did before. We can see something strange happens here. If you look carefully at the chart (Figure 15-6), you might see what I have seen, which is the following: In first and second class the count number of males almost equals the number of females, but in the third class the number of males is almost double. You might intuit that from watching the

"Titanic" movie: when you see *Leonardo DiCaprio's character* traveling in third class, you can see that most of the class consists of males.

```
sns.factorplot('Pclass',data=titanic_df,hue='Sex',kind='count')
```

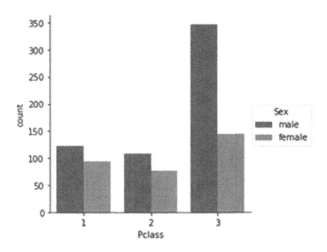

Figure 15-6. *The Pclass/sex count*

Digging Deeper

For now, we think you have some good understanding, but from now on we will go deeper. Therefore, we will not only depend on the information from columns, we also will extract and fabricate the column dimensions to get more and more information.

We need to extract more features. By saying that, we mean we will create new columns that contain knowledge that was hidden. For instance, we need to calculate the number of children who were in the ship. We can extract it from the Age column with some associations from the Sex column, and save it as the person column (Figure 15-7), as in the following code:

```
def titanic_children(passenger):
    age , sex = passenger
    if age < 16:
        return 'child'
    else:
        return sex
titanic_df['person'] = titanic_df[['Age','Sex']].apply(titanic_
children,axis=1)
```

	PassengerId	Survived	Pclass	Name	Sex	Age	SibSp	Parch	Ticket	Fare	Cabin	Embarked	person
0	1	0	3	Braund, Mr. Owen Harris	male	22.0	1	0	A/5 21171	7.2500	NaN	S	male
1	2	1	1	Cumings, Mrs. John Bradley (Florence Briggs Th...	female	38.0	1	0	PC 17599	71.2833	C85	C	female
2	3	1	3	Heikkinen, Miss. Laina	female	26.0	0	0	STON/O2. 3101282	7.9250	NaN	S	female
3	4	1	1	Futrelle, Mrs. Jacques Heath (Lily May Peel)	female	35.0	1	0	113803	53.1000	C123	S	female
4	5	0	3	Allen, Mr. William Henry	male	35.0	0	0	373450	8.0500	NaN	S	male
5	6	0	3	Moran, Mr. James	male	NaN	0	0	330877	8.4583	NaN	Q	male
6	7	0	1	McCarthy, Mr. Timothy J	male	54.0	0	0	17463	51.8625	E46	S	male
7	8	0	3	Palsson, Master. Gosta Leonard	male	2.0	3	1	349909	21.0750	NaN	S	child
8	9	1	3	Johnson, Mrs. Oscar W (Elisabeth Vilhelmina Berg)	female	27.0	0	2	347742	11.1333	NaN	S	female
9	10	1	2	Nasser, Mrs. Nicholas (Adele Achem)	female	14.0	1	0	237736	30.0708	NaN	C	child

Figure 15-7. *The modified Titanic DataFrame*

Now, let's see if the new feature can help us to gain a hypothesis.

```
sns.factorplot('Pclass',data=titanic_
df,hue='person',kind='count')
```

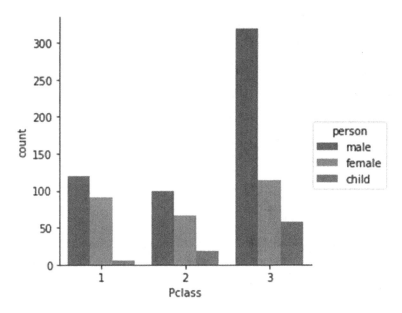

Figure 15-8. *The Pclass/person count*

As always, we will make a factorplot to see if we gain some knowledge or not. As you see in Figure 15-8, the count number of children (child) in third class is huge compare with both first and second class. But the count number of males still is almost the same, so let us find the total count of people per age.

We can done this with the hist() function that calculates the histogram of the age; simply, it counts the frequency of the variable within an interval.

```
titanic_df['Age'].hist(bins=70)
```

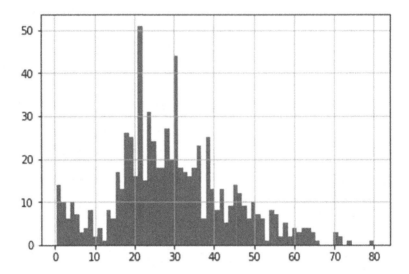

Figure 15-9. *The Age histogram*

As you can see in Figure 15-9, the frequency of people on the ship who are between 16 and 35 is much greater than the people above that age or children below it.

Let's go a step further and count the frequency of male/female per age. We do it by stacking multiple figures and creating what's called `FacetGrid`. This `FacetGrid` is composed of two charts: each of them is a kdeplot type that represents either male or female, and each `kdeplot` represents the Age of the owing Sex type.

So, to simplify the process, you can find all the other visualizations in the code accompanying this book. Go check it and see if you can extract more information and more understanding from this dataset.

Preprocessing Dataset

If you take a look in this table's features/columns from left to right, you will see the following:

- **PassengerId:** This column contains the ID of each observation, and it is an almost useless feature for any machine learning model; we cannot extract any correlation between this feature and the target/output.

- **Survived:** This column is the output feature, sometimes called the target or response; it contains values per observation—either 1 if the passenger survived or 0 if not.

- **Pclass:** This column contains the class of each passenger on the ship; it's values are either 1, 2, or 3.

- **Age:** This column contains the age of each passenger on the ship, and it is a good feature. But with some tweaking, we can extract a new feature from it: whether the passenger is a child or not, and that's of course with the help of the Sex column.

But, if you take a careful look at the Age column, you will see that it contains some null/empty values. Theoretically of course, we can fill these values. Using some statistics, we can assume that this column follows some unknown distribution, and most of the data is repeated as a phenomenon called the distribution mean.

So, without digging into the rock of statistics, we can ensure that filling the missing values with the most repeated ones will do the job, and by saying "most repeated," we mean the mean value of the column.

Calculating the mean is not that hard, and thankfully, the pandas library provides us with wonderful functionalities that help us not waste a lot of time. The function mean() calculates the mean of the Age column easily.

```
titanic_df['Age'].mean()
# 29.69911764705882
```

Now what remains is to fill the empty value in that column with this value, and again we can do that by the fillna() function: by passing a certain value to it, we can fill all the empties/nulls in that column.

```
titanic_df['Age'] = titanic_df['Age'].fillna(titanic_df['Age'].
mean())
```

In the Titanic dataset, the Cabin column does not provide us with any useful knowledge; besides, it is mostly null values. So we will not use it, because it is useless and will influence any machine learning model. The processing step for this column is to remove it from the DataFrame.

```
titanic_df.drop('Cabin',axis=1, inplace=True)
```

As an optional step, you may want to clean and use the Embarked column, but we do not recommend that. It did not give us any useful knowledge, and we recommend removing it, but we gave you this step if you wanted to try this.

```
titanic_df['Embarked'] = titanic_df['Embarked'].fillna('S')
```

After filling the empties, now let's go and check if there are any empties existing in the whole dataset or not.

```
titanic_df.isnull().values.any()
# False
```

Now, after we've ensured that there are no empties in the whole dataset, let's go and craft some new features that might help the machine learning model.

We will start with an easy one, combining both the Parch and SibSp columns, and build a new column that is Boolean. It contains either With Family or Without Family values, and those are equal to *True/False* values, therefore we consider it a Boolean column.

```
titanic_df['Alone'] = titanic_df.Parch + titanic_df.SibSp
titanic_df['Alone'].loc[titanic_df['Alone']>0] = 'With Family'
titanic_df['Alone'].loc[titanic_df['Alone'] == 0] = 'Without
Family'
```

After that, we will create a new column called person, which is similar to the Sex column, but the difference is it also tells us if the passenger is a child (if the passenger age is under 16 years).

```
def titanic_children(passenger):
    age , sex = passenger
    if age <16:
        return 'child'
    else:
        return sex
titanic_df['person'] = titanic_df[['Age','Sex']].apply(titanic_
children,axis=1)
```

Now, let's give it a look, and see what our data looks like so far (Figure 15-10).

```
titanic_df.head()
```

	PassengerId	Survived	Pclass	Name	Sex	Age	SibSp	Parch	Ticket	Fare	Embarked	person	Alone
0	1	0	3	Braund, Mr. Owen Harris	male	22.0	1	0	A/5 21171	7.2500	S	male	With Family
1	2	1	1	Cumings, Mrs. John Bradley (Florence Briggs Th...	female	38.0	1	0	PC 17599	71.2833	C	female	With Family
2	3	1	3	Heikkinen, Miss. Laina	female	26.0	0	0	STON/O2. 3101282	7.9250	S	female	Without Family
3	4	1	1	Futrelle, Mrs. Jacques Heath (Lily May Peel)	female	35.0	1	0	113803	53.1000	S	female	With Family
4	5	0	3	Allen, Mr. William Henry	male	35.0	0	0	373450	8.0500	S	male	Without Family

Figure 15-10. *The head() of the data after some preprocessing*

Now let's transform the person, alone, and embarked to one-hot encoded columns. If you do not know what one-hot encoded means, you can search for it. It's a type of transformation that basically transforms any column to a binary format.

```
person_dummies = pd.get_dummies(titanic_df['person'])
alone_dummies = pd.get_dummies(titanic_df['Alone'])
embarked_dummies = pd.get_dummies(titanic_df['Embarked'])
embarked_dummies.drop('Q',axis=1,inplace=True)
```

Also, we will transform the Pclass to on-hot-encoding form and rename its columns class_1, class_2, and class_3.

```
pclass_dummies = pd.get_dummies(titanic_df['Pclass'])
pclass_dummies.columns=['class_1','class_2','class_3']
```

The processing step that we will apply to Age is very simple; we will remove the percent of it, as there's is no age 20.2. We can achieve this by calling ceil() and applying it to the age.

And we will do the same processing step to the Fare column too.

```
titanic_df['Age'] = titanic_df['Age'].apply(math.ceil)
titanic_df['Fare'] = titanic_df['Fare'].apply(math.ceil)
```

Now, we will add all the new columns to our dataset. Using the concat() function, we can add columns to DataFrame with an axis=1 parameter, and rows with axis=0.

```
titanic_df = pd.concat([titanic_df,pclass_dummies,person_
dummies,alone_dummies,embarked_dummies],axis=1)
```

Now, let us drop all the useless columns from the DataFrame, and all the repeated/correlated (e.g., the Pclass and its classes) columns too.

```
titanic_df.drop(['PassengerId','Name','Sex','SibSp','Parch',
'Ticket','Embarked'],axis=1,inplace=True)
titanic_df.drop(['Alone','person','Pclass','Without Family',
'male','class_3'],axis=1,inplace=True)
```

At last, after finishing cleaning and extracting knowledge from this dataset, it is fair to take a last look at it (Figure 15-11) before going on to the next step. Also, it is recommended to save the data after cleaning the pipeline, to make it easier for you and for backup purposes too.

```
titanic_df.head()
```

	Survived	Age	Fare	class_1	class_2	child	female	With Family	C	S
0	0	22	8	0	0	0	0	1	0	1
1	1	38	72	1	0	0	1	1	1	0
2	1	26	8	0	0	0	1	0	0	1
3	1	35	54	1	0	0	1	1	0	1
4	0	35	9	0	0	0	0	0	0	1

Figure 15-11. *The Titanic DataFrame after the preprocessing step*

For the last step in preprocessing, we will create a checkpoint of the data, to make a backup and make sure there's no data loss.

```
titanic_df.to_csv('titanic.preprocessing.csv', index=False)
```

Building the Model

And here we are at the core of our application, building the model with TensorFlow. Now we will use all that we have learned in the previous part to build a neural network that is able to classify the observations about who survived the Titanic or not.

We will create a function that is called build_neural_network that will build the whole network for us and return the graph that we will train. The network should take an input that is equal in shape to the preprocessed Titanic dataset, and return an output that is either 0 or 1.

```
# Build Neural Network
from collections import namedtuple

def build_neural_network(hidden_units=10):
    tf.reset_default_graph()
    inputs = tf.placeholder(tf.float32, shape=[None, x_train.
    shape[1]])
    labels = tf.placeholder(tf.float32, shape=[None, 1])
    learning_rate = tf.placeholder(tf.float32)
    is_training=tf.Variable(True,dtype=tf.bool)

    initializer = tf.contrib.layers.xavier_initializer()
    fc = tf.layers.dense(inputs, hidden_units,
    activation=None,kernel_initializer=initializer)
    fc=tf.layers.batch_normalization(fc, training=is_training)
    fc=tf.nn.relu(fc)
```

```
logits = tf.layers.dense(fc, 1, activation=None)
cross_entropy = tf.nn.sigmoid_cross_entropy_with_
logits(labels=labels, logits=logits)
cost = tf.reduce_mean(cross_entropy)

with tf.control_dependencies(tf.get_collection(tf.
GraphKeys.UPDATE_OPS)):
    optimizer = tf.train.AdamOptimizer(learning_
    rate=learning_rate).minimize(cost)

predicted = tf.nn.sigmoid(logits)
correct_pred = tf.equal(tf.round(predicted), labels)
accuracy = tf.reduce_mean(tf.cast(correct_pred,
tf.float32))

# Export the nodes
export_nodes = ['inputs', 'labels', 'learning_rate',
               'is_training', 'logits', 'cost',
               'optimizer', 'predicted', 'accuracy']
Graph = namedtuple('Graph', export_nodes)
local_dict = locals()
graph = Graph(*[local_dict[each] for each in export_nodes])

    return graph

model = build_neural_network()
```

Now, after we've created the whole neural network model, we need to make sure the dataset is divided into training observations/batches for the model. So, we will create a function that takes the data and yields batches that have a size of 32, or whatever size that you set.

```
def get_batch(data_x,data_y,batch_size=32):
    batch_n=len(data_x)//batch_size
    for i in range(batch_n):
        batch_x=data_x[i*batch_size:(i+1)*batch_size]
        batch_y=data_y[i*batch_size:(i+1)*batch_size]

        yield batch_x,batch_y
```

Now we need to define some parameters for the model, such as the number of epochs, learning rate, and batch size.

```
epochs = 200
train_collect = 50
train_print=train_collect*2

learning_rate_value = 0.001
batch_size=16

x_collect = []
train_loss_collect = []
train_acc_collect = []
valid_loss_collect = []
valid_acc_collect = []
```

Now, we will create a session that we will run the whole network graph onto. We will iterate the number of epochs, and inside of each epoch we'll generate some batches that we'll feed to the model, and generate a loss that will be backpropagated to enhance the model weights.

```
saver = tf.train.Saver()
with tf.Session() as sess:
    sess.run(tf.global_variables_initializer())
    iteration=0
    for e in range(epochs):
```

```
for batch_x,batch_y in get_batch(x_train,y_train,batch_
size):
    iteration+=1
    feed = {model.inputs: x_train,
            model.labels: y_train,
            model.learning_rate: learning_rate_value,
            model.is_training:True
            }

    train_loss, _, train_acc = sess.run([model.cost,
    model.optimizer, model.accuracy], feed_dict=feed)

    if iteration % train_collect == 0:
        x_collect.append(e)
        train_loss_collect.append(train_loss)
        train_acc_collect.append(train_acc)

        if iteration % train_print==0:
            print("Epoch: {}/{}".format(e + 1, epochs),
                "Train Loss: {:.4f}".format(train_loss),
                "Train Acc: {:.4f}".format(train_acc))

        feed = {model.inputs: x_test,
                model.labels: y_test,
                model.is_training:False
                }
        val_loss, val_acc = sess.run([model.cost,
        model.accuracy], feed_dict=feed)
        valid_loss_collect.append(val_loss)
        valid_acc_collect.append(val_acc)
```

```
        if iteration % train_print==0:
            print("Epoch: {}/{}".format(e + 1, epochs),
                "Validation Loss: {:.4f}".format(val_loss),
                "Validation Acc: {:.4f}".format(val_acc))

    saver.save(sess, "./titanic.ckpt")
```

If this code is running correctly for you without any errors, you will see this progress log in your output shell:

```
Epoch: 3/200 Train Loss: 0.6199 Train Acc: 0.6770
Epoch: 3/200 Validation Loss: 0.6276 Validation Acc: 0.6425
Epoch: 5/200 Train Loss: 0.6013 Train Acc: 0.6784
Epoch: 5/200 Validation Loss: 0.6085 Validation Acc: 0.6480
...
Epoch: 198/200 Train Loss: 0.3361 Train Acc: 0.8652
Epoch: 198/200 Validation Loss: 0.4740 Validation Acc: 0.8156
Epoch: 200/200 Train Loss: 0.3361 Train Acc: 0.8652
Epoch: 200/200 Validation Loss: 0.4780 Validation Acc: 0.8212
```

And finally, after the model finishes the training, you can see an analysis of it to decide if you need to enhance the model or not (Figure 15-12).

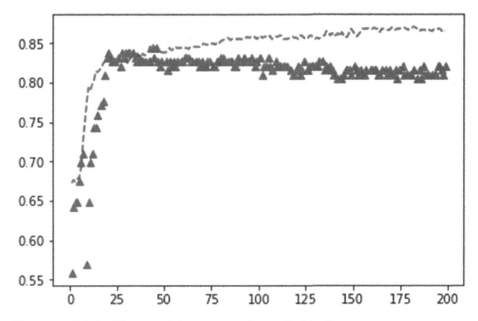

Figure 15-12. *The model progress through the dataset*

Case Study—IMDB Movie Review Data with Word2Vec

In this section we will start with the **IMDB** data and use *Word2Vec*, the most common processing algorithm with the **gensim** package. We already talked about Word2Vec in previous chapters, but in this chapter we'll try to use it with the IMDB dataset; so let's take a quick tour. In this section we have some rows/samples/observations that each one of them is either a positive or negative sample, and we will divide those samples into training and testing sets. But the new thing that we will do is to transform it as numbers as we talked about with word embeddings. Then, after the transformation, we will pass it to a new layer to feed the learning layer to complete the learning task, or save it in a pickle. In this case, we want you to learn how to use this gensim embeddings and understand the concept of Word2Vec, so you can then learn more about Word2Vec. This is a very well-used case for learning to build good models.

```
import numpy as np # linear algebra
import pandas as pd # data processing, CSV file I/O (e.g.
pd.read_csv)
import html
import os
from nltk.corpus import stopwords
import nltk
nltk.download('stopwords')
import re
from tqdm import tqdm
```

We need to load files: positive ones, negative ones, and test files.

```
path = "/content/aclImdb/"
positiveFiles = [x for x in os.listdir(path+"train/pos/")
                 if x.endswith(".txt")]
negativeFiles = [x for x in os.listdir(path+"train/neg/")
                 if x.endswith(".txt")]
testFiles = [x for x in os.listdir(path+"test/")
             if x.endswith(".txt")]
```

positiveFiles contain positive reviews.

```
positiveReviews, negativeReviews, testReviews = [], [], []
for pfile in positiveFiles:
    with open(path+"train/pos/"+pfile, encoding="latin1") as f:
        positiveReviews.append(f.read())
for nfile in negativeFiles:
    with open(path+"train/neg/"+nfile, encoding="latin1") as f:
        negativeReviews.append(f.read())
for tfile in testFiles:
    with open(path+"test/"+tfile, encoding="latin1") as f:
        testReviews.append(f.read())
```

We now need to know the size of positive reviews and negative reviews.

```
print(len(positiveReviews))
print(len(negativeReviews))
print(len(testReviews))

# Output
# 12500
# 12500
# 2
```

Let's put all types of reviews in the same DataFrame so we can see them.

```
reviews = pd.concat([pd.DataFrame({"review":positiveReviews,
                   "label":1, "file":positiveFiles}),
                  pd.DataFrame({"review":negativeReviews,
                  "label":0, "file":negativeFiles}),
                  pd.DataFrame({"review":testReviews,
                  "label":-1, "file":testFiles})
                  ], ignore_index=True).sample(frac=1,
                  random_state=1)
```

Get the data shape; it should be a number with three as the dimension of data.

```
reviews.shape
# Output
# (25002, 3)
```

Let's see the DataFrame of the data (Figure 15-13).

```
reviews[0:10]
```

	review	label	file
21939	Oh my god, what a horrible film. The film has ...	0	3942_1.txt
24113	There should be a rule that states quite clear...	0	7657_1.txt
4633	I found this to be a so-so romance/drama that ...	1	16_7.txt
17240	Forest of the Damned starts out as five young ...	0	10516_4.txt
4894	They had me from the first show.\<br /\>\<br /\>We...	1	5665_9.txt
6908	saw this in preview- great movie- wonderful ch...	1	4333_10.txt
19498	First of all this movie starts out on a really...	0	5486_3.txt
8146	I've been a fan of Xu Ke (Hark Tsui) for many ...	1	405_10.txt
13815	I can't say much about this film. I think it s...	0	1834_3.txt
6483	\<br /\>\<br /\>Everything is relative seems to be...	1	8796_8.txt

Figure 15-13. *The first ten rows of reviews*

Stop words in English are to be ignored.

```
stopWords = stopwords.words('english')
```

Define the function that does the cleaning process.

```
def CleanData(sentence):
    processedList = ""

    #convert to lowercase and ignore special charcter
    sentence = re.sub(r'[^A-Za-z0-9\s.]', r"", str(sentence).
    lower())
    sentence = re.sub(r'\n', r' ', sentence)

    sentence = " ".join([word for word in sentence.split() if
    word not in stopWords])

    return sentence

reviews.info()
```

```
<class 'pandas.core.frame.DataFrame'>
Int64Index: 25002 entries, 21939 to 235
Data columns (total 3 columns):
review    25002 non-null object
label     25002 non-null int64
file      25002 non-null object
dtypes: int64(1), object(2)
memory usage: 781.3+ KB
```

```
reviews['review'][0] reviews['review'][0]
# Output
```
'Level One, Horror.

When I saw this film for the first time at 10, I knew it would give me nightmares. It did. Surprisingly, as I recall, it was the sound as much as the sight of the monster that caused them.

Level Two, Psychoanalytic Theory.

```
CleanData(reviews['review'][0])
# Output
```
'level one horror.br br saw film first time 10 knew would give nightmares. did. surprisingly recall sound much sight monster caused them.br br level two psychoanalytic theory.

```
reviews['review'] = reviews['review'].map(lambda x:
CleanData(x))
```

```
reviews['review'].head()
# Output
```
```
21939    oh god horrible film. film right people involv...
24113    rule states quite clearly movies like resident...
4633     found soso romancedrama nice ending generally ...
17240    forest damned starts five young friends brothe...
4894     first show.br br welcome trinity county. sleep...
Name: review, dtype: object
```

```
tmp_corpus = reviews['review'].map(lambda x:x.split('.'))

#corpus [[w1, w2, w3,...],[...]]
corpus = []

for i in tqdm(range(len(reviews))):
    for line in tmp_corpus[i]:
        words = [x for x in line.split()]
        corpus.append(words)
# Output
# 100%|████████████████████| 25002/25002 [00:02<00:00,
# 10673.63it/s]

len(corpus)
# Output
# 402194

#removing blank list
corpus_new = []
for i in range(len(corpus)):
    if (len(corpus[i]) != 0):
        corpus_new.append(corpus[i])

num_of_sentences = len(corpus_new)
num_of_words = 0
for line in corpus_new:
    num_of_words += len(line)

print('Num of sentences - %s'%(num_of_sentences))
print('Num of words - %s'%(num_of_words))
# Output
# Num of sentences - 354417
# Num of words - 3265546
```

Now let's see the gensim package and how to use it with Word2Vec.

```
from gensim.models import Word2Vec
```

Let's bulid a Word2Vec model and initialize parameters.

```
# sg - skip gram |  window = size of the window | size = vector
dimension
size = 100
window_size = 2 # sentences weren't too long, so
epochs = 100
min_count = 2
workers = 4

model = Word2Vec(corpus_new)

model.build_vocab(sentences= corpus_new, update=True)

for i in range(5):
    model.train(sentences=corpus_new, epochs=50, total_
    examples=model.corpus_count)
```

After the model is trained, let's save it.

```
#save model
model.save('w2v_model')
```

Load the model into Word2Vec, which is a module in gensim.

```
model = Word2Vec.load('w2v_model')
```

Let's find the most similar movies.

```
model.wv.most_similar('movie')
# Output
[('film', 0.8756906986236572),
 ('flick', 0.6631126403808594),
 ('movies', 0.6589803695678711),
```

```
('it', 0.562816321849823),
('films', 0.5470719337463379),
('show', 0.5167748928070068),
('sequel', 0.5143758654594421),
('this', 0.5129573941230774),
('thing', 0.5066217184066772),
('really', 0.4848993122577667)]
```

The next step is to extract data using its label.

```
reviews = reviews[["review", "label", "file"]].sample(frac=1,
          random_state=1)
train = reviews[reviews.label!=-1].sample(frac=0.6, random_state=1)
valid = reviews[reviews.label!=-1].drop(train.index)
test = reviews[reviews.label==-1]
```

Let's see the shapes of the train/test datasets:

```
print(train.shape)
print(valid.shape)
print(test.shape)
# Output
# (15000, 3)
# (10000, 3)
# (2, 3)

valid.head()
```

See Figure 12-14.

	review	label	file
21572	beating bad guys... tag line movie exposes muc...	0	12438_1.txt
1806	title sequence shows credits written rainsoake...	1	6741_7.txt
4753	diego armando maradona still remains best foot...	1	4968_10.txt
18029	even first 10 minutes movie horrific. hard bel...	0	2137_1.txt
20189	hazing confused mumbojumbo wants hard evil dea...	0	11400_4.txt

Figure 15-14. *Five rows of valid DataFrame*

Now we'll do some data preprocessing, which the last iteration before we train our model.

```
num_features = 100
index2word_set = set(model.wv.index2word)
model = model
def featureVecorMethod(words):
    featureVec = np.zeros(num_features, dtype='float32')
    nwords = 0

    for word in words:
        if word in index2word_set:
            nwords+= 1
            featureVec = np.add(featureVec, model[word])

    #average of feature vec
    featureVec = np.divide(featureVec, nwords)
    return featureVec

def getAvgFeatureVecs(reviews):
    counter = 0

    reviewFeatureVecs = np.zeros((len(reviews), num_features),
    dtype='float32')
```

```
    for review in reviews:

        if counter%1000 == 0:
            print("Review %d of %d"%(counter, len(reviews)))

        reviewFeatureVecs[counter] = featureVecorMethod(review)
        counter = counter+1
    return reviewFeatureVecs

clean_train_reviews = []
for review in train['review']:

    clean_train_reviews.append(list(CleanData(review).split()))
# print(len(clean_train_reviews))\

trainDataVecs = getAvgFeatureVecs(clean_train_reviews)
# Output
Review 1000 of 15000
Review 2000 of 15000
Review 3000 of 15000
Review 4000 of 15000
Review 5000 of 15000
Review 6000 of 15000
Review 7000 of 15000
Review 8000 of 15000
Review 9000 of 15000
Review 10000 of 15000
Review 11000 of 15000
Review 12000 of 15000
Review 13000 of 15000
Review 14000 of 15000

len(valid['review'])
# Output
10000
```

```
clean_test_reviews = []
for review in valid['review']:

    clean_test_reviews.append(list(CleanData(review).split()))

testDataVecs = getAvgFeatureVecs(clean_test_reviews)
# Output
Review 1000 of 10000
Review 2000 of 10000
Review 3000 of 10000
Review 4000 of 10000
Review 5000 of 10000
Review 6000 of 10000
Review 7000 of 10000
Review 8000 of 10000
Review 9000 of 10000

print(len(testDataVecs))
# Output
10000
```

Case Study—Image Segmentation

You might wonder what image segmentation is. In computer vision, image segmentation is the process of partitioning a digital image into multiple segments. The goal of segmentation is to simplify and/or change the representation of an image into something that is more meaningful and easier to analyze. Let's understand image segmentation using a simple example. Consider Figure 15-15.

Figure 15-15. *An example image that we are going to segment*

We can divide or partition the image into various parts called segments. It's not a great idea to process the entire image at the same time, as there will be regions in the image that do not contain any information. By dividing the image into segments, we can make use of the important segments for processing the image. That, in a nutshell, is how image segmentation works.

An image is a collection or set of different pixels. We group together the pixels that have similar attributes, using image segmentation. Take a moment to look at Figure 12-16 (it'll give you a practical idea of image segmentation):

Object Detection

Instance Segmentation

Figure 15-16. *The difference between object detection and instance segmentation*

So, let's now build an application that is able to segment any image and extract instances from it. To start doing this, we need to import all the packages we are going to use. It seems that there's a new package, skimage; this package contains a lot of operations that help you to deal with images data.

```
import os
import sys
import random
import math
import numpy as np
import skimage.io
import matplotlib
import matplotlib.pyplot as plt
import warnings
warnings.filterwarnings("ignore")
```

Now we need to illustrate a new architecture model called Mask R-CNN. Data scientists and researchers at Facebook AI Research (FAIR) pioneered a deep learning architecture, called Mask R-CNN, which can create a pixel-wise mask for each object in an image. This is a really cool concept, so follow along closely!

Mask R-CNN is an extension of the popular Faster R-CNN object detection architecture. Mask R-CNN adds a branch to the already existing Faster R-CNN outputs. The Faster R-CNN method generates two things for each object in the image:

1. Its class

2. The bounding box coordinates

   Mask R-CNN adds a third branch to this that outputs the object mask as well. Take a look at Figure 15-17 to get an inside look at how Mask R-CNN works.

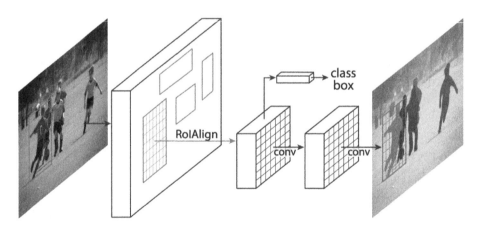

Figure 15-17. *How Mask R-CNN works*

3. We take an image as input and pass it to the ConvNet, which returns the feature map for that image

4.   The region proposal network (RPN) is applied on these feature maps. This returns the object proposals along with their object score.

5.   An RoI pooling layer is applied on these proposals to bring down all the proposals to the same size.

6.   Finally, the proposals are passed to a fully connected layer to classify and output the bounding boxes for objects. It also returns the mask for each proposal.

First, we will download the model that we are going to use from GitHub by using the command:

```
git clone https://github.com/matterport/Mask_RCNN.git
```

Then we should set the path of the model, to make sure our code sees the model downloaded.

```
# Root directory of the project
ROOT_DIR = os.path.abspath("/content/Mask_RCNN")
```

Then we will import the model and its visualization and utilities.

```
# Import Mask RCNN
sys.path.append(ROOT_DIR)  # To find local version of the
library
from Mask_RCNN.mrcnn import utils
import Mask_RCNN.mrcnn.model as modellib
from mrcnn import visualize
# Import COCO config
sys.path.append(os.path.join(ROOT_DIR, "samples/coco/"))
# To find local version
import coco

%matplotlib inline
```

After this, we are going to set the logs folder for future analysis and debugging. Also, we are going to load the weight from the h5 data file.

```
# Directory to save logs and trained model
MODEL_DIR = os.path.join(ROOT_DIR, "logs")

# Local path to trained weights file
COCO_MODEL_PATH = os.path.join(", "mask_rcnn_coco.h5")

# Download COCO trained weights from Releases if needed
if not os.path.exists(COCO_MODEL_PATH):
    utils.download_trained_weights(COCO_MODEL_PATH)
```

Now we need to set the image directory that our model will read the data from, and set the machine configuration. Also, we will instantiate the model and load its weight.

```
# Directory of images to run detection on
IMAGE_DIR = os.path.join(ROOT_DIR, "images")

class InferenceConfig(coco.CocoConfig):
    # Set batch size to 1 since we'll be running inference on
    # one image at a time. Batch size = GPU_COUNT * IMAGES_PER_GPU
    GPU_COUNT = 1
    IMAGES_PER_GPU = 1

config = InferenceConfig()
config.display()

# Create model object in inference mode.
model = modellib.MaskRCNN(mode="inference", model_dir='mask_
rcnn_coco.hy', config=config)

# Load weights trained on MS-COCO
model.load_weights('mask_rcnn_coco.h5', by_name=True)
```

Now we will create the class names; these names come from the COCO dataset that the model was trained on.

```
# COCO Class names
class_names = ['BG', 'person', 'bicycle', 'car', 'motorcycle',
               'airplane', 'bus', 'train', 'truck', 'boat',
               'traffic light', 'fire hydrant', 'stop sign',
               'parking meter', 'bench', 'bird', 'cat', 'dog',
               'horse', 'sheep', 'cow', 'elephant', 'bear',
               'zebra', 'giraffe', 'backpack', 'umbrella',
               'handbag', 'tie', 'suitcase', 'frisbee',
               'skis', 'snowboard', 'sports ball', 'kite',
               'baseball bat', 'baseball glove', 'skateboard',
               'surfboard', 'tennis racket', 'bottle', 'wine
               glass', 'cup', 'fork', 'knife', 'spoon', 'bowl',
               'banana', 'apple', 'sandwich', 'orange',
               'broccoli', 'carrot', 'hot dog', 'pizza',
               'donut', 'cake', 'chair', 'couch', 'potted
               plant', 'bed', 'dining table', 'toilet', 'tv',
               'laptop', 'mouse', 'remote', 'keyboard',
               'cell phone', 'microwave', 'oven', 'toaster',
               'sink', 'refrigerator', 'book', 'clock',
               'vase', 'scissors', 'teddy bear', 'hair drier',
               'toothbrush']
```

Now we need to test if the model that we loaded is working correctly, so we will load a test image and feed it to the model and see the output.

```
# Load a random image from the images folder
image = skimage.io.imread('/content/Mask_RCNN/
images/1045023827_4ec3e8ba5c_z.jpg')
```

```
# original image
plt.figure(figsize=(12,10))
skimage.io.imshow(image)
```

Figure 15-18. *The image contains some pedestrians that the network should extract*

As you can see in Figure 15-18, the image contains many objects, and the network should extract the objects and classify their labels. When Mask R-CNN extracts each object, it generates the bond box of the object to tell where the object is, and its label too. There's another output that we consider amazing: it creates a mask-like boundary over the object.

To do that, the network classifies each pixel as to whether it belongs to the given object or not.

Now let's see the Mask R-CNN output; to do that, we write a simple line of code that makes the network prediction work.

```
# Run detection
results = model.detect([image], verbose=1)

# Visualize results
r = results[0]
visualize.display_instances(image, r['rois'], r['masks'],
r['class_ids'], class_names, r['scores'])
```

Figure 15-19. *The extracted output of the network*

As you see in Figure 15-19, the network output extracted the pedestrians exactly. It even extracted the person who is inside the car on the right. Isn't that awesome work? But it's not only pedestrians/persons that the network extracts; there are many classes that the network can classify. You can see the class variables in the preceding code to see how many classes and what classes/objects that Mask R-CNN can extract.

To extract a certain object inside the image, you can simply iterate over the objects until you find the wanted one, and do whatever you want (Figure 15-20).

```
mask = r['masks']
mask = mask.astype(int)
mask.shape

for i in range(mask.shape[2]):
    temp = skimage.io.imread('/content/Mask_RCNN/
    images/1045023827_4ec3e8ba5c_z.jpg')
    for j in range(temp.shape[2]):
        temp[:,:,j] = temp[:,:,j] * mask[:,:,i]
    plt.figure(figsize=(8,8))
    plt.imshow(temp)
```

Figure 15-20. *The each object segmented from the network*

Summary

In this chapter, we showed you some examples to learn how to apply the knowledge you have gained from this book. All the applications in this book are designed to make sure that you learn every single concept from tabular dataset to text to images dataset, and apply these concepts in a practical manner.

We hope that you have enjoyed this chapter, as there's no theory and it contains a lot of code, and enjoyed the whole book too.

By ending this chapter, you have finished the journey of learning what the deep learning pipeline is and how to apply it in real life.

Index

A

Activation functions, 289, 293
   binary step function, 299, 300
   deep learning model, 297
   linear activation
      function, 300–302
   mathematical equations, 297
   neural network architecture, 297
   perceptron and neural
      network, 297
   placement of, 298
   recap, 305
   ReLU function, 304
   role of, 298
   sigmoid/logistic activation
      function, 302, 303
   swish activation function, 305
   works in neuron, 299
Adadelta, 350, 351
Adaptive gradient, 349, 350
Adaptive moment estimation, 352
Aggregation function, 118
AND Boolean function, 286
AND Boolean gate operation, 283
Annotation, 22
Artificial neural network
      (ANN), 22, 60

Artificial neuron, 280, 284
Association rule learning, 16
Atom extraction, 261, 262

B

Backpropagation, 294
Backpropagation, convolution
      layer, 397–399
Backpropagation through
      time (BPTT)
   architecture, 424, 425
   circled multiplication, 426
   cross-entropy loss, 424
   definition, 424
   feed backward, 426
   gradients, 425
   time step, 424
   variables, 427
Bag-of-words (BoW) model, 204–206
Batch gradient descent
   concept, 308
   pros/cons, 309
Batch normalization, 360, 361
Behavioral data available, 285
Bias neuron, 289
Bidirectional RNN
      (Bi-RNNs), 445, 446

Q

R

Printed in the United States
By Bookmasters